Lawrenceville Press

An Introduction to Computing Using Macintosh Works

Microsoft® Works version 2

Bruce Presley
William Freitas

Lawrenceville Press

First Edition

ISBN 0-931717-86-8 (softcover)
ISBN 0-931717-87-6 (hardcover)

Printed in the United States of America

All orders, including Canadian, foreign, FPO and APO addresses should be placed with:

Lawrenceville Press
P.O. Box 704
Pennington, NJ 08534-0704
(609) 737-1148

This text is available in both hardcover and softcover editions.

16 15 14 13 12 11 10 9 8 7 6 5

PREFACE

We believe the best way to introduce students to computing is with an introductory course that covers a brief history of computing, applications software (word processing, data base, and spreadsheet), and a discussion of the role computers play in modern society. These goals are accomplished by this text which is designed to serve both the needs of students who will complete only an applications course, as well as those who will go on to take subsequent computer courses. The emphasis of this text is on the concepts of computing and problem solving using Works so that students learn how computers can be applied to a wide range of problems. The text is written for a one or two-term course. No previous computer experience is assumed.

Design and Features

FORMAT Each chapter contains numerous examples and diagrams printed in a two color format to help students visualize new concepts.

OBJECTIVES An outline of the significant topics that should be emphasized is presented at the beginning of each chapter.

CONCEPTS of APPLICATION Each of the application areas begins with an introductory section which describes the application and its uses. In this way, students are taught the purpose of the application without being overly concerned with the specific software. If the student then goes on to use another software package, he or she will fully understand the general concepts behind each application.

HANDS-ON PRACTICE In the applications chapters each new concept is presented, discussed and then followed by a hands-on practice which requires the student to test newly learned skills on the computer. The practice sections also serve as excellent reference guides to review applications commands.

CHAPTER SUMMARY At the end of each chapter is an outline that briefly discusses the concepts covered in the chapter.

VOCABULARY A vocabulary section which defines the new terms used is given at the end of each chapter.

REVIEW PROBLEMS Numerous review problems are presented for each section of the chapter, providing immediate reinforcement of new concepts. Answers to all review problems are included in the Teacher's Resource Package described below.

EXERCISES Each of the applications chapters includes a set of exercises of varying difficulty, making them appropriate for students with a wide range of abilities. Answers to all exercises are included in the Teacher's Resource Package described below.

HISTORY of COMPUTING Before learning to use the applications software, Chapter 1 introduces students to a history of computing and covers the vocabulary needed to understand the concepts presented in later chapters.

DRAWING Works' built-in drawing tools are introduced, allowing text and numbers to be emphasized and graphics to be produced.

SOCIAL and ETHICAL IMPLICATIONS Because computers play an important role in modern society, Chapter 11 discusses the social and ethical consequences of living in a computerized society. Advances in computer-related technology that will impact on the student's world are also discussed. Telecommunication is explained, and the Works Communication application introduced.

CAREERS in COMPUTING It is hoped that many students will become interested in careers in computing based upon their experience in this introductory course. A section in Chapter 11 outlines different computer careers and the educational requirements needed to pursue them.

APPENDICES Summaries of Works commands are presented in appendices at the end of the text for easy reference.

Teacher's Resource Package

When used with this text, the Lawrenceville Press Teacher's Resource Package provides all the additional material required to offer students an excellent introductory computer applications course. These materials, along with the text, place a strong emphasis on developing student problem-solving skills. The Package divides each of the chapters in the text into a series of lessons which contain the following features:

- **ASSIGNMENTS** - Reading and problem assignments are suggested for each lesson.

- **DISCUSSION TOPICS** - Additional material is provided which supplements the text and can be used in leading classroom discussions. Often this includes explanations of advanced commands or concepts not covered in the text.

- **TRANSPARENCY MASTERS** - Most lessons contain transparency masters which often present diagrams of the different applications screens.

- **WORKSHEETS** - Included in each lesson is a worksheet containing problems which are meant to be completed in the computer lab. These problems supplement those in the text, giving students additional reinforcement of the concepts they have just learned. Many of these problems make use of the data files included on the Master Diskette described below.

- **MASTER DISKETTE** - A Master Diskette that contains files to be used in conjunction with text problems and worksheets is included in the Teacher's Resource Package. These files are especially helpful in allowing students to work with large amounts of data without first having to type it into the computer. Student diskettes can be easily made by following the directions included with the Master Diskette.

In addition to the material in the lessons, the following features are found at the end of each chapter:

- **TESTS** - Comprehensive end of chapter tests are provided as well as a mid-term and final examination. A full set of answers and a grading key are also included.

- **ANSWERS** - Complete answers are provided for the Review and Exercise problems presented in the text. Where appropriate, answers have also been included on the Master Diskette.

As an added feature, the above material is contained in a 3-ring binder. This not only enables pages to be removed for duplication but also for the insertion of additional teacher notes.

Acknowledgments

The authors would like to thank the following people whose talents contributed to the production of this text.

For their careful review of the text while it was being written we are especially grateful to Arlene Yolles of Ridgefield High School in Ridgefield, Connecticut, Clyde Knowlton of the Horseheads Central School District in Horseheads, New York, Pat Reisdorf of the Foxcroft School in Middleburg, Virginia, Eric Neufer of the Hun School in Princeton, New Jersey and Carroll Melnyk of the Lubbock Independent School District in Lubbock, Texas. Many of their suggestions have been incorporated in this text.

The imaginative graphics designs were produced by Gregg Schwinn, Elizabeth Dole, Alan Chin-Lee and Marge Vining. We very much appreciate both their effort and willingness to work under demanding deadlines.

Thanks are due Art Rogers and Jeri Monastero at SuperType of the Palm Beaches, and Heffernan Press, Inc., especially Bill Daley who supervised the printing of the text. For their help with the Works software we wish to thank Ellen Mosner, John Neilson, and Robert Orndorf of the Microsoft Corporation.

The success of this and many of our other texts is due to the efforts of Heidi Crane, Vice President of Marketing at Lawrenceville Press. She has developed the promotional material which has been so well received by schools around the world.

We would like to thank the Saint Andrew's School for allowing us the flexible schedules to produce this text. A very special note of appreciation is due our colleague in the Computer Science department and friend, Ruth Wagy, who has generously shared with us materials developed in her applications courses. She has also helped test this text in her classes and has offered many valuable suggestions on ways in which it could be improved. David Attis, one of our most talented students, was especially helpful in reviewing the Practices, Reviews and Exercises.

Finally, we would like to thank our students, for whom and with whom this text was written. Their candid evaluation of each lesson and their refusal to accept anything less than perfect clarity in explanation have been the driving forces behind the creation of *An Introduction to Computing Using Microsoft Works.*

About the Authors

Bruce W. Presley, a graduate of Yale University, taught computer science and physics at The Lawrenceville School in Lawrenceville, New Jersey for twenty-four years where he served as the director of the Karl Corby Computer and Mathematics Center. Mr. Presley was a member of the founding committee of the Advanced Placement Computer Science examination and continues to serve as a consultant to the College Entrance Examination Board. Presently Mr. Presley, author of more than a dozen computer text books, is president of Lawrenceville Press and teaches computing applications and physics at the Saint Andrew's School in Boca Raton, Florida.

William R. Freitas, a graduate in computer science of Rutgers University, is director of development at Lawrenceville Press where he has co-authored several programming texts as well as a number of Teacher's Resource Packages. Mr. Freitas currently teaches computing applications and Advanced Placement Computer Science at the Saint Andrew's School in Boca Raton, Florida.

Table of Contents

Chapter Four - Introducing the Data Base

Chapter Five - Creating a Works Data Base

Chapter Six - Manipulating Data with the Data Base

Chapter 1

An Introduction to Computers

Objectives

After completing this chapter you will be able to:

1. Define what a computer is.
2. Discuss the history of computers.
3. Understand how computers work.
4. Name the components of a modern computer system.
5. Understand the advantages of using a computer.
6. Know what software and hardware are.

This text is about computers: their history, how they process and store data, how they can be programmed and the role they play in modern society. We will employ a popular computer program named Microsoft Works to teach you how to use the computer to word process and produce data bases and spreadsheets. Each of these applications will be explained as we proceed.

There are three reasons for learning how to use a computer. The first and most important is to develop problem-solving skills. This is done by learning how to analyze a problem carefully, developing a step-by-step solution, and then using the computer as a tool to produce a solution.

A second reason for learning about computers is to become acquainted with their capabilities and limitations. Because you are a part of a society which is becoming increasingly computerized, learning to use a computer is probably the best way to become familiar with one.

Finally, using a computer can be fun. The intellectual challenge of controlling the operations of a computer is not only rewarding but also an invaluable skill. The techniques learned in this class can be applied to your other subjects, and to your personal or business life as well.

1.1 What is a Computer?

A computer is an electronic machine that accepts information (called "data"), processes it according to specific instructions, and provides the results as new information. It can store and move large quantities of data at very high speed and even though it cannot think, it can make simple decisions and comparisons. For example, a computer can decide which of two numbers is larger or which of two names comes first alphabetically and then act upon that decision. Although the computer can help to solve a wide variety of problems, it is merely a machine and cannot solve problems on its own. It must be provided with instructions in the form of a computer "program."

A program is a list of instructions written in a special language that the computer understands. It tells the computer which operations to perform and in what sequence to perform them. In this text we will use a computer program called Microsoft Works.

THE HISTORY OF COMPUTERS

Many of the advances made by science and technology are dependent upon the ability to perform complex mathematical calculations and to process large amounts of data. It is therefore not surprising that for thousands of years mathematicians, scientists and business people have searched for "computing" machines that could perform calculations and analyze data quickly and accurately.

1.2 Ancient Counting Machines

As civilizations began to develop, they created both written languages and number systems. These number systems were not originally meant to be used in mathematical calculations, but rather were designed to record measurements. Roman numerals are a good example of this. Few of us would want to carry out even the simplest arithmetic operations using Roman numerals. How then were calculations performed thousands of years ago?

Calculations were carried out with a device known as an abacus which was used in ancient Babylon, China and throughout Europe until the late middle-ages. Many parts of the world, especially in the Orient, still make use of the abacus. The abacus works by sliding beads back and forth on a frame with the beads on the top of the frame representing fives and on the bottom ones. After a calculation is made the result is written down.

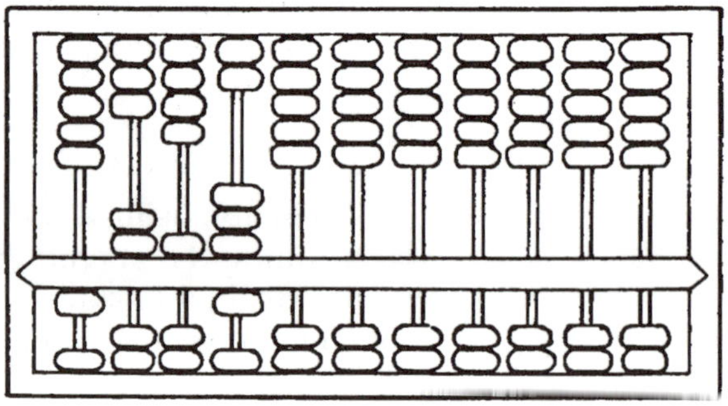

The Abacus is a calculating device used in the Orient

1.3 Arabic Numerals

Toward the end of the middle ages, Roman numerals were replaced by a new number system borrowed from the Arabs, therefore called Arabic numerals. This system uses ten digits and is the system we still use today. Because the Arabic system made calculations with pencil and paper easier, the abacus and other such counting devices became less common. Although calculations were now easier to perform, operations such as multiplication and division were able to be done by only those few mathematicians who were well educated.

1.4 The Pascaline

One of the earliest mechanical devices for calculating was the Pascaline, invented by the French philosopher and mathematician Blaise Pascal in 1642. Pascal was employed in the recording of taxes for the French government, a tedious job that often kept him up until the early hours of the morning. Being a gifted thinker, Pascal thought that the task of adding numbers should be able to be done by a mechanism that would resemble the way a clock keeps time.

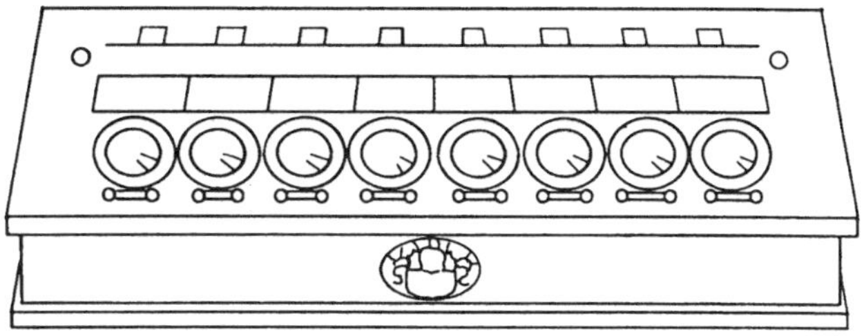

The Pascaline was a mechanical calculating device invented by Blaise Pascal in 1642

The Pascaline he invented was a complicated set of gears which could only be used to perform addition and not at all for multiplication or division. Unfortunately, Pascal never got the device to work properly.

1.5 The Stepped Reckoner

Later in the 17th century, Gottfried Wilhelm von Leibniz, a famous mathematician who is credited with being one of the developers of calculus, invented a device that was supposed to be able to add and subtract, as well as multiply, divide and extract square roots. His device, the Stepped Reckoner, included a cylindrical wheel called the Leibniz wheel and a moveable carriage that was used to enter the number of digits in the multiplicand.

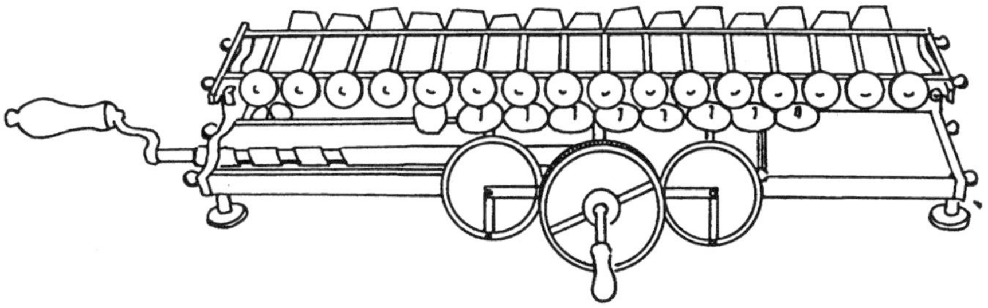

The Stepped Reckoner was another early attempt at creating a mechanical calculating device

Although both Pascal's and Leibniz's machines held great promise, they did not work well because the craftsmen of their time were unable to make machined parts that were accurate enough to carry out the inventor's design. Because of mechanically unreliable parts, the devices tended to jam and malfunction.

1.6 Jacquard's Loom and the Punched Card

In 1810 Joseph Jacquard, a French weaver, made a revolutionary discovery. He realized that the weaving instructions for his looms could be stored on cards with holes punched in them. As the cards moved through the loom in sequence, needles passed through the holes and picked up threads of the correct color or texture. By rearranging the cards, a weaver could change the pattern being woven without stopping the machine to change threads.

Jacquard's loom was the first device to make use of punched cards to store information

The weaving industry would seem to have little in common with the computer industry, but the idea that information could be stored by punching holes on a card was to be of great use in the later development of the computer.

1.7 Babbage's Difference and Analytical Engines

In 1822 Charles Babbage began work on the Difference Engine. His hope was that this device would calculate numbers to the twentieth place and then print them at forty-four digits a minute. The original purpose of this machine was to produce tables of numbers that would be used by ship's navigators. At the time navigation tables were often highly inaccurate due to calculation errors. In fact, several ships were known to have been lost at sea because of these errors. Again because of the mechanical problems that had plagued Pascal and Leibniz, the Difference Engine never worked properly.

Undaunted, Babbage later planned and began work on a considerably more advanced machine, called the Analytical Engine. This machine was to perform a variety of calculations by following a set of instructions, or "program", entered into it using punched cards similar to the ones used by Joseph Jacquard. During processing, the Analytical Engine was to store information in a memory unit that would allow it to make decisions and then carry out instructions based on those decisions. For example, in comparing two numbers it could be programmed to determine which was larger and then follow different sets of instructions. The Analytical Engine was no more successful than its predecessors, but its design was to serve as a model for the modern computer.

Babbage's chief collaborator on the Analytical Engine was Lady Ada Augusta, Countess of Lovelace, the daughter of Lord Byron. Interested in mathematics, Lady Lovelace was a sponsor of the Engine and one of the first people to realize its power and significance. She also tested the device and wrote of its achievements in order to gain support for it. Because of her involvement she is often called the first programmer.

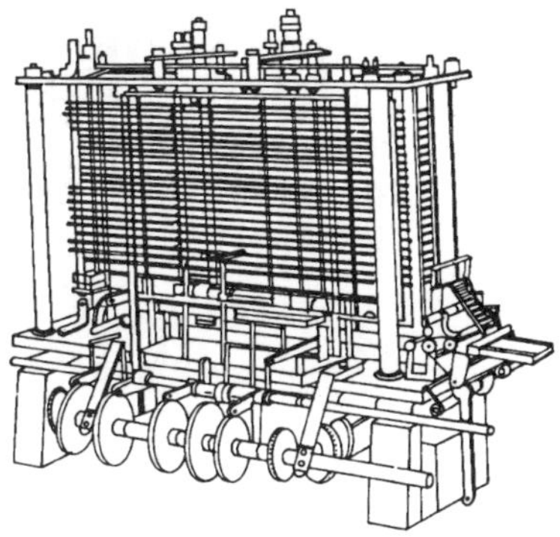

Babbage's Analytical Engine was a calculating machine which used punched cards to store different directions

Babbage had hoped that the Analytical Engine would be able to play chess, thinking out and making brilliant moves. Lady Lovelace, however, said that the Engine could never "originate anything", meaning that she did not believe that a machine, no matter how powerful, could think. To this day her statement about computing machines remains true.

1.8 The Electronic Tabulating Machine

By the end of the 19th century, U.S. Census officials were concerned about the time it took to tabulate the count of the continuously increasing number of Americans. This counting was done every ten years, as required by the Constitution. The Census of 1880, however, took nine years to compile, making the figures highly inaccurate by the time they were published.

To solve the problem, Herman Hollerith invented a calculating machine that used electricity rather than mechanical gears. Holes representing information to be tabulated were punched in cards similar to those used in Jacquard's loom, with the location of each hole representing a specific piece of information (male, female, age, etc.). The cards were then inserted into the machine and metal pins used to open and close electrical circuits. If a circuit was closed, a counter was increased by one.

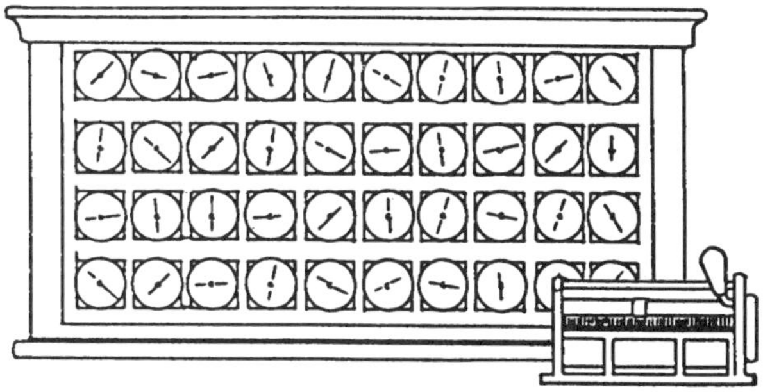

Hollerith's calculating machine, invented for the census of 1880, used elctricity instead of gears to perform calculations

Hollerith's machine was immensely successful. The general count of the population, then 63 million, took only six weeks to calculate, while full statistical analysis took seven years. This may not sound like much of an improvement over the nine years of the previous census, but Hollerith's machine enabled the Census Bureau to make a far more detailed and useful study of the population than had previously been possible. Based on the success of his invention, Hollerith and some friends formed a company that sold his invention all over the world. The company eventually became known as International Business Machines (IBM).

1.9 The Electro-Mechanical Computer

By the 1930's, key-operated mechanical adding machines had been developed which used a complicated assortment of gears and levers. Scientists, engineers and business people, however, needed machines more powerful than adding machines; machines capable of making simple decisions such as determining which of two numbers was larger and then acting upon the decision. A machine with this capability is called a computer rather than a calculator. A calculator is not a true computer because, while it can perform calculations, it can not make decisions.

The first computer-like machine is generally thought to be the Mark I, which was built by a team from IBM and Harvard University under the leadership of Howard Aiken. The Mark I used mechanical telephone relay switches to store information. The machine accepted data on punched cards, processed it and then output the new data. Because it could not make decisions about the data it processed, the Mark I was not, however, a real computer but was instead a highly sophisticated calculator. It was, nevertheless, impressive, measuring over 51 feet in length and weighing 5 tons! It also had over 750,000 parts, many of them moving mechanical parts which made the Mark I not only huge but unreliable.

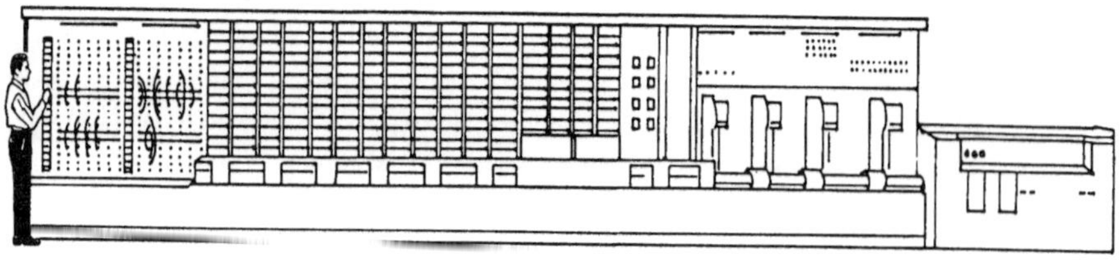

The Mark I weighed over 5 tons and was 51 feet long

1.10 ENIAC, the First Electronic Computer

In June 1943, John Mauchly and J. Prosper Eckert began work on the Electronic Numerical Integration and Calculator, or ENIAC. It was originally a secret military project which began during World War II to calculate the trajectory of artillery shells. Built at the University of Pennsylvania, it was not finished until 1946, after the war had ended. But the great effort put into the ENIAC was not wasted. In one of its first demonstrations it was given a problem that would have taken a team of mathematicians three days to solve. It solved the problem in twenty seconds.

ENIAC was different from the Mark I in several important ways. First, it occupied 1500 square feet, which is the same area taken up by the average three bedroom house and it weighed 30 tons.

Second, it used vacuum tubes instead of relay switches. It contained over 17,000 of these tubes, which were the same kind used in radio sets. Because the tubes consumed huge amounts of electricity the computer produced a tremendous amount of heat and required special fans to cool the room where it was installed. Most importantly, because it was able to make decisions, it was the first true computer.

Because it was able to make decisions, ENIAC was the first true computer

ENIAC had two major weaknesses. First, it was difficult to change its instructions to allow the computer to solve different problems. It had originally been designed only to compute artillery trajectory tables, but when it needed to work on another problem it could take up to three days of wire pulling, replugging and switch-flipping to change instructions. Second, because the tubes it contained were constantly burning out, the ENIAC was unreliable.

1.11 The Stored Program Computer

In the late 1940's, John von Neumann considered the idea of storing computer instructions in a central processing unit, or CPU. This unit would control all the functions of the computer electronically so that it would not be necessary to flip switches or pull wires to change the instructions. Now it would be possible to solve many different problems by simply typing in new instructions at a keyboard. Together with Mauchly and Eckert, von Neumann designed and built the EDVAC (Electronic Discrete Variable Automatic Computer) and the EDSAC (Electronic Discrete Storage Automatic Computer).

With the development of the concept of stored instructions or "programs", the modern computer age was ready to begin. Since then the development of new computers has progressed rapidly, but von Neumann's concept has remained, for the most part, unchanged.

The next computer to employ von Neumann's concepts was the UNIVersal Automatic Computer, called UNIVAC, built by Mauchly and Eckert. The first one was sold to the U.S. Census Bureau in 1951.

Computers at this time continued to use many vacuum tubes which made them large and expensive. UNIVAC weighed 35 tons. These computers were so expensive to purchase and run that only the largest corporations and the U.S. government could afford them. Their ability to perform up to 1000 calculations per second, however, made them popular.

1.12 The Transistor

It was the invention of the transistor that made smaller and less expensive computers possible, with increased calculating speeds of up to 10,000 calculations per second. Although the size of the computers shrank, they were still large and expensive. In 1963, IBM, using ideas it had learned while working on projects for the military, introduced the first medium-sized computer named the model 650. It was still expensive, but it was capable of handling the flood of paper work produced by many government agencies and businesses. Such organizations provided a ready market for the 650, making it popular in spite of its cost.

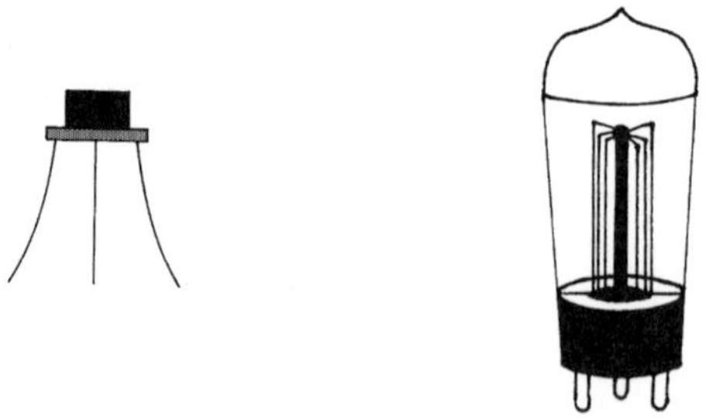

One transistor (not shown to scale) replaced many tubes, making computers smaller, less expensive and more reliable

These new computers also saw a change in the way data was stored. Punched cards were replaced by magnetic tape and high speed reel-to-reel tape machines. Using magnetic tape gave computers the ability to read (input) and write (output) data quickly and reliably.

Another important advance occurring at this time was the development of programming languages. Previously, computers had to be programmed by setting different switches to their On or Off positions. The first programming languages were very similar, being strings of 1's and 0's representing the status of the switches (1 for On and 0 for Off). These were called "low-level" languages. Languages such as FORTRAN (FORmula TRANslator), which was the first popular "high-level" language, allowed programmers to write in English-like instructions that had commands such as READ and WRITE. With them, it was possible to type instructions directly into the computer, eliminating the time consuming task of re-wiring.

One of the most widely used high-level programming languages today is COBOL. COBOL was first developed by the Department of Defense in 1959 to provide a common language for use on all computers. In fact, COBOL stands for COmmon Business Oriented Language. The designer of COBOL was Grace Murray Hopper, a Commodore in the Navy at the time. Commodore Hopper was the first person to apply the term "debug" to the computer. While working on the Mark II computer in 1945, a moth flew into the circuitry, causing an electrical short which halted the computer. While removing the dead moth, she said that the program would be running again after the computer had been "debugged". Today, the process of removing errors from programs is still called debugging.

A number of new high-level languages have been developed since that time: *BASIC* is a popular language used on microcomputers. *C* is a language designed by Bell Labs for programming large systems and is available on many computers today. Developed by the Swiss computer scientist Niklaus Wirth to teach the fundamentals of programming, *Pascal* is a language used by many schools. The latest language developed by the Department of Defense is named *Ada*, after the first programmer, Ada Augusta the Countess of Lovelace.

1.13 Integrated Circuits

The next major technological advancement was the replacement of transistors by tiny integrated circuits or "chips". Chips are blocks of silicon with logic circuits etched into their surface. They are smaller and cheaper than transistors and can contain thousands of circuits on a single chip. Integrated circuits also give computers tremendous speed allowing them to process information at a rate of 1,000,000 calculations per second.

One of the most important benefits of using integrated circuits is to decrease the cost and size of computers. The IBM System 360 was one of the first computers to use integrated circuits and was so popular with businesses that IBM had difficulty keeping up with the demand. Computers had come down in size and price to such a point that smaller organizations such as universities and hospitals could afford them.

1.14 The Microprocessor

The most important advance to occur in the early 1970's was the invention of the microprocessor, an entire CPU on a single chip. In 1970, Marcian Hoff, an engineer at Intel Corporation, designed the first of these chips. As a result, in 1975 the ALTAIR microcomputer was born. In 1977, working originally out of a garage, Stephen Wozniak and Steven Jobs designed and built the first Apple computer. Microcomputers were now inexpensive and therefore available to many people. Because of these advances almost anyone could own a machine that had more computing power and was faster and more reliable than either the ENIAC or UNIVAC. As a comparison, if the cost of a sports car had dropped as quickly as that of a computer, a new Porsche would now cost about one dollar.

1.15 Mainframe, Mini and Microcomputers

There are three general size categories by which computers are classified. The choice of which size computer to use depends on what tasks are planned for it and how much data it must store.

Mainframe computers are large computer systems costing many hundreds of thousands, if not millions, of dollars. Because they are so large, mainframes can carry out many different tasks at the same time. They are used by large corporations, banks, government agencies and universities. Mainframes can calculate a payroll, keep the records for a bank, handle the reservations for an airline or store student information for a university - tasks requiring the storage and processing of huge amounts of information.

Mainframe computers are large, often requiring their own rooms

Minicomputers are smaller than mainframes, usually taking up the space of one or two small bookcases. They are also less expensive, costing from about ten thousand to about one hundred thousand dollars. Minicomputers are used by smaller businesses, schools and research institutions. Like mainframes, minicomputers can do more than one task at a time. Although minicomputers store large amounts of data, they cannot store as much as a mainframe or process it as fast.

Minicomputers are smaller, but may be shared by many people at a time

Most people using mainframe and minicomputers communicate with them by using "terminals". A terminal consists of a keyboard where commands and data are entered and a monitor to display the output produced by the computer. The terminal is connected by wires to the computer, which may be located on a different floor or in a building a few blocks away. Some mainframe computers have over a hundred terminals attached and working at the same time.

Microcomputers are small and usually inexpensive. Often called "personal computers" or PC's, they can cost as little as one hundred dollars and fit on a desk top. Unlike mainframes and minicomputers, most microcomputers can only carry out one task at a time. During the past few years the processing speed and ability of microcomputers to store large quantities of data has increased at such a rapid rate that some of them now rival both mini and mainframe computers. The computer you will use is a microcomputer. In a microcomputer, the monitor and keyboard are attached to the computer allowing only one person to use it at a time.

1.16 How Computers Work

All computers process information, or "data." This data may be in the form of numbers, letters, words, pictures or symbols.

In order to process data, a computer must carry out four specific activities:

1. Input data
2. Store data while it is being processed
3. Process data according to specific instructions
4. Output the results in the form of new data

As an example of computer processing, it is possible to input a list containing the names and addresses of one hundred thousand people and then ask the computer to search through this data and print only the names and addresses of those people who live in Florida. Another example would be to ask the computer to add all integers from 1 to 1000 and print their sum (i.e. 1 + 2 + 3... + 1000 = ?). In each of these examples, data must be input so that it may be processed by the computer. In the first case, the input is a list of names and addresses, while in the second, a list of numbers.

1.17 The Components of a Computer

Computers contain four major components. Each component performs one of the four tasks we have described:

1. Input Device: a device from which the computer can accept data. Keyboards and disk drives are both examples of input devices. A specialized input device used on the Macintosh is the "mouse" which will be described in the next chapter.

2. Memory: an area inside the computer where data can be stored electronically.

3. Central Processing Unit (CPU): processes data and controls the flow of data between the computer's other units. It is here that the computer makes decisions.

4. Output Device: a device that displays or stores processed data. Monitors and printers are the most common visual output devices while disks drives are the most common storage devices.

The following diagram illustrates the direction in which data flows between the separate units:

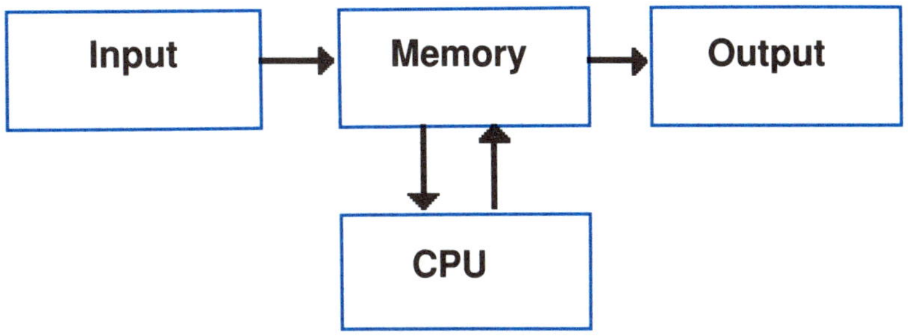

All computers accept information as input, process it (in memory using the CPU) and provide new information as output

Notice that all information first flows through the CPU. Because one of the tasks of the CPU is to control the order in which tasks are completed, it is often referred to as the "brain" of the computer. This comparison with the human brain, however, has an important flaw. The CPU only executes tasks according to the instructions it has been given; it cannot think for itself.

1.18 Advantages of a Computer

Although computers cannot think, they do have some advantages over the human brain. For example, suppose you were read a list of ten numbers (input) and were asked to first, remember them (memory), second, calculate their average (process), and third, write down the average (output). In so doing, you would perform the same four tasks as a computer. Now suppose you were read 100 or 1000 numbers and asked to calculate the average. Chances are you would get confused and tired performing all the calculations. The computer would have none of these problems. It would accurately remember all of the data and be able to quickly calculate the answers. The computer, therefore, has three important advantages over the human brain:

1. Reliable memory, with the ability to store and recall large amounts of data over long periods of time.
2. Speed, which enables it to process data quickly.
3. The ability to work 24 hours a day without rest.

Remember, however, that as reliable and fast as a computer is, it is only as "smart" as the instructions it is given by its program.

1.19 Hardware and Software

A computer requires both "hardware" and "software" to make it work. Hardware refers to the physical parts that make up a computer system and include keyboards, printers, memory, CPU's, monitors, and disk drives. Software describes the instructions or the program that is given the computer. Some software is made a permanent part of most computers, so that the tasks a computer must always be ready to perform can be carried out easily. Other software is entered into the computer only when a specific task is required. In this text we will use applications software written to perform a number of different tasks.

1.20 Memory

Most computers have two types of memory contained on chips, ROM and RAM. Read Only Memory or ROM contains the most basic operating instructions for the computer. It is made a permanent part of the computer and cannot be changed. The instructions in ROM enable the computer to complete simple jobs such as placing a character on the screen or checking the keyboard to see if any keys have been pressed.

Random Access Memory or RAM is temporary memory where data and instructions can be stored. Data stored here can be changed or erased. When the computer is first turned on this part of memory is empty and when turned off, any data it stores is lost. Because RAM storage is temporary, computers use disks as auxiliary memory storage. Before turning the computer off, the data stored in RAM can be saved on a disk so that it can be used again at a later time.

1.21 Central Processing Unit

The Central Processing Unit (CPU) directs all the activities of the computer. It can only follow instructions that it receives either from ROM or from a program stored in RAM. In following these instructions, the CPU guides the processing of information throughout the computer.

The Arithmetic Logic Unit, or ALU, is the part of the CPU where the "intelligence" of the computer is located. It can perform only two operations. It can add numbers and compare numbers. Then the question is: How does the computer subtract, multiply or divide numbers? The answer is by first turning problems like multiplication and division into addition problems. This would seem to be a very inefficient way of doing things, but it works because the ALU is so fast. For example, to solve the problem 5 × 2, the computer adds 5 two's, 2 + 2 + 2 + 2 + 2 to calculate the answer, 10. The time it takes the ALU to carry out a single addition of this type is measured in nanoseconds (billionths of a second). The other job of the ALU is to compare numbers and then decide whether a number is greater than, less than or equal to another number. This ability is the basis of the computer's decision-making power.

1.22 How the Computer Stores Data

Memory storage, both RAM and ROM, and the CPU are made of tiny chips of silicon. These chips are so small that they must be housed in special plastic cases that have metal pins coming out of them. The pins allow the chips to be plugged into circuit boards that have their wiring printed on them.

Chips are covered by intricate circuits that have been etched into their surface and then coated with a metallic oxide that fills in the etched patterns. This enables the chips to conduct electricity along the many paths of its circuits. Because there are as many as millions of circuits on a single chip, the chips are called integrated circuits.

The electrical circuits on a chip have one of two states, OFF or ON. Therefore, a system was developed that uses only two numbers, 0 and 1: 0 representing OFF and 1 representing ON. A light switch is similar to a single computer circuit. If the light is off, it represents a 0, and if on, a 1. This number system, which uses only two digits, is called the "binary" (base 2) system.

Humans find a system with ten digits, 0 to 9, easier to use primarily because we have ten fingers. The computer uses binary digits to express not only numbers, but all information, including letters of the alphabet. Because of this a special code had to be established to translate numbers, letters and characters into binary digits. This code has been standardized for computers as the American Standard Code for Information Interchange, or ASCII. In this code, each letter of the alphabet, both upper and lower case, and each symbol, digit and control function used by the computer is represented by a number. The name JIM, for example, is translated by the computer into the ASCII numbers 74, 73, 77. In turn these numbers are then stored by the computer in binary form:

Letter	ASCII	Binary code
J	74	01001010
I	73	01001001
M	77	01001101

1.23 Bits and Bytes

Each 0 or 1 in the binary code is called a "bit" (BInary digiT) and these bits are grouped by the computer into 8 bit units called "bytes". Each ASCII code is one byte in length. Note how eight 0's and 1's are used in the section above to represent each letter in JIM in binary form.

The size of the memory of a computer is measured by the number of bytes that make up its RAM. A computer might have, for example, 64K of RAM. In computers and electronics, K represents 2^{10} which equals 1024. The letter K comes from the word kilo, which means 1000, and although 1024 is more than 1000, K is still used as the abbreviation. 64K of memory, therefore, is really 64×2^{10} which is 65536 bytes.

It is possible to give a computer its instructions directly in binary code, typing in 0's and 1's using what is called "machine language". This is extremely difficult to do, which is the reason that high-level programming languages have been developed. The English word instructions from these languages are translated by the computer into binary code. The software we will use in the applications chapters of this text has already been programmed making it easy for us to use.

1.24 Applications Software

One of the most useful ways in which a computer can be used is to run commercially produced "applications software". This is software written by professional programmers to perform specific applications or tasks. In this text we will use an applications program called Microsoft Works which includes three common applications: word processing, data base and spreadsheet.

Word processing allows us to enter text from the keyboard into the computer and then manipulate it electronically. We will be able to insert and delete text, correct mistakes, move text and perform numerous other functions all on the computer screen. The text can then be printed.

Data bases allow us to store and manipulate large quantities of data using the computer. For example, a data base can store the names, addresses, grades and extra-curricular activities for all of the students in a school. It will be possible to add, delete or change data and produce printed reports using the data base.

Spreadsheets primarily store numeric data which can then be used in calculations. We will use a spreadsheet to store a teacher's grades and then calculate student averages. The primary advantage of a computerized spreadsheet is its ability to redo the calculations should the data it stores be changed.

One common factor shared by these three applications is their ability to store data on disk in a "file." A file is simply a collection of data stored on a disk in a form the computer can read. Unlike the computer's RAM memory, data placed in a file is not erased when the computer's power is turned off. This way, the applications program can access the information again and again.

A major advantage of Microsoft Works is that it is an "integrated" program. This means that a single program performs all three applications, allowing data stored in a file by one application to be transferred to another. Later in this course you will produce a data base file of names and addresses and then use this file in conjunction with a word processor file to produce personalized letters to everyone in the data base file.

Besides integrated programs like Works there are numerous other applications programs available. There are programs that can be used by musicians to produce musical scores and then play them on a synthesizer, programs that assist an architect in designing a building, programs that produce the special effects graphics that you see in the movies and on television, and much more. This book, for example, has been created and typeset using applications software.

As we progress in this text the usefulness of applications software will become increasingly obvious. With computers becoming more widely used, applications software is being written to assist people in almost every profession. Learning to use Works will give you an idea of how the computer and applications software can be applied to help solve many types of problems.

Chapter Summary

Man has searched for a machine to calculate and record data for thousands of years. The earliest of these devices were mechanical, requiring gears, wheels and levers, and were often unreliable. The advent of electricity brought about machines which used vacuum tubes, and were capable of performing thousands of calculations a minute. The unreliability of the vacuum tube lead to the development of the transistor and integrated circuit. Computers based on these devices were smaller, faster, more reliable and less expensive than before.

All computers have several parts in common: (1) an input device which allows data and commands to be entered into it, (2) some way of storing commands and data, (3) a Processing Unit which controls the processing, and (4) some way of returning the processed information in the form of output. In general, a computer is a machine which accepts information, processes it according to some specific instructions called a program, and then returns new information as output.

Today's microcomputer makes use of a CPU on a chip, the microprocessor which controls the actions of the computer. The CPU contains a special device called the Arithmetic Logic Unit (ALU) which performs any math or comparison operations. Based on von Neumann's concept, the computer stores both data and instruction in its memory at the same time. Memory comes in two forms, RAM chips which can be erased and used over, and ROM chips, which are permanent. Keyboards and disk drives are used to input data. Monitors and printers are used to output data. Because the contents of RAM are lost when the computer's power is turned off, disks are used to store data.

Vocabulary

ALU - Arithmetic Logic Unit, the part of the CPU that handles math operations.
ASCII - American Standard Code for Information Interchange, the code used for representing characters in the computer.
Bit - Binary Digit, a single 0 or 1 in a binary number.
Byte - A group of 8 bits.
CPU - Central Processing Unit, the device which electronically controls the functions of the computer.
Data - Information either entered into or produced by the computer.
Hardware - Physical devices which make up the computer and its peripherals.
Input - Data used by the computer.
K, kilobyte - Measurement of computer memory capacity, 2^{10} or 1024 bytes.
Keyboard - Device resembling a typewriter used for inputting data into a computer.
Memory - Electronic storage used by the computer.
Microprocessor - CPU on a single chip.
Monitor - Television-like device used to display computer output.
Output - Data produced by a computer program.
PC - Personal Computer, a small computer employing a microprocessor.
Peripheral - Secondary hardware device connected to a computer such as a printer, monitor or disk drive.
Program - Series of instructions written in a special language directing the computer to perform certain tasks.
RAM - Random Access Memory, memory which the computer can both read from and write to.
ROM - Read Only Memory, memory from which the computer can read only.
Software - Computer programs.
Terminal - Keyboard and monitor combination used to communicate with a mainframe or minicomputer.

Reviews

Sections 1.1-1.10

1. What is the primary difference between a computer and a calculator?

2. What is a computer program?

3. Why did early calculating devices not work well?

4. Was Pascal's Pascaline a computer? Why or why not?

5. If successful, could Babbage's Analytical Engine been considered a computer? Why or why not?

6. a) What was the first calculating machine to make use of punched cards?
b) What were the cards used for?

7. Why did scientists and business people want computers rather than calculators?

8. a) The Mark I was considered a calculator rather than a computer. Why?
b) Why was the Mark I unreliable?
c) What was the most important difference between the ENIAC and Mark I?

Sections 1.11-1.15

9. John von Neumann made one of the most important contributions to the development of modern computers. What was this contribution and why was it so important?

10. What made early computers so expensive?

11. What two innovations made the IBM Model 650 superior to earlier computers?

12. High level programming languages such as FORTRAN and BASIC were developed in the 1960's. Why were they important?

13. a) What is an integrated circuit?
b) In what ways is it superior to a transistor?

14. What invention made the microcomputer possible?

15. Compare a microcomputer with ENIAC. What advantages does the microcomputer have?

16. List three jobs which could best be performed on each of the following computers:

    a) mainframe computer
    b) minicomputer
    c) microcomputer

Sections 1.16-1.24

17. Suppose you were to use a computer to store the names of all the students in your school and then print only those names beginning with the letter "P". Explain how each of the four activities needed to process data would be performed.

18. a) List three tasks for which a computer would be better than a human working without a computer. Tell why the computer is better.
b) List three tasks for which a human would be better than a computer. Tell why the human is better.

19. a) What is computer hardware?
b) What is software?

20. Which of the four major components of a computer would be used to perform each of the following tasks?

    a) display a column of grade averages
    b) calculate grade averages
    c) store electronically a set of grades
    d) type in a set of grades
    e) decide which of two grades was higher
    f) store a set of grades outside of the computer

21. What is the primary difference between the two types of memory contained in a computer?

22. How would the computer solve the problem 138 x 29?

23. Why does the computer use binary numbers?

24. How does the computer store a person's name in memory?

25. a) What is a bit?
    b) A byte?
    c) A K?

26. How many bytes of memory does a 256K computer contain?

27. What is applications software?

Chapter 2

Introducing the Word Processor

File - Quit ⌘Q

File - Print ⌘P

Objectives

After completing this chapter you will be able to:

1. Describe what a word processor is.
2. Explain the capabilities that a word processor has that make it more powerful than a typewriter.
3. Start Works and enter the Word Processor.
4. Use the Word Processor to enter and modify text in a document.
5. Select menus from the Menu bar and choose different commands from them.
6. Save a word processed document on disk.
7. Load a previously saved document from disk into the Word Processor.
8. Print a word processed document.
9. Exit Works properly.

This chapter describes what a word processor is, and why it is a powerful tool for preparing documents. Directions for starting the computer, using disks and running the Works program are given. You will use the word processor to create, edit, print and save a document.

2.1 What is a Word Processor?

A word processor is basically a computerized typewriter. Therefore, using a typewriter and a word processor are alike in some important ways. Both use similar keyboards and both produce easy to read, professional looking documents. A word processor, however, has some powerful capabilities not shared by a typewriter. One of the most useful of these is the ability to easily make changes in a document.

The superiority of a word processor over a typewriter can be demonstrated by comparing their abilities to correct mistakes. When a typist makes a mistake on a typewriter, the error is immediately printed on the page. If the error is simple, an eraser or white-out can be used to eliminate it. If the error is large, involving many words, the typist may decide to throw the page away and start over.

When a word processor is used, the words typed are transferred from the keyboard into the computer's memory rather than on to paper. This allows a document to be edited electronically on the screen before it is printed. Instead of being forced to re-type an entire page to correct a simple error or make an editing change, a word processor allows only those words requiring changes to be re-typed. Words, phrases and even whole paragraphs can be inserted, changed or deleted. The computer automatically adjusts the position of words in the document, pushing them forward or backward as needed to accommodate the changes. Pieces of the document can also be moved or copied from one place to another. The word processor allows the document to be continually refined by making changes until what has been written truly reflects what you wish to say. This process is helpful in improving the quality of your writing.

Another useful feature of word processing is the flexibility it provides when deciding how a document is to look. Does the document look better with a half inch margin or an inch margin? Should a paper be double spaced or single spaced? Word processed documents can be displayed in different formats on the screen and compared without any re-typing. When the desired format has been determined, the document may be printed.

Text can easily be given different layouts using a Word Processor

What immediately distinguishes word processors from even the most sophisticated typewriter is that a word processor can save an entire document on a disk. The saved document can then be recalled at any time, and changes made or another copy printed. It is also possible to combine pieces of one document with another, so that lengthy paragraphs and even whole pages can be included in a new document without their having to be re-typed.

2.2 How To Use This Text

Throughout this text new commands and procedures are introduced in a two-step process. First, the command or procedure is discussed. You will be told what the command does and how to apply it, but will not use the computer at this time. Second, the discussion is followed by a section titled *Practice*. Each Practice leads you through a step-by-step example of how to use the command on the computer. You should actually perform the steps given in a Practice on the computer using Works. Practices also serve as reviews of the steps required to perform specific tasks. Because the discussion section explains the details of what is to be demonstrated, you should read it carefully before proceeding to the Practice.

2.3 Using the Mouse

The Macintosh computer comes equipped with a special input device called a "mouse":

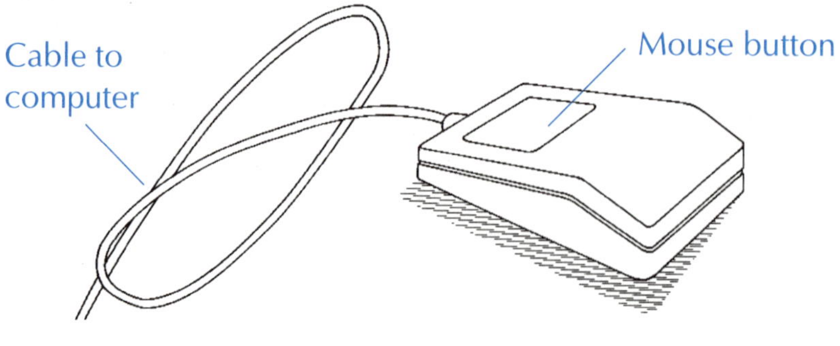

The Macintosh was one of the first personal computers to use a mouse

As you will see, the Macintosh System, the Works program and many other software packages make use of the mouse to perform different tasks. Before proceeding, you need to learn four important words that are used to describe the actions of the mouse.

Pointing:

The most basic use of the mouse is for pointing at different objects on the computer screen. When the mouse is in use an arrow called the "mouse pointer" is displayed on the screen:

Sliding the mouse along the top of the table causes the mouse pointer to move on the screen; slide the mouse to the left on the table and the mouse pointer moves to the left on the screen, slide the mouse to the right and the pointer moves to the right.

By moving the mouse, it is possible to place the pointer on different objects on the screen. Several different objects that you are likely to encounter are shown below:

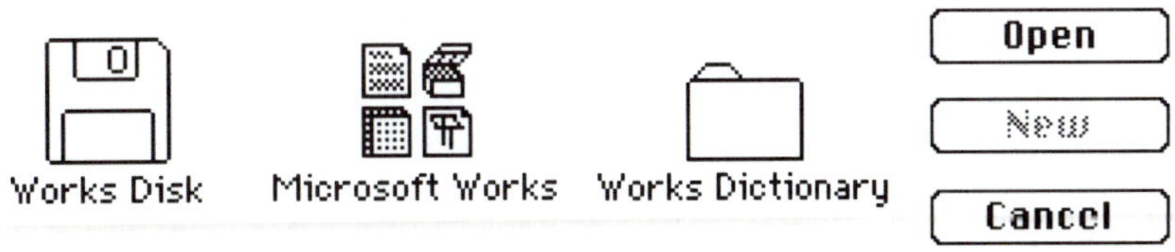

Objects such as these are common to Macintosh applications

Placing the mouse pointer on an object is called "pointing". In this text, when we say to point to an object on the screen, we mean to place the pointer on it by moving the mouse.

Clicking:

When the mouse pointer is pointing to an object, it is possible to select that object by pressing the button on the mouse and releasing it. This type of selection is called "clicking", and has different effects on different objects. When we say to select or click on an item, we mean to move the mouse pointer to it, and then press and release the mouse button.

Double-Clicking:

A special form of clicking is the "double-click". As the name implies, double-clicking requires that the mouse pointer be placed on an object and the button pressed twice in rapid succession. Double-clicking an object has different effects with different objects.

Dragging:

The last mouse technique is called "dragging". To drag an object, first place the pointer on it. Then the mouse button is pressed and held down while moving the mouse. In most cases this will move the selected object with the pointer. When we say to drag an object, we mean to place the mouse pointer on it, press and hold the mouse button and move the mouse. When the object is in the desired location, release the mouse button.

GETTING STARTED ON THE COMPUTER

You are now ready to start using the computer. This chapter takes a "hands on" the computer approach to introduce word processing and editing skills. You will learn how to start the computer and run the Works program. Simple "text" (characters, words and phrases) will be entered in the word processor to demonstrate how it may be edited, saved and printed.

2.4 Using Disks

Disks will be used both to start the computer and to save any files that you create. It is important to handle the disks carefully because they store large quantities of data in a magnetic format that is vulnerable to dirt and heat. Observing the following rules will help to insure that your disks give you trouble free service:

1. Keep disks away from electrical and magnetic devices such as computer monitors, television sets, personal stereos and any type of magnet.
2. Make sure that your disks are not exposed to either extreme cold or heat. Being made of plastic they are sensitive to temperature.
3. Be careful not to allow dust, dirt, or moisture to penetrate the disk by keeping it in a safe place when not in use.
4. Never touch the disk except by the edges of its jacket. Touching the disk's magnetic surface will usually damage it, destroying valuable data.
5. Do not bend or crimp the disk and never place paper clips on it.

2.5 Starting the Computer

Before using Works, it is first necessary to load the disk operating system (simply called the "System") into the computer's memory. The System contains special programs that the computer needs in order to run. The process of transferring the System from disk to computer memory is called "booting". The following instructions assume that you have a single disk which contains the System plus the Works program. Your disk has been prepared so that the System loads automatically. You will then tell the computer to run the Works program.

If you are using Works on a network, or if your computer has a hard drive, your instructions will be slightly different. Please check with your instructor or the Works manuals from Microsoft to determine the proper procedure for your computer.

2.6 The Open File Dialog Box

After starting Works, the following screen which is called the "Open File Dialog Box" is displayed:

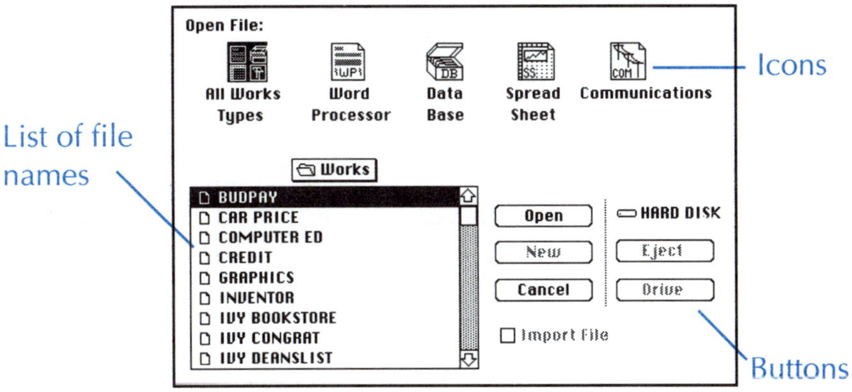

The Open File Dialog Box - yours may be slighly different

A "dialog box" is a group of options from which you may choose. Dialog boxes typically contain several different types of options. The most common of these are "buttons", "lists" and "icons".

Buttons: A button is similar to a switch that you push to initiate an action. In the Open File dialog box above, `Open` and `Cancel` are examples of buttons. To "press" a button, place the mouse pointer on the button and click once.

Note that there are several buttons shown with dimmed (lighter) text (`New`, `Eject` and `Drive`):

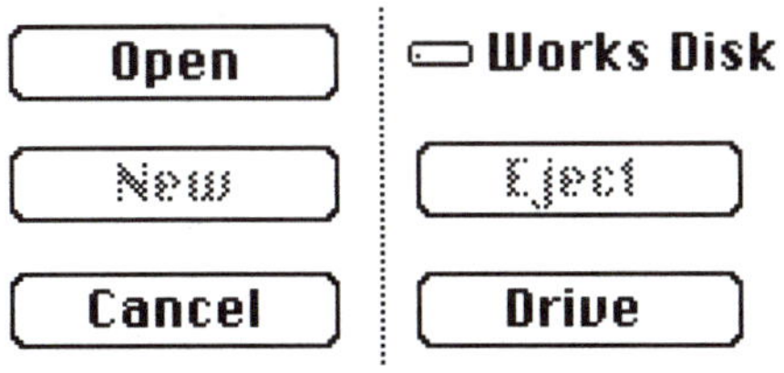

Dimmed options like the New button above have no effect at this time and may not be selected

The dimmed text indicates that these buttons will not operate at this time. Throughout all of its applications, Works uses dimmed text to designate options which are not applicable at this time.

Lists: A list is a group of items from which you may choose. The list in the Open File dialog box shows the names of files saved on your disk. To select an item from a list, the mouse pointer is placed on the item and clicked once.

Icons: Dialog boxes may contain "icons", small pictures which have an effect similar to a button. The five pictures along the top of the dialog box are icons:

To select an icon, move the mouse pointer to it and click once. In the last example, the "All Works Types" icon is selected. This is indicated by the fact that this icon is displayed in reversed text; white letters on a black background instead of black letters on a white background.

Selecting an icon has an effect on the contents of the dialog box. In this dialog box, selecting different icons controls what is displayed in the list. Selecting the "Word Processor" icon displays only word processor files in the list. Selecting "Data Base" displays only data base files, and so on.

As you progress in using Works you will have the opportunity to work with other dialog boxes and options.

2.7 About Files

The Works software is designed to work like an office. In an office, different business documents are stored in "files" in a filing cabinet. Before a file may be used, it must be taken from the cabinet and opened. In Works, each word processed document, data base and spreadsheet is stored in a different file on a disk. (Data base and spreadsheet files are explained later in this text.) Before a file may be used, it must be electronically transferred from the disk to the computer's memory. In order to create a new document, a new, empty file must first be created. New files are created using the Open File dialog box.

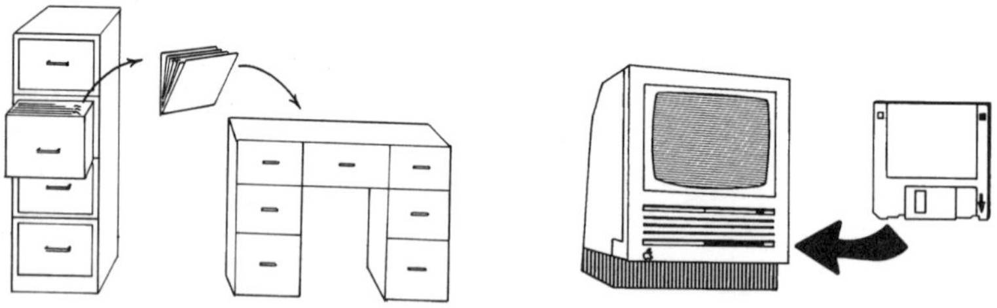

In an office, a file is taken from a cabinet and opened before it may be used. Computer files are stored on disk and opened using the Open File command.

Creating a new word processor file requires selecting two options from the Open File dialog box. First, the Word Processor icon must be selected. When this icon is selected, the New button changes from dimmed text to regular text, meaning that it is now possible to select this button, which creates an empty word processor document.

Files must be given names by which they can be identified. This is necessary so that Works can distinguish one file from another. File names can be up to 32 characters long and may contain upper- and lower-case letters, numbers and spaces. Colons (`:`) may not be used. Special symbols such as question marks and periods are legal, but should generally be avoided. Examples of legal file names are `Letter`, `CHAPTER 5`, and `2nd Memo`. It is important to give a file a name that describes what it contains. For example, a file containing a letter to Suzy Lee is better named `Suzy Lee` or `Letter to Suzy` rather than just "Letter." When a new word processor file is first saved, Works asks you to supply a name for it. This name is then used each time the file is retrieved from disk. Works keeps track of which files are word processor files, and which files were produced by other applications.

2.8 The Word Processor Screen

Word Processor documents are displayed on the Word Processor screen:

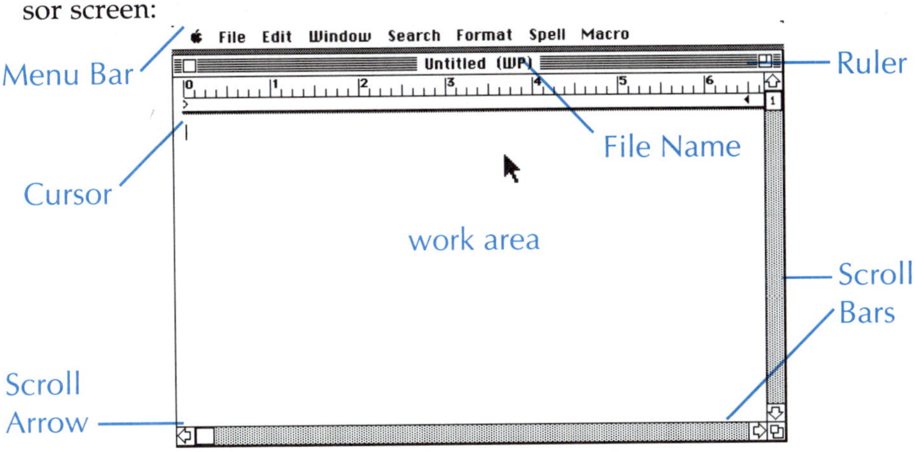

The Word Processor Screen

The Word Processor screen contains several features that will be important as you learn to use the word processor. Along the top of the screen is the Menu bar. Each word on the Menu bar is the name of a menu which contains commands which will be discussed as we proceed. Below the Menu bar is the Ruler. The Ruler is used to judge horizontal spacing and is explained in more detail later. Between the Menu bar and Ruler Works displays the name and type of file that you are using. The file name `Untitled (WP)` shown on the screen above is used temporarily by Works until you create a name for the file as described later. The `(WP)` indicates that this is a Word Processor file. At the far right and bottom of the screen are scroll bars used to display different parts of the document. The `1` in the vertical scroll bar indicates that page one of the document is currently displayed.

The center of the screen is called the Work area, and any text typed into the word processor appears here. The blinking bar at the top left-hand side of the screen is called the "cursor". It shows where characters typed into the word processor appear. Note the position of the mouse pointer in the work area. The mouse will be used to select menus from the Menu bar, and to perform certain operations on word processed files.

Whenever the Word Processor screen is displayed it is possible to enter text (characters, words and phrases) into the file whose name appears at the top of the screen. Any text typed on the keyboard appears on the screen at the current position of the cursor. As you will see, after text has been entered it is possible to make changes to it and perform several powerful operations on it.

2.9 The Computer Keyboard and Word Processing

Before proceeding, take time to familiarize yourself with some of the keys needed to do word processing. Most of the keys work just as they do on a typewriter, but some have special features. Information will be provided on additional keys as they are needed.

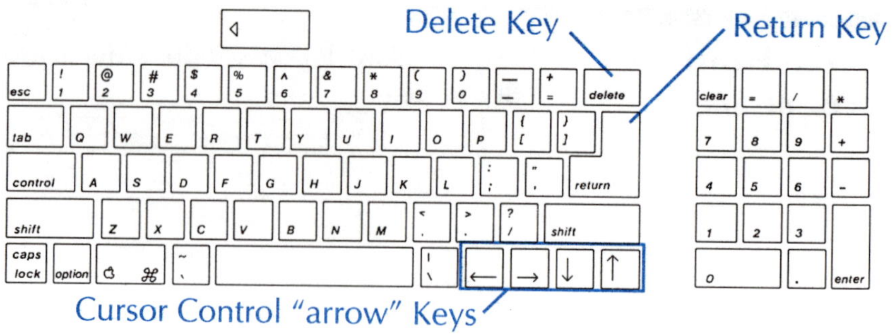

The Standard Macintosh Keyboard

Cursor Control "arrow" Keys: When the Word Processor screen is first displayed, a small blinking bar called the cursor appears in the upper left corner of the Work area. The cursor can be moved around the screen, without erasing or entering text, using the cursor control keys which are marked with arrows (up, down, left and right). To move the cursor down one line press the key marked with a down-arrow (↓). Similarly, to move the cursor up, left or right, use the keys marked with the appropriate arrows. Each of these keys is a repeat key, meaning that it will continue to move the cursor as long as the key is held down. The arrow keys can only move the cursor where text has already been typed. If you attempt to move the cursor to an area of the screen which does not contain text, the cursor does not move.

Return: In the word processor the Return key is used to end a paragraph or to terminate any line which does not reach the right-hand side of the screen. When Return is pressed the cursor moves on to the next line. Return may also be used to instruct Works to accept a menu choice or dialog box option.

Delete: The Delete key is used to erase a character. Pressing Delete erases the character directly to the left of the cursor. When a character is deleted any characters to its right are automatically moved over to close the gap left by the deleted character.

Do not confuse Delete with the left-arrow key. Both move the cursor one character to the left, but Delete erases characters as it moves, while left-arrow does not.

To insert text the cursor is first placed where the new material is to appear using the cursor control keys and then the new material typed. Works automatically inserts the characters you type at the current cursor position. Any text following the insertion is moved to the right to accommodate the inserted material. Deleting and inserting are powerful text editing features that allow almost any type of change to be made to a document.

Practice 1

In this Practice, you will turn on the computer and boot the System from disk. The Works program is then run from the same disk. If you are using Works on a network, or if your computer has a hard drive, your instructions will be slightly different. Please check with your instructor or the Works manual from Microsoft to determine the proper procedure for your computer.

You will enter text into a new file and then edit it. This Practice also demonstrates the use of the arrow and Delete keys to insert and delete characters.

1) BOOT THE SYSTEM

a. Place the disk carefully in the disk drive (the top drive if your Macintosh has two) with its label up and towards you as shown in the diagram:

b. Turn on the computer. After a few seconds, the disk drive comes on and the computer automatically loads the System from the disk.

c. After the System has booted, a screen similar to the following is displayed:

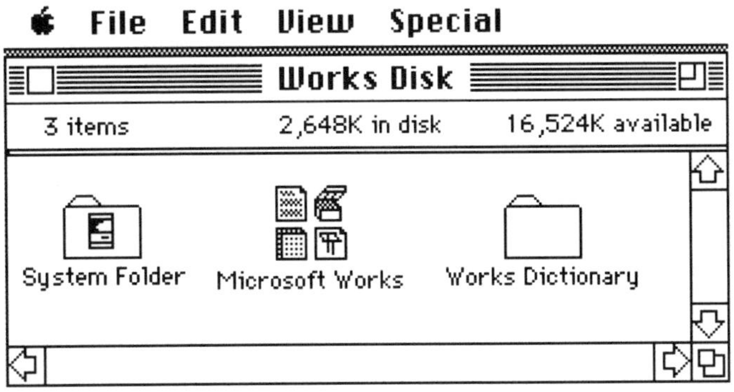

2) RUN THE WORKS PROGRAM

a. Using the mouse, position the pointer on the Microsoft Works icon:

b. Double-click on the Microsoft Works icon by pressing the mouse button twice in rapid succession.

c. The Works program will run, displaying the following copy-right screen:

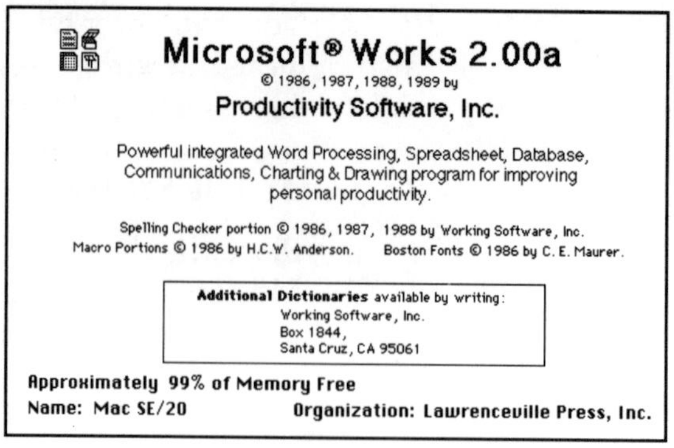

3) SELECT THE "WORD PROCESSOR" ICON

Move the mouse pointer to the Word Processor icon and click the mouse button. The icon is selected and displayed in reverse text (white letters on a black background.) Note that the `New` button is no longer displayed in dimmed text.

4) CREATE A NEW WORD PROCESSOR FILE

Move the mouse pointer to the `New` button on the dialog box and click the mouse. A new, empty word processor document named "Untitled" is displayed on the Word Processor screen. (Note the positions of the cursor and the mouse pointer on the screen.)

5) TYPE THE FOLLOWING LINE INTO THE FILE

Type the following line. Hold down the Shift key to generate the capital letters:

```
Hello, World!
```

Do not press Return.

6) ERASE THE EXCLAMATION POINT (!)

Press the Delete key once to erase the character to the left of the cursor, the exclamation point (`!`). Works automatically moves the cursor into the space formerly occupied by the erased character.

7) MOVE THE CURSOR WITHOUT ERASING ANY TEXT

Move the cursor to the right of the letter "r" by pressing the left-arrow key twice.

8) DELETE THE LETTER "r"

Press the Delete key once. The screen now contains the letters "Hello, Wold" with the "l" moving over to occupy the space where the "r" was.

9) INSERT A CHARACTER

Press the `r` key. An "r" is inserted into the line and the "ld" characters moved to the right to make room, creating "Hello, World".

10) MOVE THE CURSOR TO THE END OF THE LINE

Press the right-arrow key until the cursor is to the right of the "d" in "World". Press right-arrow again. The computer does not allow the cursor to be moved beyond the text.

11) DELETE ALL OF THE LETTERS IN THE LINE

Press Delete to erase the "d". Continue to press Delete until all of the letters have been deleted, and the cursor is at the very left side of the screen.

12) TYPE THE FOLLOWING POEM PRESSING THE RETURN KEY AT THE END OF EACH LINE:

```
Jack and Jill went up the hill,
to fetch a pail of water.
Jack fell down and broke his crown,
and Jill came tumbling after.
```

Return is pressed at the end of each line because the lines do not reach the right side of the screen. Use the Delete and arrow keys to correct any typing errors that you may have made.

<u>Check</u> - The screen should show the poem:

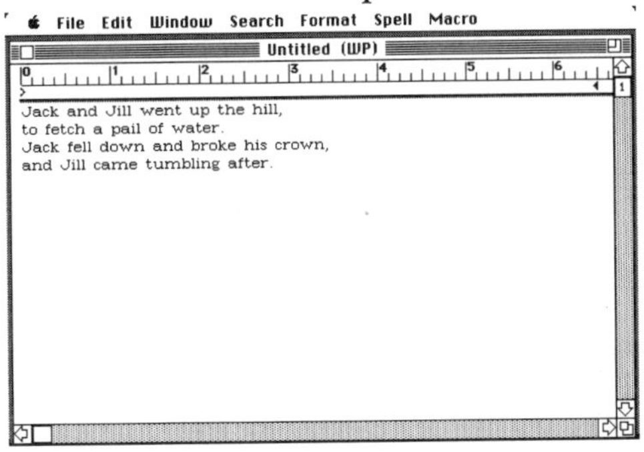

13) EDIT THE POEM

Use the Delete and arrow keys and insert new text as necessary to make the following changes in the poem:

i. insert "BIG" and a space before the word "pail"
ii. change the word "water" to "gold"
iii. change the word "crown" to "arm"
iv. change "came tumbling after" to "stood up and laughed"

<u>Check</u> - The screen should now show the edited poem:

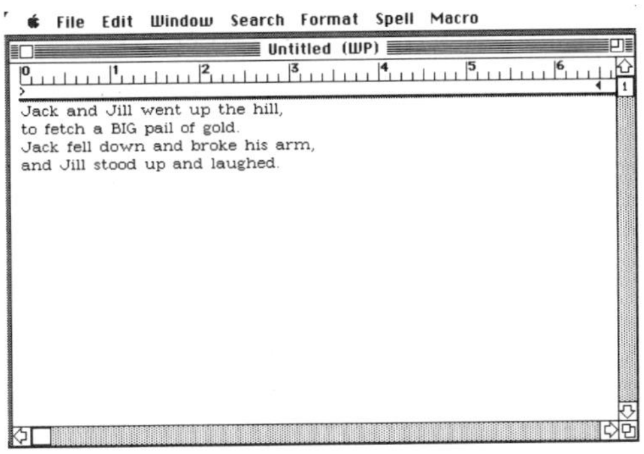

2.10 Using Menus

The topmost line of the Word Processor screen is the Menu bar. Each word on the bar is the name of a menu from which different commands may be chosen. Moving the mouse pointer to a menu name and holding down the mouse button displays the available commands on that menu. For example, placing the pointer on the word `File` and holding down the mouse button displays the File menu:

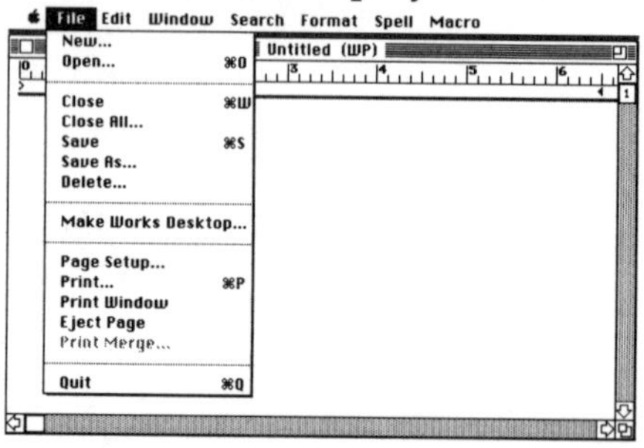

The File menu may be displayed by clicking on `File` *on the Menu bar*

Commands on the menu can then be selected by dragging the pointer down the list. Releasing the mouse button executes the highlighted command. Releasing the mouse button when no command is highlighted removes the menu from the screen and returns the cursor to the Work area.

There are times when certain menu commands will be displayed in dim text, meaning that these commands may not be selected at this time. In the File menu above the "Print Merge" command is displayed in dim text and may not be selected.

2.11 Saving a Document on Disk

Saving documents on disk is an important part of using a word processor. Because the computer's memory can only store data while the power is on, any data in memory is lost when the computer is turned off. However, if a copy of the document is saved on disk before the power is shut off, the document can later be retrieved from the disk and loaded into memory. Unfinished documents, as well as those that might need future editing or reprinting should always be saved on disk.

Another important reason for saving documents is to prevent their accidental loss. A momentary power interruption can wipe everything out of the computer's memory. Even bumping the power cord can sometimes cause the memory to be erased. It is therefore a good practice, especially when working on long documents, to save the document repeatedly. Then should a power failure occur, the document can be restored from the disk at the point where it was last saved. It is also important to save a document on disk before attempting to print it because a problem involving the printer could cause the document to be lost if it has not previously been saved.

When a document is saved, a copy of what is currently stored in the computer's memory is placed on the disk. Realize that the computer also retains the document in memory so that there are now two copies, one in memory and one on disk. The copy in memory is erased when the computer is turned off, but the copy on disk is permanent and can be recovered at any time.

Documents are saved using the Save command from the File menu. If this is the first time the file has been saved, you must then enter the file's name. Any subsequent saves will use the same name. A copy of the document in the computer's memory is then placed on the disk, using that name.

It is important to realize that any editing changes made to a previously saved file are not stored on the disk unless the file is again saved. It is also important to realize that saving an edited document replaces the original file on the disk, erasing the original.

2.12 Quitting Works

One of the most important procedures that you must learn is how to quit Works properly. Whenever you want to stop using Works either so that another program can be run or the computer turned off, the quit procedure should be performed. If Works is not properly exited files in memory can be damaged or lost. <u>Never just turn the computer off before following the quit procedure.</u> Exiting is accomplished by selecting the Quit command from the File menu. After quitting it is necessary to again run the Works program if you wish to continue working with it.

If you have created a new file or made editing changes to a previously created file, before quitting Works informs you that any new information will be lost if the file is not saved:

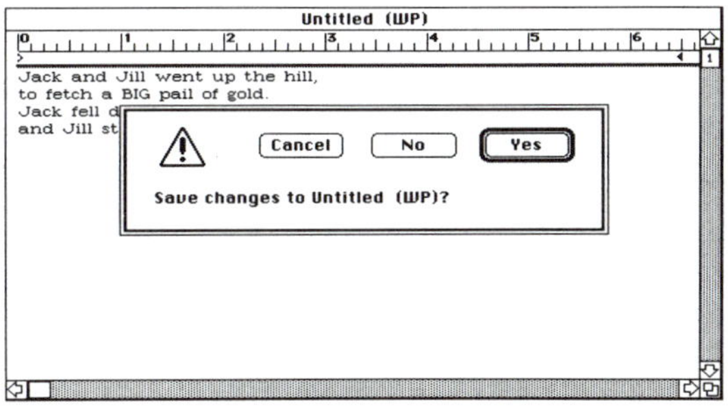

Works displays a warning box if you attempt to exit without saving

To retain the changes, use the mouse to click on the `Yes` button to save the file on disk. If you do not wish to save the new version, click on the `No` button and the previously saved version will remain on the disk unchanged. If the Quit command is selected by accident, click on `Cancel` to return to the word processor screen.

Practice 2

This Practice saves the file created in Practice 1 on disk, using the name EXAMPLE.

1) DISPLAY THE FILE MENU

a. Place the mouse pointer on the word "File" in the Menu bar.
b. Press and hold down the mouse button. The File menu is displayed.

2) SELECT THE SAVE COMMAND FROM THE FILE MENU

a. Continuing to hold down the mouse button, drag the mouse pointer down the menu until the Save command is highlighted.
b. With Save highlighted, release the mouse button to execute the Save command. Works then prompts you to enter the name of the file:

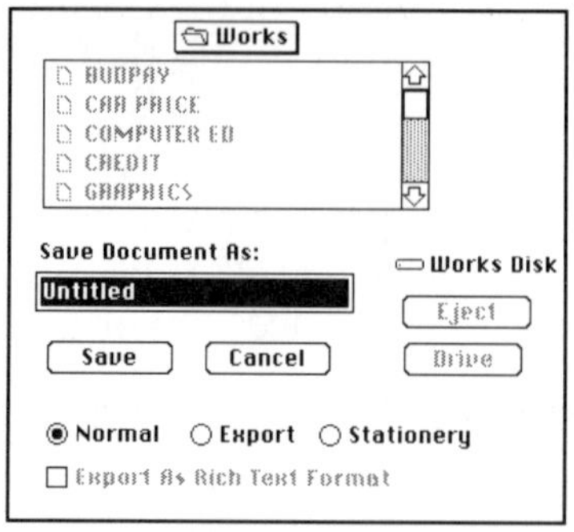

The Save command's dialog box

3) ENTER THE NAME OF THE FILE TO BE SAVED

a. The default file name "Untitled" is displayed. Type `EXAMPLE` in the Save Document As box, replacing the default name.
b. Click on the `Save` button. A copy of the file in memory is stored on disk using the name EXAMPLE. When Works removes the dialog box, note that the file name EXAMPLE (WP) is displayed at the top of the Work area.

4) PROPERLY QUIT WORKS

a. Display the File menu by moving the pointer to the word "File" on the Menu bar and holding down the mouse button.
b. Drag the mouse pointer to the bottom of the menu, highlighting the Quit command.
c. With Quit highlighted, release the mouse button.

The screen clears and the Macintosh System screen appears to inform you that Works has been exited and that the computer is now ready to run a new program. Only at this point can the computer be safely turned off. If you wish to reload Works, use the mouse to double-click on the Microsoft Works icon.

2.13 Word Wrap

When using a typewriter it is often necessary to determine if a word fits on the end of the current line being typed or if it must go on the next. Such decisions are not necessary when using a word processor because the computer determines if there is sufficient room for a word at the end of a line. If not, the word is automatically moved to the beginning of the next line in a process called "word wrap" or "wrap around".

One of the advantages of allowing Works to determine the arrangement of words on a line can be seen when deleting or inserting text. When new words are added to a line, any words to their right are moved over. If there is not enough room on the current line, those words which do not fit are moved to the next line. There may be a "domino" effect as words move from one line to the next to make room for the added text. Similarly, when deleting text, words may be moved up from previous lines to accommodate the change.

Sometimes the typist rather than the computer must determine where the end of one line and the beginning of the next are located. For example, you must specify the end of a paragraph by pressing Return, which moves the cursor to the beginning of the next line. Each time Return is pressed again a blank line is produced. Therefore, to end a paragraph followed by a blank line, press Return twice and then resume typing at the beginning of the next paragraph. Return must also be pressed to end any short lines which do not reach the right side of the screen, as in the poem entered in Practice 3.

Practice 3

This Practice demonstrates word wrap and how paragraphs are created. A new word processor file named NEWS STORY will be created.

1) BOOT THE MACINTOSH SYSTEM AND START WORKS

a. If the computer is off, turn it on and boot the Macintosh System as described in Practice 1.

b. If you have not already done so start Works by moving the mouse pointer to the Microsoft Works icon and double-clicking on it.

2) CREATE A NEW WORD PROCESSOR FILE

a. When the Open File dialog box is displayed, select the Word Processor icon by using the mouse to click on it.

b. Click once on the `New` button. A new, empty word processor document with the default file name "Untitled" is displayed on the Word Processor screen.

3) ENTER THE FOLLOWING STORY

Type the story below, allowing the computer to determine the end of lines. Press Return only at the end of a paragraph or a line which does not reach the right margin such as in the dinner menu. Leave a blank line between each paragraph, and type two spaces after each period:

```
     The annual Red Cross fund raising dinner
will be held in the main ballroom of the
downtown Hilton, at 7:30 PM next Saturday
night.  Music for dancing will be provided by
the Tom Steves Trio.  All community members
are invited, and tickets are $25.00 per
person.

     The menu for the evening's event will be:

          Fruit cup
          Roast Duck a l'Orange with Wild Rice
stuffing
```

```
          Garden salad
          Mint parfait

     After dinner, dancing will continue until
11:30 PM.  A reception will take place in the
hotel's Algonquin Room immediately following.
```

4) SAVE THE FILE ON DISK USING THE NAME NEWS STORY

a. Using the mouse, select File from the Menu bar. Press and hold the mouse button to display the File menu.
b. Drag the mouse pointer down the File menu to highlight the Save command. Release the mouse button.
c. Type the name `NEWS STORY` on the Save Document As line and click on the `Save` button. A copy of the file is saved on disk using the name NEWS STORY.

5) EDIT THE STORY

Use the Delete and arrow keys, and insert new text as necessary to make the following changes to NEWS STORY:

i. Insert the name of your town before the words "Red Cross". Note how the rest of the paragraph is adjusted to make room.
ii. The dessert has been changed from Mint parfaits to Double Chocolate Chip ice cream.
iii. The event will end at 11:00 PM and not 11:30.
iv. The location has been changed from the downtown Hilton to the Eastside Sheraton.

6) CREATE A NEW PARAGRAPH

a. Place the cursor before the "A" which begins the sentence "All community members...".
b. Press Return twice to create a new paragraph.
c. Press the Space bar 5 times to indent the new paragraph.
d. Add the following sentence to the end of the new paragraph:

```
Tickets are available from Mrs. Mitchell in the
Red Cross office during regular business hours.
```

7) ADD A HEADLINE TO THE STORY

a. Move the cursor to the very beginning of the document and add the following headline. Type 15 spaces before entering the word "FUND" to center the title:

```
FUND RAISER TO BE HELD AT EASTSIDE SHERATON
```

Note how the rest of the text moves to the right to make room for the headline.

b. Press Return twice to terminate the headline and insert a blank line between it and the rest of the story.

8) SAVE THE FILE AGAIN TO RETAIN THE EDITING CHANGES

a. Display the File menu by moving the pointer to the word File on the Menu bar and holding down the mouse button.

b. Drag the pointer to select the Save command from the menu to save the edited NEWS STORY on disk. The old file is now erased and cannot be recovered.

Check - The completed story should be similar to:

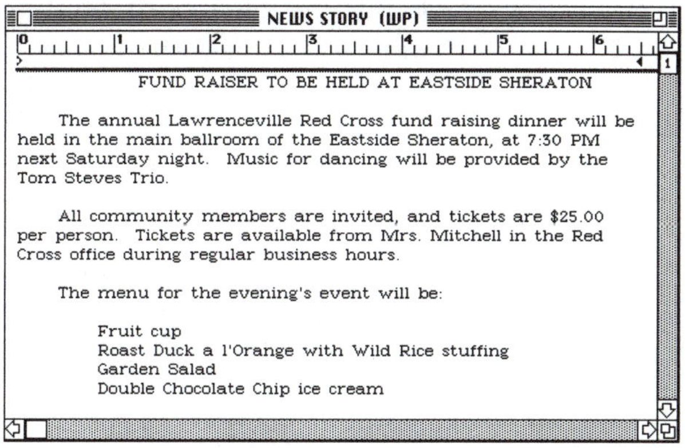

9) PROPERLY QUIT WORKS

a. Display the File menu by moving the pointer to the word File on the Menu bar and holding down the mouse button.
b. Drag the mouse to the bottom of the menu, highlighting the Quit command.
c. With Quit highlighted, release the mouse button to return to the Macintosh System screen. Note that only at this point may the computer be turned off.

2.14 Loading a Previously Saved File from Disk

Before a previously saved file may be edited it must first be transferred from the disk to the computer's memory. This is accomplished by selecting the desired file name from the list of previously saved files on the Open File dialog box:

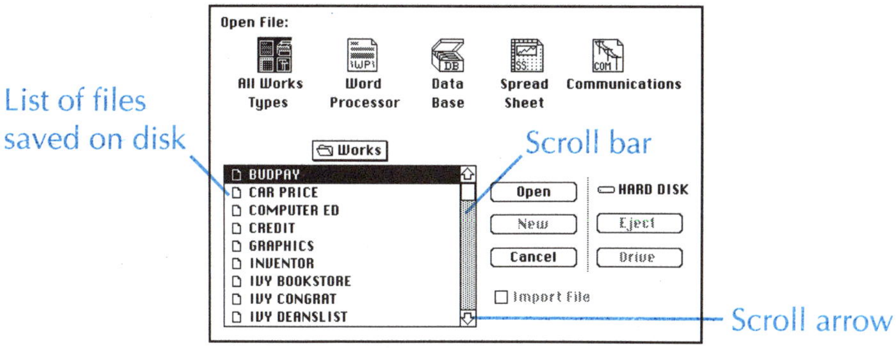

The list of file names in the Open File dialog box may be scrolled

Lists may contain more information than can be displayed on the screen at one time. For this reason they may be "scrolled." That is, it is possible to view different parts of a list by changing what part of the list is displayed on the screen. This is accomplished using the "scroll bar" at the right side of the list.

Clicking the arrow at the bottom of the scroll bar displays items further down in the list, while clicking the arrow at the top of the scroll bar displays items toward the beginning. In this way, the list box is like a window that displays only a portion of the list at a time. To bring unseen parts of the list into view the window can be moved up and down through the list using the scroll bar.

To select the file to be opened, click on the up and down arrows in the scroll bar until the desired file name is displayed in the list. The mouse pointer is then placed on the desired file's name. Once the file's name has been located, double-clicking on it transfers a copy of the file to the computer's memory, where it may then be edited. Note that you may see different file names on this list depending on what has been saved on your disk.

To limit the number of names displayed in the files list, first click on one of the icons at the top of the dialog box. For example, selecting the Word Processor icon displays only the names of word processor files.

Practice 4

In this Practice the NEWS STORY file will be transferred from the disk into the computer's memory, edited and then re-saved in its new form. If you did not quit Works at the end of Practice 3 do so now.

1) BOOT THE MACINTOSH SYSTEM AND START WORKS

a. If the computer is off, turn it on and boot the Macintosh System.
b. Move the mouse pointer to the Microsoft Works icon and double-click on it.

2) SELECT THE "WORD PROCESSOR" ICON

Place the mouse pointer on the Word Processor icon at the top of the dialog box and click on it once. The list of file names changes, displaying only word processor files.

3) SELECT THE FILE TO OPEN FROM THE FILES LIST

a. Move the mouse pointer to the list of word processor file names.
b. If necessary, click on the up and down-arrows on the scroll bar to move through the list until NEWS STORY is displayed.
c. Place the pointer on NEWS STORY and double-click the mouse button. A copy of the NEWS STORY file is transferred from the disk into the computer's memory.

4) EDIT THE FILE

Insert and delete text where necessary to make the following changes:

i. The event will start at 7:00 PM.
ii. The Schmenge Brothers Orchestra, not the Tom Steves Trio, will provide the evening's entertainment.
iii. Guests will have the choice of Fruit cup or Lime sherbet for an appetizer.

5) SAVE THE MODIFIED FILE ON DISK

a. Using the mouse, select File from the Menu bar.
b. Drag the mouse down the File menu to select the Save command and release the mouse button. The modified NEWS STORY file is saved on disk, replacing the old version.

Check - When complete, the modified file should be similar to:

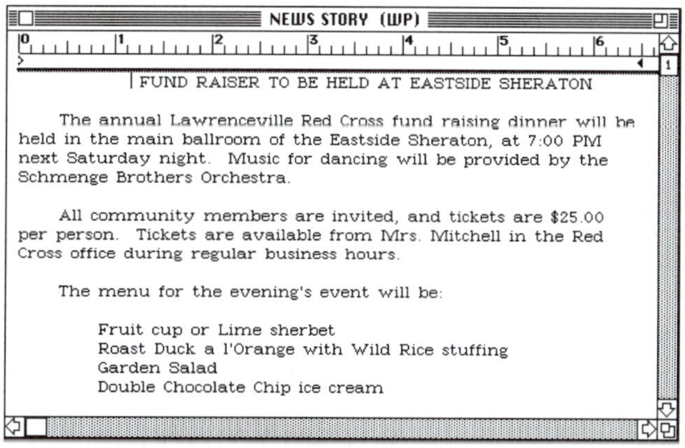

2.15 Printing a Document

Printing involves sending a copy of a document from the computer's memory to the printer. To do this, make sure that the computer is connected to a printer. Then check that the printer is turned on, is "on line" and that the paper is positioned at the top of a page. Before printing a document it should first be saved on disk so that, should an error occur and the document be erased from the computer's memory, it can be restored from the disk.

To print a document, use the mouse to display the File menu and select the Print command. The Print dialog box allows you to specify which pages, and how many copies to print:

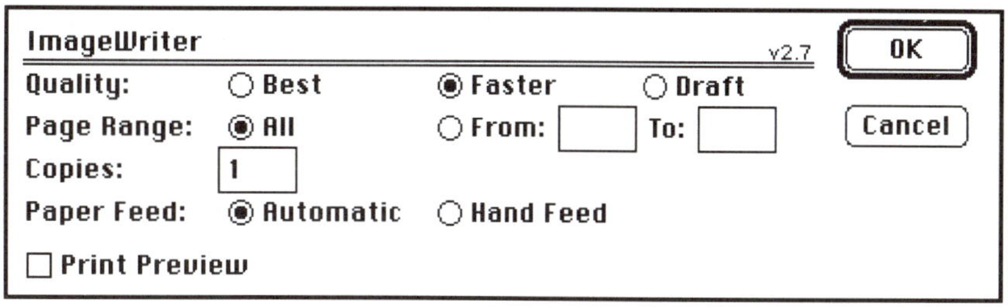

The Print command's dialog box

Because the default values are most normally used, simply click on the OK button (or press Return) and the printing begins. If more than one copy of the document is to be printed, double-click the mouse in the `Copies` box, type the number required and press Return. It is possible to interrupt the printing by holding down the Command key (the key marked ⌘) and pressing the period (.) key.

Depending on the printer you are using, it may be necessary to first tell Works what type it is. Check the Works manuals from Microsoft or with your instructor for the proper procedure if this is necessary.

Practice 5

The following Practice demonstrates how a word processor document may be printed and should only be attempted if there is a printer connected to your computer. Attempting to print without a printer attached could cause the loss of your file. Start Works if you have not already done so and open the NEWS STORY file created in the previous Practices.

1) DISPLAY THE FILE MENU

Move the pointer to File on the Menu bar and hold down the mouse button.

2) PRINT THE DOCUMENT

a. Drag the mouse down the menu to highlight the Print command. Release the mouse button to display the dialog box.
b. Click on the `OK` button to accept the default of printing 1 copy. The computer returns to the Word Processor screen when printing is completed.

3) QUIT WORKS

Select the Quit command from the File menu to exit Works.

2.16 Screen Scroll

Many documents are too long to be displayed on a single screen. For this reason, the Works screen acts like a window that displays only a portion of a document, up to 36 lines at a time. To bring unseen parts into view the screen window can be moved up and down through the document. This is referred to as "screen scroll".

The scroll bars below and on the right of the word processor screen are used to move the screen window in a document:

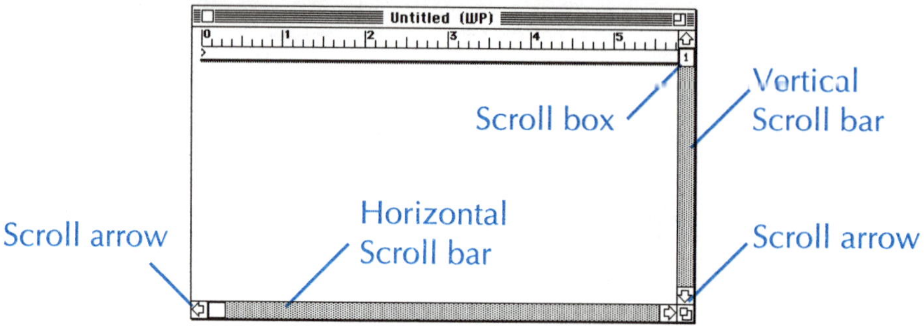

The scroll bars, scroll arrows and scroll box are used to scroll a document

Clicking on the down-arrow moves the window down one line at a time, on the up-arrow moves the window up one line. When working with long documents it can be time consuming to move the cursor in such small increments. Works can move the window in larger increments by dragging the page number box within the scroll bar. For example, dragging the box to the middle of the scroll bar causes Works to display the middle of the document. Dragging the box to the end of the scroll bar displays the end of the document. The scroll bar arrows can then be used to make fine adjustments to determine the portion of the document which is displayed.

Practice 6

This Practice demonstrates screen scroll and cursor movement. A previously created word processor file named SCROLL will be opened. Each line in SCROLL is numbered to help demonstrate screen movements.

1) BOOT THE MACINTOSH SYSTEM AND START WORKS

a. If the computer is off, turn it on and boot the Macintosh System.
b. Move the mouse pointer to the Microsoft Works icon and double-click on it. The Open File dialog box is shown.

2) OPEN THE FILE NAMED "SCROLL"

a. Click the mouse pointer on the Word Processor icon to limit the files displayed in the files list to word processor documents.
b. Move the mouse pointer to the list of word processor file names.
c. If necessary, click on the up and down-arrows on the scroll bar to move through the list until the file name SCROLL is displayed.
d. Place the pointer on SCROLL and double-click the mouse button to transfer a copy of the SCROLL file from disk into the computer's memory.

3) MOVE THE CURSOR TO THE BOTTOM OF THE SCREEN

Press the down-arrow key until the cursor is on the last line in the currently displayed window.

4) SCROLL DOWN 1 LINE

Press down-arrow again. Notice that a line disappears off the top of the screen and another appears from the bottom.

5) SCROLL DOWN 5 LINES USING THE SCROLL ARROW

Click the mouse pointer on the down-arrow in the vertical scroll bar 5 times. Note that each time down-arrow is pressed, another line scrolls off the top of the screen and the next line in the document appears from the bottom.

6) JUMP TO THE LAST LINE IN THE DOCUMENT

a. Place the mouse pointer on the page number box in the vertical scroll bar.
b. Hold down the mouse button and drag the box to the bottom of the scroll bar.
c. Release the button. The screen moves immediately to the last line in the document, line number 80 in this file. Note the "2" in the scroll box, indicating that this is page 2 of the document.

7) JUMP TO THE FIRST LINE IN THE DOCUMENT

a. Place the mouse pointer on the page number box in the vertical scroll bar.
b. Drag the box to the top of the bar and release the button. The window moves immediately to display the first line in the document.

8) MOVE DOWN HALFWAY

Drag the scroll box near the middle of the scroll bar and release the button. The text near the middle of the document is displayed.

9) SCROLL UP TO THE BEGINNING OF THE DOCUMENT

Place the mouse pointer on the up-arrow box in the vertical scroll bar. Press and hold down the mouse button. The screen scrolls up until the button is released. When line 1 is displayed, release the button.

10) QUIT WORKS

Using the mouse, select the Quit command from the File menu to properly exit Works.

Chapter Summary

A word processor is a computerized typewriter, with the addition of several powerful features. Documents ranging from research papers to business letters can be produced quickly and efficiently using a word processor. Word processing allows documents to be changed easily. Text can be inserted, deleted or modified without retyping the entire document. Formatting commands allow the appearance of text on the page to be changed. By saving the document in a file on disk, it can later be recalled, edited and printed.

Works uses a "mouse" as a special input device. An object is selected on the screen by pointing to the object and then pressing ("clicking") the mouse button. Some objects are selected by double-clicking; pressing the button twice in rapid succession. To move an object on the screen it is pointed to and dragged to its new location using the mouse.

The computer needs the Macintosh Operating System (or just System) to run. This is first loaded into the computer's memory from a disk. To run the Works program, double-click on the Microsoft Works icon on the screen. Works then loads and displays an opening copyright screen followed by the Open File dialog box. The Open File dialog box controls access to files, allowing new files to be created and previously created files to be opened.

Dialog boxes often contain buttons, lists and icons. Buttons are "pressed" by placing the mouse pointer on them and clicking once. Lists are groups of items, one of which may be selected by clicking on it. Icons are small pictures that are also selected by this technique.

Works uses menus to access word processor commands. Each menu is listed by name on the Menu bar. Clicking on the menu name displays a list of commands, and dragging the pointer to the desired command and releasing it executes that command. Many commands display a dialog box where information is entered before the command is executed. When a dialog box contains a list the pointer is used to select an option from the list and the mouse clicked.

This Chapter discussed the commands and procedures necessary for the production of word processed documents. The major steps in producing such a document are:

1) Boot the Macintosh System and load the Works program from the disk into the computer's memory.
2) Display the file to be word processed on the screen - either by creating a new file or loading a previously created file from the disk.
3) Enter or edit the document.
4) Save the document on disk.
5) Print the document if necessary.
6) Properly exit Works.

A previously saved file is opened using the Open command from the File menu or ⌘O. Saving a document is accomplished by executing ⌘S. When a file is saved it must be given a name of up to 32 characters which will then be used to identify it. Printing a document is accomplished by executing ⌘P.

The Works screen is like a window which displays a limited number of lines of a document at a time. The window may be moved through the document to display different text using the scroll bars and arrows.

Vocabulary

Arrow keys - Four keys that move the cursor up, down, right and left on the screen without changing any text.
Boot - To turn on the computer and load the operating system (the Macintosh System).
Button - Similar to a switch which initiates an action within a dialog box. Buttons are selected by clicking the mouse on them.
Character - Any letter, number or symbol which can be displayed on the computer screen.
Clicking - Selecting an object that has been pointed to by pressing the button on the mouse.
Cursor - A blinking line on the screen which indicates where characters entered from the keyboard are placed.
Cursor control keys - Keys used to move the cursor without having any effect on the text. See also Arrow keys.
Default - A command or option that is selected automatically if no other command or option is chosen.
Delete key - A key that erases the character directly to the left of the cursor.
Delete text - The removal of a character or group of characters from a document.
Dialog box - Screen used to enter information and select options required by a command.

Document - Any material that can be typed in the word processor, such as a letter, research paper or story.
Double-Clicking - Selecting an object that has been pointed to by pressing the mouse button twice in rapid succession.
Dragging - Placing the pointer on an object, then depressing the mouse button while moving the object to a new location.
Esc key - Key used to terminate (escape from) the computer's current operation.
File - Information created by Works which is stored on a disk. A word processor file stores a document.
File name - A name for a file stored on disk, up to 32 characters in length. Colons (:) may not be used in file names.
Format - The arrangement of text on a page.
Icons - Small pictures contained in a dialog box which have effects similar to buttons.
Insert text - Adding words or characters to a document.
List - Group of items from which you may choose.
Macintosh System - Operating System programs that the computer needs to run.
Menu - A list of commands that are available at a particular point in a program.
Menu bar - Line at the very top of the screen showing names of available menus.
Mouse - A device used to position the pointer on the screen.
Open File dialog box - Dialog box displayed by the Open command which contains options for creating new files or opening previously saved files.
Pointing - Placing the mouse pointer on an object on the screen.
Print command - Command on File menu which prints the currently displayed file: ⌘P.
Quit - To leave the Works program and return to the System.
Quit command - Command on File menu used to exit Works: ⌘Q.
Return key - Key used to indicate the end of an entry such as a dialog box option or response to a prompt. In word processing Return is pressed at the end of each paragraph. In general, pressing Return transfers the information typed into the computer's memory
Save - Transfer of data from the computer's memory to a file on disk.
Save command - Command on File menu used to save a file on disk: ⌘S.
Screen scroll - Moving through a document, the screen acts as a window showing only part of the document.
Scroll bars - Used to move the screen window and are located below and on the right of the screen.
Text - Any character or group of characters in a document.
Window - Part of the computer's screen displaying a file that may be used by Works.
Word processor - A computer application program that allows text to be manipulated, printed and stored.
Word wrap - When the computer decides whether to keep a word on the current line, or move it to the next based on the amount of space left on the line.
Work area - Center of the word processor screen, where text is typed and edited.

Reviews

Sections 2.1-2.6

1. What are three advantages of using a word processor rather than a typewriter to produce a letter?

2. How can using a word processor improve the quality of your writing?

3. Name three different businesses that could benefit from using word processors. Explain how each would benefit.

4. What is "pointing" and how is it done?

5. a) What is "clicking?"
   b) What is "double-clicking?"

6. What steps are required to drag an object?

7. a) Why is it important to take good care of a disk?
   b) What should be avoided when handling or storing a disk?

8. What is the Macintosh System and what is it used for?

9. What is meant by the term "booting" the computer?

Sections 2.7-2.9

10. What is a dialog box and what is it used for?

11. How do you press a button on a dialog box?

12. What does dimmed text indicate on a dialog box?

13. a) How is an icon selected?
    b) How does a selected icon appear on the screen?

14. a) What is a list?
    b) How is an item selected from a list?

15. What steps are used to create a new word processing file and display it on the screen?

16. a) What is a file?
    b) Why is a file given a name?
    c) What limitations are placed on the names which may given a file?

17. How may the cursor be moved down 3 lines and then 10 spaces to the right?

18. What is each of the following keys used for?
    a) Escape key
    b) Return key
    c) Delete key

19. What does pressing the Return key do when typing text in the Word Processor?

20. What is the difference between pressing the Delete key four times or the left-arrow key four times when the cursor is located in the middle of a line of text?

Sections 2.10 - 2.13

21. a) How are menus selected from the Menu bar?
b) How may you return directly from a menu to the work area without executing a command?

22. Give three reasons why it is useful to save a word processor file on disk.

23. If you are working on a word processor document when the power is turned off, how can you retrieve the document if it has not been previously saved on disk?

24. When a file is saved where does it go? Is it removed from the computer's memory?

25. a) Why is it important to exit Works properly?
b) List the steps required to exit Works starting from the Word Processor screen so that the file currently being worked on is saved.

26. What is "word wrap?"

27. What must be done to end a paragraph and start a new one?

28. Describe the operations necessary to change the word "men" to "people" in the sentence:

```
Now is the time for all good men to come to the
aid of the party.
```

29. a) If a previously saved file is edited will the changes be automatically made to the file on disk, or must the file be saved again?
b) What happens to an original file if an edited version of the same file is saved?

Sections 2.14 - 2.16

30. What steps must be taken to load a previously saved file from disk into the computer's memory?

31. a) Why is it important to save a document before printing it?
b) What command is used to print a document?

32. a) What is "screen scroll"?
b) Describe two ways to scroll through a document?

Exercises

1. a) Enter the following letter in the word processor in a new file:

```
                                    September 26, 1990


Mrs. Margaret Livingston
123 Main St.
Reedsburg, WI 53959

Dear Margaret,

     I am writing to let you know how much I am
enjoying my new word processor.  It has so many
advantages over my old typewriter.

     One thing that I will never miss is white-
out.  For years we used it to make corrections
and it left a thick patch on the page.

     Now corrections are handled on the computer
screen so that no one knows about my mistakes.
Once I ended up re-typing an 8 page letter to
correct the misspelling of the bank director's
name.  With my word processor it would have
taken about 1 minute to retrieve the letter from
a floppy disk and make the changes on the
screen.  The revised letter could then have been
printing while I got a cup of coffee.

     Thanks again for all your help.

                                    Sincerely,


                                    A. Secretary
```

b) Save the letter under the name MARGE on your data disk.

c) Print a copy of MARGE on the printer.

d) Edit the letter as follows:

Delete the word "old" in the last line of paragraph one.
Delete the sentence "One thing that I will never miss is white-out."
Change "For years we used it" to "For years we used white-out".
Change "so that no one knows about my mistakes" to "so that my mistakes are invisible"
Replace "A. Secretary" with your name.

Add the following lines to the beginning of the third paragraph:

`“My boss likes to make several revisions of each letter and memo that leaves the office. That means that each has to be re-typed, often several times.”`

e) Save the modified letter on your data disk.

f) Print the revised letter.

2. Word processors can be used to create documents which store a variety of different information.

   a) Enter each of the following sayings into the word processor leaving a blank line between each. Name the file BENJAMIN in honor of Benjamin Franklin who wrote many famous sayings in Poor Richard's Almanac:

```
An apple a day keeps the doctor away.

A penny for your thoughts.

Every cloud has a silver lining.

A penny saved is a penny earned.

Early to bed, early to rise, makes a man
healthy, wealthy and wise.
```

   b) Save BENJAMIN on your data disk.

   c) Print a copy of BENJAMIN on the printer.

   d) Edit the saying on each line as follows:

      Line 1: change `apple` to `orange`
      Line 2: change `penny` to `dollar`
      Line 3: change `silver` to `gold`
      Line 4: change `penny` to `quarter` (twice)
      Line 5: change `man` to `person`

   e) Save the modified BENJAMIN file on your data disk.

   f) Print the modified BENJAMIN file.

3. You are thinking of applying to several colleges around the country.

   a) Use the word processor to create a file named APPLY which contains a letter requesting information and an application from a college. Use the letter at the top of the next page as a guide, substituting your own information:

```
September 28, 1990

Ivy University
Admissions Department
1 College Court
Newton, IA 63343

Dear Sirs:

I am interested in attending Ivy University.  I
will graduate in 1990 and plan to major in
medical communications.  I have been president
of the Student Congress for 4 years and captain
of the Debate Team for 2 years.  I have varsity
letters in three sports and was a member of the
All-state gymnastics and swim teams.  My current
grade point average is 3.95.

Please send a course catalog and application to
me at this address:

     A. Student
     223 Main Street
     Anytown, USA 11111

Thank you very much.

Sincerely,


A. Student
```

b) Save the APPLY letter on your data disk.

c) Print the APPLY letter.

d) The good news is that the new grades are out and you finally got that 4.0. Change your GPA in APPLY.

e) The bad news is that you lost the recent Student Congress election. Change the file to read "3 and a half years".

f) Change the name and address of Ivy University to a school you would like to attend and print the new letter. Be sure to change the school's name in the first sentence as well.

g) Save the updated APPLY letter on disk.

4. Your cousin is visiting you from out of town. Using the word processor, create lists of directions in a file named DIRECTIONS that your cousin can follow to go from your house to the following places:

   a) Your school. Be sure to describe what time school gets out and where your cousin should meet you.

b) The local fast food restaurant.

c) The closest grocery store to your house.

d) Your video rental club. Be sure to include your membership number in the directions so that your cousin can rent some videos.

e) Your cousin is not the brightest person in the world. Leave complete instructions describing how to use your VCR to play a video.

f) Save DIRECTIONS on disk and print a copy.

5. Your school newspaper has an opening for an arts critic. Use the word processor to create a review of the last movie, concert, play or art show you attended in a new file named CRITIC. Save and print a copy of CRITIC.

6. A word processor can be used as a diary. Create a new file named DIARY and make a journal entry describing what you did last week. Be sure to include your plans for the upcoming weekend. Save and print a copy of your diary page.

7. Your English teacher has asked you to write an original essay entitled "How I spent my summer vacation." Use the word processor to produce a small version of this essay. Save the essay on disk in a file named ESSAY and then print a copy of it.

8. Use the word processor to produce an advertisement for an upcoming dance or other special event. Save the file on your data disk under the name ADVERTISEMENT and print a copy. A possible example is shown below:

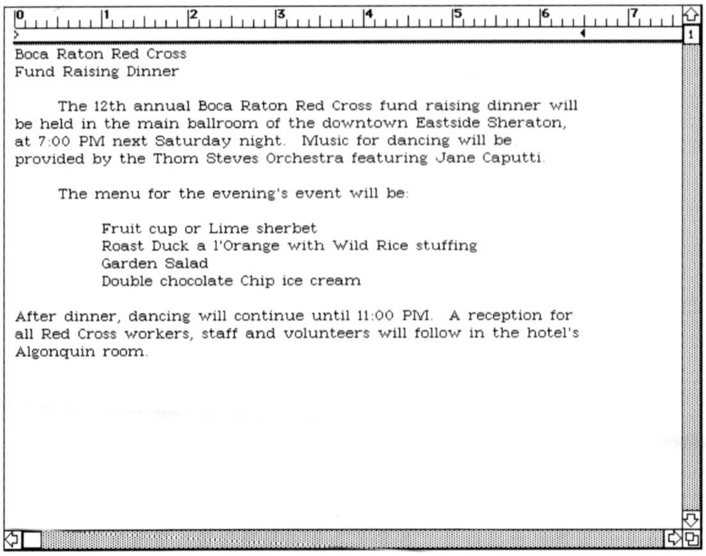

Boca Raton Red Cross
Fund Raising Dinner

The 12th annual Boca Raton Red Cross fund raising dinner will be held in the main ballroom of the downtown Eastside Sheraton, at 7:00 PM next Saturday night. Music for dancing will be provided by the Thom Steves Orchestra featuring Jane Caputti.

The menu for the evening's event will be:

Fruit cup or Lime sherbet
Roast Duck a l'Orange with Wild Rice stuffing
Garden Salad
Double chocolate Chip ice cream

After dinner, dancing will continue until 11:00 PM. A reception for all Red Cross workers, staff and volunteers will follow in the hotel's Algonquin room.

Chapter 3

Manipulating Text with the Word Processor

File - Close ⌘W

File - Page Setup

Format - Justification

Edit - Undo ⌘Z

Edit - Copy ⌘C

Search - Find ⌘F

Search - Go to Page # ⌘G

Search - Replace ⌘R

Spell - Correct Spelling

Objectives

After completing this chapter you will be able to:

1. Manipulate windows.
2. Use formatting to control the placement of text on the page.
3. Create tables in documents using indents and tabs.
4. Create headers and footers for printed documents.
5. Emphasize areas of text using underlining, bold characters and line spacing.
6. Move text from one position to another.
7. Copy blocks of text in a document.
8. Use the Find and Replace commands.
9. Use the spelling checker to proof a document.

Chapter 2 introduced the options necessary to create, edit, save and print Word Processor documents. In this chapter techniques that improve the appearance and readability of such documents are covered. Included are:

- formatting features that control the arrangement of text on a page, such as margins, paragraph alignment (flush left, flush right, justified or centered), tabs and pagination (how text is divided into pages).
- options that manipulate blocks of text, including cut-and-paste features that move and copy text from one place to another.
- techniques to search for specific text in a document, replace text with different text, and locate and correct misspelled words.

Many of the word processing options discussed in this chapter are powerful tools, capable of manipulating text in ways that go far beyond what a typewriter can do. After familiarizing yourself with these tools, you will understand why word processing has achieved such widespread popularity.

Formatting is the process of creating or changing the way a word processed document appears. As will be described below, formatting involves the placement of text in a document, including the control of spacing between words and lines, and the placement and style of text.

3.1 Using Windows

Each document in Works is displayed in a "window" on the screen:

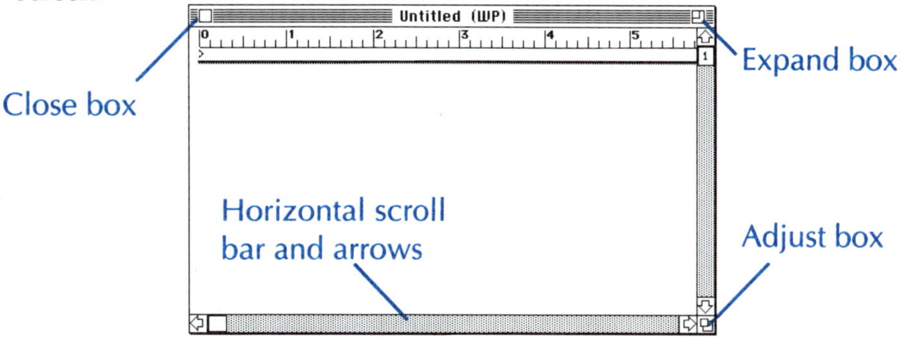

Each window has its own Close, Expand and Adjust boxes

In the last chapter you used the vertical Scroll bar on the right side of the window to scroll through a document. There are also several other window options which you should be aware of.

Close Box:

When you are finished working with the file displayed in a window, you may close the window by clicking the mouse pointer on the Close Box at the upper left-hand corner of the window. Closing the window removes it from the screen.

Adjust Box:

The size of the window may be changed by using the Adjust box in the lower right-hand corner. Dragging this box causes the window to be re-sized, wider or more narrow, taller or shorter. This will be of use later when we have several windows open at the same time.

Expand Box:

Works can be told to automatically expand the window to fill the screen by clicking the mouse pointer on the Expand box located at the top right-hand corner of the window. Clicking on the Expand box again returns the window to its previous size.

Horizontal Scroll Bar:

Windows may also be scrolled horizontally to display information which is off the screen to either side. To scroll horizontally, either click on the right or left arrow, or use the mouse to drag the scroll box as you did when scrolling vertically in the last chapter.

3.2 The Command Key

The Command key is located at the bottom of the keyboard, next to the space bar. Sometimes called the "Open-Apple" or "Propeller key" it is used to execute a variety of commands as we will see.

The Command key can be used to execute commands without a menu

One application of the Command key is to execute menu commands without using the mouse. For example, in the File menu the Save command has the notation ⌘S next to it:

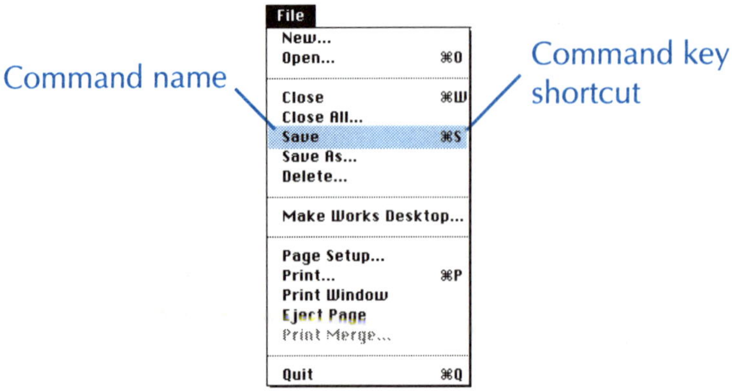

Command key shortcuts are listed in menus next to their commands

This means that holding down the Command key and pressing **S** at the same time will execute the Save command without first displaying the menu. This shortcut can save time because you do not have to take your hands off of the keyboard. Another shortcut is the Print command which can be executed by pressing ⌘P. Other Command key shortcuts will be discussed as we proceed.

3.3 Tabs and Tab Stops

Tabs are used to position text within a line or to create tables of data. Works has default tab stops at every half inch. Pressing the Tab key moves the cursor to the next tab stop to the right.

Default tab stops are generally used for indenting text from the margin. When beginning a new paragraph, pressing Tab once indents the first line half an inch before entering text. When creating the heading of a letter, your address and the date should be aligned near the right side of the page. By using the same number of tabs, the cursor may easily be placed at the desired location before each line is typed. While default tabs are initially set to every half inch, they can be changed to any desired interval.

Although tabs move the cursor more than one space, they are generated by a single keystroke and may be inserted into text or deleted from text as any other character. Pressing the Tab key does not actually insert the number of individual space characters needed to move the cursor to the next tab stop. Instead, a code is placed in the text which tells the computer to move to the next tab stop. Deleting a tab requires that only the code be deleted. The text will automatically be moved to the left to fill the space created by removing the tab.

It is possible to insert a Tab into a previously entered line of text. After a line has been typed, positioning the cursor in the line and pressing Tab will move the characters to the right of the tab to the next tab stop.

3.4 The Ruler

Directly above the work area is a ruler that is used to measure distances from the left side of the page. This ruler gauges the placement of horizontal formatting features including tabs, margins and indents (to be discussed later in this chapter). Each vertical line on the ruler represents one tenth of an inch, and full inches are indicated by a number. Below the ruler is the format line. The triangles on the format line mark the left (▶) and right (◀) edges of the current paragraph.

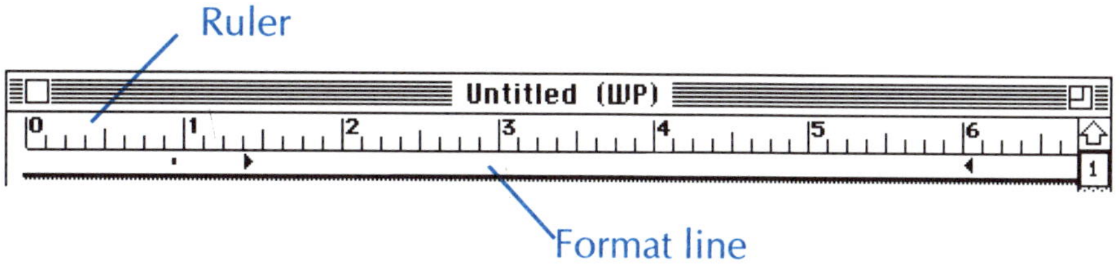

The Ruler and Format line are used to set margins and indents

3.5 Setting Individual Tab Stops

In addition to the default tab stops, Works allows individual tab stops to be set anywhere on the line. These differ from default tab stops in that, rather than appearing at regular intervals, individual tab stops may be inserted anywhere on the line.

It is also possible to remove tab stops. Setting an individual tab stop automatically removes any default stops to its left. That is, setting an individual tab stop at 1.4 inches removes the default stops at .5 and 1.0 inches. The stop at 1.5 inches is not effected.

There are several different types of tab stops. The default tab stop alignment is Left-aligned, meaning that text entered at that stop will be aligned at the stop's left. Left-aligned stops are marked with a ⊢ on the ruler. It is also possible to create right-, center- and decimal-aligned tab stops which are marked with an ⊣ , ┼ and :⊣ respectively. A right tab aligns the end of the text at the stop while a center tab centers the text equidistant over the stop. Decimal tabs are used to align columns of numbers with their decimal points at the stop. Examples of each stop are shown below with the corresponding ruler:

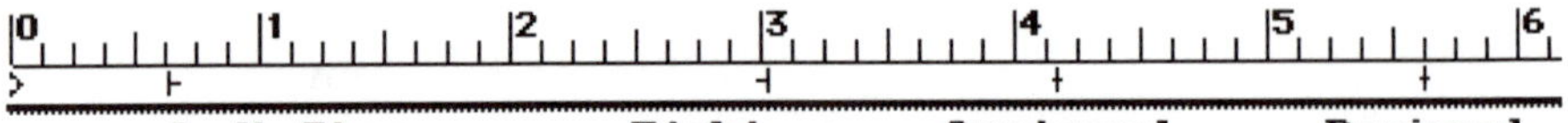

Left Stop	Right	Centered	Decimal
Name	Amy	Eppelman	12.34
Address	Philadelphia	PA	1234.567
Phone	123-4567	(215)	123

The Ruler shows the locations and alignment of tab stops

Individual tab stops are set using the mouse and the format line. Clicking the mouse once in the format line inserts a new left-aligned tab stop:

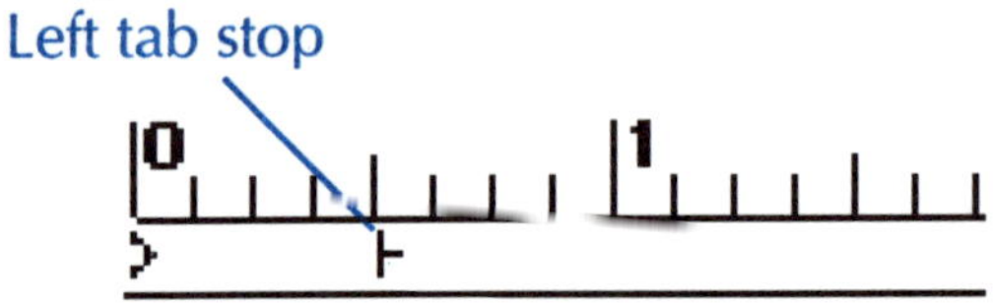

Left tab stop in Format line

Note the left-aligned marker shown on the format line. Dragging this marker to a new location changes the position of the stop. To change the alignment of the stop, click on the marker. One click produces a left-aligned stop. Clicking on that marker changes the stop to right-aligned. Clicking again on that maker changes the stop to centered, and clicking again changes the stop to decimal aligned. To return to left-aligned, click on the stop a fourth time.

To remove a specific stop, drag its marker below the format line, into the work area. Releasing the mouse button completes the procedure, removing the marker. Any text which was aligned at that stop is automatically reformatted. All tab stops that are set or cleared are retained when the file is saved on disk, so that the next time it is loaded the file will have the same stops.

It is important to note that tab stops are considered part of a paragraph's format. That is, it is possible to have different tab stops set for different paragraphs in the same document. Therefore, when you set a tab stop, only the text in the paragraph which currently contains the cursor is effected.

Practice 1

This Practice demonstrates how to use tabs, and set and clear tab stops.

1) BOOT THE MACINTOSH SYSTEM AND START WORKS

a. Following the directions given in Chapter 2, boot the Macintosh System.
b. Click the mouse on the Microsoft Works icon to start Works. The Open File dialog box is displayed.

2) OPEN A NEW WORD PROCESSOR FILE

a. Move the pointer to the Word Processor icon and click the mouse. The icon is displayed in reverse text (white letters on a black background.)
b. Move the mouse pointer to the New button and click the mouse. A new, empty word processor document named "Untitled" is displayed on the Word Processor screen.

3) INSERT THREE TABS

Press the Tab key 3 times. Because you have placed three tabs into the document, the cursor moves 1.5 inches to the right on the screen, the position of the third default tab stop.

4) DELETE THE TABS

Press the Delete key 3 times to remove the tabs. Each time the key is pressed the cursor moves 0.5 inches to the left. By deleting these markers you have not affected the tab stops in any way, only removed the tab characters from this line.

5) ENTER THE FOLLOWING TEXT

Type:

```
This is a test sentence.
```

Do not press Return.

6) INDENT THE SENTENCE BY INSERTING A TAB

a. Hold down the left arrow key to move the cursor to the beginning of the line.
b. Press the Tab key once to insert a tab character at the cursor's position. The sentence is indented one half inch, to the position of the first default tab stop.

7) INSERT LEFT-ALIGNED TAB STOPS AT 1 AND 3 INCHES

a. Place the mouse pointer below the 1 inch marker on the format line.
b. Click the mouse once. A left-aligned tab stop is inserted at the position of the pointer and a marker (⊦) is displayed on the format line. Because the position of the first tab stop has been changed, the text on the screen is now indented 1 inch.
c. Place the mouse pointer below the 3 inch marker on the format line.
d. Click once. A second left-aligned tab stop is inserted at the position of the pointer and another marker is displayed.

8) ENTER THE FOLLOWING TABLE

a. Use the right-arrow key to move the cursor to the end of the current line.
b. Press the Return key twice to insert a blank line.
c. Start the following table at 1 inch. Use Tabs to move from column to column, pressing Return at the end of each line:

Semester	GPA
Fall, 1989	3.0
Spring, 1989	3.1
Fall, 1990	3.05
Spring, 1990	3.2

9) SAVE THE FILE USING THE NAME "TAB TEST"

a. Hold down the Command key and press the `S` at the same time (⌘S) to execute the Save command. The Save dialog box is displayed.
b. The default file name "Untitled" is shown. Type `TAB TEST` on the Save Document As line, replacing the default name.
c. Click on the `Save` button. A copy of the file in memory is stored on disk using the name TAB TEST.

<u>Check</u> - Your document and ruler should be similar to the following:

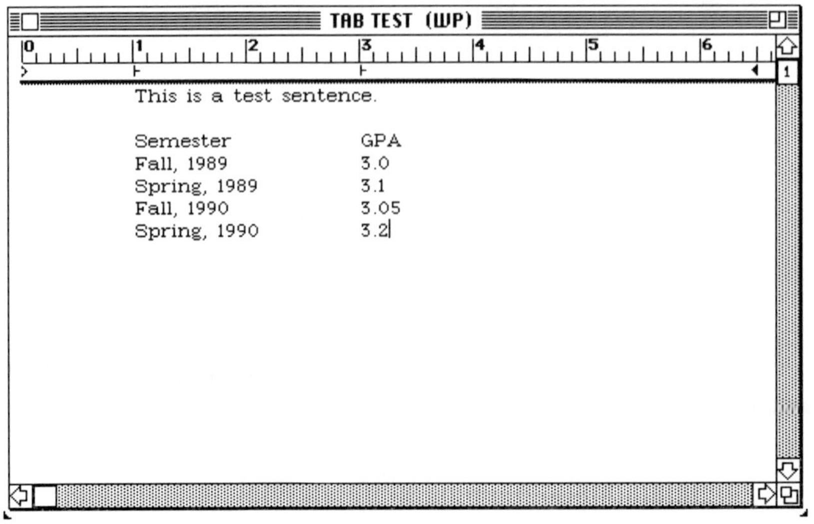

3.6 Opening and Closing Files

You will often need to work on more than one file after booting Works. When this is the case, the current file that you are working on should be saved, and then "closed". Closing a file means that it is removed from the computer's memory. Selecting the Close command from the File menu closes the currently displayed file and clears the screen. If you attempt to close a file which has been edited but not saved, Works warns you before proceeding:

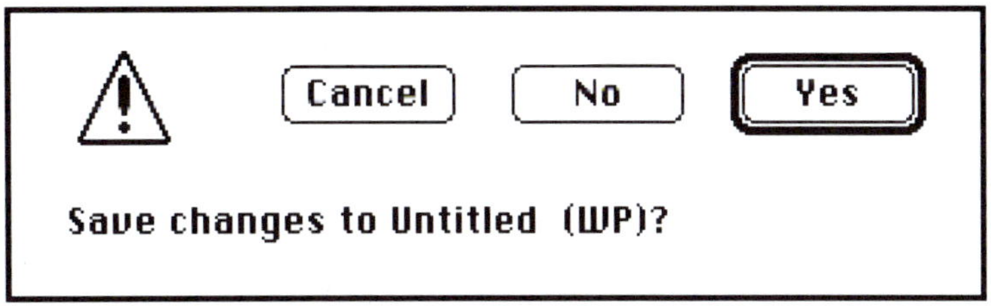

Works displays a warning box before Closing a modified file

If you wish to save the changes before closing, click on the Yes button (or press Return to accept the Yes default). If instead you wish to close the file without saving the edited version, click on the No button. The Command key shortcut for Close is ⌘W.

Once the file has been closed, you may wish to open a previously saved file. For this reason, Works automatically displays the Open File dialog box, allowing you to select from a list of previously saved files. If instead you wish to create a new file, click on the Word Processor icon, and then on the New button. It is a good practice to close any open files when you are through with them. This way, should an accident such as a power failure occur, the closed files will not be in jeopardy.

3.7 Formatting Text

Books, newspapers and other printed materials use a variety of techniques to arrange text on a page. While you may not recognize the terms that are used to describe such techniques, you are familiar with them from publications you have seen.

Arrangements of text are called "formats." A document's format includes the size of its margins, how text lines up within those margins, the spacing between lines and paragraphs, and how the document is divided into pages. Format also includes the arrangement of text into tables composed of columns and emphasized text such as underlined or boldface (darker) letters.

3.8 Setting Margins

One way to affect the appearance of a document is by changing its margins. Margins are the blank spaces between the edges of the paper and the text. Works' default settings are 1 inch margins on the left, right, top and bottom, on an 8.5 inch by 11 inch page:

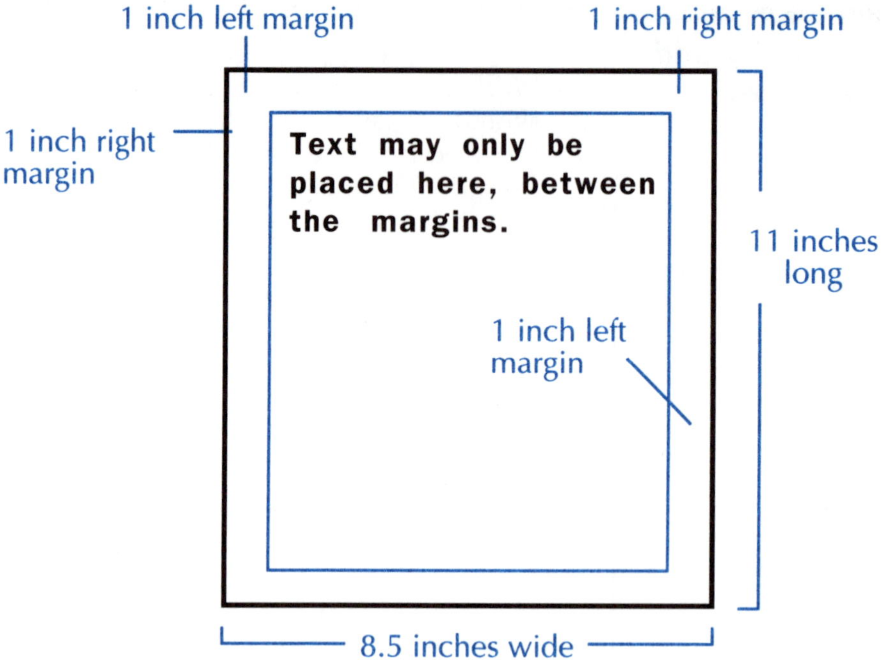

Works' default margins are 1 inch around the top, bottom and sides

Margins can be widened or narrowed as desired. Changes to the margin settings have an inverse affect on the number of characters that will fit on a line. Widening a margin decreases the amount of text that a line can contain, while narrowing a margin increases the line's capacity.

The length of a line of text that will fit across a page is determined by subtracting the size of left and right margins from the width of the page. Using the default margins of 1" on an 8.5" page yields a line 6.5" long (8.5" - 1" - 1" = 6.5").

Options for setting margins are displayed by executing the Page Setup command from the File menu. When executed, Page Setup displays a dialog box containing options which affect the document's format. Current settings are also shown:

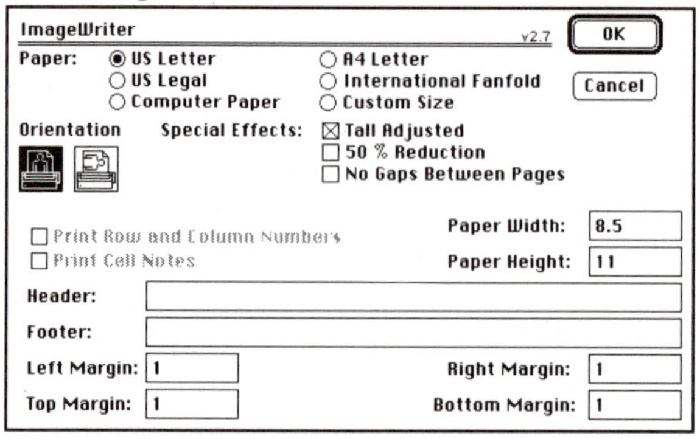

The Page Setup dialog box

Top, bottom, left and right margins each have their own entry box. For example, to change the bottom margin of a document to 0.75", double-click the mouse in the Bottom Margin box, type the new value, 0.75, and click on **OK**. Works then sets the document to the new margin settings. Because new margin settings are not automatically reflected in previously typed text, margins should be set once when the file is first created, before any text is entered. When the file is saved, it retains the current margin settings.

3.9 Headers, Footers and Page Numbers

Works can place a one line message at the top and bottom of each page when a document is printed. This message is often used to indicate the current page number. A message which is automatically printed at the top of each page is called a "header." Similarly, a message which is printed at the bottom of each page is called a "footer." Headers and footers are created on the Page Setup dialog box shown above.

To create a header or footer for a document, the cursor is placed at the desired option in the Page Setup dialog box and the text for the header or footer typed. When the document is printed, the text will be printed above or below the document in the margin on each page. To remove a header or footer, the cursor is moved to the desired option and the Delete key used.

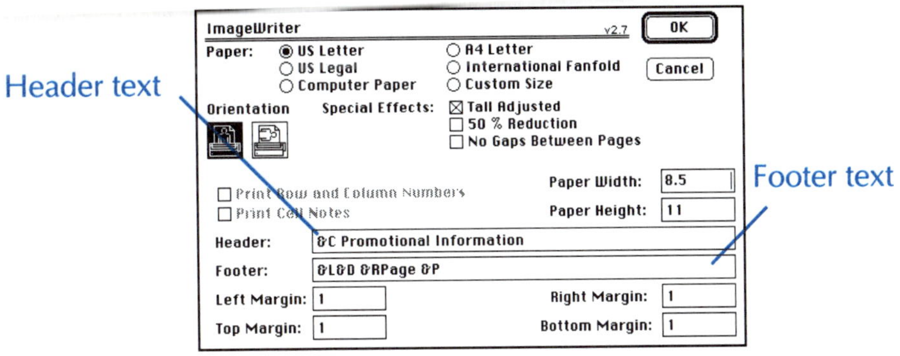

Header and Footer text is entered on the Page Setup dialog box

It is also possible to include special codes in the header or footer that will be translated when the document is printed. For example, a common use for headers and footers is to indicate the current page number. This can be accomplished by using a footer (or header) such as: `Page &P`. The "`&P`" is a code which tells Works to print the current page number. When a document is printed with this footer, `Page 1` is printed at the bottom of page 1, `Page 2` at the bottom of page 2 and so on. Other codes make it possible to change the alignment of the header or footer text, making it centered above or below the page, or aligned with the right margin. Codes which may be included in the header or footer are shown below:

Code	Action
&D	Print the current date
&F	Print the file name
&T	Print the current time
&C	Center the following text
&L	Align the following text with the left margin (default)
&R	Align the following text with the right margin

Multiple codes may be combined in a single header or footer. For example, the text

`My Report &C&D &RPage &P`

would produce a printed header similar to:

```
My Report          10/14/90          Page 1
```

Practice 2

To demonstrate the different formatting options, the following Practice sessions in this chapter use Ivy University's promotional file named IVY PROMO which is stored on your data disk.

In this Practice you will create a header and footer for the IVY PROMO document. TAB TEST should still be displayed from the last Practice.

1) CLOSE THE TAB TEST FILE

Press ⌘ `W` to execute the Close command and close TAB TEST. The Open File dialog box is displayed.

2) OPEN THE IVY PROMO FILE

a. Click on the Word Processor icon to limit the file names displayed in the list to only word processor files.
b. Scroll through the files list until IVY PROMO is visible. Double-click on IVY PROMO. The file is loaded into memory and displayed on the screen.

3) DISPLAY THE PAGE SETUP DIALOG BOX

a. Display the File menu by moving the pointer to the word "File" on the Menu bar and holding down the mouse button.
b. Drag the mouse pointer down the menu, highlighting the Page Setup command.
c. With Page Setup highlighted, release the mouse button to display the dialog box. Note that the cursor is already in the Header box.

4) ENTER THE TEXT FOR THE HEADER

We want a centered header which shows the purpose of the document so type:

`&CPromotional Information`

5) ENTER THE TEXT FOR THE FOOTER

a. Press Tab once to move the cursor to the Footer option. The footer to be created has the current date at the left side of the page, and the page number at the right.
b. Type `&D` to have Works print the current date. The date will be printed at the left margin because this is the default.
c. Press the space bar and type `&R` to right justify the following text.
d. Type `Page &P` to print the current page number. Your footer should be similar to:

`&D &RPage &P`

e. Click on OK to remove the dialog box and include the new header and footer in the document.

6) **SAVE THE MODIFIED FILE**

Press ⌘ S to save the modified file on disk. The header and footer just created are now stored in the document.

7) **PRINT THE DOCUMENT USING THE SHORTCUT**

Make sure that your computer is connected to a printer, and that the printer is on line with the paper positioned at the top of a page. Press ⌘P (the Print command shortcut) and click on OK to print a copy.

Check - Each page of the printed copy should contain the centered header "Promotional Information" and a footer with the current date at the left margin and the proper page number at the right.

3.10 Indents

It is important to realize that a document's margins are set for the entire document, and may not change from paragraph to paragraph or page to page. It is possible, however, to alter the width of the lines in a specific paragraph by using "indents".

Indents are temporary increases in the size of a margin. The default indent is 0", meaning that lines of text in a paragraph will extend from the left to the right margin. It is possible to set off a paragraph (such as a long quotation) from the rest of the text by specifying left and right indents. This causes the paragraph to have a smaller line length. For example, it is possible to set the left and right indents to 1". Should this be done, the length of the current line would be 4.5 inches: the normal 6.5" line (8.5" page width - 1" left margin - 1" right margin) minus the amount of the indents (1" on the left and 1" on the right). The resulting text would be similar to:

```
This is a normal paragraph. Each full line
extends from the left margin to the right
margin.
```

```
    This paragraph is indented. The
    lines extend from the left to the
    right indent, making for a smaller
    line length.
```

The paragraph above has both left and right indents, but it is also possible to have only a left or only a right indent. Indents are set using the format line below the screen ruler:

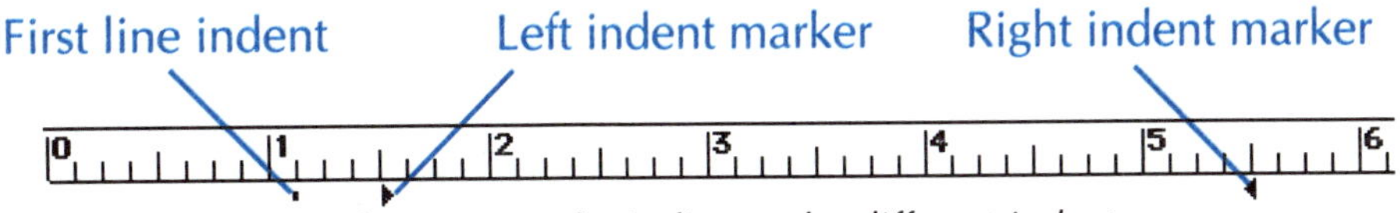

The screen ruler indicates the different indents

To set an indent, the indent markers are dragged to a new position on the format line. Setting an indent affects only the paragraph which currently contains the cursor. When the cursor is moved to a paragraph for which an indent has already been set, the indent markers on the format line automatically move to show the size of the indent.

A special type of indent is the "first line" indent. As its name implies, the first line indent affects only the first line in the paragraph. Normally, the first line indent and left indent are set to the same value. However, by making the first line indent smaller, it is possible to create what is called a "hanging indent" which is useful for creating lists, or when typing bibliography entries for a research paper:

```
This paragraph has a first line indent,
     and is an example of "hanging
     indentation." Hanging indents are
     useful in lists and bibliographies.
```

3.11 Double and Single Spacing

Single spacing places text on each line of the printed page while double spacing inserts a blank line between lines of text. Double spacing can make a document more readable and leaves room for notes to be written between lines, which is especially helpful when rewriting or editing a document. Examples of both formats are given below:

Single Spaced:

```
     This paragraph is single spaced. There
is little room between the lines for notes
or comments, but more information can be
placed on each page. Most printed text, in-
cluding this book, is single spaced.
```

Double Spaced:

```
     This paragraph is double spaced. Note

how room is left between each line for notes

or comments. Double spacing is used mostly

for academic papers and drafts.
```

Single and double spacing are set using the Spacing command from the Format menu. Like indents, Spacing is applied only to the paragraph which currently contains the cursor. This allows one paragraph in a document to be single spaced and another double spaced. Single spacing is the default.

To set double spacing, first place the cursor in the paragraph to be double spaced. Then drag the mouse pointer down the Format menu until the Spacing command is highlighted. When highlighted, the Spacing choices are shown on a small "sub-menu" just to the right of the command:

Highlighting the `Double` option on the sub-menu and releasing the mouse button double-spaces the current paragraph. The double spacing is displayed on the screen, leaving any paragraphs above and below unchanged. To switch back to single spacing, display the Format menu and use the mouse pointer to select `Single` from the Spacing sub-menu. Works also allows other spacing options, but these formats are rarely used. Any spacing options set are retained when the file is saved on disk.

3.12 Using the Mouse to Move the Cursor

When the mouse pointer is moved through the text of a document, it changes from the arrow to a new shape called the text or "I–Beam" pointer: I This allows you to place the cursor in a document using only the mouse, rather than the arrow keys. This technique is especially helpful when working with long, multi-screen documents. To move the cursor using the mouse, place the I-Beam pointer at the desired cursor position in the document, first scrolling as necessary. Clicking the mouse button once will move the cursor to the location of the I-Beam pointer. Because this technique is often used before inserting text, it is sometimes referred to as creating an "insertion point". It is also useful for selecting the proper paragraph when applying formatting options such as the indents and spacing described above.

Practice 3

This Practice demonstrates the use of indents and double spacing. Start Works if you have not already done so, and open the IVY PROMO Word Processor document.

1) CREATE 1 INCH PARAGRAPH INDENTS

a. Using the mouse, move the I-Beam pointer into the paragraph which begins "Ivy University is one of. . .".
b. Click once to place the cursor at the I-Beam's position.
c. Move the mouse pointer into the format line above the document. Note how the pointer's shape changes back to an arrow when the pointer is moved from the text.
d. Place the pointer on the left indent marker (▶) on the format line. Drag the marker to just below the 1 inch marker on the ruler and release the mouse button. The current paragraph is reformatted and displayed on screen with a 1 inch left indent. Note the hanging indent caused by the first line indent.
e. Drag the first line indent marker (▪) to just below the 1 inch marker. This removes the hanging indent.
f. Drag the right indent marker (◀) to just below the 5 inch marker. The paragraph is reformatted with a 1 inch right indent. Note how the rest of the document is unchanged.

2) NOTE THE INDENT MARKERS

a. Move the mouse pointer into the next paragraph, which begins "Located in. . .". Click once to place the cursor in this paragraph. Because this paragraph has no indents, the indent markers are automatically returned to the edge of the format line at the top of the screen.

b. Move the mouse pointer back into the first paragraph. Click once to place the cursor in this paragraph. Note how the indent markers are adjusted in the format line.

3) PLACE THE CURSOR IN THE PARAGRAPH TO BE DOUBLE SPACED

Move the mouse pointer into the next paragraph, which begins "Located in. . .". Click once to place the cursor in this paragraph.

4) DOUBLE SPACE THE PARAGRAPH

a. Drag the mouse pointer down the Format menu and highlight the Spacing command. The Spacing sub-menu appears to the right of the command.
b. Drag the mouse to the right and highlight Double. Release the button. Works double spaces the current paragraph as shown on the screen.

5) SAVE THE FILE

Press ⌘ S to save the modified file on disk.

Check - The first paragraph should be indented, and the second double spaced as shown on the screen:

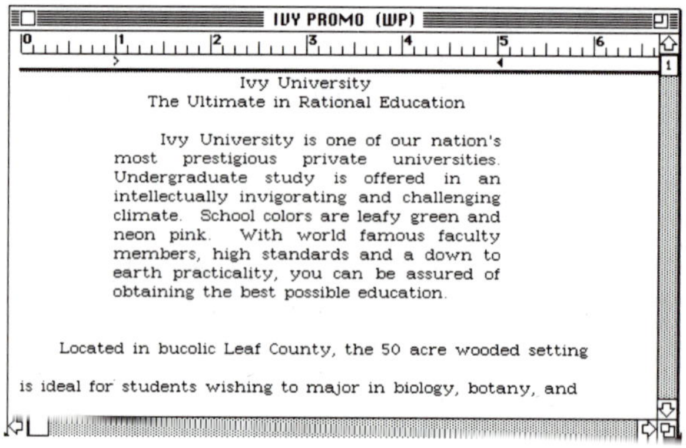

3.13 Paragraph Alignment

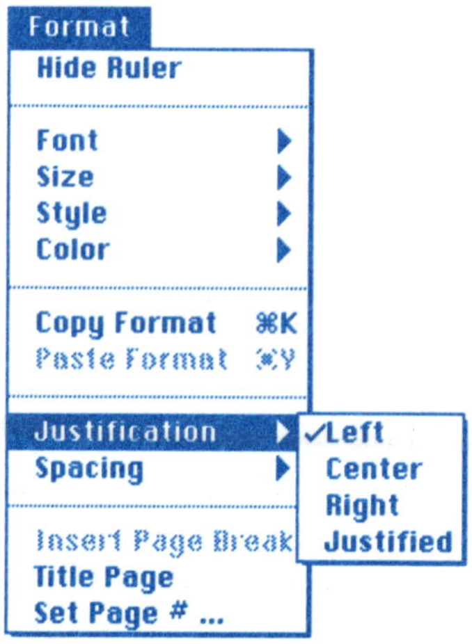

Works provides four ways to align text in a paragraph relative to the margins (or indents): left, centered, right and justified. These formats are selected by choosing the desired alignment from the Justification command on the Format menu.

Left-justified, the default, means that each line begins at the left hand margin. The resulting right margin is jagged. This is the format produced by a typewriter, and the one most often used in letters or research papers.

Centered is the alignment most often used for headings and titles. It involves positioning a line so that it is equidistant from the left and right margins. When this option is selected, Works automatically calculates the proper position of the text and then centers it.

Right-justified is the opposite of left justification: each line extends to the right margin while the left margin is jagged. This format is rarely used.

Justified creates straight paragraph borders at both margins. To justify a paragraph, the computer automatically places extra spaces between words to fill up each line. As a result the rightmost word in each line is pushed over to the right margin. Justified formats are common in newspapers and books; this textbook for example.

Selecting an alignment option affects only the paragraph that the cursor is in. When selected, the paragraph is reformatted on the screen, showing the new alignment. Examples of each of the alignments is shown below:

Left:

```
    This text is left-justified, the
default alignment.  Notice how the length of
each line is different.  In a left aligned
paragraph the right margin appears jagged.
This format is often called "ragged right"
for this reason.
```

Centered:

```
 This text is centered. Notice that each of
   the lines is placed halfway between the
  margins. Centered text is most often used
                 for titles.
```

Right:

```
         This text is right-justified. Each of
      the lines reaches the right margin. The
    effect of a right-justified paragraph is
                 that the left margin is jagged.
```

Justified:

```
    This text is justified. Each of the lines
is  extended  to  reach  the  right  margin.  The
effect  of  justifying  a  paragraph  is  that  the
borders  on  each  margin  appear  straight.  Note
the  extra  spaces  between  some  words  that  are
used to extend the lines to the right margin.
```

3.14 Undo

At times you will execute a command, only to find that you have made a mistake. For example, suppose you justified a paragraph by mistake. Works supplies a way to reverse the affects of the last command executed with Undo. Executing the Undo command from the Edit menu reverses the effect of the previous command. If you execute a command by mistake, executing Undo (⌘Z) will undo any changes made by that command. Undo only works for the command just executed, and it is not possible to undo the effect of the second or third previous command.

Practice 4

This Practice demonstrates different text alignments. Start Works if you have not already done so, and open the IVY PROMO document. You will modify the file by centering the two title lines and justifying the first paragraph. Undo will be used to remove an alignment.

1) CENTER THE FIRST TWO LINES IN THE DOCUMENT

a. Place the cursor in the first line of the document, the title which reads "Ivy University".
b. Drag the mouse down the Format menu and highlight the Justification command.
c. Drag the mouse to the right and select `Center` from the submenu. The line is centered on the screen.
d. Move the I-beam pointer onto the next line in the document and click once to display the cursor.
e. Select Justification from the Format menu and pick `Center` from the submenu.

2) JUSTIFY A PARAGRAPH

a. Place the I-beam pointer in the indented paragraph that begins "Ivy University is one . . ." and click once to display the cursor.
b. Drag the mouse down the Format menu and highlight the Justification command.
c. Select `Justified` from the submenu. The paragraph is reformatted on the screen.

3) RIGHT ALIGN THE NEXT PARAGRAPH

a. Place the cursor in the next paragraph, which begins "Located in. . .".
b. Drag the mouse down the Format menu and highlight the Justification command.
c. Select `Right` from the submenu. The paragraph is right-justified on the screen.

4) UNDO THE LAST FORMATTING COMMAND

Drag the mouse down the Edit menu and select the Undo command. The effect of the previous command (right justify) is undone, and the paragraph is returned to its original state.

5) SAVE AND PRINT THE MODIFIED FILE

a. Press ⌘S to save the modified file on disk. When IVY PROMO is next loaded, the titles will be centered and the first paragraph justified.
b. Press ⌘P and click on OK to print the document. Note that the titles are centered and the first paragraph justified on the printed copy. After the first page has printed, press ⌘. (period) to terminate the printing.

Check - The title should be centered and the first paragraph justified as shown on the screen:

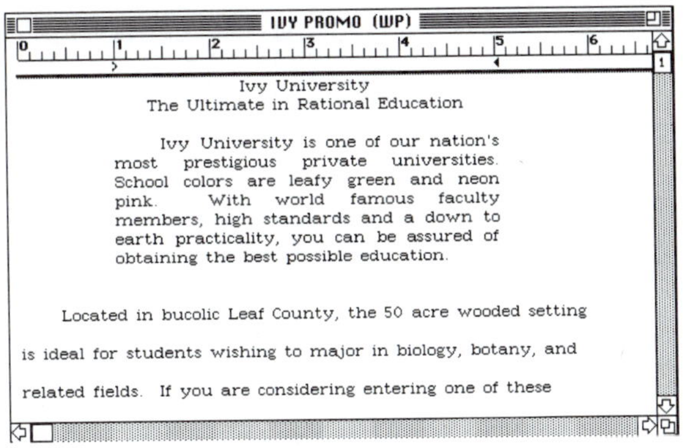
IVY PROMO (WP)

Ivy University
The Ultimate in Rational Education

Ivy University is one of our nation's most prestigious private universities. School colors are leafy green and neon pink. With world famous faculty members, high standards and a down to earth practicality, you can be assured of obtaining the best possible education.

Located in bucolic Leaf County, the 50 acre wooded setting is ideal for students wishing to major in biology, botany, and related fields. If you are considering entering one of these

3.15 Selecting and Deleting Blocks of Text

When editing it is often necessary to remove large amounts of text from a document. In the last chapter the Delete key was used to remove text one character at a time. This is cumbersome when the amount of text to be deleted is more than a word or two. To speed deleting, Works allows the text to be removed to be selected by dragging the mouse over it. Selected text is shown on the screen in reversed colors and is therefore said to be "highlighted". The highlight can contain any amount of text from a single word to several pages. When the Clear command is executed from the Edit menu, all of the highlighted text is removed.

This is normal text.

This is highlighted text.

Highlighted text appears in reverse: white letters on black

Highlighting is controlled by dragging the I-beam pointer over text using the mouse, forming a "block". Be careful when using this technique to include only the text to be deleted in the highlight. If you delete a block by mistake, immediately executing the Undo command (⌘Z) will replace it. Should you highlight a block and then decide not to delete it, click the mouse once anywhere in the document to remove the highlight.

It is possible to replace blocks of text using a similar technique. First highlight the block to be replaced, and then type the new text. The highlighted block will be erased, and replaced with what you type. A single word may be selected by double-clicking on it. The highlight will extend from the first character to the space after the word (if there is one). The highlighted word may then be replaced by typing a new one, deleted using Clear, or formatted using one of the formatting commands.

Practice 5

This Practice demonstrates the selection and deletion of blocks. Start Works if you have not already done so, and open the IVY PROMO document. You will select and delete different blocks of text. Undo will be used to restore a deleted block.

1) SELECT AND DELETE A SENTENCE

a. Place the cursor at the beginning of the second sentence in the first paragraph, before the "U" which begins the sentence "Undergraduate study is. . .".
b. Drag the mouse to the end of the sentence, being sure to include the spaces after the period. Note how the text is highlighted as the pointer passes over it.
c. Drag the mouse down the Edit menu and select Clear. All of the highlighted text is deleted.

2) DELETE THE NEXT PARAGRAPH AS A BLOCK

a. Place the cursor at the beginning of the next paragraph, which begins "Located in. . .".
b. Drag the pointer to the end of the paragraph, highlighting the entire paragraph.
c. Drag the mouse down the Edit menu and select Clear to remove the entire paragraph.
d. Press ⌘ Z to execute Undo and reverse the effects of the previous command. The paragraph is restored.

3) DELETE A WORD AS A BLOCK

a. Place the pointer on the word "Located" at the beginning of the paragraph.
b. Double-click the mouse. Note how the entire word is selected.
c. Select Clear from the Edit menu. The word is deleted.
d. Press ⌘ Z to reverse the effects of the previous command, restoring the word.

<u>Check</u> - Your file should be similar to:

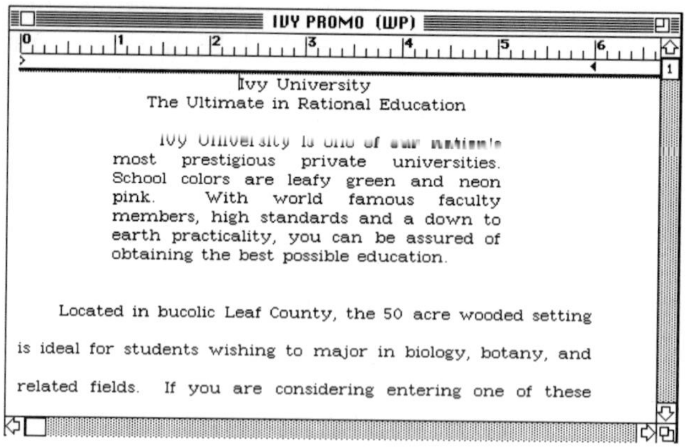

3.16 Formatting a Block

Often a group of paragraphs in a document will need to have the same format. When this is the case it is not necessary to execute the Paragraph command for each paragraph. Instead, the paragraphs may be highlighted as a block, and the formatting commands executed. When executed, the selected format will be applied to all of the paragraphs in the block. This is the case for most Works commands. If a block is highlighted when a command is executed, the command will affect only the text in that block. An example was the Clear command performed in the last Practice. When Clear was selected, all of the text in the highlighted block was removed. To justify an entire document you would first enter the text and then drag the mouse to highlight the entire document and select the Justified option using the Format menu. The entire document is then justified.

3.17 Pagination

Pagination is the division of a document into page-sized sections for printing. Using the specifications for page length and margins, Works calculates the number of lines that fit on each printed page. Do not confuse screen pages which display 20 to 30 lines of text with printed pages which usually contain 50 to 60 lines.

A "page break" is the location in a document where one printed page ends and another begins. Works automatically indicates page breaks with a dotted line drawn across the screen. After making an editing change, Works automatically recalculates the page breaks and displays the updated markers.

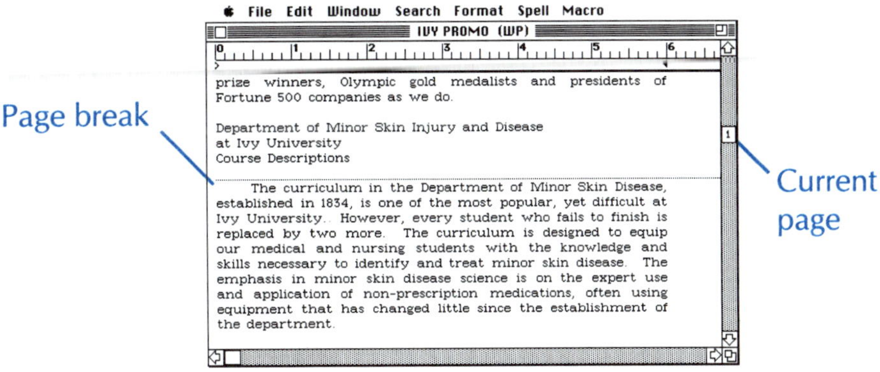

Works indicates page breaks with a dashed line across the screen

Some types of material call for starting a new page before completing the previous one: the beginning of a new chapter, a change in subject matter, or the presentation of a table or chart are three examples. You can cause the computer to advance to the next page regardless of the number of lines left on the current page by creating a "manual page break". To do this place the cursor where the new page is to start, and select the Insert Page Break command from the Format menu. A dotted line is then shown across the screen. Manual page breaks can be removed by placing the cursor anywhere on the line just below the page break marker and selecting the Remove Page Break command from the Format menu. Note that this is a case where the commands shown on a menu change depending upon the placement of the cursor. If the cursor is on a line just below a manual page break, the Format menu includes the Remove Page Break command. If the cursor is anywhere else in the document, the menu includes the Insert Page Break command instead.

Practice 6

This Practice demonstrates block formatting and automatic and manual page breaks. Start Works if you have not already done so and open the IVY PROMO document.

1) JUSTIFY THE DOCUMENT AS A BLOCK

a. Place the cursor at the beginning of the paragraph that begins "Ivy University is one of. . .".
b. Drag the mouse to the end of the document, creating a highlighted block which contains everything but the titles. Note how the screen scrolls to include the text in the highlight.
c. Execute the Justification command from the Format menu and select `Justified` from the submenu. The document is reformatted on the screen.

2) LOCATE THE PAGE BREAK MARKERS

a. Click the mouse in the text to remove the highlight.
b. Use the vertical scroll bar to scroll towards the top of the document. Note the location of the page break markers and the justified paragraphs.

3) INSERT A MANUAL PAGE BREAK

a. Place the cursor at the beginning of the paragraph that begins "Ivy University is one of. . .".
b. Drag the mouse down the Format menu and select the Insert Page break command. A dotted line appears across the screen to indicate the position of the manual page break.

4) DELETE THE MANUAL PAGE BREAK

a. Place the cursor on the line directly below the manual page break dotted line marker if it is not already.
b. Select the Remove Page break command from the Format menu. The dotted line disappears, indicating that the manual page break has been deleted.
c. Press ⌘S to save the modified file on disk. The next time it is opened, IVY PROMO will have justified paragraphs.

3.18 Character Formats - Font, Size and Style

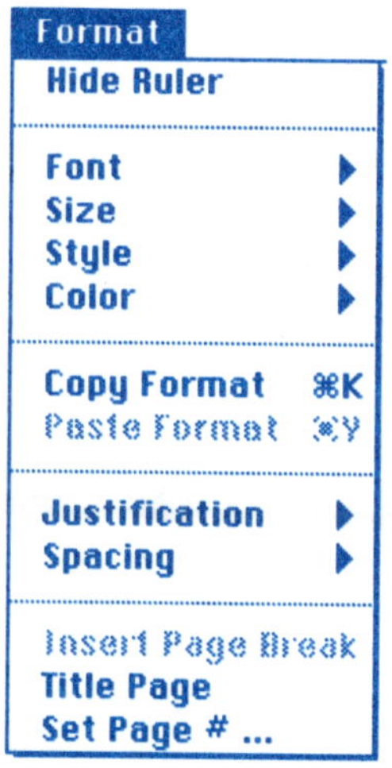

Works' Format menu has a number of commands which affect the way that individual characters appear, both on the screen and when printed. These are Font, Size and Style, which are used to emphasize different parts of text in a document.

The following steps are required to create emphasized text:

1. The pointer is positioned over the first character of the text to be emphasized.
2. The mouse is dragged to the end of the text to be emphasized, highlighting a block.
3. The Format menu is displayed and the desired command highlighted, displaying a submenu.
4. The formatting option is selected from the submenu. All highlighted characters are affected and will be emphasized when printed. The emphasized text is displayed on the screen.

Each formatting command is listed below, along with some of their more common options.

Font Command

A "font" is a description of the shape of a set of characters. The standard Works font is named Boston, but depending on your printer there are several others from which you may choose.

Courier: This is Courier. ABCDEF abcdef 1234567890

Helvetica: This is Helvetica. ABCDEF abcdef 1234567890

Times: This is Times. ABCDEF abcdef 1234567890

Size Command

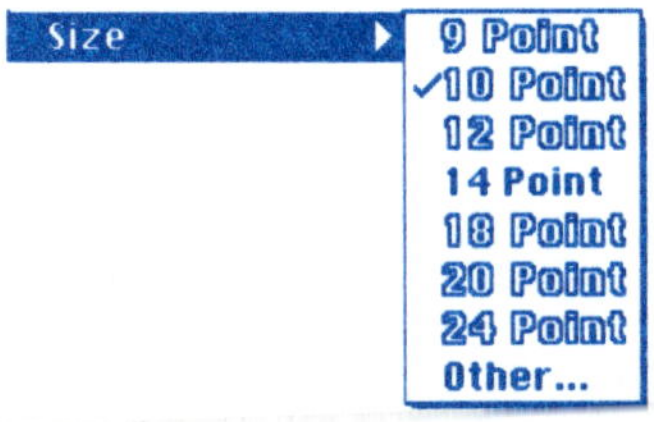

Characters can be displayed in different sizes. The standard Works size is 10, but there are several others from which you may choose.

This is 10 point text.

This is 12 point text.

This is 18 point text.

Style Command

Style can be used to add extra emphasis to selected characters. The standard style is Normal, meaning no extra emphasis. Because they are used often, some Style options have Command key shortcuts which can be executed by holding down the Command key and pressing the appropriate letter. For example, emphasized text can be reset to Normal by highlighting it and pressing ⌘N.

Bold: **Bold text** is printed darker than plain text so that words and phrases printed in bold stand out on the page. It is most frequently used for titles and headings. The shortcut for bolding highlighted text is to press ⌘B.

Italic: *Italic text* is printed on a slant. Italics are most frequently used when referring to titles. The shortcut for italic text is ⌘I.

Underline: Underlined text is another character format used to emphasize words or phrases. The shortcut for underlined text is ⌘U.

In review, to emphasize a section of text, place the pointer on the first character in the block and drag the mouse over the text to highlight a block. Then execute the desired command from the Format menu (or use a Command key shortcut). Once a block has been emphasized it stays that way until you change it. Any new text inserted inside a block will also be emphasized. As an example, a new character inserted between two bold characters will automatically be bold.

Practice 7

This Practice demonstrates the use of the Font, Size and Style commands. Start Works if you have not already done so and open the IVY PROMO file.

1) HIGHLIGHT THE BLOCK TO BE BOLD

a. Place the cursor before the "I" in the "Ivy University" title at the top of the document.
b. Drag the mouse to the end of the line, highlighting the entire first line.
c. Drag the mouse down the Format menu and place the pointer on the Style command.
d. Move the pointer to the right and select `Bold` from the submenu. The highlighted text is shown as bold on the screen.

2) ITALICIZE THE NEXT LINE

a. Place the cursor before the "T" in "The Ultimate. . ." on the next line.
b. Drag the mouse to the end of the line, highlighting the entire line.
c. Drag the mouse down the Format menu and place the pointer on the Style command.
d. Select `Italic` from the submenu. The block is now italicized as shown on the screen.

3) UNDERLINE THE FIRST LINE IN THE NEXT PARAGRAPH

a. Place the cursor before the "I" in "Ivy University is one of. . .".
b. Drag the mouse down onto the next line, and then to the right to highlight the entire sentence.
c. Drag the mouse down the Format menu and place the pointer on the Style command.
d. Select `Underline` from the Style submenu. The sentence is underlined.

4) REMOVE UNDERLINES FROM PART OF THE SENTENCE USING A COMMAND KEY SHORTCUT

a. Place the cursor on the space between "University" and "is".
b. Drag the mouse to the end of the sentence.
c. Make this text plain by holding down the ⌘ key and pressing `N` (for Normal). The highlighted text changes to normal on the screen and only "Ivy University" is underlined.

5) INCREASE THE SIZE OF THE TITLE

a. Place the cursor before the "I" in the "Ivy University" title at the top of the document.
b. Drag the mouse to the end of the line, highlighting the entire title.
c. Drag the mouse down the Format menu and select the Size command.
d. Select `18 Point` from the submenu. The highlighted text is shown as bold and 18 points high on the screen.

6) CHANGE THE FONT OF THE NEXT LINE

a. Place the cursor before the "T" in "The" in the next line.
b. Drag the mouse to the end of the line, highlighting the title.
c. Drag the mouse down the Format menu and select Font.
d. Select `Helvetica` from the submenu. The shape of the letters changes on the screen.

7) SAVE AND PRINT THE DOCUMENT

a. Press ⌘ S to save the modified file on disk. The next time IVY PROMO is loaded the formatted text (bold, italic, Helvetica, etc.) will be present.
b. Press ⌘ P and click on **OK** to print the file. After the first page has printed, press ⌘ . (period) to terminate printing. Note how the formatted text in the printout resembles that shown on the screen. This is one of the main benefits of using a Macintosh, its ability to display formatted text on the screen as it will be printed.

Check - The title should be in bold, 18 point text, the next line in italic Helvetica, and the "Ivy University" in the first sentence underlined:

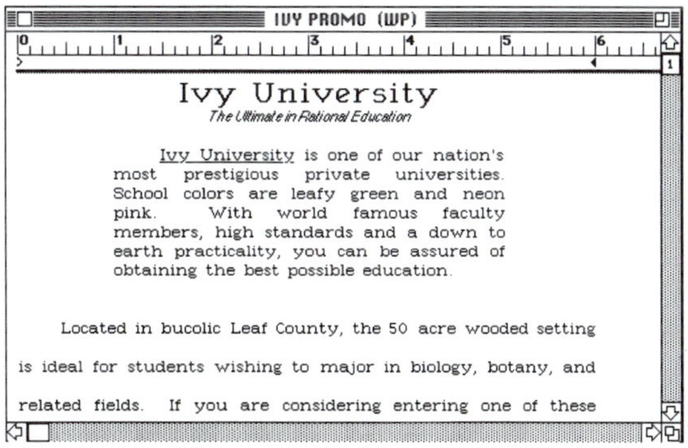

3.19 Moving a Block

One of the most powerful editing tools that a word processor provides is the ability to move a block of text from one area of a document to another. For example, a sentence can be moved from one paragraph and placed on the next page. Text moved can be as small as a single character or word or as large as an entire page or even a group of pages. Works automatically closes the space that formerly held the moved text and opens new space to receive it, rearranging the rest of the document to accommodate the change. Whole paragraphs or groups of paragraphs can similarly be re-positioned by moving them from one place in a document to another.

Moving a block of text is a four step process:

1. Place the cursor before the first character in the block to be moved. Drag the mouse over the text to be moved, creating a highlighted block.
2. Execute the Cut command from the Edit menu which removes the highlighted text from the screen.
3. Place the cursor at the new location for the moved block.
4. Execute the Paste command from the Edit menu which inserts the previously cut text into the document at the cursor's position.

When the Paste command is executed, the block is inserted at the position of the cursor. Text currently stored in that location is moved down to make room from the new block. The Command key shortcut for Cut is ⌘X and for Paste is ⌘V.

3.20 Copying a Block

Works can also copy blocks of text. While Move deletes a block from its original position and reproduces it in another location, the Copy command retains the original and creates an exact duplicate in a new location.

The procedure for copying is similar to that for moving a block. To copy a block of text, the block is highlighted and the Copy command executed from the Edit menu. The cursor is then moved to the position where the copy is to be placed and the Paste command executed. The Command key shortcut for Copy is ⌘C.

Practice 8

This Practice demonstrates the use of block move and copy. Start Works if you have not already done so and open the IVY PROMO document. A block consisting of a sentence will be moved, and then an entire paragraph copied.

1) HIGHLIGHT THE BLOCK TO BE MOVED

a. Place the cursor at the beginning of the sentence which begins "There is a. . ." in the second paragraph.
b. Drag the mouse to highlight the sentence. Be sure to include the period at the end of the sentence and the spaces after the period in the block.

2) MOVE THE HIGHLIGHTED BLOCK

a. Select Cut from the Edit menu. The text is removed from the screen.
b. Place the cursor before the "W" that begins the sentence "With world famous. . ." in the first paragraph.
c. Select the Paste command from the Edit menu. The sentence is inserted in the paragraph.

3) HIGHLIGHT THE BLOCK TO BE COPIED

a. You will produce a copy of the first paragraph at the end of the document. Place the cursor before the "I" in the first paragraph, which begins "Ivy University is. . .".
b. Drag the mouse to the end of the paragraph, including the final period.

4) COPY THE HIGHLIGHTED BLOCK

a. Execute the Copy command using the shortcut ⌘C.
b. Use the scroll bars and mouse to place the cursor after the last line in the document.
c. Paste the block using the shortcut ⌘V. The paragraph is inserted at the bottom of the document.

d. Scroll back to the top of the document and verify that the original paragraph is still there.
e. Press ⌘ S to save the modified document on disk.

Check - The sentence about visiting the school should be moved from the second paragraph to the first and a copy of the first paragraph placed at the bottom of the document.

3.21 Searching For Text in a Document

The Find command operates differently than the commands you have studied so far. Executed from the Search menu, Find does not involve entering text or editing it. Rather the computer scans a document looking for a particular combination of letters called the "search text". This text may be a single letter, a word or a phrase and is entered at the Find What option in the Find dialog box:

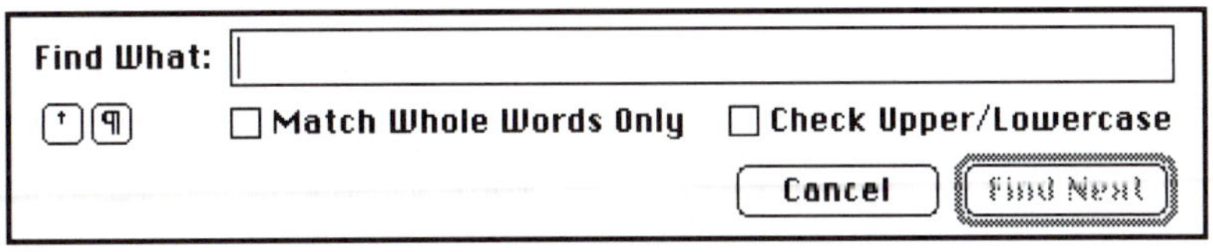

The Find command's dialog box

Starting from the current cursor position, the computer moves through the document looking for a sequence of letters that matches the search text. If a match is found, the scanning stops allowing the document to be read or edited. The search can then be repeated until all occurrences of the search text have been found. Find is useful when trying to locate a specific word or passage in a large document. The Command key shortcut for Find is ⌘ `F`.

Note that Find begins its search at the current cursor position. To search the entire document the cursor must first be moved to the beginning of the file before executing the Find command. When new search text is entered, any old search text is automatically removed from the dialog box. The search text must be 80 characters or less.

Find has a number of different options. Normally, Works ignores case differences (i.e., upper and lower case) during a search. If the search text is `Dog`, Works will find `dog`, `Dog`, `DOG`, etc. The Check Upper/Lowercase option tells Works to find only text with the same capitalization as the search text. For example, a Check Upper/Lowercase search for `CAT` will not find `Cat` or `cat`.

It is important to realize that a match is also considered to be found when the search text is located within another word. For example, specifying a search text of `the` will not only find "the" but also `they`, `theory`, `another`, etc. Such false finds can be eliminated by using the Match Whole Words Only option. When selected, this option only finds an occurrence of the search text when it is not part of another word.

Click on the `Find Next` *button in the Search dialog box to locate the next occurence of the search text*

If you want to continue to search for the same text, clicking on the `Find Next` button will repeat the last Find command performed, using the same search text and options. Clicking on the Cancel button terminates the search.

3.22 Finding Special Characters

The Find dialog box has two options which allow special characters to be located:

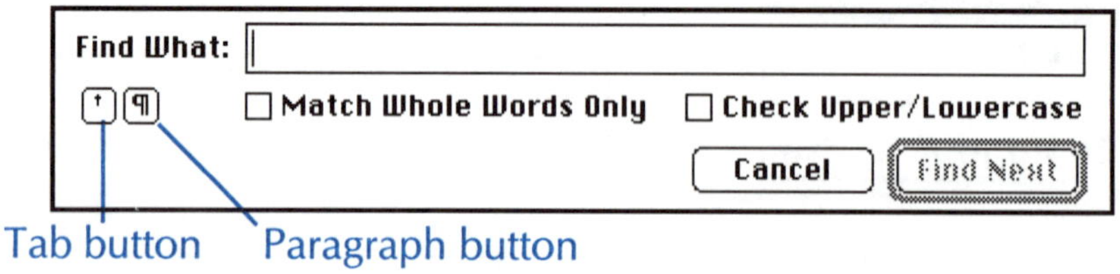

The Tab and Paragraph buttons are used to search for special characters

Clicking on the tab button inserts a tab character into the search text. Clicking on the paragraph button inserts a return character into the search text. Careful use of these buttons can help eliminate false finds. For example, suppose you wish to locate only occurrences of the word "The" which begin paragraphs. If all paragraphs are indented with a single tab, clicking on the tab button and then typing "the" for the search text will locate only these words.

3.23 The Go To Page Command

Often you know that the text that you wish to locate is on or after a certain page. The Go To Page # command from the Search menu, ⌘G, allows you to move the cursor directly to the top of any page in a document. This can be much quicker than using the scroll bars, especially when the document is long. Once you have jumped to the desired page, the mouse can be used to place the cursor at the desired location on that page. A benefit of this command is that it limits the amount of text that is checked by the Find command, making the Find quicker. For example, if you wish to locate the occurrence of some text which is on page 15 or later, you can use the Go To Page # command to jump to page 15 and then execute the Find command.

Practice 9

This Practice demonstrates the Find command. If you have not already done so, start Works and open IVY PROMO. You will search for each occurrence of the word "bandage".

1) EXECUTE THE FIND COMMAND

a. Make sure that the cursor is at the top of the document.
b. Select the Find command from the Search menu. The Find dialog box is displayed.

2) ENTER THE SEARCH TEXT

Type the word `bandage` on the Find What line and click on the Find Next button. There is a slight pause as Works searches the document. The first "bandage" found is in the course description for class 101.

3) REPEAT THE FIND USING THE SAME SEARCH TEXT

To repeat the command using the same search text, simply click on the Find Next button. The cursor moves to the next occurrence of "bandage".

4) FIND THE REST OF THE OCCURRENCES OF BANDAGE

a. Continue to click on Find Next until all occurrences of the word "bandage" have been found. How many did you find?

b. When all occurrences of the search text have been found, Works displays the following message:

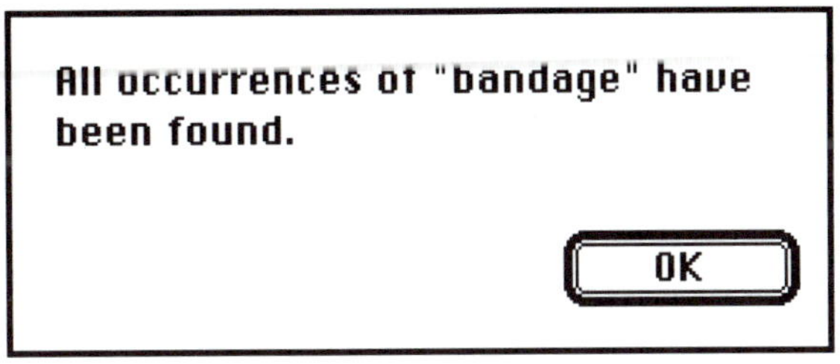

Click on OK to continue.

5) GO DIRECTLY TO THE TOP OF PAGE 1

a. Press ⌘ G to display the Go To Page # dialog box.

b. Type 1 and click on OK. Works jumps directly to the top of the document and displays page 1.

3.24 Replacing Text

The Replace command (⌘R) locates text in a document just as the Find command does, but then replaces it with another piece of text that you supply. This makes it easy to create different versions of the same document that have some specified differences. For example, Works could be used to create a letter requesting a college interview with Ivy University. After printing the letter, the Replace command could be used to change each occurrence of "Ivy University" to "Trenton State" and then to "New Brunswick College" and so on. Thus all the letters needed could be easily created without having to type each one separately; the master letter is typed once and the name of the school changed using Replace:

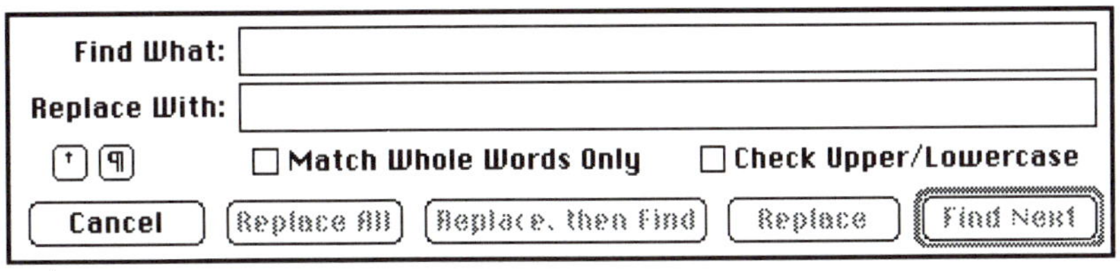

The Replace dialog box

The Replace command can be dangerous. If the search text is not clearly defined unwanted replacements may be made. For example, a search text of `the` will affect any word that contains "the", such as `they`, `theory`, `another`, etc. One way to avoid unwanted replacements is to define the search text very carefully. For example, specifying `the` followed by a space as the search text will avoid the replacements described above. Another way is to use the Match Whole Words Only option. When selected, this option only replaces occurrences of the search text when it is not part of another word. The tab and paragraph buttons may be used in either the search or replace text.

Like the Find command, Replace starts its search from the current cursor position and can be made to replace only upper and lower case matches. Replace also has the option of replacing all occurrences with the new text, or one at a time, prompting you to verify that each change should be made. It is usually advisable to verify each replacement before it is made, thereby avoiding unwanted changes. When entering new find and replace with text, any old text is automatically deleted when the new text is entered.

Practice 10

Ivy University is considering updating its image by changing its name. This Practice will use the Replace command to change each occurrence of "Ivy University" to "Modern College" in the IVY PROMO file. This will allow the administration to see how the document looks with the new name. If you have not already done so, start Works and open the IVY PROMO file.

1) MOVE THE CURSOR TO THE BEGINNING OF THE DOCUMENT

Press ⌘ G and jump to page 1 if is not already displayed.

2) EXECUTE THE REPLACE COMMAND

a. Press ⌘ R. The Replace dialog box is displayed. Note that the last search text, bandage, may be displayed from the previous Practice.

b. Type `Ivy University` for the Find What text, replacing any old text that might exist.

c. Press Tab once to move the cursor to the Replace With box and type `Modern College`.

d. Click on the `Find Next` button to execute the command.

3) REPLACE EACH OCCURRENCE

a. Works moves the cursor to the first occurrence of Ivy University. From the dialog box

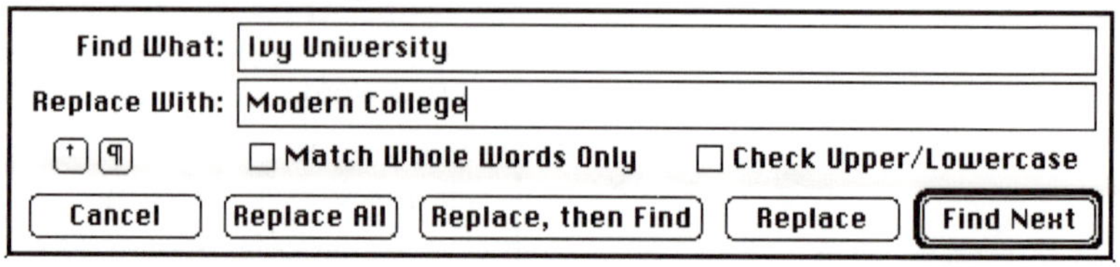

click on the `Replace` button to replace the highlighted text with Modern College.

b. Click on `Find Next` to have Works move the cursor to the next occurrence of Ivy University. Click on Replace to replace it with Modern College.

c. For each Ivy University found, click on the Replace, then Find button to make the replacement and then locate the next occurrence. When Works has completed executing the Replace command, it leaves the cursor at the position where the last replacement was made and displays the message:

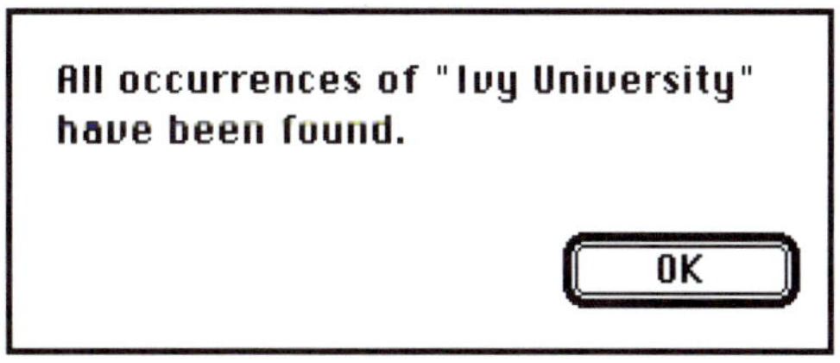

Click on OK. All occurrences of Ivy University have now been changed to Modern College. Scroll through the document to verify that the changes have been made.

d. Press ⌘S to save the modified document on disk.

e. Press ⌘W to close the file.

3.25 Using the Spelling Checker

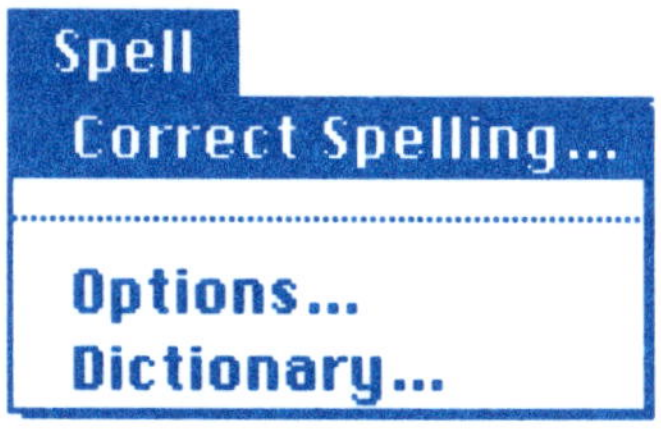

One of the most useful features of a word processor is its ability to check the spelling of the words in a document. In Works, this is accomplished by executing the Correct Spelling command from the Spell menu. When this command is executed, Works starts at the beginning of the document and compares each word in it to a dictionary file. During the spelling check the cursor changes to a rotating circle to inform you that a check is being performed. Words in the document not found in Works' dictionary are displayed in a dialog box. From this box you have the option of typing a correction or having Works produce a list of suggested spellings from which you may select:

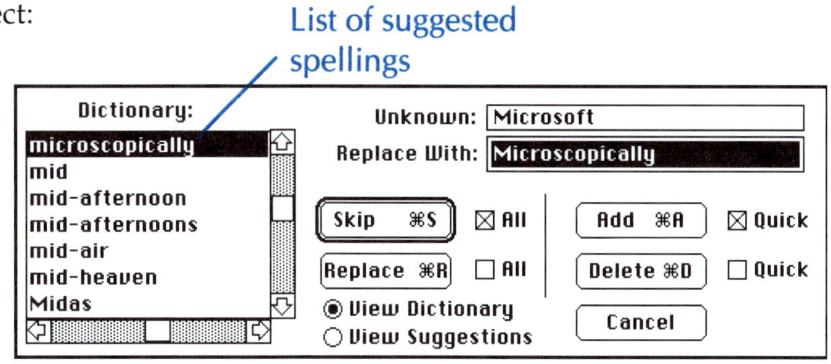

The Spell dialog box offers a list of suggestions for an unknown word

Because the dictionary file does not contain every word in the English language, it is possible that Correct Spelling may come across a word that it does not have in its dictionary. (Proper names are a common example.) When this happens you have two options. If the word is spelled correctly you can tell Works to skip it and proceed to the next misspelled word. If the word is one that you will use often in your writing, such as your name, you can have Works add the word to its dictionary. Once added to the dictionary file, such words are no longer considered misspelled when they appear in a document.

The first time that the Correct Spelling command is used, you may be asked to tell Works the location of the dictionary file (normally the `MsWorksDict` file in the folder named `Works Dictionary`):

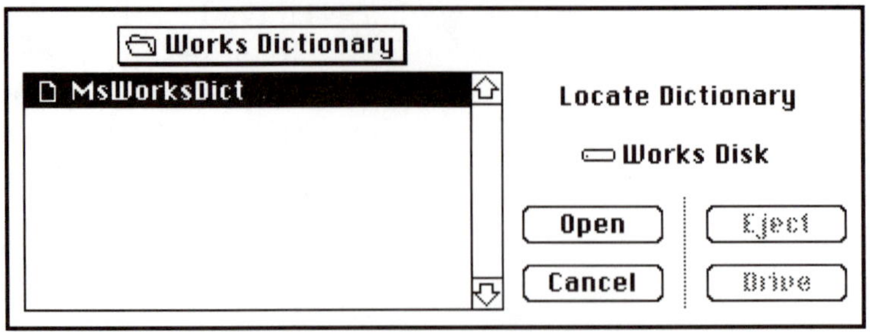

Works needs to be told the location of the dictionary file

Use this dialog box to inform Works of the location of the dictionary file. Once Works knows the location of the dictionary this step need not be repeated. If your dictionary file is located on a different disk, place that disk in the drive when this box is displayed.

Practice 11

Ivy University is about to print a course description in the school newspaper. This Practice will use the Correct Spelling command to verify the spelling in that document before sending it to the paper. Start Works if you have not already done so. You may be asked to enter a disk containing the Works dictionary file when executing the Correct Spelling command.

1) OPEN THE IVY NEW COURSE FILE

a. Click on the Word Processor icon to limit the files displayed to only word processor documents.
b. Scroll through the files list until IVY NEW COURSE is displayed.
c. Double-click on IVY NEW COURSE to open the file.

2) EXECUTE THE CHECK SPELLING COMMAND

Select the Correct Spelling command from the Spell menu to start the spelling check. Insert the dictionary disk if you are asked to do so. There is a pause as Works checks the spelling, and the cursor is displayed as a rotating circle. Works finds a word that may be misspelled and displays it in the Correct Spelling dialog box.

3) SKIP THE MISSPELLED WORD

Because "spreadsheet" is spelled correctly, click on the Skip button to skip this word. Works continues to check for misspellings.

4) CORRECT THE NEXT MISSPELLED WORD

Works finds the word "Instructio", checks its dictionary and displays the most probable spelling "Instruction" on the Replace With line. Because "Instruction" is the word we want, click on the Replace button to accept the suggested spelling and have it replace the misspelled word in the file. Works continues to check the spelling.

5) CORRECT THE NEXT MISSPELLED WORD

a. Works finds the word "computr" and suggests the spelling "computing".

b. Because the suggestion is not the one we want, use the up scroll-arrow to scroll through the dictionary list and locate the correct spelling, "computer".

c. Double-click on "computer" to replace the misspelled word with it. Works then continues to check the spelling.

6) SKIP THE PROPER NAME

a. Click on the Skip button to ignore the spelling of the name "Wagy", which is correct.

b. When the spelling check is finished Works displays the following screen asking if the skipped words should be ignored the next time this document is checked:

Click on the No button.

c. Works then displays a dialog box telling the number of words checked and the number of errors:

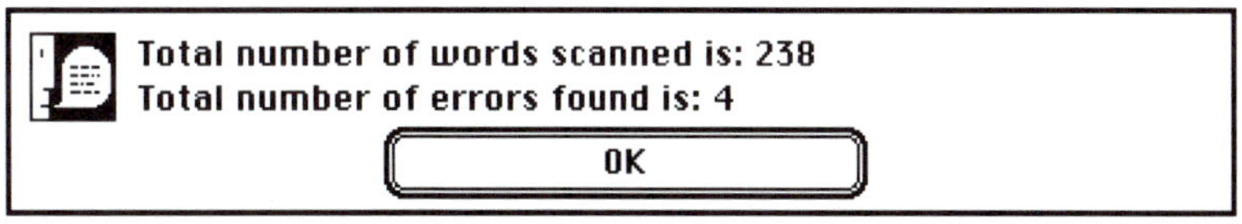

Click on the OK button to remove the box.

7) SAVE AND CLOSE THE CORRECTED FILE

a. Press ⌘S to save the corrected file.

b. Press ⌘W to close the file.

3.26 Superscripts and Subscripts

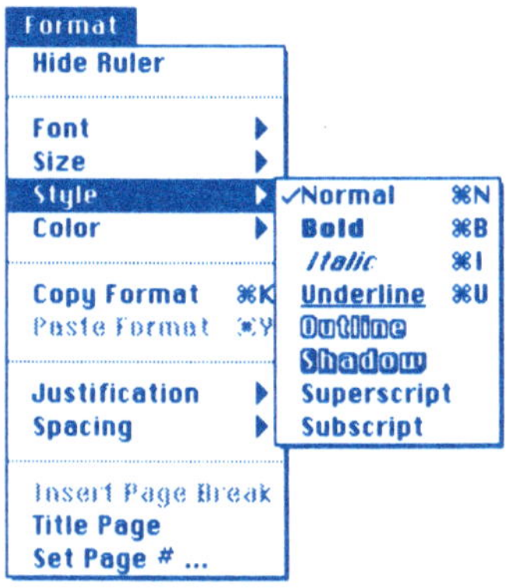

Many times a word processed document must contain a "superscript" or "subscript". A superscript is a section of text which is raised slightly above the current line while a subscript is printed slightly below the current line. Superscripts and subscripts are most often used to indicate footnotes or other reference material in research papers, or in mathematical and scientific formulas. For example:

Dr. Sulfuric^4 proved that the formula for water is H_2O.

The "4" after Dr. Sulfuric is a superscript representing a footnote reference, while the "2" in H_2O is a subscript. It is possible to emphasize more than one character in a superscript or subscript. The following line has "super" as a superscript, and "sub" as a subscript:

This is a ^{super}script and this is a $_{sub}$script.

Both superscripts and subscripts are created using the Style command from the Format menu in a process similar to making bold or underlined text:

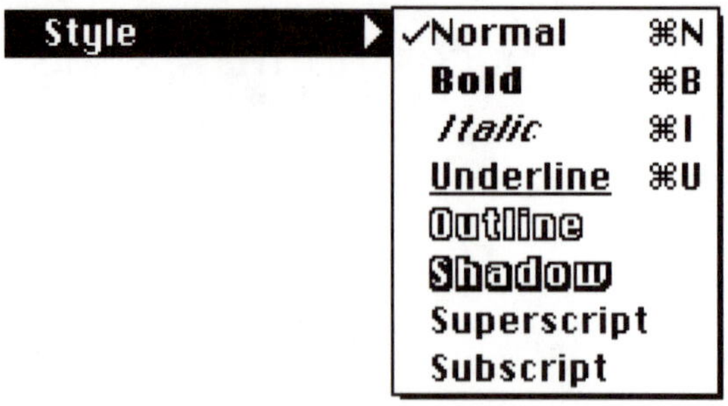

The Style submenu controls sub- and superscripts

The block to be emphasized is highlighted by dragging the mouse over it, and the desired format option selected using the Style command from the Format menu. Like other text formats superscript and subscript text are shown on the screen as they will print.

Practice 12

In this Practice you will create the superscripts and subscripts shown in the examples in the section above. Start Works if you have not already done so. The Open File dialog box should be displayed.

1) CREATE A NEW WORD PROCESSOR DOCUMENT

Double-click on the Word Processor icon to create a new file.

2) ADD TEXT TO THE DOCUMENT

Type the following two lines, leaving a blank line between them:

```
Dr. Sulfuric4 proved that the formula for
water is H2O.

This is a superscript and this is a subscript.
```

3) CREATE THE FOOTNOTE SUPERSCRIPT

a. Place the cursor before the "4" after Dr. Sulfuric's name.
b. Drag the mouse to highlight the "4".
c. Execute the Style command from the Format menu, and select `Superscript` from the submenu. The "4" is shown on the screen as a superscript.

4) CREATE THE FORMULA SUBSCRIPT

a. Place the cursor before the "2" in "H2O".
b. Drag the mouse to highlight the "2".
c. Execute the Style command from the Format menu, and select `Subscript` from the submenu. The "2" is shown on the screen as a subscript.

5) CREATE THE "SUPER" SUPERSCRIPT

a. Place the cursor before the first "s" in "superscript" in the line which begins "This is a superscript. . .".
b. Drag the mouse to the first "r" in "superscript", highlighting "super".
c. Execute the Style command from the Format menu, and select `Superscript` from the submenu. The "super" is shown on the screen as a superscript.

6) CREATE THE "SUB" SUBSCRIPT

a. Place the cursor before the first "s" in "subscript".
b. Drag the mouse to the "b", highlighting "sub".
c. Execute the Style command from the Format menu, and select `Subscript` from the submenu. The "sub" is shown on the screen as a subscript.

7) SAVE AND PRINT THE FILE

a. Press ⌘S to execute the Save command.
b. Type `SCRIPT TEST` and click on Save to save the file on disk.
c. Press ⌘P and click on `OK` to print the file. Both lines should print as shown below:

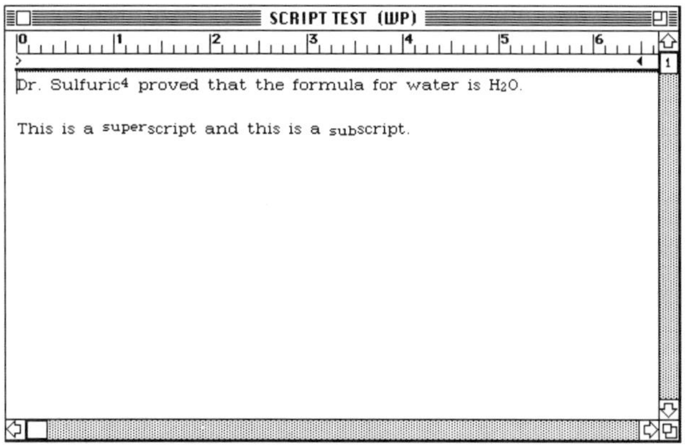

3.27 *Where can you go from here?*

The last two chapters have introduced you to the concepts of word processing. You can now create, edit, print and format documents using the word processor. Works has several other word processing options available that you may wish to learn about. The best place to begin is by reading the Word Processor sections of the Works manual supplied by Microsoft.

For many users, the ability to word process documents justifies the expense of purchasing a personal computer. There are dozens of word processing software packages available, many of which have features and options not included in Works. Some of the most popular are MacWrite, Microsoft Word and Word Perfect. Because you have learned the Works word processor, you will be able to easily learn and use another word processing package such as the ones named above. Word processing is a valuable skill, not only for school work but in your personal and professional life as well.

Chapter Summary

This chapter explained how text in a Word Processor document can be formatted to improve its appearance and readability. Windows are employed by Works to display documents on the screen. A window can be closed, adjusted, expanded and scrolled.

Tables can be created in a document using tabs, margins and indents. Works has default tab stops at every half inch. Individual tab stops may be set and cleared using the mouse. These stops may be left, right, center or decimal aligned.

To remove a file from the computer's memory it must be closed, ⌘W. This frees computer memory and protects the file from an accident such as a power failure. To reverse the effects of the last command issued the Undo command from the Edit menu, ⌘Z, is used. Note that it is possible to execute menu commands without the mouse by using the Command key.

Margins are the blank spaces between the edges of the paper and text. Works' default margin settings can be changed using the Page Setup command from the File menu. When a margin is changed it affects all of the document from the first page to the end of the document. The Page Setup command also controls the creation of headers and footers. A header is a line printed at the top of each page, and a footer at the bottom of each page. Page numbers, file names, dates and times can be printed in either headers or footers.

Indents are additions to the margins and are set by dragging the indent markers on the format line. Setting an indent affects only the paragraph which currently contains the cursor. Single and double spacing are controlled by the Spacing command from the Format menu. When line spacing is set it affects all text in the current paragraph, or in the selected block.

Works provides four ways to align text also using the Justification command from the Format menu: left, right, centered and justified. Left alignment creates a straight left hand border and a jagged right hand border. Right alignment is the opposite, creating a straight right border and a jagged left border. Centering positions a line equidistant from the left and right margins. Justified alignment creates straight borders at both margins.

Pagination is the division of a document into page-sized sections for printing. Works automatically displays the position of page breaks with a dotted line, allowing you to determine how text will be divided when printed. After an editing change, Works recalculates the position of the page breaks. When it is necessary to end the current page manual page breaks may be inserted using the Insert Page Break command from the Format menu and removed using the Remove Page Break command.

Blocks are highlighted sections of text created by dragging the mouse. Blocks may be deleted, moved or copied. A block is deleted by executing the Clear command from the Edit menu and formatted by executing any of the format commands. To Move a block of text from one location within a document to another the block is defined, the Cut command from the Edit menu executed (⌘X), the cursor moved to the new location and then the Paste command executed from the Edit menu (⌘V). To Copy a block of text so that it appears both at its original location and at a new location the above procedure is used except the Copy command (⌘C) rather than Cut is selected.

The Work's Format menu contains options which affect the way that the font, size and style of characters appear on the screen and when printed. Text to be formatted is first highlighted and then the appropriate selection made from the Format menu. Bold ⌘ B), italic (⌘I) and underline (⌘ U) styles may be selected to format text. Text may be printed in superscript (raised slightly) or subscript (lowered slightly) by highlighting the text and then using the Style command from the Format menu.

The Find command from the Search menu (⌘F) allows a document to be searched for a particular combination of characters called the search text. The Replace command from the Search menu (⌘ R) locates a search text in a document and replaces it with different text. To move the cursor to the top of any page in a document the Go To Page # command from the Search menu (⌘G) is used.

One of the most powerful features of the Works Word Processor is the Correct Spelling command on the Spell menu. Correct Spelling compares the words typed in a document to a dictionary file. If a word is found which is not in the file, Works can replace it with the correct spelling, or will allow you to type a correction.

Vocabulary

Block - A highlighted section of text, created by dragging the mouse, which may contain anything from a single character to an entire document. Once highlighted, operations such as Copy and Move may be performed on the block or text formats such as bold applied.
Bold text - Darker letters, used for emphasis.
Centered text - Text positioned evenly between the left and right margins.
Close - To remove a file from the work area when it is no longer needed: ⌘ W.
Command key - Key used to execute menu commands without using the mouse. Abbreviated as ⌘.
Copy text - Creates an exact copy of a highlighted block in a new location:⌘C.
Delete text - Removes a highlighted block from a document using the Clear command from the Edit menu.
Double space - Leaving a blank line between each line of text when a document is printed.
Find - The computer searches a document for specified text: ⌘ F.
Font - Description of the shape of a set of characters such as Boston or Helvetica.

Footer - Line which is printed at the bottom of each page.
Format - The way that text appears on a page, including options such as font, indents, emphasized text and headers and footers.
Format menu - Menu from which formatting options such as font, style, size and justification are set.
Go To Page # command - Used to move the cursor directly to the top of a specified page: ⌘G.
Header - Line which is printed at the top of each page.
Highlighted text - Text that has been selected as a block by dragging the mouse.
I-beam pointer - Shape the mouse pointer becomes when moved into the text of a document. Clicking the mouse places the cursor at the current location of the I-beam pointer.
Indent - Paragraph formatting option which increases the left or right margin.
Justification - See Paragraph alignment.
Justified - Paragraph format in which each line of text is made to extend from the left margin to the right by adding extra space between words.
Left alignment - Default paragraph format where text is even with the left hand margin, while the right side is ragged.
Margin - Blank spaces on a printed page which surround text.
Move text - Removes a highlighted block from its current position and places it in a new one:⌘ X and ⌘V.
Pagination - Works calculates and displays a dotted line showing where text will be broken into pages when printed.
Paragraph alignment - How text is printed in relation to the margins: left (default), right, centered or justified.
Paragraph format - Use of options affecting a paragraph including alignment, spacing, tabs and indents.
Replace text - The computer replaces one specified piece of text with another: ⌘R.
Right alignment - Paragraph format where text is set even with the right hand margin, while the left side is ragged.
Ruler - Line at the top of the work area showing placement of tab stops, indents and margins.
Search - Locate specific text in a document: ⌘S.
Search text - Text entered by the user to be found or replaced.
Single space - Leaving no space between each line of text when a document is printed.
Spelling checker - Words in a document not found in Works' dictionary file are displayed along with possible correct spellings.
Style - How text is displayed; for example, bold or italic.
Subscript - Text printed slightly below the normal line.
Superscript - Text printed slightly above the normal line.
Tab stop - Position(s), shown on the ruler, where the cursor jumps to when the Tab key is pressed. Used to create columns or indent text.
Text format - How the letters making up the text are printed: bold, underlined, italic, superscript, subscript or plain.
Undo command - Reverses the effect of the last command issued: ⌘Z.
Unjustified - Left-aligned text, with the right side jagged.
Window - Area of the screen where data is displayed.

Reviews

Sections 3.1-3.4

1. List three ways that a word processor can manipulate text that cannot be done on a typewriter.

2. a) What steps are required to make the window containing a document smaller?
b) To make the window fill the screen?
c) How may you close the window which contains a document?

3. What is the Command key used for? Give two examples.

4. a) What are tab stops used for?
b) What is a default tab stop?

5. a) What is the ruler and what is it used for?
b) What do the triangles below the ruler indicate?

Sections 3.5-3.11

6. Explain what each of the following tab stops does:
a) left-aligned
b) right-aligned
c) center-aligned
d) decimal-aligned

7. a) Explain the steps required to set a center-aligned tab stop at 2.7".
b) How can the tab stop described in (a) be removed?
c) How can you tell where tab stops have been set?

8. If a file is saved are the tab stops saved with it?

9. a) How do you close the currently displayed file?
b) What happens to a file when it is closed? Is it automatically saved on disk?

10. a) What is meant by formatting text?
b) List five publications in which you have seen formatted text and describe the formats used.

11. a) List the steps required to change the margins of a document so that the left margin is at 2 inches and the right margin at 3 inches.
b) How long is a line of text after these margins have been set? (Assume an 8.5 x 11 inch sheet of paper.)
c) How can you tell where the margins have been set when working on the word processor screen?

12. a) Explain the steps required to have Works print the header "My Summer Vacation" and a footer containing the current date and page number on each page of a document.
b) What additional steps are required to center the header and footer?

13. What is the difference between an indent and a margin?

14. Explain the steps required to indent a paragraph 1" on the left and 0.5" on the right.

15. a) Why might you want text to be double spaced?
b) List the steps required to double space only the second paragraph in a document that contains five paragraphs.
c) Will the second paragraph appear double spaced on the screen?

16. Explain how the mouse can be used to move the cursor to the middle of the third paragraph in a document.

Sections 3.12-3.16

17. a) What is meant by "justified" text?
b) Explain how to justify a paragraph.

18. a) What is meant by "centered" text?
b) What type of text is usually centered?

19. a) What is meant by text that is "left-aligned?"
b) What types of documents are usually formatted using left-alignment?

20. If you make a mistake in formatting a paragraph what is usually the fastest method of correcting the error?

21. a) What is meant by a "block" of text?
b) How can you tell which text is included in a block?

22. List the steps required to delete the second paragraph in a five paragraph document.

23. Explain how to replace a block of text with new text entered from the keyboard.

24. What is the easiest way to justify the text in a whole document?

25. a) What is meant by "pagination?"
b) How is pagination indicated on the word processor screen?
c) Explain two situations when you might want to control the pagination in a document.
d) How can you add a page break in the middle of a page?
e) How can you remove the page break set in part (d)?

Sections 3.17-3.19

26. List the steps required to bold the first line of text and underline the second line in a word processed document.

27. Explain the steps required to center the title of a document and then change it to Helvetica in 18 point type.

28. a) What is meant by "moving" a block of text?
b) List the steps required to move the second paragraph in a document to a point directly after the fourth paragraph.

29. a) What is meant by "copying" a block of text?
b) What is the difference between moving and copying a block of text?

Sections 3.20-3.25

30. a) What is meant by searching for text?
b) Give three examples where you might use the Find command.

31. List the steps required to find each occurrence of the name "Judith Habersham" in a document.

32. If the Find command is instructed to search for the text to, which of the following words will be found?

```
Toby
alto
Otto
rot
tomorrow
```

33. What is the quickest way to move the cursor to the top of page 23 in a long document?

34. a) What is the Replace command used for?
b) Give three examples where the Replace command might be used.

35. When using the Replace command to replace the word hat with cap, how can you avoid changing the letters "hat" when they appear within another word such as chatter?

36. a) Explain what steps must be taken to have Works check the spelling of a document starting from the beginning.
b) What does Works do when it finds what it considers a spelling error?
c) Is it possible that Works might indicate an error when a word is spelled correctly? How is this possible?

37. Can you add words to the Works dictionary? If so, how?

38. What is the difference between a superscript and a subscript?

Exercises

1. The file on your data disk named PARTY gives directions from the school to a party but is listed out of order. Use Cut and Paste to place the list in proper order and then print a copy.

2. Exercise 8 in Chapter 2 asked you to create an advertisement for an upcoming school event in a file named ADVERTISEMENT.

   a) Open the ADVERTISEMENT file and use formatting options such as tabs, centering, different fonts and styles to make it more attractive. For example:

   b) Use the Correct Spelling command to check the spelling in ADVERTISEMENT. Make any corrections required and then save and print a copy.

3. The file named OPENINGS on your data disk contains several lines which could be used to start a short story.

   a) Choose one of the lines, delete the rest using blocks and then write a paragraph using the opening line.

   b) Use the Correct Spelling command to check the spelling in your story. Make any corrections and then save and print a copy.

4. The Copy command is useful when text must be repeated in a document.

   a) Use the Copy command to create a file called MY NAME which contains your name 50 times, each name on a separate line. Hint: consider using a block with more than 1 line.

   b) Add a header to this file which prints the page number on each page. Save MY NAME on disk and then print a copy of this file.

5. Exercise 5 in Chapter 2 asked you to write a review of a recent movie or concert and save it in a file named CRITIC.

   a) Load CRITIC and add a bold, centered headline which reads "Critic's Corner".

   b) Underline any titles in the review, such as the title of the movie, an album or song title, etc.

   c) The paper's editors like all submissions to be doubled spaced. Format your review to conform with their wishes.

   d) Use the Correct Spelling command to check the spelling in your review. Make any corrections required. Save the file and print a copy of the modified review.

   e) Justify the text in the review so that it looks more like a newspaper article. Save the modified review and print a copy of it.

6. It is often necessary to create tables in documents using tabs.

   a) Use the word processor to create the following table. Use tabs to create the columns and bold the column headings:

Opponent	**Record**
Audubon	7-4
Cherry Hill East	7-4
Cherry Hill West	4-7
Collingswood	2-8
Gulf Stream	6-5
Haddon Heights	10-1
Pine Crest	1-10

   b) Add a third centered column titled Division to the table:

Division
I
IV
IA
III
IV
V
I

   c) Save the document under the name TABLE and print a copy.

7. In exercise 3 in Chapter 2 you created a file named APPLY which contained an application letter for a college.

   a) Correct the spelling in the document.

   b) Using the Replace command, change the name of the college in APPLY to Trenton State University and print a copy of the new letter.

   c) Change the college name from Trenton State University to New Brunswick College. Print a copy of the new letter.

   d) Change the body of the letter only to double-spaced.

   e) Save and print a copy of the modified letter.

8. You are to create a two-page newsletter on any topic that you wish. The newsletter must contain the following features:

   At least 4 different stories.
   A page header which shows the page number.
   Two advertisements.
   Bold, centered headlines.
   Justified paragraphs.
   Correct spelling.
   At least 1 table.
   At least 1 superscripted footnote. Place the footnote references on the last page.
   Consider using tabs to create more than one column per page (like a newspaper). Note that text in columns created this way cannot be justified.

   An example newsletter design is shown on the next page.

I.U. News Page 1

Ivy University News - "All the News that Fits"

We Win!

Kansas City: Today the Ivy University Roaring Tigerlilies again proved that they were a force to be reckoned with as they bested the Overbrook Rams, 2-1. Overbrook took the lead early on but was soon shut down by the mighty Tigerlily defense. Coach Riley said that "The team has never, ever, ever played better." For complete details please see the Sports section.

Steves' Election Bid Fails

In a surprising come-from-behind victory, dark-horse candidate J.T. Willbury today defeated incumbent Thom Steves in the Student Congress presidential race. Steves, a 3 and a half year veteran, lost by a huge margin to the newcomer Willbury. The final tally was:

Candidate	Votes
Steves	57
Willbury	3,461
Undecided	289

More election results - page 3

Editorial Comment - by *Dana A. Clarke*

It comes as no surprise to those who have followed this year's Student Congress elections that Thom Steves was not re-elected. What is surprising is the actual number of people who realized that for the last 3 and a half years this guy has been sandbagging it. If ever there was a case for impeachment, this was it. The well-oiled political machine that passed as Steves' campaign staff was a joke. His grandiose plans to have the cafeteria serve chocolate milk never materialized, as did the student trip to the Bahamas. Those of us (cont., next page)

9. The school literary magazine would like to print the essay you wrote for Chapter 2 exercise 7. Load the ESSAY file and make the following changes:

   a) Add a centered header showing your name.

   b) Add a footer which prints the page number.

   c) The body of the essay should be double spaced.

   d) Add a bold, centered title.

   e) Correct the spelling in the document.

   f) Save the modified file and print a copy for the magazine.

10. Load the file named COMPUTER ED from your data disk and make the following changes. Save the modified file and print a copy when the changes are complete:

Center and bold title in 18 point type —— Computers in Education

Justify all paragraphs

Over the past ten years it has become obvious that computers will increasingly play a role in education. The invention of the microcomputer has made it possible for schools to purchase large number of computers at affordable prices. In many schools these computers have been placed in computer laboratories, while in other schools they have been distributed to classrooms. Now that the computers are available for student use, educators have been discussing how they should be used. Below are a few examples of how schools are using their computers.

Center title in 12 point type —— Computer Aided Instruction

Underline 2nd sentence ——

A number of computer programs have become available which instruct students in different academic disciplines. These programs have been especially effective in instructing students in languages and mathematics. When used with elementary school students, computer aided instruction has been found to keep students interested in a subject while entertaining them at the same time. Mrs. Groves, a teacher at West Lawrence Grade School, said, "When used as part of a complete learning system, computers help reinforce skills learned in the classroom."

Center title in 12 point type —— Applications Programs

Many students are now taking courses which introduce them to applications software. They are taught how to use word processing, data base and spreadsheet software. Most students find that knowing how to use such software can help them in their other courses. Mr. Ronald Johnson of Ivy University said, "Our students are especially interested in learning how to use integrated software like AppleWorks and Microsoft Works."

Center title in 12 point type —— Writing Programs

Italicize "BASIC" and "Pascal" ——

Students who would like to pursue careers in computing often elect to take courses which teach them how to write computer programs. The languages most often learned are BASIC and Pascal. Besides learning to program, these courses teach valuable problem-solving skills.

Chapter 4

Introducing the Data Base

Objectives

At the end of this chapter you will be able to:

1. Describe what a data base is.
2. Give examples of manual (non-computerized) and computerized data bases.
3. Describe common data base operations.
4. Explain why a computer is useful for manipulating a data base.
5. Define what records, fields and entries are.
6. Plan and design a form for a computerized data base using appropriate field names.
7. Plan a query of a data base to obtain desired information.

This chapter provides an introduction to data bases and how they organize and store information. Specific tasks that are performed using a data base are covered as examples. Specialized terms that describe the operations and structure of a data base are defined. Attention is given not only to understanding what a data base is, but also to the planning and design considerations that make them more efficient and easy to use.

Chapter Five provides step-by-step instructions for creating and manipulating a computerized data base using Works. Because a knowledge of data base concepts and terminology is required, it is important to thoroughly understand the material in this chapter before proceeding to the next.

4.1 What is a Data Base?

A data base is simply a group of related pieces of information. You are familiar with several different manual (non-computerized) data bases: the card catalog in a library, a recipe file box, an office "Rolodex" file for phone numbers and a filing cabinet storing a school's student records are all examples of data bases. Each item in a data base is related to each of the others in some way. For example, each card in a card catalog records some information about a specific book in a library.

One way to think of a data base is as a collection of forms, each storing the same type of information. An example of such a form would be a card in a library's card catalog which stores the reference number, title, author and publisher data for a single book:

Number: SP125

Title: *Patchwork Quilts Through the Ages*
Author: Dr. Rosey Greer
Published: Scrapwork Press, New Haven, Conn., 1982

The cards in a library card catalog are examples of records

Each card is organized so that the different pieces of information appear at the same locations. A book's reference number is in the upper left corner, title on the first line of the card, author on the second line, and so on for every card in the catalog. A consistent design makes it easy for your eyes to pick out needed information when scanning through a stack of cards.

4.2 Computerized Data Bases

As you have discovered using the word processor, the computer is a powerful tool for storing and manipulating information. The speed and storage capabilities of the computer make it an ideal tool for managing large amounts of information in the form of data bases.

Today almost all businesses and organizations use computer data bases in some way. A data base can be used by a bank to store the account information of its depositors or by a school to store student records. Department and grocery stores keep track of the different items they have for sale, their prices and how many of each are in stock in a computer data base. The size of such data bases can become very large. A major advantage of using a computer is its ability to look through a large data base for a specific piece of information in a very short amount of time. In addition, because the computer can store information about thousands of items on a small disk, the amount of space needed to store a large data base is substantially reduced.

Computerized data bases can be used to organize information about virtually any area of knowledge: agriculture, biology, economics, education, law, medicine and more. It is even possible to have a data base which stores information about other data bases. Any information that can be stored in a list or on individual forms can be put into a data base. Governments maintain thousands of computer data bases on information ranging from births and deaths to taxes. Many historians refer to our present time as the "Information Age" primarily because of the ability computers and data bases have given us to store and manipulate huge amounts of information. Clearly then, because data bases are becoming more important to the world in which we live it is increasingly necessary to learn what they are and how to use them.

4.3 Data Base Terminology

Like the documents produced by the word processor, the information in a computer data base is stored on disk in a file. A data base file has its own special structure, and differs from a word processor file or a file for some other application. Information on a single item in a data base is called a "record". For example, the catalog card for *Patchwork Quilts Through the Ages* could be thought of as a single record which is different from the record or card for any other book. A data base file, therefore, is a collection of related records. In Works, approximately 6,000 records may be stored in a single data base file.

Information within a record is separated into "fields". Author, title and reference number are three separate fields in a single catalog card record. It is important to note that each record in a data base has the same fields, but that the data stored in each field differs from record to record. In the card catalog, each card has a place for a reference number, title, author's name, etc., but no two cards have the same reference number. The order and placement of fields in a record is called a "form".

The data stored in an individual field in a single record is called an "entry". For example, in the card catalog Author is a field; a place for an author's name appears in each record. Dr. Rosey Greer is an entry in that field; the author of a specific book.

Naturally, the size of a record depends on the number of fields it contains. It is not uncommon for a data base to have as few as two fields, such as a name and phone number. On the other hand, large business or scientific data bases may contain hundreds of fields in each record. In Works, each record may contain up to 60 fields. The following diagram shows the differences between a record, field and entry using the card catalog as an example:

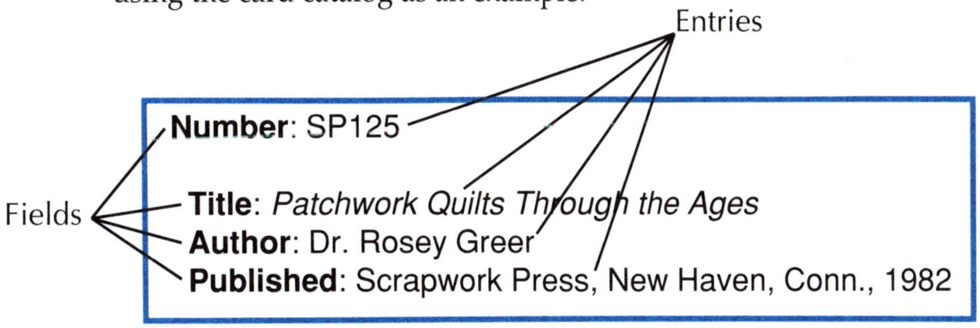

4.4 Field Names and Types

To illustrate how a data base is designed and implemented on the computer we will describe how Ivy University, better known as I.U., stores its student records in a computerized data base. When storing information in a data base the computer needs to be given a specific name for each field in the record. This "field name" is required so that the computer can distinguish between the different pieces of data stored in the record. Works field names may be up to 64 characters long.

Fields are often classified by the type of data that they store. There are a few basic field types in a computerized data base. For example, fields which store only words are called "character" fields. At I.U. the name and address for each student are stored in character fields.

Another commonly used field type is the "numeric" field. As the name implies, numeric fields store only numbers. Ivy University's data base stores student grade point averages (GPA) in a numeric field. Because numeric fields store only numbers the data they store can be used in mathematical calculations.

In addition to character and numeric data, Works allows dates and times to be stored in fields. Dates are stored in either long form (June 4, 1990) or short form (6/4/90). Times are stored in 24-hour form (14:30) or 12-hour form (2:30 PM). Seconds may also be shown (2:30:15 PM). Data stored in time or date fields may be used in calculations which will be explained in Chapter 6.

4.5 A Simple Data Base

To review what has been discussed so far, let us look at the manual system currently used by Ivy University to record student data. We will later convert this into a computerized data base. Each record currently uses the following form:

Name
Address
Date Admitted
GPA
Tuition Paid

A sample record showing only fields, no entries

All of the information above for a single student is considered to be a record. Each record contains five fields, which are defined below by describing their types and the information they store:

Name: Student's name stored in a character field.

Address: Student's school (dorm) address stored in a character field.

Date Admitted: Date the student was admitted to the University. Works automatically makes this a date because of the way in which the data is entered.

GPA: A numeric field which stores the student's grade point average.

Tuition Paid: Whether or not the student has paid the tuition for this semester. To save space, a code of Y represents Yes and a code of N represents No.

Here are sample records for three I.U. students:

Name: Matilda Rose
Address: 435 Frelinghuysen Hall
Date Admitted: 2/14/88
GPA: 3.4
Tuition Paid: Y

Name: Sam Adams
Address: 121 Carey Quadrangle
Date Admitted: 3/12/89
GPA: 1.5
Tuition Paid: N

Name: Roberta Poisson
Address: 8P Corwin Place
Date Admitted: 6/27/89
GPA: 4.0
Tuition Paid: N

Three example records from the University student data base

Notice how each of the records has the same form containing the same fields, but that the entries differ from record to record. It is also possible for a record to have "empty" entries; that is, a field which does not yet store any data. As an example, when new students enroll they have no value for their GPA, so that field is left blank. When their first semester is over, their record may be updated and the new GPA value stored in the field.

4.6 Common Data Base Operations

Data bases become useful when searching, querying, and sorting operations can be performed on them. The power of a computerized data base is that these operations may be performed on large quantities of data very quickly.

Searching:

The simplest data base operation is the "search". When users search a data base, they ask the computer to locate the first record which contains some specific text, either a letter, number, word or group of words. Each record in the data base is then checked, starting from the first, to see if it contains the requested information in any of its fields. If it does, the cursor jumps to that field. A subsequent search will locate the next field containing the desired text and so on until no field can be found.

Search is limited because it locates any field that contains the search text. For example, asking Works to search for "5" in the three student records above will first locate the 5 in the Address field of Matilda Rose's record. On the next search it locates the 5 in the GPA field of Sam Adams' record.

Querying:

More powerful than the Search is the Query which allows you to display all records which meet certain criteria. Criteria are conditions such as 'greater than' or 'not equal to' that can be applied to specific fields. For example, using the proper criteria it is possible to display only records which have 4.0 in the GPA field, or all students who were admitted between 5/1/87 and 5/16/89. Criteria can be joined together making complex conditions which limit the number of records displayed. This makes querying a powerful tool for gathering specific information from a large data base. Some example criteria are:

Which students are from Maine?
Show all students with the Last Name "Lee".
Show all students with a GPA less than 2.0 who were admitted before 1/1/86.

It should be obvious that a data base can only be queried for information that it stores in its records. That is, it would be impossible to search Ivy's student data base to determine the average rainfall in New Jersey because this involves asking the data base for information it does not store.

Reports:

Information taken from a data base is called a "report" and consists of data from specific records and fields. Reports can contain many pieces of data, or just one. For example, there may be hundreds of students from Maine, but Roberta Poisson has only one value for her current GPA. Reports generated with Works can contain titles, and calculate totals, subtotals and averages. Reports can also make use of formatting options such as bold or centered text like the Word Processor. Reports may be printed on paper or displayed on the screen.

Reports can differ based on the person who is using them. Different reports may contain different information, or the same information in a different order. For example, the university's business department would need to have a report which included the tuition paid information, but is probably not interested in the student's GPA. Chapter 6 will explain how a Works data base report is designed and printed.

Sorting:

It is easier to locate specific information in a data base if the records are arranged in order based on the data stored in a specific field. A student data base would be easier to search for a specific student's information if the records in it were ordered alphabetically by last name. To then find Roberta Poisson's grade point average it would not be necessary to look at every record in the file, but to simply go directly to the name "Poisson". Reports are also easier to read and understand when the information presented is in order.

Ordering records in a data base is called "sorting". A sort is performed based on the value of one field called the "key field" which is chosen by the user. When a data base is sorted, the position of a record in the file is changed based on the value stored in its key field. In the student records example above, the key field is the name field, so the records appear in order by name. When the computer performs a sort, it has been programmed to know that the character "A" is less than "B" and that 1 is less than 2 and so on. If the key is a date field, the data base program knows that 1/1/89 is less than 6/27/89, etc. This is called "chronological order". Here are the three student records sorted by date admitted:

Name: Matilda Rose
Address: 435 Frelinghuysen Hall
Date Admitted: 2/14/88
GPA: 3.4
Tuition Paid: Y

Name: Sam Adams
Address: 121 Carey Quadrangle
Date Admitted: 3/12/89
GPA: 1.5
Tuition Paid: N

Name: Roberta Poisson
Address: 8P Corwin Place
Date Admitted: 6/27/89
GPA: 4.0
Tuition Paid: N

The records sorted in chronological order by date admitted

It is important to realize that a computer data base file can be easily sorted on different key fields as the need arises. One report may need the data ordered by last name, and another by GPA or admit date. Here are the same three student records sorted in descending order (high to low) by GPA:

Name: Roberta Poisson
Address: 8P Corwin Place
Date Admitted: 6/27/89
GPA: 4.0
Tuition Paid: N

Name: Matilda Rose
Address: 435 Frelinghuysen Hall
Date Admitted: 2/14/88
GPA: 3.4
Tuition Paid: Y

Name: Sam Adams
Address: 121 Carey Quadrangle
Date Admitted: 3/12/89
GPA: 1.5
Tuition Paid: N

The same records sorted in descending order by GPA

In a computer data base the records may be sorted quickly using any field as the key field because the information is stored in the computer's memory, and not on paper forms. Sorting is often not possible in a manual data base without a large amount of work. For this reason most libraries must maintain two separate manual card catalogs to have their books listed by both author and subject, which often leads to errors, mis-filed cards, etc.

Libraries must maintain two separate manual card catalogs in order to have their records sorted by both title and subject

Modifying: From time to time, data base files must be modified to be kept current: old information removed, outdated information updated, and new information added. At the end of each school year Ivy must remove any graduating seniors from its student data base. This involves "deleting" certain records from the data base file. New GPAs must be calculated for the remaining students and placed in the GPA field. Changing the information stored in a field is called "updating" the file. Finally, the names and related data of any new students who have been accepted must be added to the file.

A definite advantage of a computerized data base is the ease in which it may be modified. Like the word processor, changes made to a data base file can be made on the screen and stored electronically. When all of the desired changes have been made, the modified data base can be saved on disk for future use. A change to a manual data base would require that the appropriate record be located and then physically changed, using an eraser or by rewriting the information onto a new form.

4.7 Planning a Data Base

A great deal of time and thought should go into the planning of a data base before it is created. Carefully planning a data base will save time and eliminate frustration later. Below are listed three steps for planning a data base.

Steps for Planning a Data Base

1. Determine what data should be stored in each record. This is best accomplished by examining the needs of the different users of the data base. Start by creating a general list on paper of the data available. Eliminate any information that is not directly related to the overall purpose of the data base.

2. Examine the specific operations to be performed on the data base. Do the operations require any information that is missing from the current list? Will there be a need to separate the first name from the last? Is there a need for a complete mailing address or will a street address be enough? Make any changes required to the list produced in step 1.

3. Create a list of fields and field names using the list from step 2. Use this list to create a description of the data stored in the different fields, their types (character, numeric, date, etc.), and the operations performed with them. Produce a sample form for a single record on paper.

In step 2 it is helpful to create examples of the reports that may be needed by sketching them on paper. This makes it easy to see what information is required by each report.

Careful planning requires information about both the user of the data base and the operations that will be performed on it. Data base designers often spend a great deal of time talking to the user(s) of a proposed data base and analyzing their needs before making any decisions about fields, types, forms, reports, etc. It is also important to realize that most data bases are accessed by more than one user, each of whom has different requirements and will perform different operations. The time spent planning makes it easier for each user to get the fullest use from the information stored in the data base and avoids having to later make major modifications to the data base. Producing sample records and reports on paper helps to define the data base and shows where potential errors may occur. Only after the design has been checked by hand should the computer be used to actually create the data base.

4.8 Planning Records and Fields

The two most important questions when designing a data base are "What information should be stored?" and "What operations will be performed on that information?". Deciding what information to store depends on what the data base will be used for. A student data base would not contain any information about salaries or how many desks are in certain classrooms, only information that is directly related to the students. Each record in a student data base would probably contain the following fields at a minimum:

Student Name
Address
Date student was admitted
Current GPA
Has tuition been paid?

The first step in designing a record is to list the possible fields

It is important to realize that each record stores all of the information above for a single student, and that the data base will contain one record for each student enrolled.

Next, the operations performed on the data base should be considered. Ivy University keeps its student records in order by last name. So that the records may be sorted based on the last name only, two separate fields have to be created to store the student name; a first name field and a last name field:

First Name
Last Name
Address
Date student was admitted
Current GPA
Has tuition been paid?

Next, make certain that those fields are enough to perform all operations

Finally, the administration would like to be able to send warning letters to each student who has a low GPA. In order to use the data base to produce complete mailing labels, the address field must be expanded to include separate fields for a city, state and zip code:

First Name Last Name Street address City State Zip code Date student was admitted Current GPA Has tuition been paid?

By considering the uses for the data, a proper record may be defined

Several problems have been avoided by carefully considering the uses for this data base before it is created. For example, the ability to produce mailing labels is a valuable asset of a student data base. Had this not been planned for, a great deal of work would have to be done either to later modify the data base or to create some manual system for recording student addresses. Storing a complete student mailing address in separate fields allows the university to more fully use the power of the computer data base.

4.9 Choosing Field Names

Each field must have a distinct name to distinguish it from the other fields in a record. A well chosen field name describes the data stored in that field, making it easy to determine its use. Below are good examples of field names for the student record data base:

Data	**Field name**
First Name	`First Name`
Last Name	`Last Name`
Street address	`Address`
City	`City`
State	`State`
Zip code	`Zip`
Date student was admitted	`Admit Date`
Current GPA	`GPA`
Has tuition been paid?	`Paid`

Most computer data bases have a limit on the number of characters in a field name. Choosing the shortest possible name which accurately describes the contents of the field is therefore important. This is why the name `Address` rather than Street Address, was chosen to represent the street address field. In general, a name of ten to fifteen characters or less should be able to describe the data stored in any field. However, should it be required, Works allows up to 64 characters per field name, including spaces and punctuation marks.

4.10 Form Design

The order in which the different fields appear in a record is called the "form". It also includes the amount of space that each field has when displayed on the screen.

The form can be changed at any time by inserting or deleting fields. For example, if Ivy University's Dean wants the student's age added to the data base this can be done by placing a new field on the data base form. This would automatically add the new field to all of the records in the data base.

If a data base is originally well planned the form should have to be changed infrequently. Adding and deleting fields can make the records a "hodge-podge" of data, limiting the usefulness of the data base.

4.11 Viewing Records

Works has two different ways of displaying records on the screen. First is the "Form view". In Form view all of the fields for a single record are displayed. This is most often used when updating a record, or when adding a new record to the file. Below is an example of a record displayed in Form view:

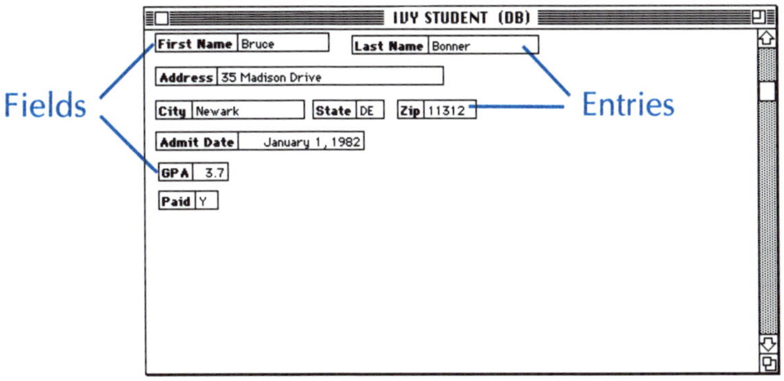

A single record in Form view

The second display method is the "List view". In List view, up to 21 different records may be displayed on the screen at one time. However, because the screen is limited to a width of 80 characters, not every field may be displayed. Like the word processor, the data base screen may be scrolled up and down by moving the cursor, allowing other records to be displayed. Listed below are student records from the I.U. data base in List view:

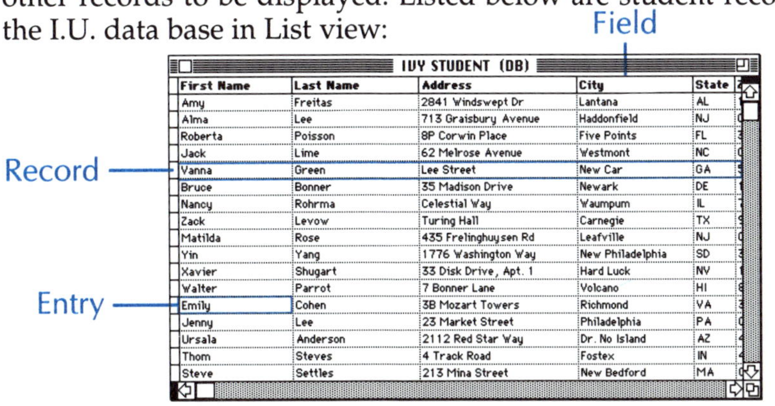

Multiple records in List view. Note how some fields are not shown

Note that due to width restriction of the screen the Admit Date, GPA and Paid fields are not currently displayed. They are, however, still stored in the record and may be viewed by switching to Form view.

After the form's design has been determined it is a good idea to give some thought to the way that reports will look. Sketch sample designs of the different required reports showing field names and the amount of space to be given each field. Just as related fields should be grouped together in the form, they should also be printed together in a report. As when designing the form, it is important to consider the user of the report. As you progress you will also have to consider such points as how the data in the report should be sorted and when to print totals and other information.

Chapter Summary

A data base is an organized collection of related information. Information in a data base is divided into records, each of which stores a complete set of data about a specific item. Different pieces of data within a record are called fields and the arrangement of the fields within a record is called a form.

A field name is required so that the computer can distinguish between different pieces of data stored in a record. Fields which store only words are called character fields while numeric fields store only numbers. Works includes a date/time field which stores either dates or times. The data stored in an individual field in a single record is called an entry.

The speed and storage capabilities of the computer make it an ideal tool for managing large amounts of information in the form of data bases. Information in a computerized data base is stored on disk in a file. Data bases are used by many organizations (businesses, governmental agencies, educational institutions, etc.) and may become very large. They can be used to organize information about almost any area of knowledge.

Data bases become useful when searching and sorting operations can be performed on them. When a search is performed the user asks to see the first record which contains specific information. The computer then searches each record until a field containing the sought information is located. A subsequent search locates the next occurrence of the information.

Records in a data base can also be queried. Unlike a search, a query allows the search to be limited to specific fields, and can apply criteria such as 'equal to' or 'greater than'.

Placing the records in a data base in order is called sorting. A sort is performed based on the value of one field called the key field. When a data base is sorted, the position of a record in the file is changed based on the value stored in its key field. For example, sorting on a name field in a data base arranges the records in alphabetical order based on names.

Information taken from a data base is called a report. Reports may include many pieces of data, or just one. Work's reports can contain titles, calculate totals, and make use of formatting options.

A data base may be modified: old information removed, outdated information updated and new information added. Removing records from a data base is called deleting from the file. Changing information stored in a field is called updating the file.

Before a data base is created, a great deal of planning should go into its design. Who will use the data base and how they will use it should be considered as part of the planning process. Choosing appropriate fields, field names, types and field lengths makes a data base complete and easy to use. A hastily designed data base usually requires a large amount of work to reorganize it after it has been created.

The order in which the different fields appear in a record as well as the space allocated to each field is called the form. In a well designed data base the form should have to be changed infrequently.

Vocabulary

Character field - A field which stores only characters such as a name or address.
Criteria - Rule a field must satisfy in order to have the record displayed which contains the field. For example, "GPA is less than 2.0".
Data base - A collection of related information.
Data base file - A file on disk which is created by the data base application and which stores a computerized data base.
Date field - A field which stores a date.
Entry - The information stored in one field in one record.
Field - A specific piece of information stored in each record, such as Last Name.
Field name - Name by which the computer identifies the different pieces of information in a record.
Form - The arrangement, length and order of the fields in a data base record.
Form View - The fields for a single record displayed on the screen. Useful when updating a record.
Format - How the records in a data base are displayed, Form view (one at a time) or List view (many at a time).
Key Field - Field which stores the data used when determining the order during a sort.
List View - Up to 21 records displayed on the screen at one time.
Modify - To change the contents of a record or entry.
Numeric field - A field which contains only numbers.
Query - Limiting the number of records that are displayed using criteria that displayed records must meet. A query is based on criteria which refer to specific fields and contain comparisons such as 'is less than' or 'is not equal to'.
Record - A complete collection of data for one item.
Report - Information extracted from a data base, usually printed on paper.

Search - Operation where the computer searches through the fields in a data base, displaying the first one to contain a specified text.
Sort - Places the records stored in a data base in order based on the value stored in one field.
Time field - A field which stores a time.
Update - See Modify.

Reviews

Sections 4.1-4.3

1. Why do historians refer to our present time as the Information Age?

2. a) What is a data base?
   b) What is a record?

3. a) Give two examples of manual data bases with which you are familiar.
   b) Describe the data stored in each.
   c) Describe the different fields stored by a single record in each of the manual data bases.

4. What capabilities of the computer make it an ideal tool for managing data bases?

5. What determines the size of a single record in a data base?

6. Can the following be considered to be data bases? Why or why not?

   a) a phone book
   b) just the yellow pages in a phone book
   c) patient files in a doctor's office
   d) a grocery list
   e) a school yearbook

7. The following information is found in the white pages of a phone book:

```
  . . .
Capeletti, Rod      712 Adams Ave.     212-0907
Caputti, Jane       80 Scarlet Ct.     123-4567
Caputti, Jane N.    255 Camden Ave.    555-1234
Caputti, M.         77 Sunset Strip    911-1111
  . . .
```

   a) What information would constitute a single record?
   b) Describe the separate fields in such a record.
   c) What information does each field store?

8. How would the information stored in a doctor's patient files be broken into records? Describe some of the possible fields and the data stored in them.

9. List five governmental agencies that might use a computerized data base. Explain what each agency would store.

10. Show what the form for a student record in your school's computer data base might look like.

Sections 4.4-4.6

11. a) What is the difference between character and numeric fields?
    b) What is a date field?

12. How many character, numeric and date fields are there in a single student record shown in Section 4.5?

13. Is it possible to enter data in to certain fields and leave others empty in the same record?

14. Choose appropriate field names and types for the following data:

    a) a person's name.
    b) a phone number.
    c) the color of a car.
    d) an item's price.
    e) whether an item is on sale or not.
    f) the day a person was born.

15. Answer the following questions based on the three sample student records given in Section 4.5:

    a) How many students have not paid their tuition?
    b) Which students were admitted before 1988?
    c) What are the names of the students with a GPA below 2.0?
    d) How many students live in the Carey Quadrangle?

16. a) What does it mean to search a data base?
    b) Give 3 examples of searches that could be performed on the student data base in your school's computer.

17. What is the difference between searching and querying a data base?

18. Which of the following operations constitute a search and which a query of a data base?

    a) Which records contain the name George?
    b) Which students have not paid their tuition?
    c) Which students were expelled last year?
    d) Show all records containing a 35.
    e) List all students who are over 21 years old.

19. a) What is a report?
    b) Describe two different reports that could be generated using the student records described in Section 4.5.

20. What field are the records in a phone book sorted on?

21. Describe a situation that would require a phone book record to be:

    a) updated
    b) added
    c) deleted

22. What fields other than Name and GPA could the records in the I.U. student data base be sorted on? Give a reason for having the data base sorted this way.

Sections 4.7-4.10

23. Why is it important to plan a data base before using the computer?

24. Why might it be better to store the first name and last name of students in separate fields rather than in the same field in the Ivy student data base?

25. a) What should be considered when choosing a field name?
b) What is the maximum length Works allows a field name to be?

26. a) What is a data base form?
b) Can the design of a form be changed after a data base has been produced on the computer?

27. What is the difference between displaying records in Form view or List view? What is the advantage of each?

28. a) What information should be stored in a computerized data base listing the cars for sale at an automobile dealership?
b) Describe a record from such a data base, including the information to be stored in each of its fields.
c) Using appropriate field names design a form for the data base.

Exercises

For each of the exercises below you will be asked to design a form for the data base. This should be done using paper and pencil, following the steps given in Section 4.7. You should be careful to select appropriate field names, and give consideration to their types and lengths. When you have completed each design type it into the word processor and produce a printed copy. Save the printed copy so that the design can be used in the next chapter to assist in producing a computerized data base.

1. Ivy University Bookstore has decided to store their inventory information in a data base. A partial list of items, their prices and quantity in stock is displayed below. Design a form for the Bookstore that includes fields for the example information listed below:

Item	**Quantity in stock**	**Price per item**
Ball point pen	2,300	$0.39
Felt tip pen	3,800	$0.79
Notebook	574	$1.89
Loose leaf paper	112	$6.55
3-ring binder	743	$4.75

2. Many people use a computerized data base in place of an address book. Design a data base form that includes the name, address, phone number and birthdate for each person in such a data base. Include two additional fields which could be used to store useful information about the person.

3. Fantasy Wheels, Inc. is an automobile dealership that sells exotic used cars. They want to store their inventory of cars in a data base. Produce a form for them that includes all of the information listed below. Fields for up to 3 accessories per car should be allocated in the design. The data for one of Fantasy's cars is shown below:

1969 Maserati
color: blue
interior: black
accessories: radio, 4 speed, sunroof
paid: $9,800
asking price: $21,600
date acquired: 5/9/88

4. You are to produce a questionnaire to survey a group of students in your school. In the next chapter the results of the survey will be stored in a computerized data base.

    a) Using the word processor, create a questionnaire which asks students to supply the following information about themselves:

First Name	List your favorite:
Last name	Course in school
Age	Rock band
Birthdate	Sport
Class	Hobby
Height	Food
Weight	Automobile
Sex	Television program

    Rate yourself as a dancer:
    Excellent, Good, Fair, Poor, Don't dance

    b) Produce 25 copies of your questionnaire and hand them out to students who are your friends and to students who you do not know well. Try to get a good mix of males and females as well as students with a variety of interests.

    c) Produce a form for the data acquired by the survey. Be certain to group related fields and to select appropriate field names and types.

5. Your school is going to computerize its report card system using a data base. At a minimum, each report card will contain a student name, the names of the classes that student is enrolled in and the grades received in the classes. Acting as the data base designer, answer the following:

    a) Before a data base can be created it is important to talk to the users of the data base. Make a list of these people and the questions you will ask them.

    b) Design a form that could be used to store the data base. The school would like to mail report cards directly to students' homes so be sure to include room for a complete mailing address.

    c) It will be necessary to search the report card data base from time to time. Give a list of possible queries that the school might perform on the data base. Does the form designed in part (b) make it possible to perform these queries? Make any necessary changes to the form.

    d) Besides the report cards themselves, give three examples of printed reports that might be produced using the data base. Does the form produced in part (b) contain all the information needed to produce these reports? Make any necessary changes to the form.

e) Give three examples of when it would be necessary to update the report card data base.

6. Your local library is considering computerizing its card catalog using a data base.

   a) Give three benefits of having the card catalog stored in a data base. Can you think of any drawbacks to the computerized system? List them.

   b) Design a form for the card catalog data base. Be sure to include all of the information currently included on the manual cards.

   c) Using the design from part (b), give three different key fields for sorting this data base. For each key field, describe why the data base might be sorted on this field.

7. Because the computerized card catalog designed in exercise 6 was such a success, the library would also like to store its lending information in a data base and keep track of its overdue books.

   a) Produce a form for a borrowed book record. Include the name of the borrower, the title and reference number of the book, the date it was borrowed and the date the book must be returned.

   b) Give three examples of printed reports that might be produced using this data base. Include a design for a report listing overdue books.

   c) Give reasons for having the data base sorted on the borrower's name, title, and due date fields.

8. Companies often use computerized data bases to keep track of their inventory.

   a) Design a form for an inventory which contains three fields: the product identification code, the product name and the amount of that product "on hand" (actually in the warehouse).

   b) Often the computer is located in a different building then the warehouse where the inventory items are stored. Using the word processor, create a printed form which could be used by a warehouse worker to record the amount on hand for a specific item. Include a title describing the purpose of the form, and leave room for the product's identification code and name.

   c) The manager of purchasing needs to know when to reorder products. Using the design in part (a), create a query that displays only those records with an amount on hand that is less than 100.

d) Design a printed report for the purchasing manager showing items that need to be reordered. Note the field names used on the report, and include titles.

e) There is often a delay between when a product is ordered and when it arrives in the warehouse. Add a field to your form named "Ordered:" which stores the amount of a product that has been ordered, but has not yet arrived. Modify the query in part (c) to display only those records for items which have an on hand amount less than 100 and have not yet been reordered.

9. Some scientific experiments require that data be recorded over a period of weeks, months or even years.

a) Design a form for a computerized data base to store the results of a weather experiment. Each record should contain fields which store the date, time, temperature, amount of rain fall, and sky conditions (clear, cloudy, etc.) for a single observation.

b) Using the field names from part (a) and criteria such as 'equals', 'greater than' and 'less than or equal to', create queries which display only the records which meet the following criteria:

Sunny days only
All cloudy days with no precipitation
The weather on March 15, 1989
The weather for the month of July, 1989
All rainy days in April

Chapter 5

Creating a Works Data Base

Format - Set Field Attributes

Organize - Find Field ⌘F

Format - Show Form ⌘L

Format - Show List ⌘L

Organize - Record Selection

Organize - Show All Records

Edit - Insert Record ⌘I

Edit - Cut ⌘X

Objectives

At the end of this chapter you will be able to:

1. Design a form for a data base record using Works.
2. Enter data into the new data base, record by record.
3. Save the data base in a file on disk.
4. Use the Find Field command to locate text in a data base.
5. Save an updated data base in the same file on disk.
6. Display the data in both Form view and List view.
7. Print the contents of a data base on a printer.
8. Query the data base for specific information.
9. Change the data stored in a record or field.
10. Add records to and delete records from a data base.

This chapter describes the steps necessary to create a computerized data base using Works and perform some common operations with it: search, query and update. A record form will be created and records entered into the data base. The data base is then saved on disk in a file and searched for text. Commands which update and save the information stored in the data base are introduced. Queries will be defined and applied so that only records which meet certain criteria are displayed. Chapter Six covers the creation of printed reports using the information in a data base as well as ways of ordering the records to make those reports easier to read and understand.

5.1 Creating a New Data Base

To create a new Works data base, double-click on the Database icon on the Open File dialog box. A blank data base Form is then displayed, along with a dialog box asking for the name of a field:

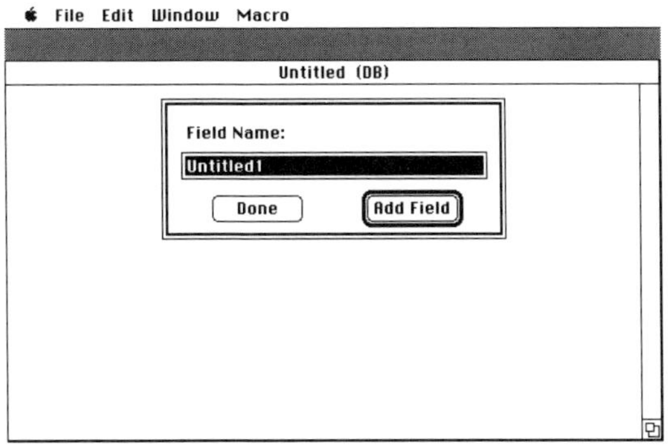

The Add Field dialog box allows a new field to be added to a form

The name and placement of each field in the data base is entered on this screen. In Macintosh Works, field names must begin with a letter and may not contain certain special characters such as hyphens or asterisks but may contain spaces.

5.2 Creating the Data Base Form

We will design a form for the Ivy University student data base discussed in Chapter Four. Each record stores the data for one student using the field names listed on the next page:

Field name	**Data**
`First Name`	student's first name
`Last Name`	student's last name
`Address`	street address
`City`	city
`State`	state
`Zip`	zip code
`Admit Date`	date student was admitted
`GPA`	grade point average
`Paid`	paid tuition bill? (Y or N)

The first step in creating a new data base is to enter the field names and their positions. It is important to place related fields near each other so that the form is easier to use and understand. As an example, the field for the student's last name should be placed next to the field for the first name. Other fields that should be grouped together are Address, City, State and Zip.

To create a form, the field name is typed in the Field Name dialog box. Clicking on the `Add Field` button places the field onto the form. A default field width (the space reserved to display the data stored in that field) is indicated by the entry box shown following the field name:

Fields have names and widths

Additional fields may then be added until the form is complete. When all of the fields have been added, clicking the `Done` button terminates field entry and an empty record is displayed, ready to receive data.

5.3 Changing Field Widths and Positions

Normally, a field's width will be changed from its default to accommodate the specific data to be entered for that field. This is accomplished using the mouse to drag the entry part of the field. When the mouse pointer is placed on the edge of the entry box, it changes to a new shape:

The Width pointer may be used to lengthen or shorten the entry box

This new pointer indicates that the width of the field may now be changed by dragging. Fields may be made longer or shorter:

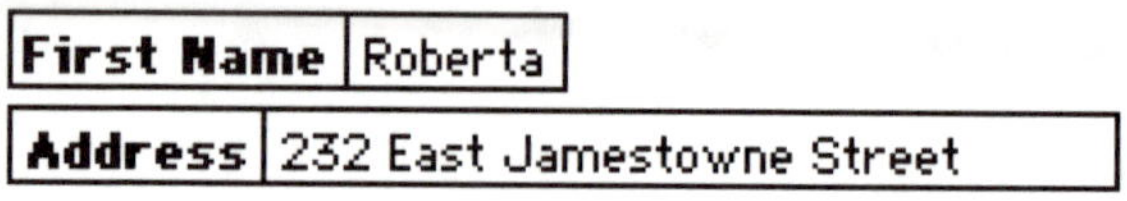

Field lengths may be changed to accomodate the data they store

You should create a field which is wide enough to display all of the data in that field. This does not have to be exact and may always be changed later. For example, for a field storing a person's first name, a field which can display only 5 characters is too short, while 30 characters is probably too long. Somewhere between 10 and 20 characters is best. Also, a field's width is not permanent and may be changed later. It is important to realize that a field's width only determines the number of characters displayed on the screen, not the number of characters actually stored in that field. The actual number of characters stored in a field depends on the number of characters entered from the keyboard, up to 250.

When Works adds new fields to a form, it simply places them in a column at the side of the screen. While this format is usable, it is usually not the best arrangement. For this reason, Works allows fields to be moved on a form to create a better arrangement. When the mouse pointer is placed on a field name, it changes to a hand shape which can be used to "grab" and move the field to a new location on the form:

The Grabbing hand pointer is used to move fields on the form

When the pointer is this shape, dragging the mouse causes the field under the hand to be moved. When the mouse button is released, the field is placed on the form in the new location.

Practice 1

In this Practice you will create a form for the student data base by entering the field names. The widths will then be changed, and fields moved to new locations on the form.

1) START WORKS

Following the directions given in Chapter 2, boot the Macintosh System. Double-click on the Microsoft Works icon to start Works and display the Open File dialog box.

2) CREATE A NEW DATABASE

From the Open File dialog box, double-click on the Data Base icon to create a new data base file. A blank form is shown with the Field Name dialog box.

3) PLACE THE FIRST NAME FIELD ONTO THE FORM

a. Type `First Name` in the Field name box.
b. Click on the `Add Field` button to place the field onto the form. Works shows an entry box following the field name to indicate where data stored in that field will be displayed.

<u>Check</u> - Your screen should show the First Name field:

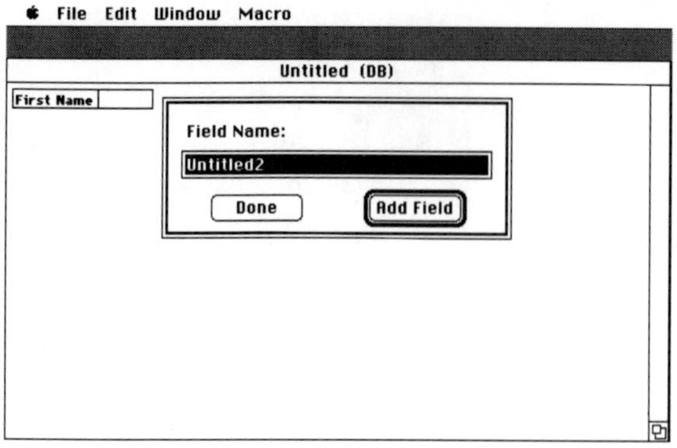

4) PLACE THE LAST NAME FIELD ONTO THE FORM

a. Type `Last Name` in the Field name box.
b. Click on the `Add Field` button to place the new field onto the form, below First Name. Your screen should show the two fields.

5) COMPLETE THE FORM BY ENTERING THE REST OF THE FIELDS

Next, the field for the address should be placed on the form. Using the steps described above, complete the record form by adding the rest of the fields listed below:

Field Name
`Address`
`City`
`State`
`Zip`
`Admit Date`
`GPA`
`Paid`

When the form is complete, click on the `Done` button to terminate field entry and remove the Field Name dialog box. Your form should be similar to:

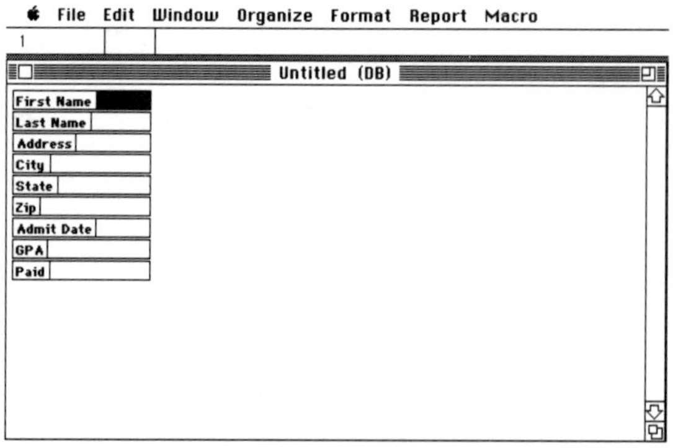

6) CHANGE THE WIDTH OF THE FIRST NAME FIELD TO DISPLAY MORE CHARACTERS

a. Place the mouse pointer on the end of the entry box of the First Name field. The pointer changes to a double-arrow.

b. Hold down the mouse button and drag the pointer to the right, expanding the entry box.

7) **CHANGE THE WIDTH OF THE OTHER FIELDS**

Using the procedure described in step 6 above, change the widths of the rest of the fields until they are similar to the following form:

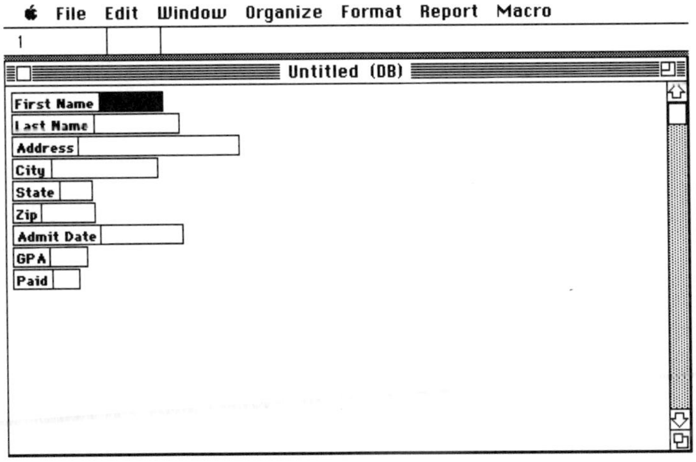

8) **CHANGE THE POSITION OF THE LAST NAME FIELD**

a. Place the mouse pointer on the field name of the Last Name field. The pointer changes to the grabber hand shape.
b. Hold down the mouse button and drag the field toward the upper right. Place the field next to (not on top of) the First Name field and release the button. The field placements should be similar to:

9) **MOVE THE OTHER FIELDS**

Using the procedure described in step 8 above, position the rest of the fields until they are similar to the following form:

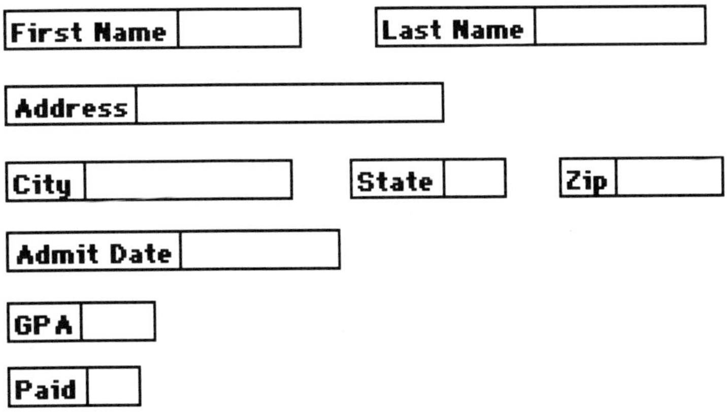

5.4 Entering Records in a New Data Base

After a form has been completed, data can be entered into the records.

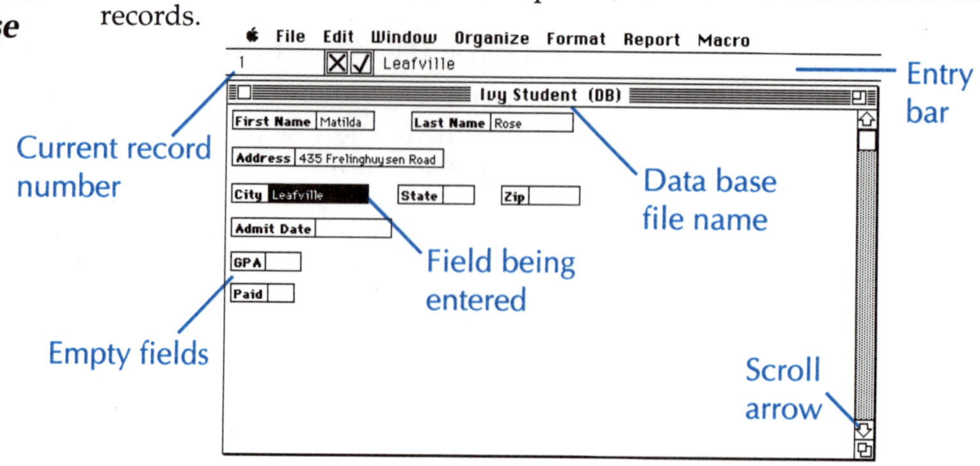

A sample record shown in Form view

Each field name is displayed with space to enter data for that field. Empty fields (fields with no data stored in them) are indicated by empty entry boxes. To enter data into a field, the pointer is moved to that field, the mouse clicked, and the data typed. As the data is typed it is shown on the Entry bar at the top of the screen. Clicking on the Check box transfers the data into the field so that it is displayed on the form. If you make a mistake before transferring the data, click on the X box to erase the current entry and start typing from the beginning of that field. When all of the fields in a record have been entered, clicking the down scroll-arrow clears the screen and a new, empty form is displayed. Works keeps track of how many records have been entered and which record is currently displayed and shows this information at the top of the screen.

Works can store 250 characters of data in a single field, but the number of characters displayed on screen depends on the field's width. Any characters beyond the width are still stored, just not displayed. When the pointer is clicked on a field the actual contents of that field are displayed on the Entry bar.

5.5 Saving a Data Base on Disk

Executing the Save command from the File menu (⌘S) saves the current data base in a file on disk. When a data base is saved, a copy of each of the records currently in the computer's memory is made on disk. Once a file has been saved, it may be opened later and the data stored in it displayed, printed or changed. It is important to periodically save a data base when it is being worked on so that, should an accident such as a power failure occur, it would be possible to recover the file from disk. After it has been saved, the file should be closed using the Close command, ⌘W, if it will not be worked on at this time.

Practice 2

In this Practice you will enter data into three student records and save the data base in a file on disk.

1) TYPE A STUDENT'S FIRST NAME

a. Click on the First Name field to select it. Note the 1 at the top of the screen indicating that this is the first record in the file.
b. Type `Matilda` and click on the Check box. If you make a mistake, retype the data and again click on the Check box.

2) ENTER THE STUDENT'S LAST NAME

a. Click on the next field, Last Name.
b. Type `Rose` and click on the Check box.

3) COMPLETE THE STUDENT RECORD

a. Enter the following data for the rest of the fields:

Address: `435 Frelinghuysen Road`
City: `Leafville`
State: `NJ`
Zip: `18049`
Admit Date: `2/14/88`
GPA: `3.4`
Paid: `Y`

b. After entering the data for Paid, click once on the down scroll-arrow. The screen is cleared and a new, empty form is shown into which the data for another record may be typed. Note the "2" at the top of the screen indicating that this is the second record in the data base file.

4) ADD THE FOLLOWING TWO STUDENT RECORDS

Following the steps above, enter the next records into the file:

First Name: `Sam`
Last Name: `Adams`
Address: `121 Carey Quadrangle`
City: `Leaftown`
State: `PA`
Zip: `19717`
Admit Date: `3/12/89`
GPA: `1.5`
Paid: `N`

First Name: `Roberta`
Last Name: `Poisson`
Address: `8P Corwin Place`
City: `Five Points`
State: `FL`
Zip: `33434`
Admit Date: `6/27/89`
GPA: `4`
Paid: `N` (Do not click on the scroll-arrow after this field.)

<u>Check</u> - The final record entered should be similar to that shown below. Note the "3" at the top of your screen for third record:

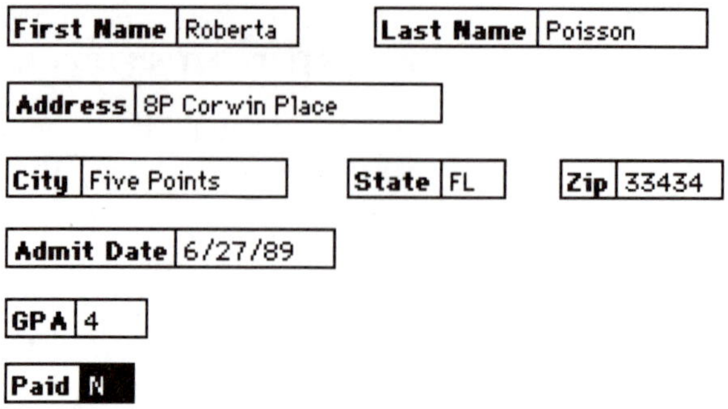

5) SAVE THE DATA BASE ON DISK USING THE NAME STUDENT

a. Press ⌘ S to display the Save dialog box.
b. Type the file name `STUDENT` and click on the `Save` button. The data base containing the three new records is saved in a file on disk using the file name STUDENT.

5.6 Changing the Data Stored in a Field

It is possible to change the data stored in a field. Changes to the entry in a field are made by clicking the pointer on the desired field, typing the new data and clicking the Check box. The new data then replaces the old in that record. This process is called "updating" and is covered in more detail later.

You may also edit the contents of a field by selecting it, which displays the data on the Entry bar. The mouse and Delete key can then be used to edit the entry, and characters may be inserted or deleted. When the Check box is clicked the edited data is copied from the Entry bar and placed in the field. If you choose not to make the update, clicking the X box instead erases your changes and restores the former entry.

Before the data in a record may be changed it must be displayed on the screen. The scroll bars and arrows are normally used for this purpose. It is also possible to scroll through the data base using the arrow keys to move the highlight from field to field. In both cases, the current record number is shown at the top of the screen to the left of the Entry bar. It is possible to scroll through the data base record by record by placing the pointer on a scroll arrow and holding down the mouse button.

Practice 3

In this Practice you will modify data stored in the STUDENT data base. Start Works and open the STUDENT file if you have not already done so.

1) SCROLL TO THE BEGINNING OF THE FILE

Click on the up scroll-arrow until the first record in the file is displayed. Note the "1" at the top of the screen indicating the record number.

2) SCROLL FROM RECORD TO RECORD

a. Click once quickly on the down scroll-arrow. Record 2 is displayed as indicated by the 2 at the top of the screen. (Note: if you do not click quickly the screen will scroll and another record will be displayed. Should this occur, simply scroll back up to record 2 using the up scroll-arrow.)
b. Click once quickly on the down scroll-arrow again. The screen moves to the third record and a 3 is shown.

3) CHANGE THE LAST NAME FIELD IN RECORD 3 USING EDIT MODE

A mistake has been made entering the last name of the student in record 3. Roberta Poisson's last name should be "Poston".

a. With record 3 displayed, click on the Last Name field. Note that the contents of the field, Poisson, are shown on the Entry bar.
b. Click before the second "s" on the Entry bar. The cursor is displayed on the Entry bar.
c. Drag the pointer over the second "s", highlighting just that letter.
d. Type the new character, `t`. The "t" is inserted at the current cursor position, replacing the highlighted "s".
e. Click the pointer just before the "i", and drag the mouse to highlight only that letter.
f. Press Delete to remove the "i". The proper last name, Poston, is shown on the Entry bar.
g. Click on the Check box. The edited name is placed in the Last Name field on the form.

4) REPLACE THE CITY WITH ORLANDO IN RECORD 3

a. Data in a field does not have to be edited but may be replaced as a whole. With record 3 still displayed, click on the City field.
b. Type the new city data, `Orlando`, and click on the Check box. The old city is replaced.

5) SAVE THE MODIFIED DATA BASE FILE ON DISK

Press ⌘`S`. The modified data base is saved on disk.

<u>Check</u> - Your record should be similar to:

First Name	Roberta	**Last Name**	Poston		
Address	8P Corwin Place				
City	Orlando	**State**	FL	**Zip**	33434
Admit Date	6/27/89				
GPA	4				
Paid	N				

5.7 Modifying the Record Form

It is sometimes necessary to make changes to the record form; fields may need to be renamed, added, deleted or moved, or field widths changed. Fields can be moved by dragging them to a new position on the form, or widths can be changed by dragging the entry box. To modify the form it is possible to make changes to any record. Those changes are then reflected in every record in the data base. For example, if a new field is added to record 5, it will appear in every record in the file. If the width of the Last Name field is increased in record 3, it will automatically be increased in all of the records in the data base. Remember, changing a field width has no effect on the data stored in the field, only its appearance on the screen. Fields will be inserted and deleted in Chapter 6.

To rename a field, double-click on the field's name. This displays the same Field Name box that was used when entering new fields:

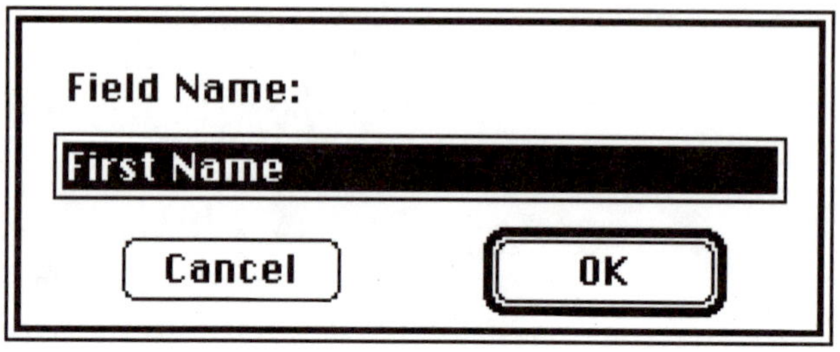

The Field name box is also used to rename a field

Type the new name and click on `OK` to change the name of the field. This changes the name of the field in every record, but has no effect on the data stored in that field.

5.8 Formatting Data using Field Attributes

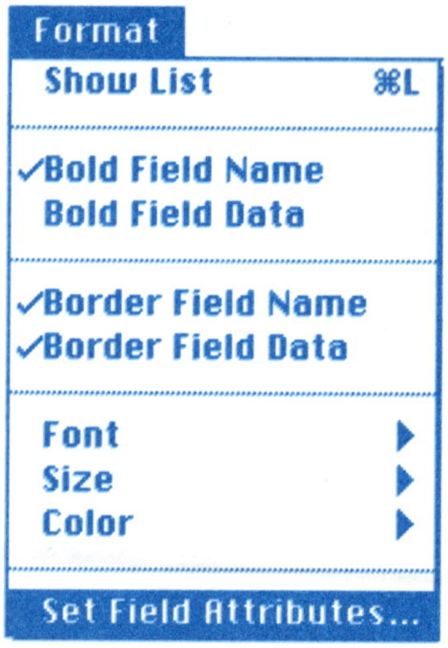

Works has a number of commands which change the way in which data stored in a field is displayed. These commands, called "field attributes", have no effect on the data stored in the field, only on the way that Works displays the data. To apply a field attribute, double-click on the entry box of the field to be formatted and select the desired attribute(s) from the Set Field Attributes dialog box. The selected attribute is then applied to that field in every record. For example, if a field is to contain numbers with decimals, it should be formatted using the Fixed attribute. Selecting Fixed causes Works to display the data stored in that field with a fixed number of decimal places:

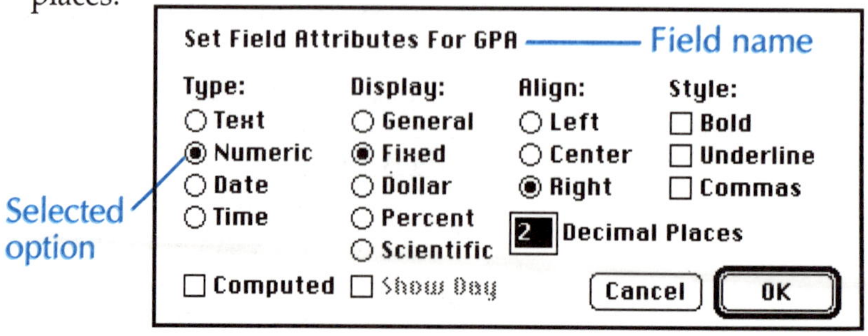

The Set Field Attributes box allows formatting options to be applied

Dots are used to indicate the selected options. The default value of 2 decimal places can be changed by typing the desired number and clicking OK. Any number entered into a field formatted with Fixed will be displayed with the specified number of decimal places. For example, we would like all GPA values to be displayed with 1 decimal place. By double-clicking on an entry in the GPA field and selecting Fixed, we can specify the value 1 in the Decimal Places box. Now all GPA values will be displayed with 1 decimal place (e.g., 4 will be displayed as 4.0, etc.). Field attributes can be set in Form view or List view. It is important to note that applying a formatting option to a field affects that field in all of the records, not just the one currently displayed.

Another useful numeric field format is the Dollar attribute. A field formatted with the Dollar command displays numbers as dollar amounts, such as $1000.00. The Dollar command also allows the number of decimal places to be specified, again using the Decimal Places box. When formatting dollar values, the default of 2 decimal places is usually used. A special format is Commas option in the Style list. Selecting Commas includes commas in the number to separate thousands and millions. For example, the entry 1000 stored in a field formatted with the Dollar and Commas attributes would be displayed as $1,000.00:

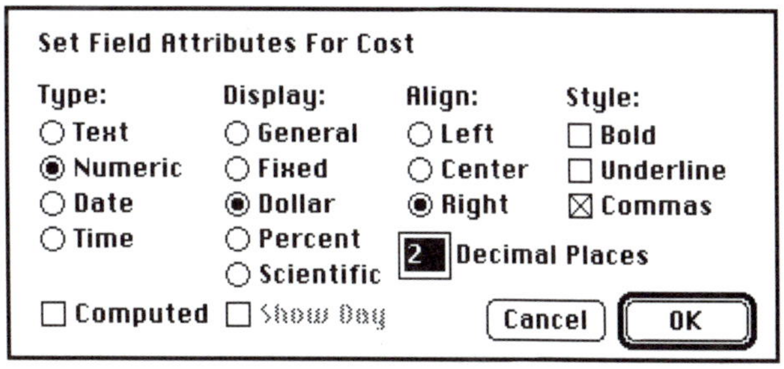

A field formatted with these options displays dollar amounts with commas

Other attributes include displaying data as right-justified, left-justified or centered in the entry box. Text formats such as underlined and bold may also be selected. Dates can be displayed using abbreviations (`10/5/91`) or spelled out (`October 5, 1991`).

Practice 4

In this Practice you will modify the student record form by changing the width of the Address field and formatting GPA to display 1 fixed decimal place. Start Works and open the STUDENT data base if you have not already done so.

1) CHANGE THE WIDTH OF THE ADDRESS FIELD

a. Place the pointer on the end of the Address field entry box. Note how the pointer changes.
b. Drag the pointer approximately 5 characters to the right. The width of the entry box is increased.

2) FORMAT THE GPA FIELD FOR 1 DECIMAL PLACE

a. Place the pointer on the entry box in the GPA field.
b. Double-click on the GPA entry to display the Set Field Attributes dialog box.
c. In the Type column, click on Numeric. Note how the dot moves to indicate which option has been selected. The Display options change from dimmed text and may now be selected. A dot is shown next to the default, Fixed, to indicate that it is selected.
d. The Decimal Places box is shown with the default value of 2. Type the new value, `1`, and click on `OK` to apply the format. Any value now entered into the GPA field in any record will be displayed with 1 decimal place.
e. If it is not already, scroll to display Roberta Poston's record. Click once on the GPA entry. Note that the field contains only a "4" (as shown on the Entry bar), but is displayed as 4.0 in the record due to the field attribute just applied.

Check - The modified form should be similar to (note the GPA value):

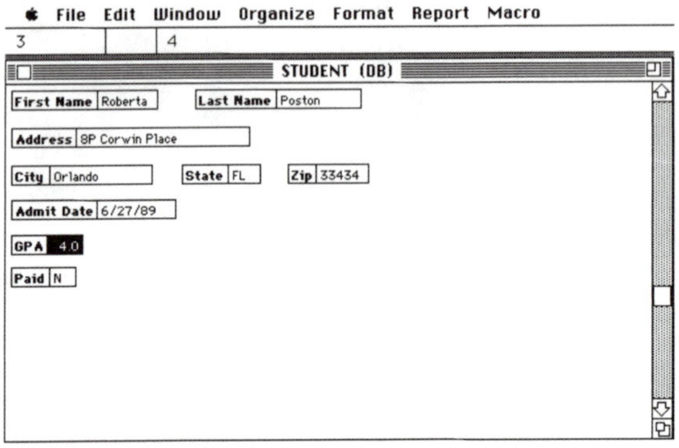

3) SAVE AND CLOSE THE MODIFIED FILE

a. Press ⌘`S` to save the modified file on disk. When next retrieved, the STUDENT data base will have the new form including the GPA field attributes.
b. Press ⌘`W` to close the STUDENT file and remove it from the computer's memory.

5.9 Finding Text in a Record

Works can be told to locate those records in a data base which contain a certain word or phrase. This operation is called "searching" and is executed using the Find Field command from the Organize menu, ⌘`F`. You are then prompted to enter the text to be found, the "search for text." Once entered, the computer compares that text to the data stored in each field in the file. The first record for which a match is found is then displayed on the screen. Pressing ⌘`F` repeats the search using the same search for text, and the next record containing the text is located and displayed. After the last occurrence of the search for text is found, Works displays a message:

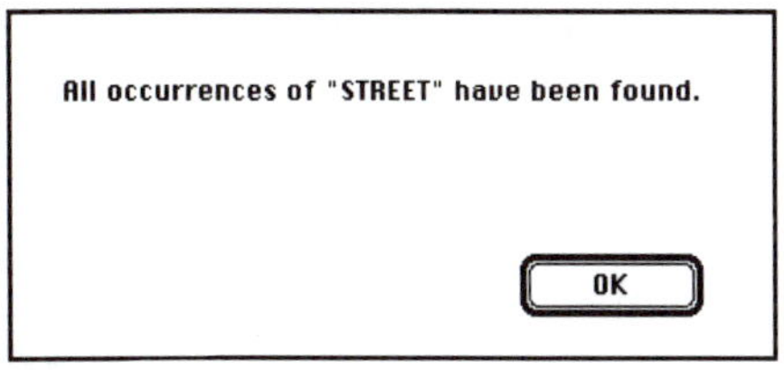

Works informs you when all occurrences of the text have been found

To search for different text, press ⌘F again and enter a new search for text.

The Find Field command cannot be used to search for text in a specific field because a match is considered found if the search for text is contained anywhere in a record. For example, supplying "et" for the search for text would locate a record which has "Janet" in the First Name field as well as a record which has the word "Street" in the Address field. Also, Find Field is not affected by upper and lower case letters, so that entering "et" finds any combination of upper and lower case letters so long as "e" is followed by "t"; Etonic, beets, STREET, etc.

It is sometimes the case that the search for text is not found in any of the records in the data base. When this occurs, Works displays the message "Not found".

Practice 5

This Practice demonstrates the Find Field command with different search texts. To demonstrate this command on a large number of records, the IVY STUDENT data base file stored on your data disk will be used. Start Works if you have not already done so.

1) OPEN THE IVYSTU DATA BASE ON YOUR DATA DISK

a. Click once on the Data Base icon on the Open File dialog box.
b. Scroll through the list of previously saved file names and double-click on IVY STUDENT to open the file and view the data.

2) EXECUTE THE SEARCH COMMAND

a. Display the Organize menu.
b. Drag the mouse down the menu and execute Find Field. Works displays the Find Field dialog box:

3) TYPE THE SEARCH FOR TEXT

Type `street` in the box and click on the `Find Next` button. Works searches for the first occurrence of the text "street" and displays that record.

4) REPEAT THE SEARCH SEVERAL TIMES

a. Press ⌘F. Note that the old search for text, street, is displayed.
b. Click on `Find Next`. Works searches for the next occurrence of street and displays that record.
c. Press ⌘F and click on `Find Next`. Works repeats the search for street and displays the next record. Note that the street's found may appear in any field, including Address and Last Name.
d. Continue the above process until all of the "streets" have been found, and Works displays the message:

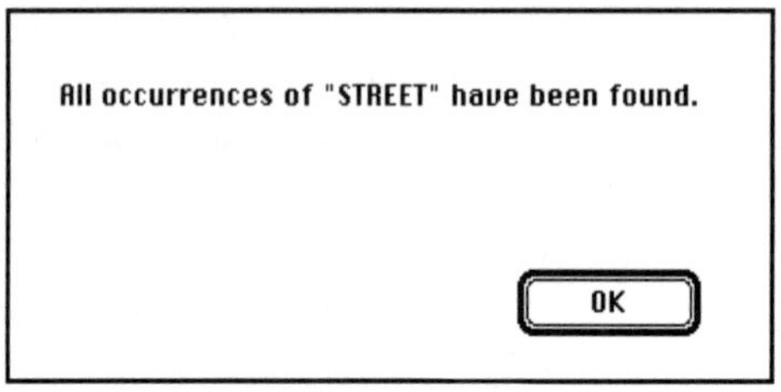

Click on OK to remove the message.

5) ENTER A NEW SEARCH FOR TEXT

a. Press ⌘F.
b. The old search for text, street, is shown.
c. Type `zzz` replacing the old text and click on `Find Next`. Because no records are found that match the search for text, Works displays the message:

Click on OK to remove the message.

5.10 List View and Form View

Selecting Show List from the Format menu (⌘L) displays the contents of the data base file in List view:

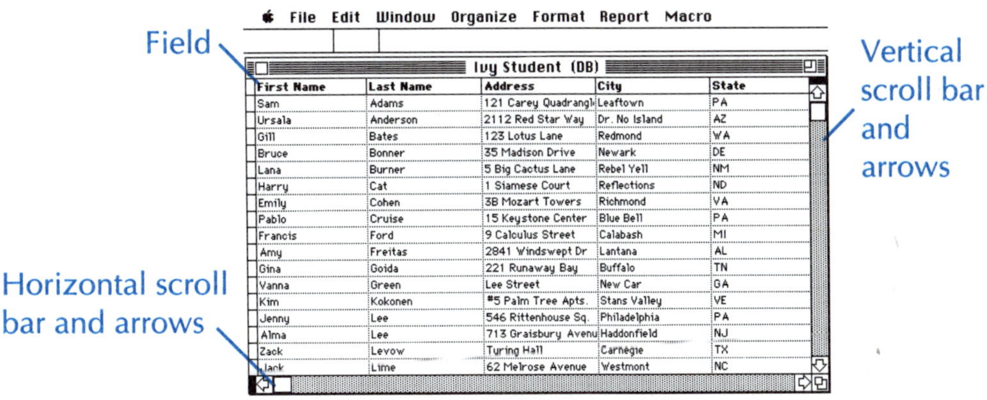

List view displays some of the fields for several records

In List view, the first few fields for several records are displayed. List view is useful because it allows records to be compared to one another. Note that only the first fifteen or so characters of the data stored in a field are currently displayed (e.g., the Address field). The rest of the data is still stored in the entry, only not displayed. Later we will learn how to increase the size of a field in List view to show all of the data stored in it.

In List view the screen can be scrolled to view fields or records which are not currently visible. The horizontal scroll bar displays additional fields, while the vertical scroll bar displays different records.

One of the difficulties with List view is that all of the fields for a single record may not be displayed on the screen at one time. For example, it is no longer possible to determine if Sam Adams has paid his tuition simply by looking at the screen because the Paid field is no longer displayed. For this reason Works allows you to switch between List view and Form view by pressing ⌘L. Form view displays all of the fields for a single record.

When switching between List and Form views, the highlight always remains on the same record in the same field. For example, if the Paid field in record 3 is highlighted in List view when ⌘L is pressed, record 3 is displayed in Form view with Paid highlighted. If the highlight is then moved to First Name in record 1 and ⌘L again pressed, the screen switches to List view and the highlight remains on First Name in record 1.

Most of the commands which may be executed in Form view may also be executed in List view. For example, the Find Field command (⌘F) may be used in either view. It is also possible to change the contents of a record while in List view by clicking on the desired entry, typing the new data and clicking the Check box. Because it shows all of the fields, most data base operations are normally performed in Form view to ensure that the proper record are field is used. List view is best used for those operations which involve determining the relationships between records.

5.11 Modifying the List View Screen

In List view, the width of each field (the amount of space it takes up on the screen) may be changed from the default by dragging. Placing the pointer on the line which divides the field names changes it to the width shape. Dragging the pointer to the right increases the field width, to the left decreases it. It is again important to note that changing a field width has no effect on the data stored in the field, only its appearance on the screen. Also, changing a field width in List view has no effect on the Form view, and vice versa.

Works saves the List view screen layout of a data base along with the data it stores. If a data base file is saved after a field width has been changed, the next time the file is opened it will have the new width.

Practice 6

This Practice shows the difference between Form and List views. Field widths will be changed and Find Field executed in List view. Start Works and open IVY STUDENT if you have not already done so.

1) SWITCH BETWEEN FORM AND LIST VIEW

a. Press ⌘L to display the data base in List view.
b. Click on the right scroll-arrow to display the GPA and Paid fields at the end of the record. Note how the screen scrolls to reveal the other fields.
c. Click on the left scroll-arrow to display the First Name field.
d. Click on the Last name field in the 4th record, highlighting it.
e. Press ⌘L to display the data base in Form view. Note that the highlight remains on the Last Name field in record 4.
f. Press ⌘L again. The file is displayed in List view with the highlight on Last Name in the 4th record.

2) CHANGE LIST VIEW FIELD WIDTHS

a. Move the pointer to the line which separates First Name from Last Name, above the first record. The pointer changes to the width change shape.
b. Drag the line about 5 spaces to the right. The First Name field is widened and can now display more data.
c. Move the pointer to the line which separates Last Name from Address. Change the widths of each field until the List view screen is similar to:

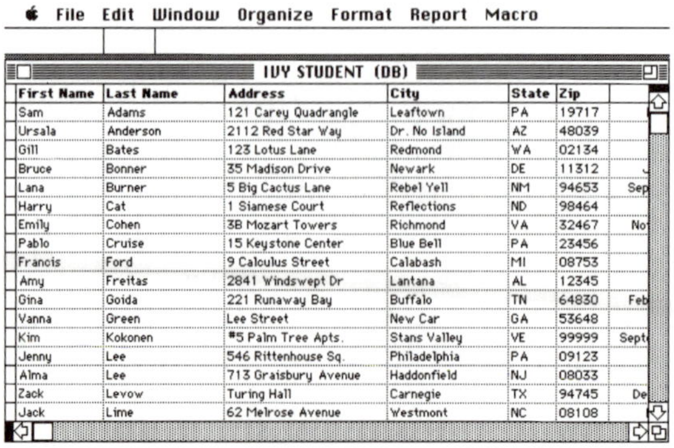

First Name	Last Name	Address	City	State	Zip	
Sam	Adams	121 Carey Quadrangle	Leaftown	PA	19717	
Ursala	Anderson	2112 Red Star Way	Dr. No Island	AZ	48039	
Gill	Bates	123 Lotus Lane	Redmond	WA	02134	
Bruce	Bonner	35 Madison Drive	Newark	DE	11312	J
Lana	Burner	5 Big Cactus Lane	Rebel Yell	NM	94653	Sep
Harry	Cat	1 Siamese Court	Reflections	ND	98464	
Emily	Cohen	3B Mozart Towers	Richmond	VA	32467	No
Pablo	Cruise	15 Keystone Center	Blue Bell	PA	23456	
Francis	Ford	9 Calculus Street	Calabash	MI	08753	
Amy	Freitas	2841 Windswept Dr	Lantana	AL	12345	
Gina	Goida	221 Runaway Bay	Buffalo	TN	64830	Feb
Vanna	Green	Lee Street	New Car	GA	53648	
Kim	Kokonen	#5 Palm Tree Apts.	Stans Valley	VE	99999	Sept
Jenny	Lee	546 Rittenhouse Sq.	Philadelphia	PA	09123	
Alma	Lee	713 Graisbury Avenue	Haddonfield	NJ	08033	
Zack	Levow	Turing Hall	Carnegie	TX	94745	De
Jack	Lime	62 Melrose Avenue	Westmont	NC	08108	

3) EXECUTE THE FIND FIELD COMMAND IN LIST VIEW

a. Press ⌘F to display the Find Field dialog box.
b. Type `street` at the prompt and click on `Find Next`. Works searches for the first occurrence of the text "street" and highlights that field.

4) REPEAT THE SEARCH SEVERAL TIMES

a. Press ⌘F again and click on `Find Next`. Works repeats the search and highlights the next field which contains "street".
b. Continue to use Find Field until all of the occurrences of "street" have been found. Click on **OK**.

5) SAVE THE MODIFIED FILE ON DISK

Press ⌘S to save the modified file on disk. The next time it is opened, IVY STUDENT will have the modified List view screen.

5.12 Printing a Data Base

After it has been created it is often necessary to produce a printout of the contents of a data base. Normally, this requires the creation of a report as described in Chapter 6. However, it is possible to print the records displayed on the current screen using the Print Window command from the File menu. Print Window produces a listing of the data shown on the screen, from either List view or Form view.

Note that some additional information is printed besides the contents of the records. The field name, and entry box are two examples. Even with this information included, the printout is not as easy to read as we would like, but it can be used to verify the format and contents of the records. Better formatted printouts called reports are described in Chapter 6.

Practice 7

In this Practice you will print the contents of the IVY STUDENT data base on the printer using the Print Window command. Start Works and open IVY STUDENT if you have not already done so.

1) PRINT CONTENTS OF THE DATA BASE

a. If it is not already, display the data base in List view by pressing ⌘L. Make sure that the computer is connected to a printer, and that the printer is turned on.
b. Using the mouse, display the File menu.
c. Drag the mouse down the menu and select the Print Window command. Works prints the contents of the current screen on the printer. The fields not currently visible are not printed.

2) PRINT A SINGLE RECORD

a. Switch to Form view by pressing ⌘L.

b. Select the Print Window command from the File menu. Works prints the contents of the current screen on the printer. Because only one record is currently displayed, the printout contains the data for that record. Note the field names and entry boxes included in the printout.

5.13 Using Record Selection to Perform Queries

The Find Field command is limited because it cannot be restricted to a specific field. Specifying a search for text of "Adams" would not only locate Sam Adams' record, but also anyone who lives on Adams Street or comes from Adamsville, etc. Also, Find Field does not have the important capability of searching for more than one search for text at a time. That is, we cannot use Find Field to locate the records of all students who come from Maine or Vermont in a single command. Find Field's most serious limitation is that the result of a search is always a single record. There is no way for Find Field to locate and display all of the records that contain "Adams" in one operation; ⌘F must be pressed until each record has been located.

Works can be made to display only those records which contain specific data by applying "selection rules." A selection rule is a description of the data that the displayed record must contain. Unlike the Find Field command, a selection rule refers to a specific field and may contain more than one search for text. In addition, a selection rule can locate and display more than one record at a time. For example, a selection rule can locate and display all of the records where the last name is "Adams".

Selection rules are defined using the Record Selection command from the Organize menu, which displays a dialog box:

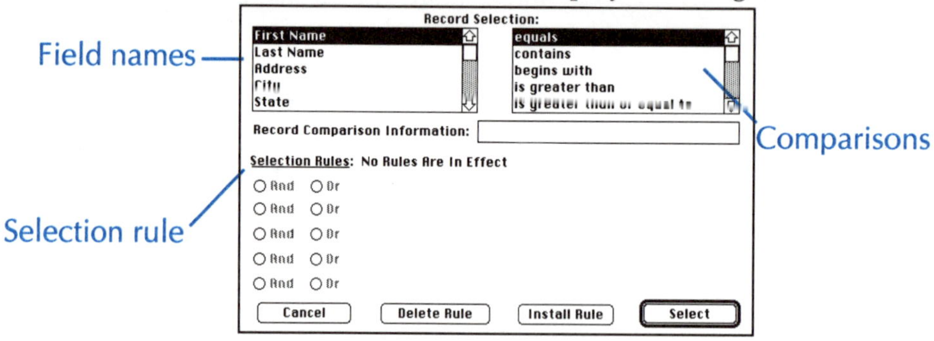

The Record Selection dialog box is used to create selection rules

Different "criteria" which describe the desired records are then entered in this dialog box. Clicking on the `Select` button applies the selection rule so that only those records which meet the criteria are displayed. The other records are still in the file, only not displayed at this time. Those records which do not meet the selection rule's criteria are therefore said to be "hidden".

Criteria are created by choosing a field name and comparison from the lists, and typing the text for that field to be compared to. The following selection rule would display the records of all students with the last name "Adams":

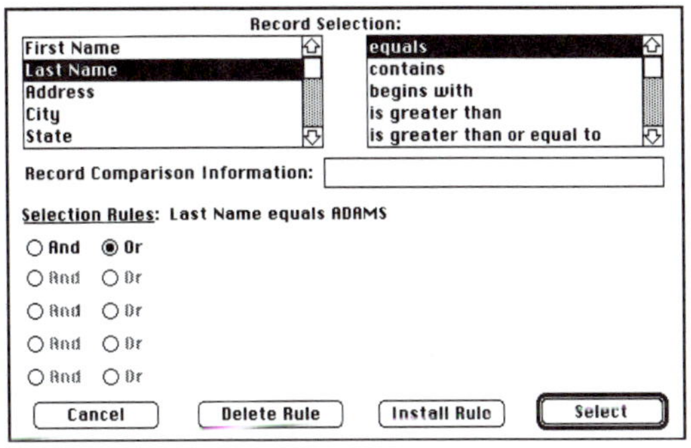

When the Select button is clicked, only records with a last name of "ADAMS" will be displayed

Students who live on Adams Street or from Adamsville, etc. would not be displayed. Like the Find Field command, selection rules ignore upper and lower case differences.

To cancel a selection rule the Show All Records command is executed from the Organize menu. Works then removes the selection rule and displays all of the records. Executing Record Selection again displays the dialog box, allowing you to create a new selection rule.

Because they show relationships between records, queries are normally applied from the List view screen, but they can also be used in Form view. If no records meet the criteria, Works displays the message "No records match your selection rule". After a selection rule has been applied, Works requires that the queried database be saved before it may be closed, even if no changes have been made to the data.

Note that if the Print Window command is issued when a selection rule is applied, only the records displayed by the selection rule will be printed.

Practice 8

In this Practice you will apply two different selection rules to the IVY STUDENT data base and note their effects. Start Works and open IVY STUDENT if you have not already done so. We will apply the rules "PAID equals N" to get a list of all students who have not yet paid their tuition and "Last Name equals Lee".

1) DISPLAY THE SELECTION RULE SCREEN

a. Display the data base in List view if it is not already by pressing ⌘L.
b. Select Record Selection from the Organize menu to display the Record Selection dialog box.

2) SELECT THE FIELD TO BE INCLUDED IN THE SELECTION RULE

a. Scroll through the field list until the Paid field is visible.
b. Click on Paid to include that field in the rule. Paid should be highlighted in the list. Note that the comparison we want,

equals, is the default and is already highlighted in the list.

3) **ENTER THE COMPARISON INFORMATION**

Type `N` and click on the `Install Rule` button. The rule displayed is "Paid equals N". When applied, this rule will display only those records with an N stored in the Paid field.

4) **APPLY THE SELECTION RULE TO THE DATA BASE**

a. Click on the `Select` button to apply the selection rule to the data base. Only those records which have an N stored in their Paid field are now displayed.
b. If the Paid field is not currently visible on your List view display, scroll to the right. Verify that only records with an "N" in the Paid field are displayed.

5) **REMOVE THE SELECTION RULE**

Execute the Show All Records command from the Organize menu. The selection rule is removed, and all of the records in the data base are again displayed.

6) **CREATE AND APPLY A NEW SELECTION RULE**

a. Execute the Record Selection command from the Organize menu to display the dialog box. The old selection rule is shown.
b. Click on the `Delete Rule` button to remove the old rule. No rules are currently selected.
c. Select Last Name from the field list. The default comparison "equals" is still selected.
d. Type the comparison data `Lee` and click on `Select`. Only those students with the last name of "Lee" are displayed. Note that records containing data such as "Lee Street" are not displayed.
e. Select Show All Records from the Organize menu to remove the selection rule. All records are displayed.
f. Press ⌘S to save the file on disk.

5.14 Using Ranges to Create Complex Queries

It is possible to include comparison information for more than one field in a selection rule. For example, applying the rule

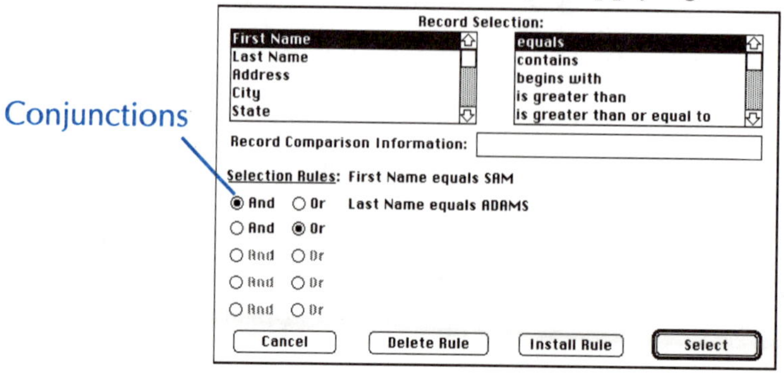

The And conjunction allows two rules to be joined

displays records for only those students named "Sam Adams".

Previous queries displayed records when the value stored in a field was equal to the value specified in the selection rule. Other comparisons may be performed in a selection rule by selecting the desired comparison from the list:

Comparison
`equals` (default)
`contains`
`begins with`
`is greater than`
`is greater than or equal to`
`is less than`
`is less than or equal to`
`is not equal to`
`is blank`
`is not blank`

For example, it is possible to create the rule:

```
GPA is greater than 3.5
```

When applied, this selection rule displays only those student records which store a GPA value greater than 3.5. Queries like this are said to contain "ranges" because there are multiple values of GPA which meet this criteria. Also, a single range can be used to take the place of several separate queries: GPA is greater than 3.5 instead of GPA equals 3.6, GPA equals 3.7, GPA equals 3.8, and so on.

Text may also be included in a range. For example, to display those students whose last names come before Jones alphabetically, the rule

```
Last Name is less than Jones
```

is used. Do not use quotes when entering comparison information. If the rule were typed with quotes around "Jones", Works would display an error message.

It is possible to put limits on both ends of a range by using "conjunctions." Conjunctions are operators which join two or more rules together to form one large selection rule. Available conjunctions include "And" and "Or". For example, it is possible to specify the following selection rule for the GPA field:

```
    GPA is greater than 1
And GPA is less than 2
```

When this selection rule is applied, only records with a GPA entry which is greater than 1 and less than 2 (between 1 and 2) are displayed. Queries may also be joined with the "Or" conjunction to produce a selection rule which has different parts. When selection rules are joined with "Or", records are displayed if any of the conditions are met. For example, applying the GPA selection rule

```
   GPA equals 2.5
Or GPA is greater than 2.7
```

displays the records for all students with either a GPA equal to 2.5 or greater than 2.7. As another example, to display all students who come from Maine or New Hampshire, the proper selection rule is:

```
   State equals ME
Or State equals NH
```

Different fields may also be combined using "And" and "Or". The selection rule

```
   Last Name equals Smith
Or GPA is greater than 3.0
```

displays every record which contains Smith in the Last Name field, and every record which has a GPA greater than 3.0. For example, the record for student Jim Smith would be displayed even if he had a GPA of 2.0. To display only the people named Smith who also have GPA's over 3.0, use the "And" conjunction:

```
    Last Name equals Smith
And GPA is greater than 3.0
```

Practice 9

In this Practice you will apply two complex queries to the IVY STUDENT data base and note their effects. Start Works and open IVY STUDENT if you have not already done so. We will first apply a selection rule to list all students with a GPA of 3.0 or better.

1) DEFINE A NEW SELECTION RULE

a. If it is not already, display the data base in List view by pressing ⌘L. Scroll to the first record in the file.
b. Select Record Selection from the Organize menu to display the dialog box.
c. If the previous selection rule is shown, click on the `Delete Rule` button to remove it.
d. Highlight the GPA field in the list of fields.
e. Highlight "is greater than or equal to" in the list of comparisons.
f. Type the comparison information, 3, and click on `Install Rule`.

2) APPLY THE SELECTION RULE AND VIEW THE RECORDS

a. Click on `Select` to apply the selection rule. Only records with a GPA of 3.0 or greater are now displayed.
b. Scroll through the records to verify that only those with a GPA greater than or equal to 3.0 are displayed.

3) DEFINE AND APPLY A NEW SELECTION RULE

a. A selection rule which displays all students from Maine or New Hampshire will be created. Select Record Selection from the Organize menu to display the dialog box.
b. Click on the `Delete Rule` button to remove the previous selection rule.
c. Highlight the State field.

d. "Equals" is already selected so type the comparison data `ME`.
e. Click on `Install Rule`. The rule is displayed:

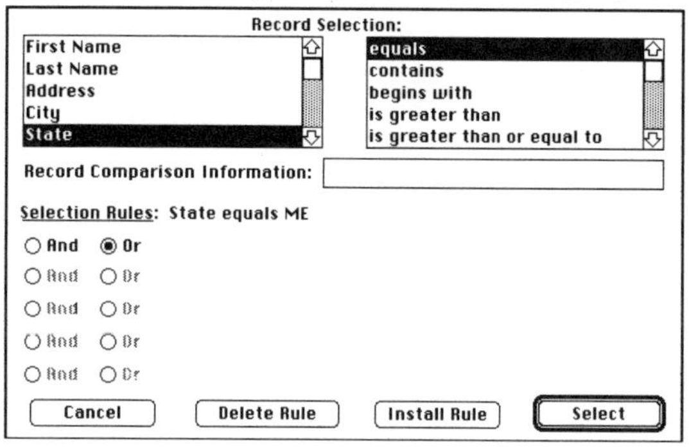

f. State and "equals" are still selected. Type the second comparison information, NH.
g. Click on `Install Rule`. The rule is displayed:

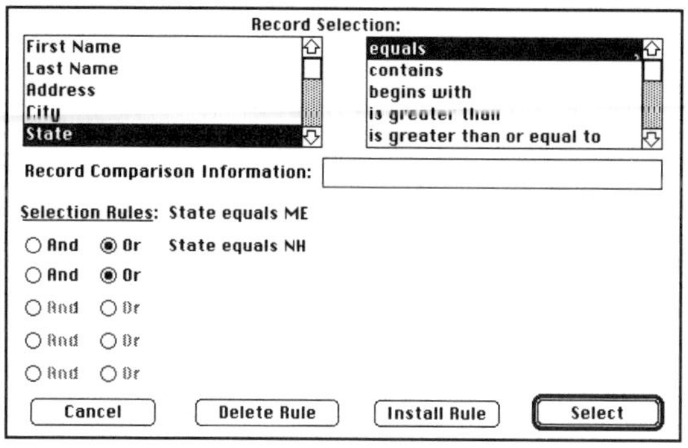

Note that "Or" is selected by default.

h. Click on `Select` to apply the rule. Only records for students from Maine or New Hampshire are now displayed.

4) REMOVE THE SELECTION RULE AND SAVE THE FILE

a. Select Show All Records from the Organize menu to remove the selection rule and display all records.
b. Press ⌘S to save the file on disk.

5.15 Updating Data in a Record

Any time a data base is displayed in either Form view or List view it is possible to change the contents of a field. This is called "updating a record" and is accomplished by clicking the pointer on the desired field, typing the new data or editing the old, and clicking on the Check box. If the file is then saved on disk, the new data stored in that field is retained.

The ability to update records is important because the data stored in a data base often changes; a person may move and have a new address, the price of an inventory item may go up or down, a student receives a new GPA at the end of a semester, etc. For example, suppose Ivy University's registrar receives a check from student Bruce Bonner to pay his tuition bill. Ivy's student data base can be accessed and a "`Y`" stored in the Paid field of Bruce Bonner's record, replacing the N. Should a selection rule such as "show all records where Paid equals N" then be applied, Bruce's record would no longer be listed. It is important to realize that simply changing the value on the screen does not mean that it is changed in the file. The file must be saved on disk after the change is made. Should there be a power failure before you save the file, the change would not appear the next time the file was opened. Therefore, as a precaution you should frequently save a data base file (⌘S) when updating records.

Because an update usually involves a specific record, a Find Field or Selection rule is often used to locate the record to be updated. In the example above, the Find Field command could be used to move the highlight to each record containing the text "Bonner". The correct record would then be easy to locate and the update made.

As we have stated before, List view is limited because it only displays the first few fields in a record. It is possible that an update may require changing the data in a field not currently displayed on the screen. When this occurs, the desired record is first located in the file (using a Find Field or Selection rule if necessary). The display is then switched to Form view (⌘L) which displays all of the fields for that record, and the update then made. Switching to Form view makes it easy to insure that Bruce Bonner's record is updated, and not some other student's.

Practice 10

In this Practice you will update two records in the IVY STUDENT data base to reflect new information. Start Works and open IVY STUDENT if you have not already done so.

1) LOCATE THE DESIRED RECORD IN THE FILE

Update: Student Jenny Lee has moved to 23 Market Street.

a. Display the data base in List view if it is not already by pressing ⌘L.
b. Press ⌘F to execute the Find Field command.
c. Type the search for text, `Lee`, and click on `Find Next`.
d. There are several Lee's in the file as well as someone who lives on Lee Street. If it is not already, continue to use Find Field until the highlight is on Jenny Lee's record.

2) ENTER THE NEW DATA FOR THE ADDRESS FIELD

a. Click on the Address field in Jenny Lee's record.
b. Type `23 Market Street` and click on the Check box. Her new address is now stored in the field, replacing the old data.

3) LOCATE THE DESIRED RECORD IN THE FILE

Update: Student Bruce Bonner has paid his tuition bill.

a. Press ⌘F to execute the Find Field command.
b. Type `Bonner` and click on `Find Next`.
c. Continue to use Find Field until the highlight is on Bruce Bonner's record.

4) SWITCH TO FORM VIEW AND ENTER THE NEW DATA

a. The Paid field is not displayed on the screen in List view. Press ⌘ L to switch to Form view.
b. Click on the Paid field.
c. Type a capital Y and click on the Check box. A "Y" is now stored in the Paid field in Bruce's record.

5) SAVE THE FILE TO RETAIN THE UPDATES

Press ⌘ S to save the file on disk. Both changes will be present in the file the next time IVY STUDENT is opened.

5.16 Adding Records

It is often necessary to add new records to a data base; new students enroll in a school, a store adds a new item to its inventory, etc. New records can be added to a data base in two ways: appended at the end of the file, or inserted into the file. In both cases it is usually easiest to add a new record using Form view because it displays all of the fields for the new record.

Appending a record is a simple process. In Form view, scrolling to the end of the data base displays an empty record located at the end of the file. The data for the new record is then typed onto that form. When the file is saved the new record is stored on disk. In List view, a record may be appended by scrolling to the first empty record at the end of the file and typing the new data there.

Works allows a new record to be inserted in a data base using the Insert Record command from the Edit menu, ⌘ I. Any new records inserted are placed in the file above the current record. Executing the Insert Record command from Form view displays a new, empty form. The new data is then entered on that form. Insert Record in List view inserts an empty row into which data may be entered. After inserting the data for any new records the file must be saved on disk to retain them.

Practice 11

A new student, Steve Rohrman, has enrolled in Ivy University and you will insert his record into the student data base. Start Works and open the IVY STUDENT file if you have not already done so.

1) MOVE THE HIGHLIGHT TO WHERE THE NEW RECORD WILL BE INSERTED

a. Press ⌘L to display the data base in List view if it is not already.
b. Scroll through the file until Matilda Rose's record is visible.
c. Click the pointer on any field in Matilda Rose's record.

2) EXECUTE THE INSERT RECORD COMMAND

a. Display the Edit menu.
b. Drag the mouse down the menu to execute the Insert Record command. A new, empty record is shown.

3) ENTER THE DATA FOR THE NEW RECORD

Type the following data for each field:

First Name: `Steve`
Last Name: `Rohrman`
Address: `212 Phillips Ave.`
City: `Magnolia`
State: `NJ`
Zip: `28131`
Admit Date: `10/16/88`
GPA: (leave blank)
Paid: `Y`

4) SAVE THE MODIFIED FILE

Press ⌘S to save the modified file on disk. The next time that IVY STUDENT is opened Steve Rohrman's record will be in the file.

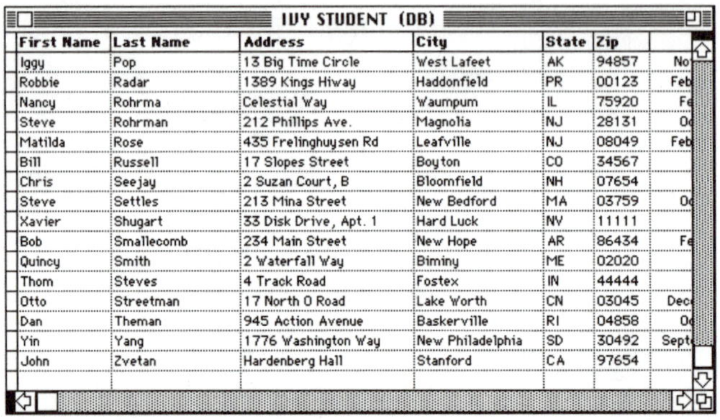

IVY STUDENT (DB)

First Name	Last Name	Address	City	State	Zip	
Iggy	Pop	13 Big Time Circle	West Lafeet	AK	94857	No
Robbie	Radar	1389 Kings Hiway	Haddonfield	PR	00123	Feb
Nancy	Rohrma	Celestial Way	Waumpum	IL	75920	Fe
Steve	Rohrman	212 Phillips Ave.	Magnolia	NJ	28131	O
Matilda	Rose	435 Frelinghuysen Rd	Leafville	NJ	08049	Feb
Bill	Russell	17 Slopes Street	Boyton	CO	34567	
Chris	Seejay	2 Suzan Court, B	Bloomfield	NH	07654	
Steve	Settles	213 Mina Street	New Bedford	MA	03759	O
Xavier	Shugart	33 Disk Drive, Apt. 1	Hard Luck	NV	11111	
Bob	Smallecomb	234 Main Street	New Hope	AR	86434	Fe
Quincy	Smith	2 Waterfall Way	Biminy	ME	02020	
Thom	Steves	4 Track Road	Fostex	IN	44444	
Otto	Streetman	17 North O Road	Lake Worth	CN	03045	Dec
Dan	Theman	945 Action Avenue	Baskerville	RI	04858	O
Yin	Yang	1776 Washington Way	New Philadelphia	SD	30492	Sept
John	Zvetan	Hardenberg Hall	Stanford	CA	97654	

5.17 Deleting Records

Just as it is necessary to add new records to a data base, records must often be deleted; a student graduates or drops out of school, a store decides to no longer carry an item, etc. In Works, the Cut command from the Edit Menu (⌘X) deletes the current record. Records may be deleted from either Form or List view. Because of the possibility of damaging the data base by removing the wrong record, you must be sure before executing the Cut command. When the file is then saved on disk, the deleted record is no longer stored. As when updating a record, it is often convenient to locate the record to be deleted using a Find Field or Selection rule.

In Works, the data to be Cut must first be selected. This can be done by placing the pointer on the first field in the record and dragging to the end, but there is a faster way. In List view, at the very left of each record is a "record selector" box:

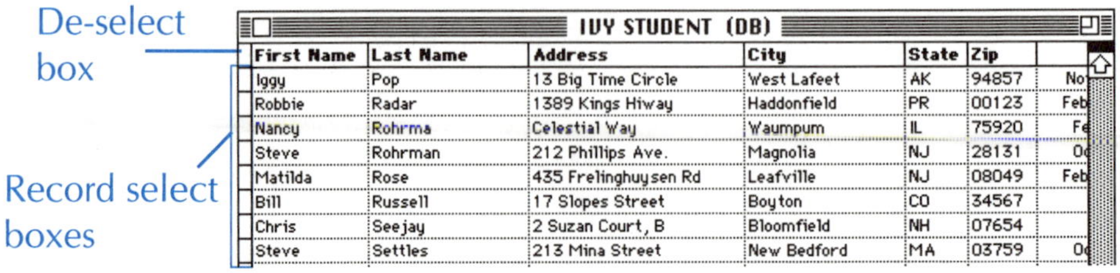

IVY STUDENT (DB)

First Name	Last Name	Address	City	State	Zip	
Iggy	Pop	13 Big Time Circle	West Lafeet	AK	94857	No
Robbie	Radar	1389 Kings Hiway	Haddonfield	PR	00123	Feb
Nancy	Rohrma	Celestial Way	Waumpum	IL	75920	Fe
Steve	Rohrman	212 Phillips Ave.	Magnolia	NJ	28131	O
Matilda	Rose	435 Frelinghuysen Rd	Leafville	NJ	08049	Feb
Bill	Russell	17 Slopes Street	Boyton	CO	34567	
Chris	Seejay	2 Suzan Court, B	Bloomfield	NH	07654	
Steve	Settles	213 Mina Street	New Bedford	MA	03759	O

Clicking on the record select box selects an entire record

Clicking on this box selects the entire record. The highlight can be removed by clicking on any field or by clicking on the "de-select" box shown in the diagram above. Because of the ease in selecting records in List view, we will perform our deletions there.

Practice 12

Student Bob Smallecomb has dropped out of Ivy University and you will remove his record from the data base. Start Works and open the IVY STUDENT file if you have not already done so.

1) LOCATE THE RECORD TO BE DELETED

a. If it is not already, switch to List view using ⌘L.
b. Use the Find Field command to locate the record for Smallecomb.
c. Click on the record selector box next to Bob Smallecomb's record. The entire record is highlighted.

2) EXECUTE THE CUT COMMAND

With Bob Smallecomb's record highlighted, press ⌘X to execute the Cut command. The entire record is removed from the screen.

3) SAVE THE MODIFIED FILE

Press ⌘S to save the file, without Bob Smallecomb's record, on disk.

Chapter Summary

This chapter covered the basics of creating and using a computerized data base in Works. Before a new data base is created on the computer it should first be carefully planned, using pencil and paper as described in Chapter 4. Once planned, the first step in creating a new Works data base is to define the record form by entering the field names in the Field Name dialog box. A field may be moved on the form by grabbing it with the mouse and moving it to a new location. When the record is complete Works displays an empty record in Form view, where data may be entered into the file record by record.

Data is entered into a field by clicking on it and then typing the data. Works can store up to 250 characters in a single field, but the number displayed depends on the field's width. Changes to the entry in a field can be made by clicking on the field, typing the new data and clicking on the Check box. Replacing old data with new is called updating.

It is possible to make changes to the data base form in any record. These changes are then reflected in every other record. The width of a field is changed by dragging its entry box. A field name is changed by double-clicking on it and entering the new name.

The way in which data is displayed by a field can be changed by double-clicking on the field's entry box and then selecting the desired attribute from the Set Field Attributes dialog box. For example, numeric fields can be formatted to display a specific number of decimal places or dollar amounts.

Once created, there are two ways to view a Works data base: Form view and List view. Form view shows all of the fields for one record while List view shows only the first few fields for a number of records. Form view is useful for making changes to a record. List view makes it easy to see the relationships between the data stored in many records. Pressing ⌘L switches from one view to the other. The records displayed on the current screen may be printed using the Print Window command from the File menu.

Works has two ways of locating specific data within a data base file. The first is by using the Find Field command from the Organize menu, ⌘F. Find Field performs a general search which allows a search for text to be entered and then moves to the first record which has that text stored in any of its fields. Subsequent searches for the same text are performed by pressing ⌘F which locates a single record each time. More specific than Find Field is to perform a query by applying selection rules using the Record Selection command from the Organize menu. With this command, only records which fit certain criteria (rules) are displayed. For example, using a selection rule it is possible to display the records for all students from Maine, or all students with a GPA greater than 3. Queries for which multiple values will meet the criteria contain ranges.

Because the data stored in a data base changes, Works can insert new records into a file using the Insert Record command from the Edit menu (⌘I) and delete existing records using the Cut command from the Edit menu (⌘X). When changes have been made to a data base, the data base file must be saved on disk to ensure that the changes will be present the next time the file is used. The Save command from the File menu (⌘S) saves the current file on disk.

Vocabulary

Conjunctions - Operators such as "and" and "or" used to join criteria in a selection rule.
Criteria - Description of the data that records must meet to be displayed. Refers to the contents of specific fields. Also called a "selection rule."
Cut command - Removes the current record from the data base: ⌘ X.
Field attribute - Determines how the data in a field will be displayed.
Find Field command - Performs a general search which displays the next record containing a specified search for text in any field: ⌘F.
Form - The arrangement and number of fields in a record.
Form view - All of the fields for a single record displayed on the screen at one time. Useful when updating a record or adding new records.
Hidden records - Records which do not meet the currently applied selection rule's criteria, and are not displayed but remain in the file.

Insert command - Adds a new, empty record to the data base before the current record: ⌘ I.
List view - Displays the first few fields for a number of records. Useful when comparing records to one another or determining the results of a query.
Range - Selection rule criteria that includes an operator such as 'less than' or 'greater than'.
Search for text - Text entered by the user during a Find Field which records are compared to.
Selection rule - Limiting the number of records in a data base that are displayed by defining criteria that they must meet.
Update a record - Changing the contents of an entry or entries in a record.

Reviews

1. What is the difference between a data base form and a record?

Sections 5.1-5.8

2. a) List the steps necessary to design a new data base which stores information about the members of the Computer Club.
b) Design a form for the Computer Club data base. Include the field names you believe the club wants to store for each of its members. Be sure to group related fields.

3. a) List the steps necessary to create the Computer Club form on the computer from the design created in Review 2.
b) Create sample data for one member of the Computer Club and explain how it would be entered into the computer.

4. Explain how to move field names around on the form created in Review 3 above so that all address fields are on the same line.

5. a) If the name Joseph Josiah Kropeudopolis is entered into the Computer Club data base only part of it is displayed. What happens to the undisplayed part of the name?
b) How can Works be instructed to display the complete name?

6. If a mistake is detected after a name has been entered into the Computer Club data base, how can it be corrected?

7. Explain the steps required to save the above data base naming it COMPUTER CLUB.

8. Explain how to change a field name after a data base has been created and data entered.

9. a) What steps are required to format a field to display dollar amounts with commas?
b) How does formatting a field to dollars affect the data in stored that field?

Sections 5.9-5.14

10. a) How can the Computer Club data base be searched for the name Kropeudopolis?
b) What will happen if there are 3 members with that name? How may all three be found?
c) What will happen if a member lives at 35 Kropeudopolis Boulevard?
d) How does Works respond if a search is performed and there is no Kropeudopolis in the data base?

11. a) Describe what is displayed by the List view of a large data base. How much of each field is displayed?
b) How is it possible to display all of the fields in only the fifth record of a data base?

12. a) What steps are required to increase the width in List view of the Last Name field in the IVY STUDENT data base?
b) If a file is saved after the List view format has been changed, what format is displayed when the file is next accessed; the original or the changed format?

13. a) How can information displayed on the screen be printed?
b) Will information not on the screen, but in the data base be printed by step (a)?

14. What are the differences in using Find Field or Record Selection to search a data base?

15. What is meant by the term "criteria?" Give 2 examples of criteria.

16. a) List the steps required to display all records in the IVY STUDENT data base which contain the name Harold in their First Name fields.
b) Which records containing the following entries would be displayed?

```
John Harold
Harold Smarold
35 Harold Street
H. Arold Smythe
C. Tharold Jones
Heidi Smythe-Harold
Harold T. Harold
```

17. a) List the steps required to display all records in the IVY STUDENT data base for students who have not paid their tuition.
b) If the Print Window command is issued while the selection rule in part (a) is applied, what will be printed?

18. a) What happens to records that are "hidden" when a selection rule is applied?
b) How may hidden records be displayed?

19. What is meant by a "range" in a selection rule? Give 2 examples.

20. Write queries which display the following when applied to the IVY STUDENT data base:

    a) students with GPA's less than 1 and greater than 3.
    b) students from CA and OR.
    c) students with zip codes between 10016 and 11514.
    d) students whose last names are Jones and who are from FL.
    e) students who have GPA's above 3.0 and who have not paid their tuition.

Sections 5.15-5.17

21. A new student, Elise Reilly, has enrolled at Ivy University. Explain the steps required to add her data to the IVY STUDENT data base. Because you are not sure where she fits alphabetically in the file, start by locating the position in the file where Elise's record should be added.

22. The Ivy University administration is discussing upgrading its standards by not allowing students with GPA's below 1.5 to enroll next year. Explain the steps that would be required to locate and delete those students from the IVY STUDENT data base.

Exercises

1. In Exercise 2 of Chapter 4 you designed a record form for a data base that would act as an address book.

   a) Using this form create the data base using Works and save it on disk using the name ADDRESS. Enter data into the file for a minimum of 10 of your friends.

   b) Using a selection rule, display only the people in ADDRESS who were born between 1965 and 1970.

   c) You've made a new friend, Amy Eppelman. Add her data to ADDRESS:

   ```
   Amy Eppelman
   713 Graisbury Avenue
   Haddonfield, NJ 08033
   (213) 555-1324
   Born 7/5/65
   ```

   d) Amy Eppelman has moved. Change her address and phone number to:

   ```
   343 Nenue Street
   Honolulu, HI 98765
   (767) 145-5937
   ```

   e) You have decided that the first person in the file is no longer your friend. Delete that record from ADDRESS.

   f) You would like to get some of your birthday purchases out of the way. To prepare to buy presents, use a selection rule to display only those people who have birthdays before January 1, 1975.

   g) Print the displayed data base in List view with the selection rule created in part (f) applied.

   h) Save ADDRESS on disk.

2. On your data disk is a data base named INVENTOR which stores information about inventions: the name of the invention, the year it was invented, and the name and nationality of the inventor.

   a) Create and apply the following queries to INVENTOR, printing a copy of the displayed data base in List view after each:

      Display all inventors who are from the United States.
      List all inventors from France whose inventions were produced between the years 1900 to 1930.
      Display all inventions produced by Galileo.
      List all inventions from Russia produced after 1960.

b) Last week your friend Julie Fritz invented a Peanut Butter and Tunafish sandwich. Add a new record to INVENTOR file which chronicles this event and save the modified file on disk.

3. Exercise 3 in Chapter 4 required you to design a record form for a car dealer's inventory data base.

   a) Using the form produced in that exercise, create a data base named FANTASY that records Fantasy Wheel's inventory. The first record should contain the car data shown in Exercise 3.

   b) Add the following cars to the Fantasy data base:

1972 Corvette
color: red
interior: green
accessories: radio, automatic, air
paid: $8,500
asking price $25,800
date acquired: 10/12/88

1984 Ferrari
color: grey
interior: black
accessories: 4 speed, convertible
paid: $22,000
asking price: $38,500
date acquired: 7/12/84

1987 Porsche
color: black
interior: white
accessories: 4 speed, air
paid: $22,300
asking price: $46,000
date acquired: 5/27/89

1975 Aston Martin
color: red
interior: black
accessories: radio, air
paid: $56,700
asking price: $120,000
date acquired: 10/6/87

1985 Porsche
color: red
interior: blue
accessories: radio, 4 speed
paid: $31,000
asking price: $62,000
date acquired: 10/11/88

1988 Ferrari
color: red
interior: black
accessories: radio, air, 4 speed
paid: $72,300
asking price: $102,000
date acquired: 2/17/89

1958 Thunderbird
color: white
interior: red
accessories: radio, air
paid: $14,500
asking price: $31,000
date acquired: 2/14/85

1978 Triumph
color: green
interior: white
accessories: 4 speed, air
paid: $4,560
asking price: $7,200
date acquired: 5/18/86

   c) Fantasy Wheels has had a great day and sold the 1985 Porsche. Delete its record from the data base.

   d) A customer has come into Fantasy's show room who wants to buy his wife a red sports car as a Valentine's day present. Produce a listing which displays only red cars in List view.

   e) Print the displayed records in List view for the red cars displayed in part (d).

f) Fantasy has had the 1969 Maserati painted purple, added air conditioning and raised the asking price to $29,000. Modify the record for the Maserati accordingly and save the modified file on disk.

4. Holiday Airlines has weekly flights to the Bahamas and has decided to computerize its reservation system. Holiday owns one airplane which has 20 seats numbered as shown below:

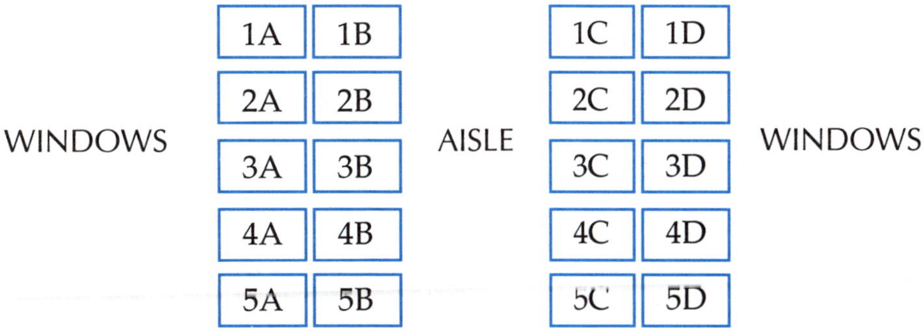

a) Design a database form for Holiday Airlines to store the seat number, seat location (aisle or window), whether it is in the first class section or not, and name and phone number of each passenger on its plane.

b) Create the database on the computer and name it HOLIDAY. Add an empty record for each seat on the plane. Enter the word "Empty" into the passenger name field of each record. Make all seats in rows 1 and 2 the first class section.

c) Make the following reservations by updating the proper records in the database. Use queries to locate seats for passengers with preferences:

Mr. & Mrs. A. Schwartzenegger
Phone#: 407-858-6321
Mr. Schwartzenegger: window seat, first class
Mrs. Schwartzenegger: aisle seat (next to her husband)

Mr. Bruce Presley
Phone#: 305-592-7847
aisle seat

Ms. Heidi Crane
Phone#: 609-896-9165
window seat, first class

Mr. John Heacock
Phone#: 212-885-7436
window seat

Mrs. Ruth Wagy
Phone#: 407-324-7588
No preference

Mr. & Mrs. Russell Ball
Phone#: 217-358-7671
Mrs. Ball: aisle seat, first class
Mr. Ball: window seat (next to his wife)

d) The reservation desk at Holiday needs to know the seat numbers of all empty seats. Create and apply a selection rule which does this and print the list.

e) Holiday Airlines has held a promotional contest and you have won 5 free trips to the Bahamas. Make 5 reservations using the names and phone numbers of friends.

f) The Holiday flight is about to take off for the Bahamas and the cabin staff needs to know the seat numbers and names for each passenger. Create and apply a selection rule showing only the occupied seats in List view and print the list.

g) Passenger Presley has changed his mind and would now like a seat in the first class section. Create and apply a selection rule which lists all empty aisle seats in the first class section. If such a seat is available, change Mr. Presley's reservation. Save the modified file on disk.

5. Chapter 4 exercise 8 asked you to create a form for a company's inventory data base.

   a) Using that form, create a new data base named PRODUCT which contains data for the following items:

Prod. ID	**Prod. Name**	**On Hand**	**Ordered**
A1000	Widgets	920	0
A2050	Wadgets	675	0
A3400	Wudgets	35	750
B1000	Flanges	330	0
B1005	Gadgets	78	0
B2005	Wonkers	2112	182
C2000	Springs	535	0
E3300	Rollers	23	444
E5000	Sanders	1778	0
F6005	Cutters	252	530
G1000	Slicers	150	0
G3350	Piercers	935	273
G4050	Smashers	471	624
J2005	Grinders	23012	0
J3000	Punchers	578	0
K5050	Pullers	100	0
M2900	Pushers	7565	0
M6770	Washers	5	1929
N1800	Wetters	378	0
Q2505	Zonkers	942	38

b) Apply a selection rule in List view that displays only those products with less than 100 items on hand which have not yet been reordered.

c) Print the displayed data base in List view with the selection rule created in part (b) applied.

6. Exercise 9 in Chapter 4 described a data base to record weather observations.

   a) Using your form design, create a new data base named WEATHER to store observations.

   b) Add the following records to WEATHER:

Date	Time	Temp F	Rain	Sky
1/8/60	3:00 PM	79	0	Partly Cloudy
11/5/61	5:46 AM	67	0	Sunny
4/20/62	6:19 PM	57	1.1	Cloudy
6/5/65	5:26 PM	29	.43	Cloudy
12/21/67	10:59 PM	46	0	Clear
10/15/68	7:15 AM	81	.2	Windy
3/16/70	4:00 PM	49	0	Partly Cloudy
7/12/72	1:00 PM	78	0	Sunny
12/11/73	12:59 AM	47	0	Hazy
7/19/74	6:49 AM	56	0	Sunny
10/31/75	9:15 AM	49	.3	Windy
11/16/77	11:50 PM	74	0	Clear
1/1/80	3:43 PM	32	0	Partly Cloudy
2/6/81	6:55 PM	21	.1	Cloudy
2/27/82	8:20 PM	90	1.2	Partly Cloudy
7/19/83	5:01 AM	72	0	Partly Sunny
5/19/84	7:46 AM	62	0	Sunny
6/27/85	2:28 PM	68	.3	Cloudy
12/23/86	12:59 PM	36	0	Clear
5/19/87	2:49 AM	55	.75	Cloudy
8/24/87	5:33 AM	76	.5	Hazy
11/5/88	6:45 AM	44	.1	Windy
3/24/88	2:33 PM	66	.7	Cloudy
10/22/88	10:15 AM	83	.2	Windy

   c) Add a record to the file describing today's weather and save the file on disk.

   d) Using a selection rule in List view display only those days when it rained or when the temperature was below freezing.

   e) Print the records displayed in part (d).

   f) Display only those records for days when clouds were visible.

7. On your data disk is a data base named CAR PRICE which contains information about the price of new cars. Each record contains the following fields:

    Make
    Model
    Base price
    Price with air conditioning
    Price with stereo
    Price with sunroof

    Produce queries which answer the following questions and print the results.

    a) Which cars have a base price under $12,000?

    b) Which cars can be purchased with air conditioning for under $11,250?

    c) Your friend Bob needs a new car but does not have much money. Display in List view all cars with stereos which cost $9,000.

    d) The price for a Porsche 944S with sunroof has gone up $199. Make this change and save the modified file on disk.

Chapter 6

Manipulating Data with the Data Base

Organize - Sort ⌘A

File - Print ⌘P

Report - New Report

Report - Select Report

Organize - Record Selection

Report - Duplicate Report

Totals Page - Sum This Field

Objectives

After completing this chapter you will be able to:

1. Use sorting to change the order in which records are displayed.
2. Plan and produce printed reports containing specific information from the data base.
3. Load and modify previously created report definitions.
4. Print totals in a report.
5. Add a computed field to a data base.

The previous two chapters described the commands necessary to create and manipulate a data base using Macintosh Works. It is only after a data base has been created that one of its most powerful features can be employed: the ability to produce printed reports detailing the information stored in its records. In this chapter the commands necessary to produce such reports will be discussed, as well as ways of ordering the data to make the reports more readable. A powerful Works feature which allows a field in a record to be calculated based on the data stored in other fields will be introduced.

6.1 Sorting Records in a Data Base

Data stored in a data base can be made easier to use if the records are in order based on the data stored in a specified field, called the "key field". For example, it is easy to locate students in the IVY STUDENT data base because the records are in order alphabetically by Last Name. Placing a data base in order is called "sorting" and is accomplished using the Sort command from the Organize menu, ⌘A. To sort a data base click on the desired key field (the field that contains the values on which to base the ordering). Executing the Sort command displays the Sort dialog box:

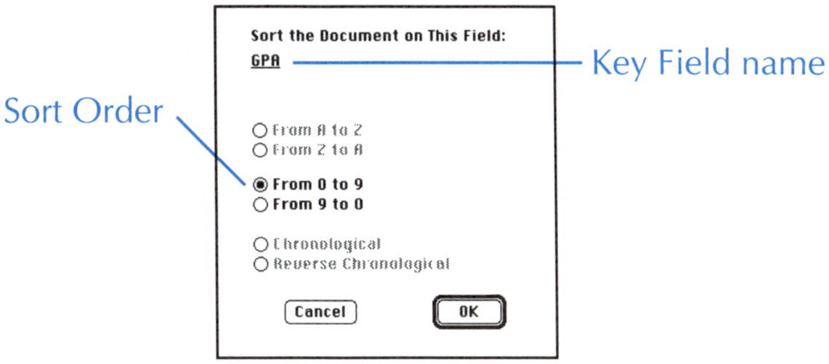

The Sort dialog box shows the key field name and the sort order

The example dialog box above would sort the file based on the values stored in the GPA field. Sorting may be performed in ascending (low to high) or descending (high to low) order. Different options will be available depending on the type of the field: `From A to Z` and `From Z to A` for character fields, or `From 0 to 9` and `From 9 to 0` for numeric. Should the key field be a date or time, "chronological" order is used. `Chronological` means earliest to latest (Jan, Feb, Mar, ... Dec, or 1:00 AM, 2:00 AM, etc.) and `Reverse Chronological` order is latest to earliest (Dec, Nov, ... Jan, etc.). Ascending order is the default option for all field types.

After a key field and sorting order have been specified, Works changes the order in which the records are displayed based on the values stored in the key field. If sorted using the example shown in the dialog box above, a student record with a GPA of 4.0 would be moved before any records with a GPA of 3.9, and so on. If the data base is then saved on disk, the records are stored in the newly sorted order, so that the next time the file is opened it will be sorted. Because sorting changes the order in which the records are placed in the file, a data base should be saved after it is sorted if the new order is to be retained.

Practice 1

In this Practice you will sort a data base and print a copy of the sorted version.

1) START WORKS AND OPEN THE IVY STUDENT DATA BASE

a. Boot the Macintosh System and start Works.
b. Click once on the Data Base icon on the Open File dialog box.
c. Double-click on IVY STUDENT in the list of file names to open the file.
d. If it is not already, display the data base in List view by pressing ⌘L. Note that IVY STUDENT is in order by Last Name.

2) SPECIFY A DESCENDING SORT BASED ON THE GPA FIELD

a. If it is not currently on the screen, scroll to display the GPA field. Click once on the GPA field in any record.
b. Select the Sort command from the Organize menu. The Sort dialog box is shown. Note that the default order is ascending, "From 0 to 9".
c. Click on `From 9 to 0` to select a descending sort which will sort the records in descending order (high to low) based on the value stored in the GPA field.

3) SORT THE RECORDS AND VERIFY THE RESULTS

a. Click on OK. After a slight pause the records are rearranged and displayed in their new order on the screen.
b. Verify that the records are now in descending order by GPA by scrolling through the data base.

4) SORT THE DATA BASE IN ASCENDING ORDER ON THE LAST NAME FIELD

a. If it is not currently on the screen, scroll to display the Last Name field. Click once on the Last Name field in any record.
b. Press ⌘A to display the Sort dialog box. Note that ascending order, "From A to Z" is the default.
c. Click on OK. The records are sorted and displayed in their new order.
d. Scroll through the data base to verify that the records are sorted by Last Name.

5) SAVE THE MODIFIED FILE

Press ⌘S to save the modified file on disk.

6.2 Parts of a Printed Report

Once a computerized data base has been created its versatility becomes apparent as people access the information it stores in different ways. One of the most common ways to use the information in a data base is the printed report. A report allows selected information from a data base to be printed in a variety of formats. For example, it is possible to produce a report which lists only the names and GPAs of each student in the IVY STUDENT data base, and another report which shows their names, addresses, and whether they have paid their tuition.

In Works, a report is organized into columns, similar to List view. While the report is printing, Works can be told to keep track of certain values and print a total at the end. A example report is shown below:

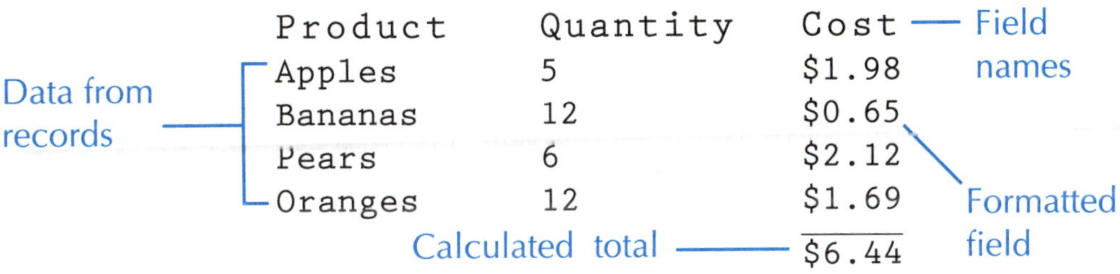

Reports print data from records in columns, similar to List view

6.3 Creating a Report Definition

Before a report may be printed a "report definition" must be created. The report definition describes the contents of the report to the computer. Creating a report definition involves choosing which fields are to appear in the report, in what order, and how much space to use for each. Once created, the report definition can be printed, producing a formatted listing of the data stored in the data base. It may also be saved with the data base, allowing the report definition to be printed again or modified later.

Executing the New Report command from the Report menu displays the Report screen where the report definition is created:

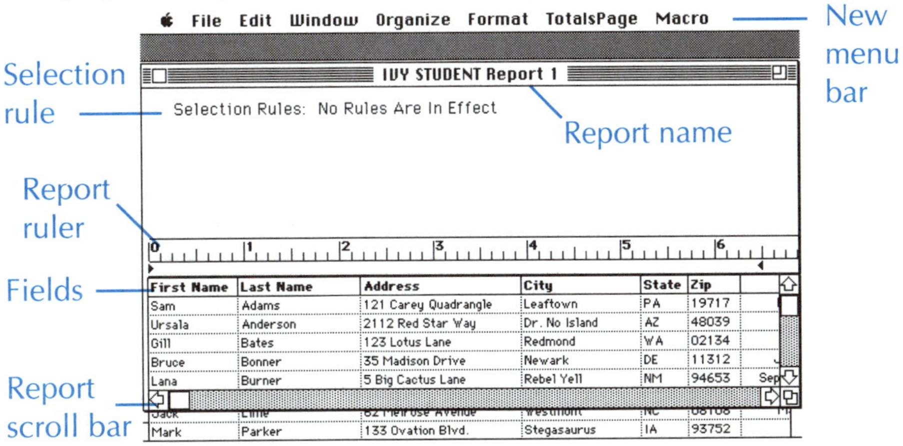

The Report Screen is displayed over top of the data base screen

Note this screen's similarity to List view. No data may be entered on the screen, only the order and widths of fields changed. Below the ruler is the format line, similar to the Word Processor. The triangles on the format line mark the left (▶) and right (◀) edges of the report and are based on the values for margins and paper size. Only the information between the triangle markers will be printed. It is possible to drag the right edge marker to change the width of the report. The name of the report definition shown at the top of the screen, `IVY STUDENT Report 1`, is a default name supplied by Works which may be changed.

Fields may be rearranged by dragging them to a new position on the screen. Widths may also be changed by dragging. To exclude a field from the report, drag it beyond the triangle marking the right edge of the report. Note that changing the width or placement of a field on the Report screen has no effect on the data base - both the Form and List views are unchanged.

Once the report definition has been created, executing the Print command (⌘P) from the File menu prints the report on the printer. Clicking on the Close box exits the Report screen and displays the data base. Reports may also be printed from the database screen using ⌘P. Before printing it is important to check that your computer is connected to a printer, and that the printer is turned on. While the report is printing, pressing ⌘. (period) will terminate the printing.

6.4 Using Print Preview

Of special use when creating reports is the Print Preview option available on the Print dialog box:

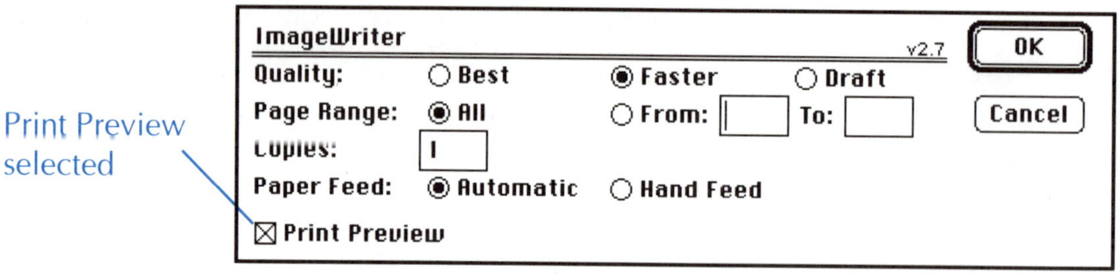

The Print Preview option can help save time and paper

When selected, this option first displays a copy of the printed report on the screen, allowing you to check it for accuracy:

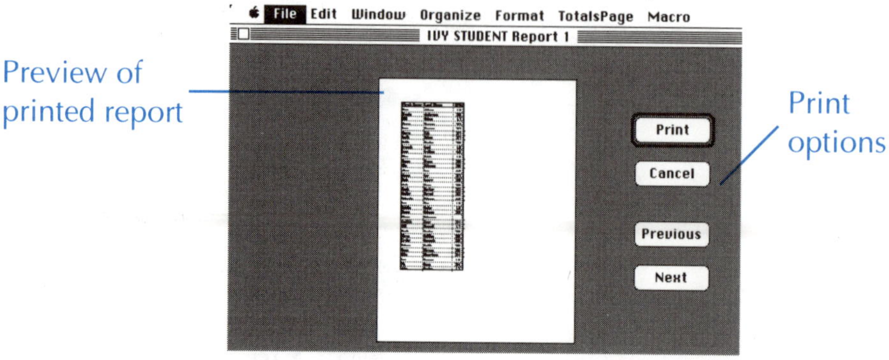

The Print Preview screen shows how the printed report will look

If the report is correct, click on **Print** to print a copy on the printer. If changes are desired, clicking **Cancel** terminates the preview and returns to the Report screen. For reports with multiple pages, the **Next** and **Previous** buttons allow you to display the different pages. Using the Print Preview option saves time and paper when creating report definitions.

Practice 2

In this Practice you will create a simple report definition for the IVY STUDENT data base and use it to print a report. The report will include only the First Name, Last Name and GPA fields. Start Works and open the IVY STUDENT data base if you have not already done so.

1) DISPLAY THE REPORT SCREEN

a. Execute the New Report command from the Report Menu to create a new report definition. The Report screen is shown.

b. Click on the Expand box in the upper right corner to enlarge the Report screen.

2) MOVE THE GPA FIELD

a. If it is not already visible, scroll to display the GPA field.

b. Place the pointer on the GPA field name. The pointer changes into the "grabbing hand" shape.

c. Hold down the mouse button and drag the field to the left. When the field is over top of the address field, release the button, changing the order of the fields:

First Name	Last Name	GPA	Address	City	State	Zip
Sam	Adams	1.5	121 Carey Quadrangle	Leaftown	PA	19717
Ursala	Anderson	3.0	2112 Red Star Way	Dr. No Island	AZ	48039
Gill	Bates	1.7	123 Lotus Lane	Redmond	WA	02134
Bruce	Bonner	3.7	35 Madison Drive	Newark	DE	11312
Lana	Burner	2.1	5 Big Cactus Lane	Rebel Yell	NM	94653
Harry	Cat	2.7	1 Siamese Court	Reflections	ND	98464
Emily	Cohen	3.1	3B Mozart Towers	Richmond	VA	32467
Pablo	Cruise	2.5	15 Keystone Center	Blue Bell	PA	23456
Francis	Ford	1.6	9 Calculus Street	Calabash	MI	08753

3) EXCLUDE FIELDS FROM THE REPORT DEFINITION

a. We wish to exclude the Address through Paid fields from the report. If it is not already visible, scroll to the right of the report definition until the right edge marker (◀) is displayed on the screen.

b. Drag the right edge marker to the left, until it is next to the end of the GPA field (just to the right of the "A" in GPA). All fields to the right of the marker will not appear in the report.

Check - Your Report screen shouldbe similar to:

First Name	Last Name	GPA	Address	City	State	Zip
Sam	Adams	1.5	121 Carey Quadrangle	Leaftown	PA	19717
Ursala	Anderson	3.0	2112 Red Star Way	Dr. No Island	AZ	48039
Gill	Bates	1.7	123 Lotus Lane	Redmond	WA	02134
Bruce	Bonner	3.7	35 Madison Drive	Newark	DE	11312
Lana	Burner	2.1	5 Big Cactus Lane	Rebel Yell	NM	94653
Harry	Cat	2.7	1 Siamese Court	Reflections	ND	98464
Emily	Cohen	3.1	3B Mozart Towers	Richmond	VA	32467
Pablo	Cruise	2.5	15 Keystone Center	Blue Bell	PA	23456
Francis	Ford	1.6	9 Calculus Street	Calabash	MI	08753

4) PREVIEW AND PRINT THE REPORT

a. Press ⌘P to display the Print dialog box.
b. Select the Print Preview option.
c. Click on OK to display the report on the Preview screen:

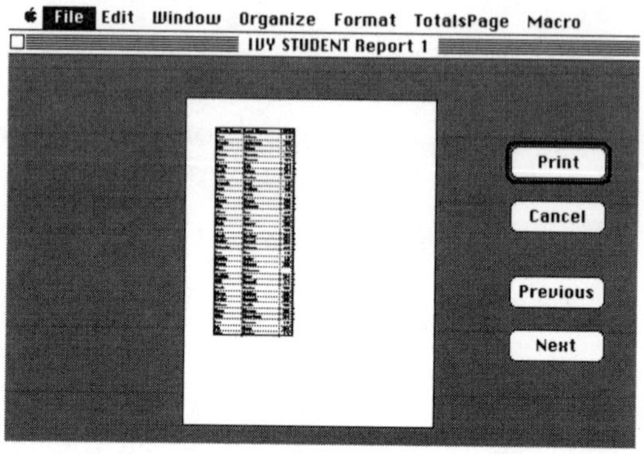

d. Click on the Print button to print the report on the printer.
e. After the report has printed, close the Report screen by clicking on the Close box. The data base is again displayed.

5) SAVE THE DATA BASE AND REPORT DEFINITION

Press ⌘S. Both the data base file and the report definition are saved on disk. When the IVY STUDENT data base is next opened it will be possible to access the report definition created in this Practice and print it again or modify it.

Check - Reports will differ depending on the printer used but your printed report should be similar to the preview screen shown above.

6.5 Planning a Report

A report should be carefully planned before creating its report definition. This is done by answering some of the same questions posed when first creating a data base:

1. What information should be included?
2. How should that information appear on the page?

The information to be included in a report is determined by analyzing the needs of the person that the report is being created for. Including unnecessary information in a report makes it harder to find desired information. It is important to consider how the different fields should appear when printed: in what order and how much space is to be given to each. Thought must also be given to formatting, field attributes and totals that are to be included as part of the report. All of these options are specified from the Report screen when creating the report definition. Planning, as we will see later, is especially important when creating complex reports.

6.6 Modifying a Report

The report definition created in Practice 2 does not print all of the fields in an IVY STUDENT record, and it is likely that different users will require reports showing the missing fields, or want the fields printed in a different order. For this reason it is possible to create up to eight different report definitions for each data base and store them on disk with the file. Report definitions have some of the characteristics of Works files: they have a specific name, may be opened, modified and saved. The difference is that a report definition is not a separate file, but part of a specific data base and may only be used when that data base is open.

The Select Report command from the Report menu allows you to access a previously created report definition, allowing changes to be made. Double-clicking on a report definition name opens that definition and displays it on the Report screen.

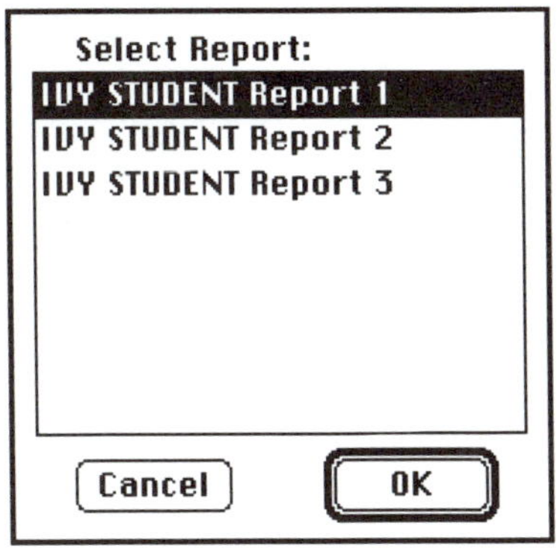

The Select Report dialog box lists the names of previously created reports

6.7 Print Preview Zoom

When a report is displayed on the Print Preview screen, the letters are small, making it hard to tell exactly what information is displayed. For this reason, it is possible to "zoom in" on a section of the Preview screen using the mouse. When the pointer is placed over the previewed report, it changes to a magnifying glass shape:

The Magnify pointer can be used to zoom in on a Print Preview screen

Clicking this pointer enlarges the data under the magnifying glass, making it easy to read. The grabbing hand pointer can then be used to scroll the enlarged report on the screen, making it possible to check the report for errors. Clicking on the Close box returns to the standard Print Preview screen.

Practice 3

In this Practice you will modify the report definition created in Practice 2 to produce a report including the student's address. Start Works and open the IVY STUDENT data base if you have not already done so.

1) DISPLAY THE PREVIOUSLY CREATED REPORT DEFINITION

a. Execute the Select Report command from the Report menu. The Select Report dialog box is displayed.
b. Double-click on IVY STUDENT Report 1 to display the report definition created in the previous Practice on the Report screen.

2) MOVE THE ADDRESS FIELD AFTER GPA

a. Place the pointer on the Address field.
b. Drag the field on top of GPA and release the mouse. The Address field is placed between Last Name and GPA.

3) MOVE THE RIGHT EDGE MARKER

The GPA field is no longer included in the report because it is to the right of the right edge marker. Drag the edge marker to include GPA.

Check - Your Report screen should look like:

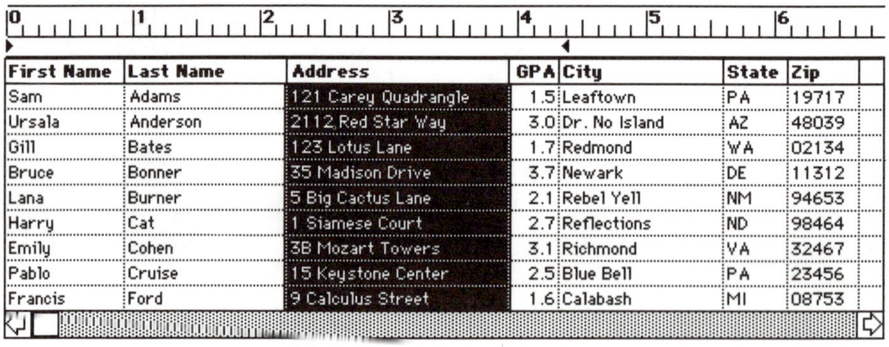

First Name	Last Name	Address	GPA	City	State	Zip
Sam	Adams	121 Carey Quadrangle	1.5	Leaftown	PA	19717
Ursala	Anderson	2112 Red Star Way	3.0	Dr. No Island	AZ	48039
Gill	Bates	123 Lotus Lane	1.7	Redmond	WA	02134
Bruce	Bonner	35 Madison Drive	3.7	Newark	DE	11312
Lana	Burner	5 Big Cactus Lane	2.1	Rebel Yell	NM	94653
Harry	Cat	1 Siamese Court	2.7	Reflections	ND	98464
Emily	Cohen	3B Mozart Towers	3.1	Richmond	VA	32467
Pablo	Cruise	15 Keystone Center	2.5	Blue Bell	PA	23456
Francis	Ford	9 Calculus Street	1.6	Calabash	MI	08753

4) PREVIEW THE REPORT

a. Press ⌘P to display the Print dialog box.
b. Select the Print Preview option.
c. Click on OK to display the report on the Preview screen.

5) ZOOM IN ON THE REPORT

a. Place the pointer over the previewed report. The pointer changes to a magnifying glass.
b. Click the mouse near the First Name field at the top of the report. The screen zooms in on the report, making the text easy to read.
c. Drag the pointer upward and to the left, displaying more of the report.
d. Click on the Close box to return to the standard Print Preview screen.

6) PRINT AND SAVE THE REPORT

a. Click on the `Print` button to print the report on the printer.
b. After the report has printed, close the Report screen by clicking on the Close box. The data base is again displayed.
c. Press ⌘S. Both the data base file and modified report definition are saved on disk.

Check - The printed report should contain the Address field.

6.8 Using and Renaming Multiple Report Definitions

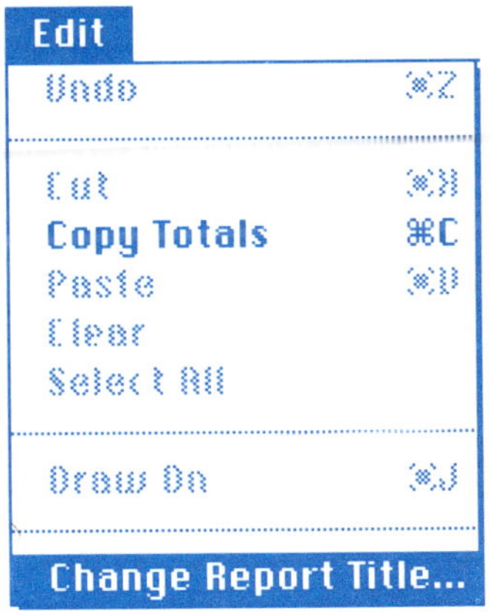

Since up to eight different report definitions can be saved with a single data base file, names are needed to distinguish one definition from another. The name of the current report definition is shown at the top of the Report screen. Works uses the default names Report 1, Report 2, etc. to name each report definition as it is defined. From the Report screen, the Change Report Title command from the Edit menu can be used to rename a report definition so that it has a more meaningful name.

Executing Change Report Title displays the dialog box

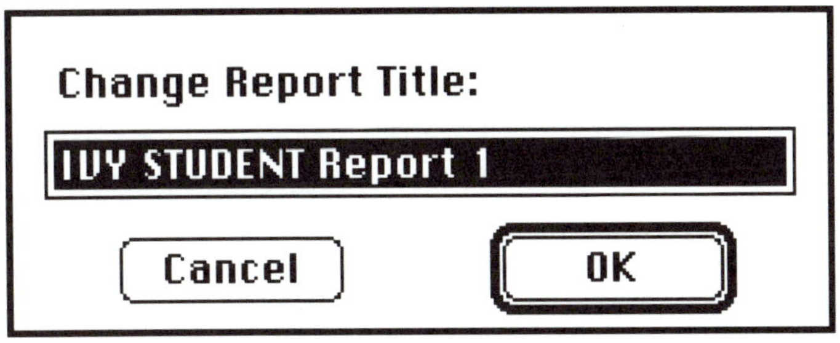

The Change Report Title dialog box

allowing a new name to be entered for the report definition. When `OK` is clicked the report definition is given the new name. Clicking instead on `Cancel` removes the dialog box from the screen without changing the name.

The Select Report command from the Report menu opens the different report definitions stored with the data base. The Window menu determines which of the open report definitions is used:

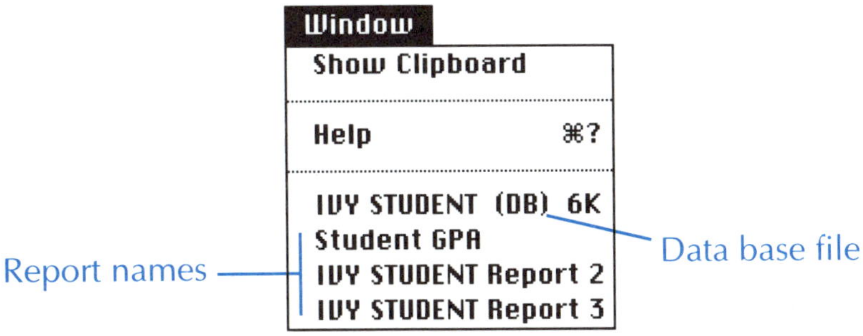

Selecting one of the report names returns to the Report screen

Selecting the report name makes that report active, so that it may then be modified or printed.

Sorting a data base file affects not only the order in which the records are displayed on the screen, but also the order in which they are printed. This makes it possible to have one report in order by Last Name, and then another by GPA. However, the key field and sorting order may not be specified from the Report screen. The Window menu can be used to return to the data base screen, where the data base may be sorted. Selecting the report definition from the Window menu returns to the Report screen where the report may again be printed, this time with the records in the new order.

Only eight report definitions may be stored with a data base at one time. To remove a report definition, execute the Erase Report command from the Report menu:

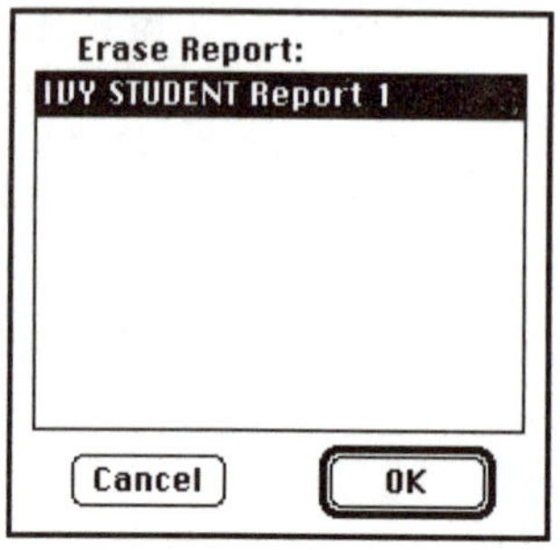

Selecting a report name from this box removes that report from the file

Double-clicking on a definition erases it from the file, and it may not be recovered. Clicking `Cancel` terminates this operation, and all report definitions are left unchanged.

Practice 4

In this Practice you will rename the current report definition and sort the data base. Start Works and open the IVY STUDENT data base if you have not already done so.

1) DISPLAY THE CURRENT REPORT DEFINITION

a. Execute the Select Report command from the Report menu. The current report definition, which has the name Report 1, is highlighted.

b. Click on `OK` to display the definition on the Report screen.

2) RENAME THE CURRENT REPORT DEFINITION

a. From the Report screen, select the Change Report Title from the Edit menu. The dialog box is shown with IVY STUDENT Report 1 as the current name.

b. Type the new name: `Student GPA`.

c. Click on `OK` to apply the new name. Report 1 is renamed Student GPA as shown at the top of the Report screen.

3) SORT THE DATA BASE

a. Select IVY STUDENT from the Window menu to display the data base. Note that the report definition name is now listed in the menu as Student GPA.

b. Click once on any GPA field.
c. Press ⌘A to execute the Sort command. The Sort dialog box is displayed.
d. Select descending order, "From 9 to 0" which will sort the records from high to low based on the GPA field.
e. Click on `OK`. The data base is sorted in descending order by GPA.

4) SAVE THE FILE AND PRINT THE REPORT

a. Press ⌘S to save the modified report definition and the data base on disk. The data base is now in order by GPA.
b. Select the Student GPA report from the Window menu to return to the Report screen.
c. Press ⌘P to display the Print dialog box.
d. Select the Print Preview option.
e. Click on `OK` to display the report on the Preview screen.
f. Click on `Print` to print the report on the printer.
g. After the report has printed, select the IVY STUDENT data base from the Window menu.

Check - The printed report should list the students in order by GPA.

6.9 Using Selection Rules with Reports

Selection rules were employed in the last chapter to limit the number of records displayed to only those which met certain criteria. When a selection rule is applied, the records printed in a report are also limited. This allows special reports to be printed which display, for example, only students with GPA's greater than 3.5 or only students from Maine or Vermont.

Selection rules may be applied from either the data base screen or the Report screen. If the New Report command is executed when a selection rule is in effect, that rule will be carried over into the report definition and displayed at the top of the screen. A selection rule applied from the Report screen is saved with the report definition and need not be reentered. This allows a report definition to specify not only *how* the data in the report is to appear, but also *which* data will be printed. For example, a report definition named Warning could be created which contains the selection rule "GPA is less than 1.5". This report would print only students with a GPA less than 1.5, no matter what other rule was currently applied to the data base.

When a selection rule is applied, the records shown on the report screen are limited to those which meet the rule's criteria. This provides an easy way to check the rule for correctness before printing the report; if records which should not appear in the printed report are displayed on the report screen, the rule is in error and must be changed.

6.10 Duplicating a Report Definition

Many printed reports have similar features. For this reason, Works allows a previously created report definition to be duplicated under a new name and then modified and saved.

To copy a report definition, the Duplicate Report command is executed from the Report menu, producing a dialog box which lists all current report definitions:

The Duplicate Report dialog box is used to create a copy of a report

Clicking `OK` copies the highlighted report definition using the next available default name (Report 2, Report 3, etc.) and displays it on screen allowing changes to be made. The copied report definition will have all of the characteristics of the original, and may be modified, printed and saved like any other report definition. The Change Report Title command from the Edit menu can then be used to change the name of the copied report definition.

Practice 5

In this Practice you will create a new report definition named Honors by copying the Student GPA report. Honors will use a selection rule to print only students with a GPA greater than 3.5. Start Works and open the IVY STUDENT data base if you have not already done so.

1) COPY THE STUDENT GPA REPORT DEFINITION UNDER THE NAME HONORS

a. Select the Duplicate Report command from the Report menu. The Student GPA report definition is highlighted in the list.

b. Click on `OK` to copy the Student GPA report definition. The copy is given the default name IVY STUDENT Report 2 and displayed on the Report screen.

c. Execute the Change Report Title command from the Edit menu. The dialog box is shown with IVY STUDENT Report 2 as the current name.

d. Type the new name `Honors`.

e. Click on `OK` to rename the report. The copied report is now named "Honors" as shown at the top of the Report screen.

2) APPLY A SELECTION RULE TO HONORS

a. Execute Record Selection from the Organize menu to display the Record Selection dialog box. If any previous rules exist click on `Delete Rule` to remove them.

b. Scroll through the fields list until the GPA field is visible. Click on GPA.
c. Select "is greater than" from the comparison list.
d. Type `3.5` for the comparison information.
e. Click on `Select` to apply the selection rule to the report definition. The Report screen is displayed with the selection rule at the top. When printed, only those records which have a GPA greater than 3.5 will be included in the report.

Check - Your report definition should be similar to the following. Note that only records which meet the selection rule's criteria are shown on the report screen:

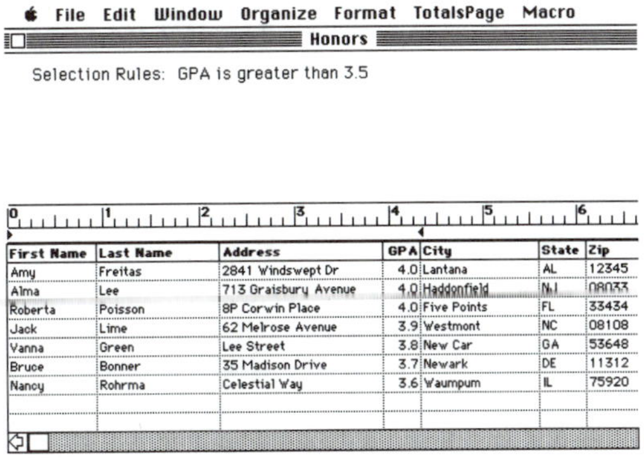

3) PRINT THE REPORT AND SAVE THE FILE

a. Press ⌘P to display the Print dialog box.
b. If it is selected, click on the Print Preview option to remove it.
c. Click on `OK` to print the report on the printer. Only those students with GPA's greater than 3.5 are printed.
d. After the report has been printed click on the Close box to return to the data base screen. Note how the selection rule applied from the Report screen had no effect on the data base itself - all records are displayed.
e. Press ⌘S to save the modified report definition and the data base on disk.
f. Press ⌘W to close the IVY STUDENT data base.

6.11 Adding Totals to Reports

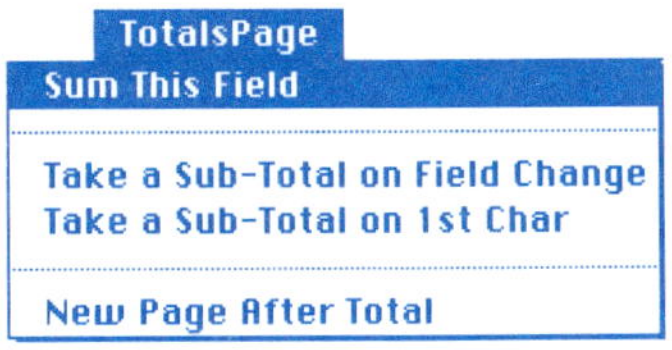

Reports can do more than just list the information stored in a data base in an organized manner. In addition to printing the contents of fields, Works reports can also calculate the total of the values printed in specified fields. These totals can then be printed at the end of the report as part of the report's summary.

To include totals in a report, the field to be totaled is selected and the Sum This Field command executed from the TotalsPage menu. The total of all of the printed entries in that field will then be displayed at the bottom of the report. Note that Sum This Field only counts entries that are printed in the report; if a selection rule is applied which excludes certain records, those values are not included in the total.

Practice 6

In this Practice you will create and print a report which includes a total. The IVY BOOKSTORE data base which stores information about products available for sale in the school's bookstore will be used. Start Works if you have not already done so.

1) **OPEN IVY BOOKSTORE AND DISPLAY THE REPORT SCREEN**

   a. From the Open File dialog box, open the IVY BOOKSTORE data base.
   b. Select New Report from the Reports menu to display the Report screen.

2) **SELECT THE FIELD TO BE TOTALED**

   Click once on the In Stock field name to highlight that field.

3) **TOTAL THE SELECTED FIELD**

   Execute the Sum This Field command from the TotalsPage menu.

4) **VIEW AND PRINT THE MODIFIED REPORT**

   a. Press ⌘P to display the Print dialog box.
   b. If it is not already, click on the Print Preview option to select it.
   c. Click on `OK` to display the report on the Preview screen. Note the total at the bottom of the In Stock column.
   d. Click on `Print` to print the report.
   e. After the report has been printed, select IVY BOOKSTORE from the Window menu to return to the data base screen.
   f. Press ⌘S to save the modified report definition and the data base on disk.

Check - Your printed report should include the total of the In Stock field, 1869

6.12 Computed Fields in a Data Base

Data base fields can store more than just information entered from the keyboard. It is possible for a field to perform a calculation using the data contained in a record and store the result as part of that record in what is called a "computed field". For example, a field in a Works data base can be told to calculate the result of the value stored in one field times the value stored in another for each record in that data base.

Computed fields are created by selecting the "Computed" option from the Field Attributes dialog box and then entering a "formula" as an entry in that field:

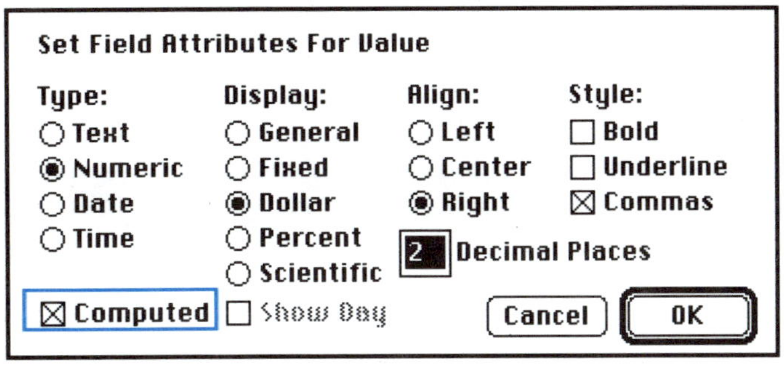

Selecting the Computed option allows a formula to be entered in a field

Normally this formula will refer to values stored in other fields in the record. To better describe formulas, we will refer to the Ivy University Bookstore data base which contains the following fields:

`Item Name`	-	The name of an item for sale
`Department`	-	The department the item is sold in
`In Stock`	-	How many of the item are currently available for sale
`Price`	-	How much the item sells for

Each record stores information about one item available for sale in the bookstore.

When creating a computed field the formula is entered into the field in either Form or List view. Works then copies that formula to every record in the data base. Formulas must begin with an equals sign (=) and may use the following mathematical operators:

Operator	**Action**
+	Add
-	Subtract
*	Multiply
/	Divide
^	Raise to a power (exponentiate)

For example, typing the formula `=100 * 5` into a computed field would cause Works to display 500 in that field for every record in the file. When a formula is entered into the field in one record, it is automatically copied by Works into that same field in every other record in the data base. Newly inserted records are given the formula automatically.

Formulas can refer to the value stored in another field by specifying that field's name in the formula. As an example, it is possible to determine the value of an inventory item in the IVY BOOKSTORE data base by multiplying the number of those items in stock (stored in the In Stock field) by the price per item (stored in Price). Thus the formula for a computed field showing the value of an inventory item would be,

```
=In Stock * Price
```

meaning multiply the value stored in the In Stock field by the value stored in Price and place the result in the computed field. It is also possible to include numeric constants in a formula. For example, the formula `=Price * 0.05` could be used to calculate a five percent sales tax on the Price field.

It is important to note that the value stored in a computed field is determined when the other values are entered into that record, not when the formula is created. This allows the computed field to store the correct value when changes are made to the data base after the field has been created. Also, a computed field is stored as part of the data base, just like any other field. The difference is that a computed field stores a formula which is evaluated by Works, and not a single value.

Practice 7

In this Practice you will modify the IVY BOOKSTORE data base to include a computed field which displays the value of inventory as described in the Section above. A new field will be added to the form and the formula entered into that field in Form view. Start Works and open IVY BOOKSTORE if you have not already done so.

1) INSERT A NEW FIELD ON THE FORM

a. If it is not already, press ⌘L to display the data base in Form view.
b. Select the Add New Field command from the Edit menu. The Field Name dialog box is displayed.
c. Type the name of the new field, `Value` and click on `Add Field`. The Value field is shown on the form.

2) SELECT THE COMPUTED OPTION

a. Click once on the Value field, highlighting it.
b. Select the Set Field Attributes command from the Format menu. The attributes dialog box is displayed. Note that the Computed option is displayed in dim text.
c. Click on Numeric. The Computed option changes from dimmed text.
d. Click on Computed, selecting it. Works now considers Value to be a computed field.
e. Click on `OK` to apply the attributes and return to the data base screen. Note the equals sign on the entry bar which is the beginning of the calculation formula.

3) ENTER THE CALCULATION FORMULA

a. Click once on the In Stock field, placing "In Stock" in the calculation formula on the Entry bar.
b. Type an asterisk (*) to indicate multiplication.
c. Click once on the Price field, including it in the formula. The formula should now read "=In Stock * Price".
d. Click on the Check box to enter the formula. Works automatically performs the calculations and stores the results in the Value field.
e. Press ⌘L to display the data base in List view. Note how Works has copied the formula to each record.

Check - Your List view should be similar to:

IVY BOOKSTORE (DB)

Item Name	Department	In Stock	Price	Value
Avocado Dip	Food	6	$0.99	5.94
Ball point pen	Pens/Pencils	150	$0.89	133.50
Chips	Food	77	$0.65	50.05
Class Ring	Clothing	50	$212.50	10625.00
Dictionary	Books	22	$12.95	284.90
Doritos	Food	145	$2.49	361.05
Felt-tip pen	Pens/Pencils	76	$0.98	74.48
Logo T-Shirt	Clothing	250	$9.99	2497.50
Pencil	Pens/Pencils	200	$0.15	30.00
Pepsi	Food	444	$0.65	288.60
School Jacket	Clothing	100	$34.95	3495.00
School Tie	Clothing	15	$17.50	262.50
Theasaurus	Books	12	$15.00	180.00
Three-Hole Paper	Paper	200	$1.98	396.00
Three-Ring Binder	Supplies	122	$3.50	427.00

4) FORMAT THE VALUE FIELD FOR DOLLAR AMOUNTS

a. With Value still highlighted, select the Set Field Attributes from the Format menu.
b. Select Dollar from the Display column.
c. Select Commas as the Style option.
d. Click on `OK` to apply the format and remove the dialog box. Note how the Value field is now displayed using dollar format.

5) MODIFY AN ENTRY

a. Click the pointer on the In Stock field in record 1.
b. Type a new amount, `105`, and click on the Check box. Note how Works automatically calculates and displays the new entry for the Value field.

6) SAVE THE MODIFIED DATA BASE

Press ⌘S to save the modified data base on the disk. The next time it is opened, IVY BOOKSTORE will have a calculated Value field.

6.13 Where can you go from here?

The last three chapters introduced the concepts of data bases; their design, creation and use. The Works data base has a number of other options not discussed in this text which you may want to explore on your own. One of the best places to begin is by reading the data base sections of the Works manual supplied by Microsoft. A powerful feature of Works is its ability to integrate the information stored in a data base file with a word processed document to produce personalized form letters. This process is called "mail merge" and is described in Chapter 9.

Larger, more powerful data base programs have even more options for generating reports and performing various operations with the data. Several of the most widely used packages for microcomputers are dBASE, 4th Dimension and FileMaker. Because you have learned how to use the Works data base it will be easier to learn a new package such as one of the ones listed above.

As the use of computerized data bases becomes more widespread the knowledge of what a data base is, and what it can be used for will be an important skill. There are many job opportunities for people to work with computer data bases. Information about careers involving computers and data bases is given in Chapter 11.

Chapter Summary

This chapter covered one of the most important aspects of the computerized database: its ability to produce printed reports detailing the information stored in its records. Works reports have several different parts, and may include a title, record list and report summary.

Report definitions are created using the New Report command from the Report menu. The Report screen is then displayed and the fields to be included in the report, their widths and placements are defined. When the data base file is then saved, any report definitions created are saved with it, and may be modified or printed later.

Up to eight different report definitions can be saved with a single data base file. Works uses the default names Report 1, Report 2, etc. to name each report definition, but these names may be changed using the Change Report Title command from the Edit menu.

With longer reports it is often necessary to organize the data in the report so that the desired information is easy to find. This may be done by sorting the data in the report or applying selection rules to it. When a data base file is sorted using the Sort command from the Organize menu, ⌘A, its records are placed in order according to the data stored in a specific field called the key field. When a report is then printed, the records are displayed in order according to that field. If a data base is saved after it has been sorted, the next time it is accessed the records will be in the sorted order. Selection rules limit the number of records displayed when a data base is printed based on certain criteria such as "GPA greater than 3.5" or "State equals ME". Selection rules may be defined from either the Report or data base screens, and are saved with the report definition.

A computed field can be created which stores a value based on the data stored in other numeric fields. This value is calculated by specifying a mathematical formula such as `=In Stock * Price` to print the product of the value stored in the In Stock field times the value stored in Price. The sum of all the entries in a numeric field can be calculated using the Sum This Field command from the Totals Page menu.

Vocabulary

Computed field - Numeric field which is calculated based on the value(s) stored in other fields using a formula.
Key field - Field which stores the data used when determining the order during a sort.
Report - Printed description of the information stored in a data base.

Report definition - Description of the order and placement of fields in a report. May include titles and summaries.
Sort - Places data base records in order, based on the value stored in a specific (key) field: ⌘A.

Reviews

Sections 6.1 - 6.7

1. a) What is meant by "sorting" a data base?
   b) Give 3 examples of how the IVY STUDENT data base could be sorted. In each example state what the key field is.

2. a) What is a report definition?
   b) What happens to a report definition when a data base is saved?

3. Explain the steps necessary to produce a report definition that produces a report similar to the following using data stored in IVY STUDENT:

Last Name	City	State
Freitas	Boca Raton	FL
Herskovitz	San Diego	CA
Presley	Lawrenceville	NJ
White	East Brunswick	NJ

. . .

4. List 3 factors which should be considered in planning a report?

5. a) How many separate report definitions may be stored with a single data base?
   b) How is a report definition selected?

6. Explain what Print Preview and Zoom do.

Sections 6.8 - 6.12

7. Explain how 3 different selection rules might be used to produce reports from the IVY STUDENT data base.

8. If a report is printed, the data base then sorted and the report printed again, will the two printed reports be different? Explain.

9. Why might you want to duplicate a report definition?

10. On your data disk is a file named CAR PRICE which lists different makes of automobiles and their prices. Explain the steps required to produce a report that lists the total of all the base prices.

11. A data base stores each student's grades in fields named Grade 1, Grade 2, Grade 3, Grade 4 and Grade 5. The grades are numeric values from 0 to 100. Explain how a field named Average can be added to the data base which calculates and stores the grade average for each student.

12. A data base named SAVINGS contains the following fields:

```
First Name
Last Name
Acct Number
Deposit Date
Withdrawal Date
Acct Balance
```

a) List the steps required to produce a report named Balance from this data base. Balance should display only the Last Name, Acct Number and Acct Balance for each depositor.
b) What additional steps are required to add a summary to the report that gives the sum of all of the account balances?
c) What formula should be entered into a new field named Interest which calculates the interest in each account by taking 5% of the account balance?
d) What steps are necessary to print a copy of the Balance report for only those customers having more than $10,000 in their account?

Exercises

1. Open the CAR PRICE data base on your data disk.

   a) Sort the records is ascending order by base price and answer the following:

      Name the three least expensive cars.
      Name the three most expensive cars.

   b) Sort the records in descending order by price with stereo and answer the following:

      Name the three most expensive cars with stereo.
      Name the three least expensive cars with stereo.

   c) Create a report definition named Inexpensive which lists the Make, Model and Base price for all cars with a base price less than $9,000.

   d) Print a copy of the Inexpensive report on the printer.

   e) Print a copy of the Inexpensive report for all cars with stereos which cost less than $10,000.

   f) Save the modified data base with the report definition on disk.

2. Open the ADDRESS data base created in Chapter 5 exercise 1.

   a) Sort ADDRESS in alphabetic order by last name.

   b) Create a report definition named Presents which lists the name and birthdate of all people in ADDRESS who will turn 18 or 21 this year.

   c) Print a copy of the Presents report on the printer.

   d) Create a report definition named Seventies which prints the name, birthday and full mailing address of each person born in the 1970's (1970 through 1979). Seventies should list the people in order by birthdate.

   e) Preview the Seventies report on screen and then print a copy on the printer.

   f) Save the modified data base with the report definitions on disk.

3. Open the INVENTOR data base on your data disk.

   a) Sort INVENTOR in ascending order based on invention date.

   b) Create a report definition named French which lists the date, invention and inventor for all French inventions.

   c) Print a copy of the French report on the printer.

   d) Duplicate the French report definition under the name New French.

   e) Modify the New French report to list the names of only French inventions from the 20th century. Print a copy of New French.

   f) Save the modified data base with the report definitions on disk.

4. Open the FANTASY data base created in Chapter 5 exercise 3.

   a) Create a report definition named Car Profit which shows the make, price paid and asking price for each car in inventory.

   b) Create a computed field named Profit which displays the profit on each sale (asking price minus the price paid).

   c) Add the Profit field to the report. Print the total of the Profit and asking price fields at the bottom of the report.

   d) Sort FANTASY in ascending order by year.

   e) Print a copy of the Profit report on the printer.

   f) Save the modified data base with its report definition on disk.

5. Open the WEATHER data base created for exercise 6 in Chapter 5.

   a) Create a report definition named Good Days which lists the date and time for each observation that had a temperature above 65 and no rain.

   b) Print a copy of the Good Days report on the printer.

   c) Duplicate a copy of Good Days under the name Bad Days. Bad Days should print only cloudy days with a temperature below 40. Be sure to change the report title and selection rule.

   d) Print a copy of Bad Days on the printer.

   e) Save the modified data base with the report definitions on disk.

Chapter 7

Introducing the Spreadsheet

File - Save ⌘S

Format - Set Cell Attributes

Edit - Paste Function

File - Print ⌘P

Objectives

After completing this chapter you will be able to:

1. Understand what a spreadsheet is and define its vocabulary.
2. Plan a spreadsheet.
3. Create a simple spreadsheet on the computer and enter data into it.
4. Perform and display the value of calculations using formulas and functions.
5. Store and retrieve spreadsheets from the disk.
6. Print a spreadsheet.

The third Works application is the spreadsheet. This chapter explains what a spreadsheet is and how to use one. We will first concern ourselves with the vocabulary of a spreadsheet and then with the specific commands needed to produce a simple one on the computer. The next chapter explains how Works is used to create larger and more powerful spreadsheets.

7.1 What is a Spreadsheet?

A spreadsheet is simply rows and columns of data. The term comes from the field of accounting where accountants keep track of business activities on large sheets of paper that spread out to form a "spreadsheet". These spreadsheets contain rows and columns of figures with totals and other calculations that relate to the flow of money in a business, but they can also be used to organize any type of numeric data.

Spreadsheets are record keeping tools that work primarily with numbers. An example of a simple non-computerized spreadsheet is the grade book used by Ivy University's chemistry professor, Dr. Sulfuric. In her grade book the names of her students run down the left side of the page, while labels running across the top of the page indicate each test and the date on which it was given:

Name	**Test 1** 9/10	**Test 2** 10/20	**Test 3** 11/15	**Test 4** 12/12
J. Smith	50	83	68	64
W. Freitas	86	89	78	88
M. Porter	78	100	90	89
B. Presley	45	78	66	78
H. Crane	66	76	78	55
M. Lee	85	74	83	66

Dr. Sulfuric's grade book

The grade book is organized into rows and columns. A row runs horizontally and stores both the name and grades for one student. The name J. Smith and the grades 50, 83, 68 and 64, which run across the page, form a row. A column runs vertically and stores a title and all of the grades for a single test. The title Test 1 and its grades run down the page from a grade of 50 to 85 forming a column.

Computerized spreadsheets appear similar to manual ones but have the added capability of using the computer to perform calculations on the data stored in the spreadsheet. If instead of storing her grades in a gradebook, Dr. Sulfuric were to use a computerized spreadsheet she would be able to have the computer calculate averages on her grades. Then if she were to change one of the grades the computer would automatically redo the calculations. This is the primary advantage of a computerized spreadsheet; the ability of the computer to perform calculations on the data stored in it and to redo the calculations when any changes are made to the data.

7.2 Cells, Labels, and Values

Computerized spreadsheets store data in a grid of columns and rows. Columns are identified by letters which run along the top of the spreadsheet. In Works these letters run from A to Z, and then AA to AZ, BA to BZ, and so on to column IV. This allows for a maximum of 256 columns. Rows are numbered on the left-hand side of the spreadsheet from row 1 to row 16,382. In most instances a much smaller number of rows and columns will actually be used to store data. Due to memory limitations some computers may not be able to store a spreadsheet as large as the maximum allows.

The diagram below shows an empty Works spreadsheet. Note the column letters running horizontally across and the row numbers running down the left hand side of the screen:

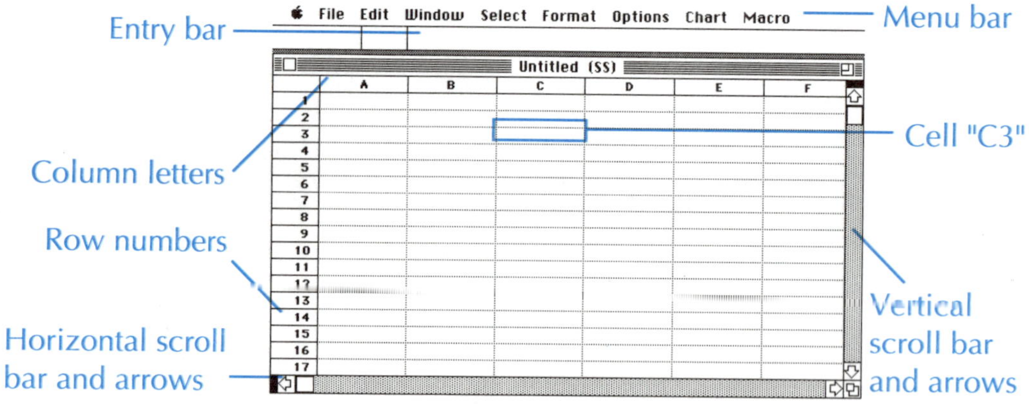

The Works spreadsheet screen

On this screen you will enter data into a spreadsheet.

Where a row and column intersect is called a "cell". A single cell is identified by its column letter followed by its row number. Therefore, the third cell from the top in column C is named C3. Each cell can store a single item of data. This system is similar to mailboxes at the post office where each "box" or cell has a name and can store information. Be careful not to confuse the name of the cell and the data it stores.

Note that the screen only displays columns A to F and rows 1 to 17. The other columns and rows can be displayed by using the mouse to "scroll" the screen. When this is done columns and rows move off the screen and new ones appear. The old columns and rows are not lost, just not displayed. In this way the screen can be considered a "window" showing only a portion of the larger spreadsheet. Scrolling moves the window around the spreadsheet without effecting any of the data stored in the cells.

Spreadsheets can store three types of data in cells: "labels", "values", and "dates". Labels are entries which store data that cannot be used in calculations, including words or letters. Values are entries that have numeric values and can be used in calculations. The student names (i.e. J. Smith) are labels, while a grade such as 50 is a value. Dates are the third type of entry that can be stored in a cell. A date is a calendar date such as 9/10/90. When setting up a computerized spreadsheet it is important to first determine what data will be stored as labels or values.

7.3 Creating a New Spreadsheet

To create a new spreadsheet double-click on the Spreadsheet icon from the Open File dialog box:

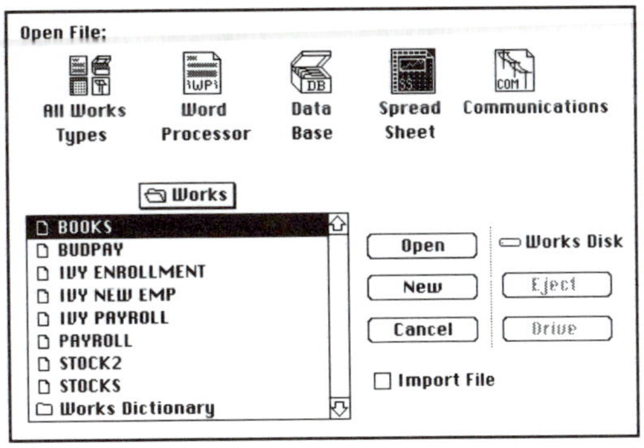

Double-clicking on the Spreadsheet icon creates a new, empty spreadsheet

To inform Works into which cell information is to be entered move the mouse pointer to that cell and click once. An outline appears around the cell, and the column letter and row number of the cell are displayed in the cell indicator at the top of the screen. When data is typed on the keyboard it first appears on the Entry bar. Two boxes also appear on the Entry bar, one containing a check and the other an X. Clicking on the Check box transfers data to the selected cell; clicking on the X box erases data from the Entry bar. (The Check box is sometimes referred to as the "accept" box, and the X box as the "reject" or "cancel" box.)

Clicking the Check box on the Entry bar would enter "Poston" into the cell

To scroll through the spreadsheet click on one of the scroll arrows. Clicking the mouse once will move the screen one row or column in the direction of the arrow. Holding the mouse down will continue the scroll in the direction of the arrow.

Practice 1

In this Practice you will create a new spreadsheet, move the cell cursor around the spreadsheet, enter data into a cell and scroll through the spreadsheet.

1) START WORKS

2) CREATE A NEW SPREADSHEET FROM THE OPEN FILE DIALOG BOX

Move the pointer to the spreadsheet icon and click twice.

3) SELECT CELL D8

a. Using the mouse move the pointer to cell D8.
b. Click once and note that an outline appears around the cell and that D8 appears in the cell indicator at the top of the screen.

4) ENTER DATA INTO CELL D8

a Type `35.7`. Note that the number appears on the Entry bar.
b. Click once on the Check box to transfer the data from the Entry bar to cell D8.

5) SCROLL THE SCREEN

a. Click on the right scroll arrow until column Z comes into view.
b. Click on the down arrow and continue clicking until row 33 comes into view.
c. Move the pointer to cell Z30 and select the cell by clicking once. Check the cell indicator to determine that you have selected the correct cell.

6) RETURN THE CELL CURSOR TO CELL A1

Using the arrows at the screen corners scroll the screen so that cell A1 is displayed.

7.4 Entering and Correcting Data in a Spreadsheet

Once a cell in a spreadsheet has been selected and data entered from the keyboard the data may be transferred into the cell in two different ways. The first method is to click the Check box on the Entry bar as was done in Practice 1. The second method is to press the Return key which transfers the data to the selected cell and then moves the highlight to the next cell in the column. This method is especially useful when long columns of numbers are to be entered into a spreadsheet.

If a mistake is made entering data before it is transferred into a cell it may deleted one character at a time by pressing the delete key or the whole entry may be erased by moving the pointer to the X box on the Entry bar and clicking once. To correct data that has already been entered into a cell the pointer is moved back to the cell, the mouse clicked once to select the cell and the new data entered by typing it and entering it. This will erase any previous data stored in the cell.

Works automatically displays values up to 12 digits in a single cell. When the value exceeds 12 digits it is expressed in scientific notation. For example, the number 333334444455555 is displayed as 3.333344E+14. Labels will be displayed in their entirety until they encounter another cell containing data.

7.5 Saving a Spreadsheet on Disk and Closing its File

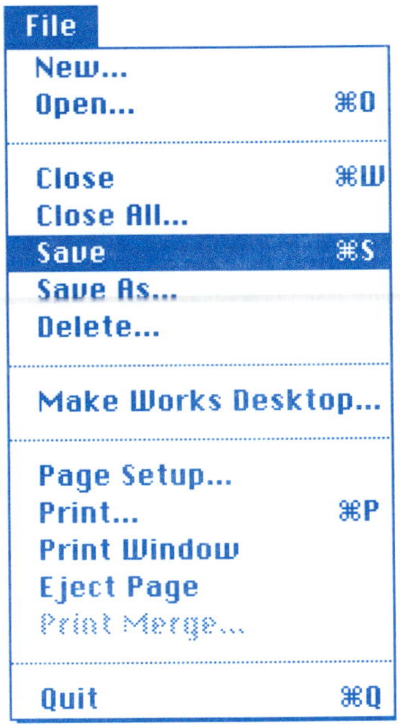

To save a spreadsheet the ⌘ key and S are pressed at the same time. This transfers a copy of the spreadsheet from the computer's memory to the disk. The first time a spreadsheet is saved a dialog box is shown asking you to enter a file name in the box containing the word Untitled. The name entered can be up to 32 characters in length. Once the name has been entered from the keyboard the pointer is moved to SAVE and clicked once. It is best to use a name which describes the contents of your spreadsheet. For example, a spreadsheet containing Dr. Sulfuric's grades could be named GRADES.

When a spreadsheet is in the computer's memory and the Save command executed, the latest version of the spreadsheet is saved replacing any earlier version. For this reason it is necessary to use the Save command after making changes to a previously stored spreadsheet.

The procedure to transfer a previously saved spreadsheet file from disk to the computer's memory is the same as that used for word processor or data base files. From the File menu select the Open command. Select the Spreadsheet icon with a single click and a list of all spreadsheet files will be displayed. Move the pointer to the selected file name and double-click.

You will often want to work on more than one file after booting Works. When this is the case, the current file that you are working on should be saved and then "closed" to free the computer memory needed to store the file. To close a file the Close command from the File menu is selected, or press ⌘ `W`.

Practice 2

In this Practice you will enter the data from Dr. Sulfuric's grade book into spreadsheet created in the last Practice.

1) ENTER THE COLUMN TITLES IN ROW 1

a. Select cell A1.
b. Type `Name` and click on the Check box.
c. Select cell C1. Column B is skipped to make the spreadsheet easier to read.
d. Type `Test 1` and click on the Check box.
e. Select cell D1.
f. Type `Test 2` and click on the check.
g. Continue this procedure to place the headings `Test 3` in cell E1 and `Test 4` in cell F1.

2) ENTER THE STUDENT NAMES

a. Select cell A4. Rows 2 and 3 are skipped.
b. Type the name `J. Smith` and press Return. Note that it is easier to enter columns of data using Return rather than the mouse since Return automatically selects the next cell in the column (cell A5).
c. With cell A5 selected type the name `W. Freitas` and press Return.
d. Continue this process to place the names:

`M. Porter`	into cell A6
`B. Presley`	into cell A7
`H. Crane`	into cell A8
`M. Lee`	into cell A9

3) ENTER THE GRADES

Select cell C4 and enter the first grade for J. Smith, a **50**. Continue entering the grades until your spreadsheet looks like the one below:

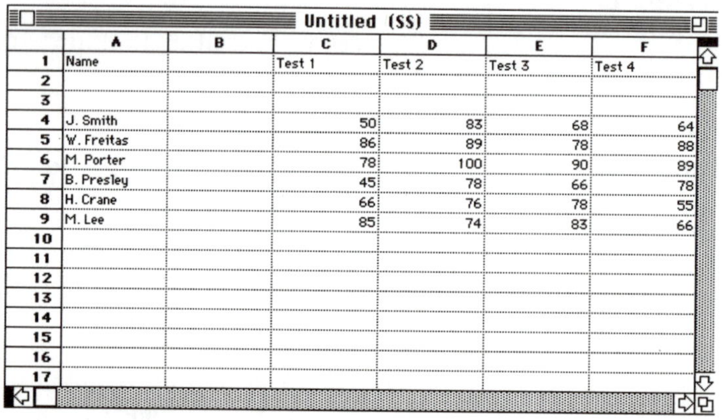

Untitled (SS)

	A	B	C	D	E	F
1	Name		Test 1	Test 2	Test 3	Test 4
2						
3						
4	J. Smith		50	83	68	64
5	W. Freitas		86	89	78	88
6	M. Porter		78	100	90	89
7	B. Presley		45	78	66	78
8	H. Crane		66	76	78	55
9	M. Lee		85	74	83	66
10						
11						
12						
13						
14						
15						
16						
17						

4) SAVE THE SPREADSHEET ON DISK

a. Press ⌘S.
b. When the dialog box appears type `GRADES` on the Save Document As line and click on the Save button. The spreadsheet is now saved on disk using the name GRADES.

7.6 Formatting Cells

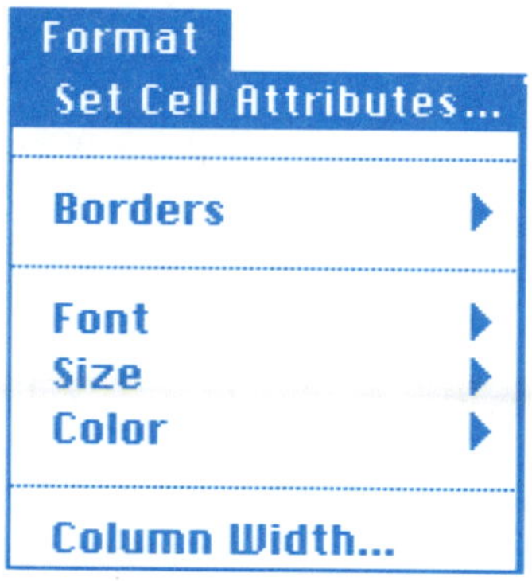

In viewing the spreadsheet created in Practice 2 there is a problem. The Test column headers are left justified while the grades are right justified. This occurs because Works left justifies labels and right justifies values. This problem can be easily rectified by using the Set Cell Attributes command from the Format menu.

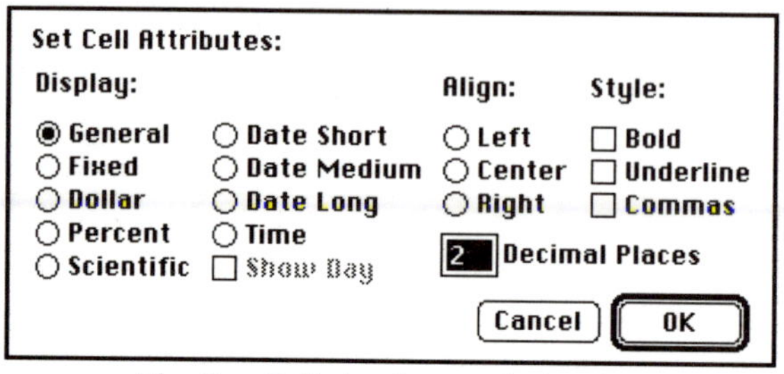

The Set Cell Attributes dialog box

To format either a single cell or a series of cells the cells are first selected and then the cell attribute selected from the above dialog box. A series of cells is selected by dragging the mouse pointer across the cells which causes the cells to be displayed in black.

The Set Cell Attributes command can also be used to format a date such as 9/10/90 when it is to be stored in a cell. To do this one of the three date formats is selected. Without formatting Works will display an incorrect value when a date such as 9/10/90 is entered.

Practice 3

In this Practice you will format the cells containing the Test labels and the dates in the GRADES spreadsheet.

1) RIGHT-JUSTIFY TEST COLUMN HEADERS

a. Select cell C1 and drag the mouse to cell F1. Note that cells D1, E1 and F1 are highlighted.
b. Select the Set Cells Attribute command from the Format menu.
c. Select Right under the Align attribute and then click on `OK`. Note how the Test column headers are right aligned.

2) ENTER THE TEST DATES

a. Move the cell cursor to cell C2.
b. Type `9/10/90` and click on the Check box. Note that numbers are displayed rather than the date. This will be corrected in step 3.
c. Select cell D2.
d. Type `10/20/90` and click on the Check box.
e. Continue this procedure to place the date `11/15/90` in cell E2 and `12/12/90` in cell F2.

3) FORMAT DATES

a. Select cell C2 and drag the mouse to cell F2. Note that the cells are highlighted.
b. Select the Set Cells Attribute command from the Format menu.
c. Select Date Short under the Display attributes and click on `OK`. Note that the dates are now displayed properly

4) SAVE AND CLOSE GRADES

a. Press ⌘S. Now the latest version of GRADES has been saved on disk, erasing the earlier version.
b. Select the Close command from the File menu. This erases the GRADES spreadsheet from the computer's memory.

<u>Check</u> - Your spreadsheet should be similar to the one shown on the next page.

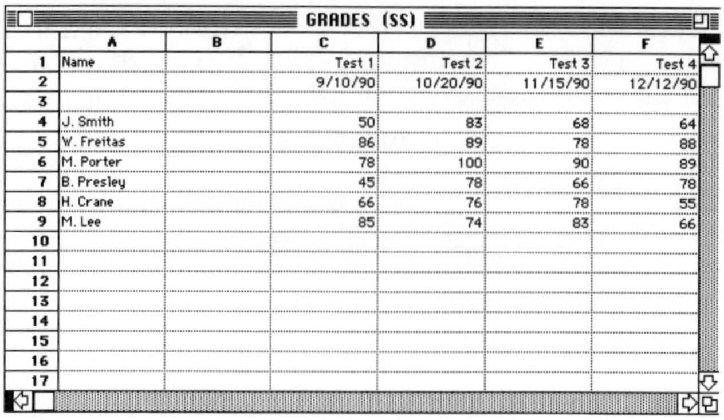

GRADES (SS)

	A	B	C	D	E	F
1	Name		Test 1	Test 2	Test 3	Test 4
2			9/10/90	10/20/90	11/15/90	12/12/90
3						
4	J. Smith		50	83	68	64
5	V. Freitas		86	89	78	88
6	M. Porter		78	100	90	89
7	B. Presley		45	78	66	78
8	H. Crane		66	76	78	55
9	M. Lee		85	74	83	66
10						
11						
12						
13						
14						
15						
16						
17						

7.7 Using Formulas to Perform Calculations

We have stated that the primary benefit of a computerized spreadsheet is its ability to perform calculations. To perform these calculations "formulas" are used. Formulas are mathematical statements used to calculate values. For example, when the mathematical formula =25 * 38 is entered in a cell the value 950 is displayed by the cell. The computer then automatically calculates the product of the two stored numbers and places it in the cell. Note that all formulas in Works must begin with equal signs (=).

The following mathematical operators may be used in writing a formula:

Addition	+
Subtraction	−
Multiplication	*
Division	/
Exponentiation	^

Exponentiation means raised to a power and uses the caret (^) symbol. For example, 2^2 = 4 and 5^3 = 125. Below are some examples of formulas that could be stored in cells:

```
=3 * 28 - 15
=25 + (19 / 22)
=3^3
=3 + 12 / 2
```

When Works evaluates a formula it reads it from left to right, but does so using the rules of order of operations. For example, what value is computed when the expression

```
=3 + 12 / 2
```

is evaluated? Does the computer add 3 and 12 and then divide by 2? If it does, the answer is 7.5. Or does the computer first divide 12 by 2 and then add 3 resulting in an answer of 9? Entering the formula we discover that the computer produces an answer of 9. It divided first and then added 3 to the result because it follows a specific order of operations when evaluating expressions.

The computer uses the following order of operations when it evaluates a formula:

FIRST: Exponents: Any number raised to a power, e.g., 2^2, is calculated first.

```
=4 + 3^2                produces the value 13
```

SECOND: Multiplication and Division: Next, the computer looks for multiplication or division signs which are of equal priority.

```
=3 + 5 * 6 / 2          produces the value 18
```

First the computer multiplies 5 and 6 to get 30, then it divides by 2 to produce 15. Finally it adds 3 resulting in the value 18. When there is more than one operation of the same priority in a formula, the computer performs them in order from left to right.

THIRD: Addition and Subtraction: The third order of operations is addition and subtraction which are of equal priority.

```
=3 * 5 + 6              produces the value 21
```

Since multiplication and division are done before addition, the computer first calculates the product of 3 and 5, which is 15. To produce the final result, 6 is added to 15, which is 21.

When parentheses are used the computer performs whatever operations are within the parentheses first. By using parentheses, you can tell the computer to change the order of operations. For example, to add 3 and 12 and then divide the result by 5 parentheses can be used:

```
=(3 + 12) / 5           produces the value 3
```

Here are a number of formulas and the results they yield:

```
=2 * 2 + 3 * 2          = 10
=25 * 8 / 4             = 50
=35 + 12 / 3            = 39
=3 + 5 * 8 + 7          = 50
=(3 + 5) * (8 + 7)      = 120
=3^2 * 8 + 4            = 76
=6 + 2^2                = 10
=(6 + 2)^2              = 64
```

If we want to store the product of the values stored in cells A5 and B7 in a cell all we need do is enter the formula =A5 * B7 in that cell. Storing the value 20 in cell B3 and the value 50 in cell C2, the formulas below would produce the following:

```
=B3 / C2                = .4
=B3 * C2                = 1000
=B3 - C2                = -30
=2 * B3 + 5 * C2        = 290
=B3 + 5 * C2 + 8        = 278
=B3 + 5 * (C2 + 8)      = 310
=(B3 + 5) * (C2 + 8)    = 1450
```

If cells C1 to C6 store values the sum of the values can be calculated with the formula:

```
=C1 + C2 + C3 + C4 + C5 + C6
```

The average of the values in cells C1 to C6 can be calculated with the formula:

```
=(C1 + C2 + C3 + C4 + C5 + C6) / 6
```

Entering an improper formula causes Works to display a dialog box containing an error message and the formula with a blinking cursor located at the error. The correction can be entered here and `OK` clicked. For example, if the formula `=(C4 + C8` is entered without the right parenthesis Works will display:

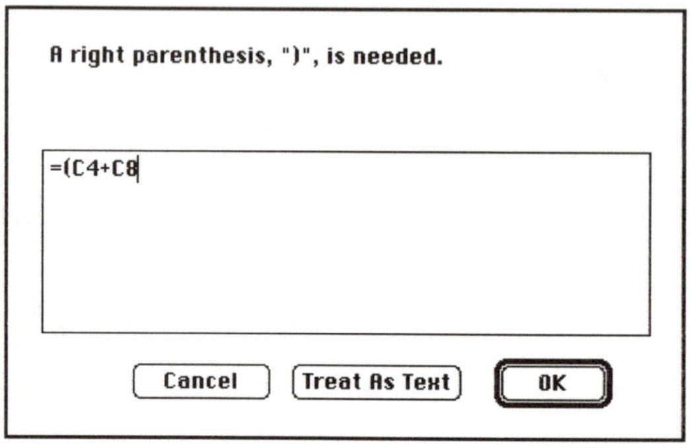

Works notifies you of the error it has detected and allows you to either correct it in this box, or to treat the entry as text (a label)

If you attempt to enter an illegal formula into a cell, Works displays `*Error*` in that cell. For example, it is illegal to divide a number by zero because this result is undefined in mathematics. Therefore, entering `=10/0` in a cell causes Works to display `*Error*` in that cell when the formula is entered.

7.8 Editing Entries and Clearing Cells

When a mistake has been made in a formula or a change is desired, the complete formula can be retyped and entered, but this is unnecessary. Works allows a cell's entry to be edited by selecting the cell and then moving the pointer to the formula on the Entry bar. The pointer is then located at the place in the formula that is to be edited and a single click given. A blinking cursor will appear at this point so that characters may be entered or deleted. When the formula has been corrected it is entered by clicking on the Check box.

To erase whatever is stored in a cell, whether it is a value, label or formula, the cell is selected, the Delete key pressed, and the Check box clicked. The contents of the cell are then erased, leaving the Entry bar blank.

Practice 4

In this Practice you will enter values and formulas into the cells of a new spreadsheet and perform calculations. Start Works if you have not already done so.

1) CREATE A NEW SPREADSHEET

Double-click on the Spreadsheet icon to create a new spreadsheet.

2) ENTER FORMULAS INTO THE SPREADSHEET

a. Select cell B5.
b. Type `=35 * 12 / 3` and click on the Check box. The result 140 is displayed in cell B5. Note that the formula used to calculate the result is shown on the Entry bar.

3) ENTER VALUES INTO THE SPREADSHEET

a. Select cell B3.
b. Enter the value `20` and click on the Check box.
c. Select cell C2.
d. Enter the value `50` and click on the Check box.

4) ENTER FORMULAS

a. Select cell D5.
b. Type each of the following formulas in cell D5 and click on the Check box each time. Note the resulting values:

Formula	**Resulting value**
`=B3 / C2`	`0.4`
`=B3 * C2`	`1000`
`=B3 - C2`	`-30`
`=2 + B3 * 5 + C2`	`152`
`=(2 + B3) * (5 + C2)`	`1210`
`=B3^2 + C2^2`	`2900`
`=(B3 + C2)^2`	`4900`
`=10 / 0`	`*Error*`
`B3 + C2`	`B3 + C2`

In the last example, the result is a label because it is not preceded by an equal sign.

5) BLANK EACH CELL

Select each cell displaying a value (B3, B5, C2, D5), press the Delete key and click on the Check box to erase the values. The spreadsheet work area should now be blank.

6) ENTER NEW VALUES

a. Select cell C1 and enter the value `50`.
b. Select cell C2 and enter the value `85`.
c. Continue entering the values:

`75` in cell C3
`83` in cell C4
`34` in cell C5
`55` in cell C6

7) CALCULATE THE SUM OF THE VALUES IN COLUMN C AND CORRECT AN ERROR

a. Select cell C8.
b. Enter the following formula exactly as shown:

```
=C1 + C2 + C3 + C4 + C5   C6
```

Note that Works displays the error dialog box with the message "There is a flawed cell representation".

c. Place the pointer between C5 and C6 in the dialog box and click. Type a + sign and click on `OK`. Cell C8 now displays the sum of the values stored in cells C1 through C6, 382.

8) CALCULATE THE AVERAGE OF THE VALUES IN COLUMN C

a. Select cell C10.
b. Enter the formula:

```
=(C1 + C2 + C3 + C4 + C5 + C6) / 6
```

The average of the values, 63.666666667, is shown in cell C10.

9) CALCULATE THE AVERAGE OF THE FIRST 3 CELLS ONLY

a. Select cell C10 if it is not already.
b. Place the pointer just to the left of the right parenthesis in the formula on the Entry bar and click once. A blinking cursor appears.
c. Press the Delete key 9 times.
d. Place the pointer to the right of the divisor 6 and click once. The cursor moves to this position.
e. Press the delete key once to delete the 6 and type 3. The formula

```
=(C1 + C2 + C3) / 3
```

should now be displayed on the Entry bar.

f. Click on the Check box. The average of the first three cells only, 70, is shown in cell C10.

10) SAVE TEST ON DISK

Press ⌘S. Type the name `TEST` and click on SAVE. A copy of the TEST spreadsheet is saved on disk.

<u>Check</u> - Your spreadsheet should be similar to the following:

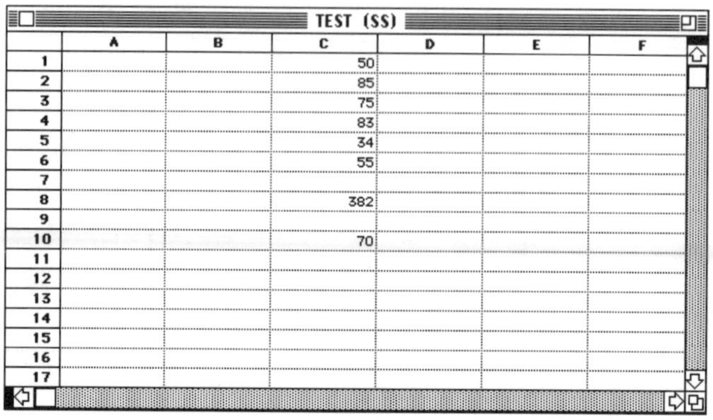

7.9 Using Functions to Perform Calculations

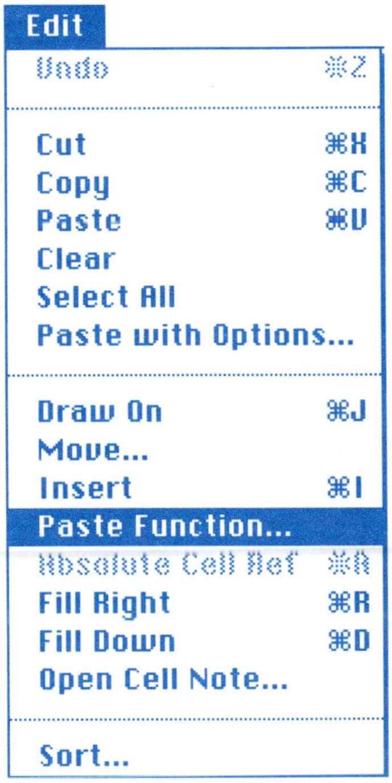

To produce commonly performed calculations Works contains built-in "functions" which may be used as part of a formula. For example, in Practice 4 we used a formula to add the values of a column of numbers stored in cells C1 to C6. Instead we could have used the Work's built-in Sum function:

```
=SUM(C1:C6)
```

The computer then automatically calculates the value of C1 + C2 + C3 + C4 + C5 + C6. The Sum function requires that the first cell name and last cell name in the sum be entered. A colon (:) is used to indicate a "range" of cells so that (C1:C6) refers to cells C1, C2, C3, C4, C5 and C6.

Values stored in a row of cells may also be summed using the Sum function. For example, to sum the cells in row 2 for the range of cells B2 to E2 we need only enter the formula

```
=SUM(B2:E2)
```

Works then sums the values in cells B2, C2, D2, and E2.

We could replace the formula in cell C10 used to average the column of grades in Practice 4 with

```
=SUM(C1:C6) / 6
```

and obtain the same result. Note that we must still divide the sum by 6 to obtain the average.

There is an easier method of averaging the values using the Average function which calculates the average of the values stored in the cells listed. To average the values for cells C1 through C6 we can use the function:

```
=Average(C1:C6)
```

There are two ways in which a formula can be entered into a cell. First it can be entered directly from the keyboard. Second, the formula can be entered by selecting the Paste Function command from the Edit menu:

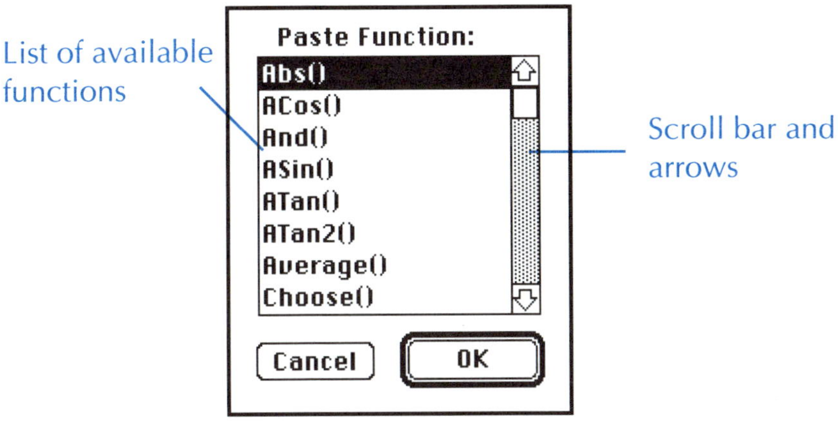

The Paste Function dialog box contains a list of available functions

The advantage of this second method is that it avoids errors in determining the range. This is especially important in large spreadsheets where the range may extend beyond a single screen. When a function is selected from the above dialog box it appears on the Entry bar. The mouse is then dragged to determine the function's range.

Practice 5

In this Practice functions will be used to sum and average rows and columns of values. Start Works and open the TEST spreadsheet created in Practice 4 if you have not already done so.

1) ENTER FUNCTION TO SUM COLUMN C

a. Select cell C8.
b. Select the Paste Function command from the Edit menu.
c. Move the pointer to the scroll arrow at the lower right hand side of the list and click until the Sum function appears.
d. Click on the Sum() function and then on `OK`. Note that =SUM() appears on the Entry bar with the cursor between the parentheses.
e. Move the pointer to cell C1 and drag the mouse to cell C6. Cells C1 to C6 are outlined.
f. Release the mouse and the range C1:C6 is entered into the function.
g. Click on the Check box and the sum 382 is displayed in cell C8.

2) ENTER FUNCTION TO AVERAGE COLUMN C

a. Select cell C10.
b. Select the Paste Function command from the Edit menu.
c. Click on the Average() function and then on `OK`. Note that =Average() appears on the Entry bar.
d. Move the pointer to cell C1 and drag the mouse to cell C6. Cells C1 to C6 are outlined.
e. Release the mouse and the range C1:C6 is entered into the function.
f. Click on the check and the average 63.666666667 is displayed in cell C10.

3) ENTER VALUES IN ROW 2

a. Select cell B2.
b. Enter the following values into the cells in row 2 (note that cell C2 already stores the value 85):

`97.8`	into cell B2
`109.4`	into cell D2
`105.8`	into cell E2

4) ENTER FUNCTION TO SUM ROW 2

a. Select cell G2. Click on the scroll arrow at the bottom of the screen to bring column G into view.
b. Using the method described in step 1 enter the function:

```
=SUM(B2:E2)
```

Click on the scroll arrow at the bottom of the screen to bring column B into view before entering the range. The sum of the values in row 2 is displayed, 398.

5) ENTER FUNCTION TO AVERAGE ROW 2

a. Select cell H2.

b. Using the method described in step 2 enter the function:

`=Average(B2:E2)`

The average of the values in row 2 is displayed, 99.5.

6) CHANGE THE VALUE IN CELL E2

a. Select cell E2.

b. Enter the new value `1495.8`.
Note that both the row's sum (cell G2) and average (cell H2) change automatically to reflect the new value.

7) SAVE AND CLOSE THE TEST SPREADSHEET

a. Press ⌘S. The modified TEST spreadsheet is saved on disk.

b. Select the Close command from the File menu to close TEST.

Check - The modified spreadsheet should be similar to:

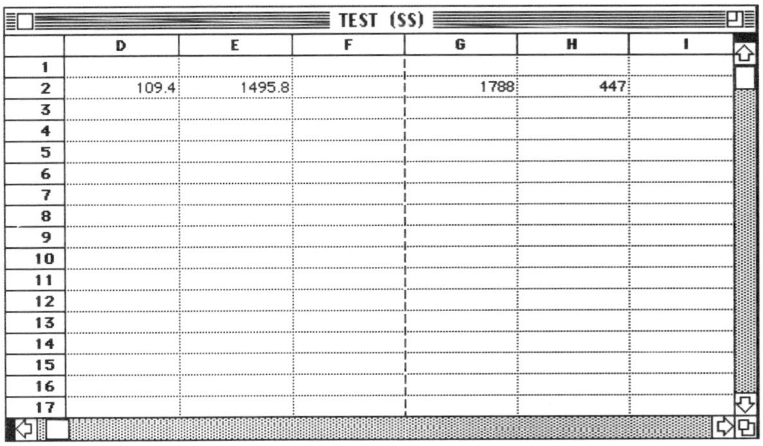

7.10 Planning a Spreadsheet

It is important to first plan a spreadsheet carefully before using the computer. This can best be done by answering the following questions:

1. What new information should the spreadsheet produce?
2. What data must the spreadsheet store to produce the new information?
3. How could the new information be produced without using a computer?
4. How should the spreadsheet be displayed on the computer?

We will use Dr. Sulfuric's grade book, shown in Section 7.1, to answer these questions:

1. Dr. Sulfuric wants to calculate each student's term average and the class average on each of her tests.
2. The data to be stored is the student names and grades.
3. Without using a computer Dr. Sulfuric could produce the class average on each test by adding all the grades for that test and dividing by the number of students (6). Each student's term average could be calculated by adding the four grades and dividing by 4.
4. How the spreadsheet should be formatted on the computer is easy to determine since we want it to look like Dr. Sulfuric's grade book. Later when we plan more complicated spreadsheets, especially those involving financial calculations, we will have to spend considerable time planning them.

Step 3 is especially important. In the process of planning how to solve a problem without the computer we must determine the sequence of steps the solution requires. Since the computer solution usually requires the same or very similar steps we can use our manual solution to assist us in developing the computer one.

Working out the details, as we have above, is very important before proceeding to the computer. In the next chapter we will expand our discussion of spreadsheet planning.

7.11 Displaying Formatted Values

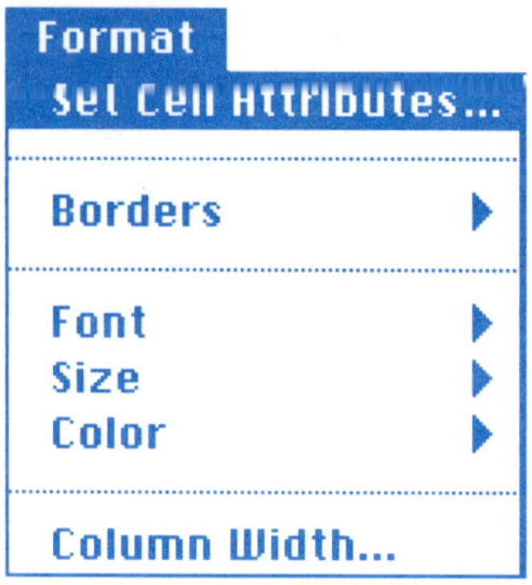

Often Works will display numbers to many more decimal places than are desired. For example, if we average the grades for Test 1 in the GRADES spreadsheet the value will be displayed as 68.333333333, when it would be better displayed as 68.3. Works can be told to limit the number of decimal places displayed by formatting a cell using the Set Cell Attributes command from the Format menu.

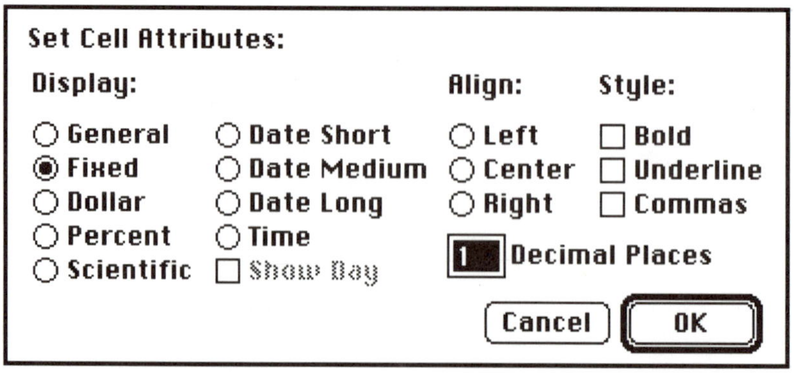

A cell formatted with these options will always display 1 decimal place

To set a cell to display 1 decimal place first select the cell, select the Set Cell Attributes command and click on Fixed. Then type 1 on the keyboard and click on OK. It is important to realize that the values stored by the computer are unchanged when the value displayed is formatted. In calculations using the cell above, 68.333333333 will be used even though 68.3 is displayed.

Practice 6

In this Practice you will enter formulas to calculate the average grade on each test and the term averages for each of Dr. Sulfuric's students in the GRADES spreadsheet. Start Works if you have not already done so.

1) OPEN THE GRADES SPREADSHEET

2) ENTER THE FORMULA TO AVERAGE GRADES FOR TEST 1

a. Select cell C11.
b. Enter the function:

```
=Average(C4:C9)
```

using the method outlined in Practice 5. The average grade on Test 1, 68.333333333, is displayed in cell C11.

3) ENTER THE FORMULAS TO CALCULATE THE OTHER TEST AVERAGES

a. Select cell D11.
b. Enter the formulas:

`=Average(D4:D9)` into cell D11
`=Average(E4:E9)` into cell E11
`=Average(F4:F9)` into cell F11

4) CALCULATE EACH STUDENT'S TERM AVERAGE

a. Select cell H4.
b. Enter the formula:

```
=Average(C4:F4)
```

The average for J. Smith, 66.25, is displayed in cell H4.

c. Repeat this process by entering the formulas:

`=Average(C5:F5)` into cell H5
`=Average(C6:F6)` into cell H6
`=Average(C7:F7)` into cell H7
`=Average(C8:F8)` into cell H8
`=Average(C9:F9)` into cell H9

5) ADD TITLES FOR THE NEW INFORMATION

a. Select cell H1 and enter the label: `Student`
b. Select cell H2 and enter the label: `Average`
c. Select cell B11 and enter the label: `Average:`

6) FORMAT THE AVERAGES TO ONE DECIMAL PLACE

a. Select cells C11 to F11 by dragging the mouse.
b. Select the Set Cell Attributes command from the Format menu.
c. Click on Fixed.
d. Type a `1` on the keyboard and click on `OK`. Note that the cells are reformatted on the screen.

e. Select cells H4 to H9 by dragging the mouse and repeat steps b through d.

f. Click on cell A1 to remove the highlight.

7) SAVE THE MODIFIED GRADES SPREADSHEET

Press ⌘S to save the revised version of GRADES on disk.

<u>Check</u> - The formatted averages for Dr. Sulfuric's class should now appear in the spreadsheet as shown below:

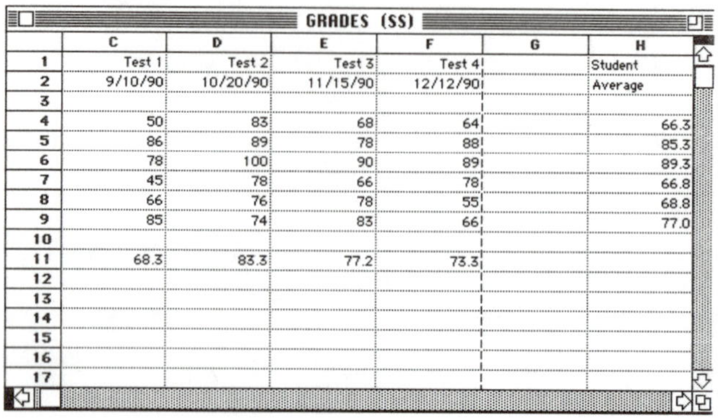

	C	D	E	F	G	H
1	Test 1	Test 2	Test 3	Test 4		Student
2	9/10/90	10/20/90	11/15/90	12/12/90		Average
3						
4	50	83	68	64		66.3
5	86	89	78	88		85.3
6	78	100	90	89		89.3
7	45	78	66	78		66.8
8	66	76	78	55		68.8
9	85	74	83	66		77.0
10						
11	68.3	83.3	77.2	73.3		
12						
13						
14						
15						
16						
17						

7.12 Printing a Spreadsheet

Before printing a spreadsheet it is important to first save it on disk. If something then goes wrong in the process of printing and the computer's memory is erased, the spreadsheet can be retrieved from disk. Also check to make sure that the printer is turned on and properly connected to your computer before attempting to print.

To print a spreadsheet the Print command is executed from the File menu. The Print dialog box is then displayed:

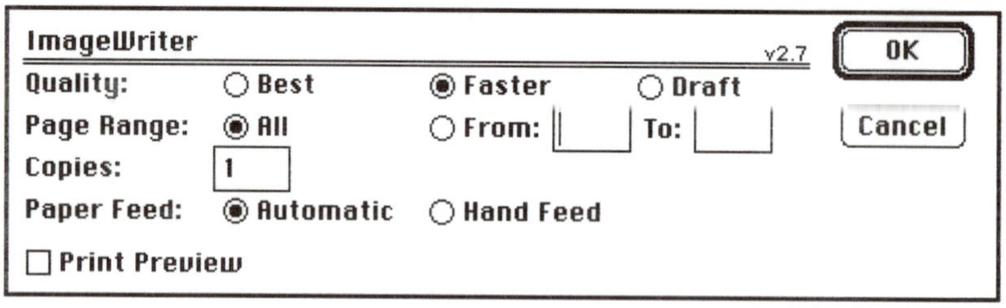

The Print dialog box

This dialog box allows you to select the Print Preview option which will display on the screen what will be printed on paper.

It is possible to print three different views of a spreadsheet:

a) <u>All cells through the last cell containing data.</u> This is done by executing the Print command from the File menu (or pressing ⌘P) without selecting any cells. If a spreadsheet is too wide to print on a single standard sheet of paper it will be printed on consecutive sheets starting from the leftmost columns and proceeding to the right. It is then possible to tape the separate sheets together to form a print-out of the complete spreadsheet.

b) Only cells which currently appear on the screen. This is done by selecting the Print Window command from the File menu.

c) Only selected cells. Cells are selected by dragging the mouse and then the Print command executed. Only the highlighted cells in the selected area are printed.

A number of changes can be made to the way in which a spreadsheet is printed by using the Page Setup command from the File menu:

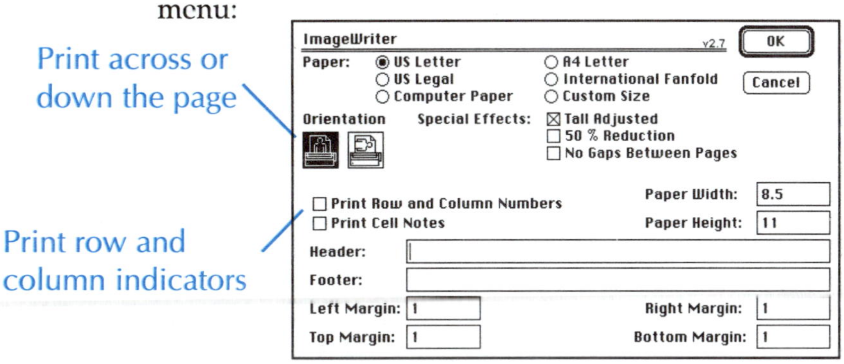

The Page Setup dialog box has several useful options for spreadsheets

If a spreadsheet is too wide to fit on a single sheet of paper it is possible to print it running down the length of the paper rather than across. This is done by selecting the right-hand option under Orientation. It is also possible to decrease the margins so that more of the spreadsheet will be printed.

Row and column numbers can be printed by selecting the Print Row and Column Numbers option from the Page setup dialog box. Headers and footers can be added by entering text into the appropriate boxes.

Practice 7

In this Practice you will print the GRADES spreadsheet in a number of different ways. Load GRADES if it is not already and make sure the printer is turned on and ready to print.

1) PRINT THE COMPLETE SPREADSHEET

a. Click on cell A1 to remove any highlight that may exists from the previous Practice.
b. Select the Print command from the File menu. When the Print dialog box is displayed click on OK. The complete Grades spreadsheet is printed. Note that two sheets of paper are needed to print the complete spreadsheet.

2) PRINT ONLY THE CELLS ON THE SCREEN

a. Make sure that cell A1 is displayed.
b. Select the Print Window command from the File menu. Only those cells which appear on the screen are printed including a part of column F.

3) PREVIEW AND PRINT CELLS FROM COLUMNS D AND E

a. Select cell D1 and drag the mouse so that cells D1 through E9 are highlighted as a block.
b. Press ⌘P to execute the Print command.
c. Click on the Print Preview option and then on OK. Note that only the selected cells are displayed on the Preview screen.
d. Click on the `Print` button to print the selected cells.

4) PRINT THE COMPLETE SPREADSHEET RUNNING DOWN THE PAPER

a. Click on any cell to remove the highlight.
b. Select the Page Setup command from the File menu.
c. Click on the right-hand Orientation option (shows page being printed down the page) and then on OK.
d. Press ⌘P to execute the Print command.
e. Click on Print Preview to remove the preview and then on OK. The complete spreadsheet is printed running down the page.

5) PRINT THE COMPLETE SPREADSHEET WITH ROW AND COLUMN NUMBERS AND A HEADER

a. Select the Page Setup command from the File menu.
b. Click on the Print Row and Column Numbers option.
c. Type "Dr. Sulfuric's Grades" on the keyboard. Note the text appears in the Header box. Click on OK.
d. Press⌘P to execute the Print command and click on OK. The spreadsheet is printed running down the page with the row and column numbers displayed along with the title.

6) CLOSE GRADES AND QUIT

a. Press ⌘S to save the spreadsheet on disk.
b. Press ⌘Q to quit Works.

Chapter Summary

This chapter covered the basics of planning and creating a computerized spreadsheet. A spreadsheet is simply rows and columns of data with rows running horizontally and columns vertically. The primary advantage of a computerized spreadsheet is that it has the ability to perform calculations on the data it stores with the calculations automatically changing to reflect any changes in the data.

In a Works spreadsheet the rows are numbered on the left-hand side and the columns identified by letters which run along the top of the spreadsheet. Where a row and column intersect is called a cell. A single cell is identified by a column letter and row number. For example, C4 names the cell located in column C at row 4.

Spreadsheet cells can store three types of data; labels, values, and dates. Labels can be words or characters and cannot be used in calculations. Values are numeric and can be used in calculations. Dates are calendar dates and can be used in certain types of calculations.

A new spreadsheet is created on the computer by double-clicking on the Spreadsheet icon in the Open File dialog box. Data is entered into the spreadsheet by moving the mouse pointer to a cell, clicking, typing the data and clicking on the Check box. The cell indicator at the top of the screen shows the current location of the cell cursor, and the Entry bar displays the contents of the cell. A series of cells may be selected by dragging the mouse pointer across them. A spreadsheet is saved on disk by pressing ⌘S.

Works automatically left justifies labels and right justifies values. To change the format of either a single cell or a series of cells, the cells are selected and then the Set Cell Attributes command executed from the Format menu. Dates are right justified and may be formatted to short (`2/5/91`), medium (`Feb 5, 1991`) or long formats (`February 5, 1991`).

Formulas are mathematical statements used to calculate values which can be stored in cells. The statement `=B3 * C4` is a formula which calculates the product of the value stored in cell B3 times the value in cell C4. All formulas must begin with an equal (=) sign.

The computer uses an order of operations in evaluating a formula. First it performs exponentiation, second multiplication and division, and third addition and subtraction. Operations of the same order are performed from left to right. The order of operations may be changed by using parentheses. For example:

```
3 + 5 * 8 + 7             = 50
(3 + 5) * (8 + 7)         = 120
```

Functions are pre-defined formulas that are used by the computer to perform common calculations. The statement `=SUM(B3:B8)` is a function. B3:B8 is called a range which may define either a portion of a row or column. This chapter covered the following functions:

Sum: `=SUM(B3:B8)`

sums the values in the column of cells B3, B4, B5, B6, B7 and B8.

`=SUM(A5:E5)`

sums the values in the row of cells A5, B5, C5, D5 and E5.

Average: `=Average(C3:C8)`

averages the values in the column of cells C3, C4, C5, C6, C7 and C8.

`=Average(B7:F7)`

averages the values in the row of cells B7, C7, D7, E7 and F7.

A single cell or range of cells may be formatted to display values to a specified number of decimal places by using the Set Cell Attributes command from the Format menu.

It is important to carefully plan a spreadsheet before using the computer. This is best done by first deciding what new information the spreadsheet will produce, what data it will store, how it can be produced without a computer, and what it should look like when displayed on the computer.

It is possible to print three different views of a spreadsheet: all cells through the last cell containing data by pressing ⌘P, only cells which appear on the screen by selecting the Print Window command, and only selected cells by dragging the mouse to select the cells and then pressing ⌘P.

Vocabulary

Cell - Where a row and column intersect. A cell is identified by its column letter and row number, for example G8.
Cell indicator - Shows the current location of the cell cursor at the top of the screen.
Check box - Indicator on Entry Bar clicked when data entered is correct. Also called "accept" box.
Column - Vertical line of data identified by a letter.
Entry Bar - Line at the top of the screen where data entered from the keyboard is displayed before it is entered into a cell.
Formatting - Determines how the data stored in a cell will be displayed.
Formulas - Mathematical statements used to calculate values which are stored in cells. The statement `=C5+D7+E8` is a formula.
Functions - Used in formulas to perform common calculations. `=SUM(B5:B10)` is a function.
Label - Words or characters stored in a cell that cannot be used in calculations.
Range - Partial row or column of adjacent cells.
Row - Horizontal line of data identified by a number.
Scroll - Moving the screen "window" to view different parts of a spreadsheet.
Spreadsheet - Rows and columns of data on which calculations can be performed.
Values - Numeric data that can be stored in cells and used in calculations.
X box - Indicator on Entry Bar clicked when data entered is incorrect. Also called the "reject" or "cancel" box.

Reviews

Sections 7.1-7.5

1. What is the primary advantage of using a computerized spreadsheet rather than a spreadsheet produced using paper and pencil?

2. a) What is a cell in a spreadsheet?
   b) What is the difference between a row and a column?
   c) What is the cell indicator?

3. a) What is the difference between a label and a value entry?
   b) What is a date entry?

4. What is the purpose of each of the following parts of the spreadsheet screen:

   a) Entry bar
   b) Cancel box
   c) Menu bar

5. a) What is the maximum number of cells permitted by a Works spreadsheet?
   b) How many value cells does the GRADES spreadsheet produced in Practice 2 contain?

6. Outline the steps required to enter the value 30.9 in cell D20.

7. a) What is the difference between a cell name and the data stored in a cell? Give an example.
   b) Can the name of a cell be changed? If so, how?
   c) Can the data stored in a cell be changed? If so, how?

8. Draw a diagram that shows all of the cells in the first three columns and five rows of a spreadsheet. Show the name of each cell and store the value 27 in cell B3.

9. a) What is the maximum number of digits Works will display in a cell?
   b) How is a value displayed if its number of digits exceeds this number?

10. a) How can spreadsheet columns that are not currently displayed be moved on to the screen?
    b) What is this action called?

11. How many of each of the following types of entries are stored in the GRADES spreadsheet shown in Practice 2?

    a) labels
    b) values
    c) dates

12. If a mistake is noticed after data has been entering into a cell, in what two ways may it be corrected?

13. What determines the maximum displayed length of a label?

14. How do you transfer a copy of a spreadsheet from the computer's memory to disk?

Sections 7.6-7.9

15. List the steps required to:

    a) right justify a row of column headers.
    b) format a column of dates to Date Long (October 28, 1991).

16. a) What is meant by order of operations?
    b) Which operation is performed first?
    c) Which operation is performed last?
    d) How may the order of operations be changed?

17. If a formula contains 3 operations all of the same order which will be performed first?

18. If `10/28/91` is entered into an unformatted cell, Works displays the value 32077. How must the cell be formatted or the entry changed to:

    a) display the result of the division?
    b) display the date 10/28/91?
    c) display the date Oct 28, 1991?

19. Write a formula which calculates each of the following:

    a) the product of the values stored in cells A1, B3 and C4.
    b) the sum of the values stored in cells A3, A4, A5, A6, A7, and A8.
    c) the average of the values stored in cells B5, B6 and B7.
    d) the average of the values stored in cells A1, B3 and C4.

20. What value would be calculated by Works for each of the following formulas?

    a) `=2 + 7 * 5 + 4`
    b) `=(2 + 7) * (5 + 4)`
    c) `=5 + 10 / 5`
    d) `=(5 + 10) / 5`
    e) `=2^3 + 4`
    f) `=15 + (12 / 4)`

21. What would be displayed by Works for each of the following if cell C15 stores the value 16 and cell D8 the value 4?

    a) `=C15 * D8`
    b) `=C15 + 5 + D8`
    c) `=C15 * 5 + D8`
    d) `=C15 * (5 + D8)`
    e) `=C15 / D8`
    f) `=C15 / (D8 - 4)`
    g) `=C15 + 4 / D8`
    h) `=C15 + (4 / D8)`
    i) `C15 + (4 / D8)`

22. If a mistake has been made in a formula what are two ways it may be corrected?

23. How can the value stored in a cell be erased?

24. What is the difference between a formula and a function?

25. a) What is meant by a range of cells?
    b) Give an example of a range of cells contained in a row.
    c) Give an example of a range of cells contained in a column.

26. Write formulas using functions that will calculate each of the following:

    a) the sum of the values stored in cells B4, B5, B6 and B7.
    b) the sum of the values stored in cells B4, C4, D4, and E4.
    c) the average of the values stored in the column of cells D7 to D35.
    d) the average of the values stored in the row of cells F3 to J3.

Sections 7.10-7.12

27. Write a formula which calculates the average of the values stored in cells B3, B4, B5, C5, D5 and E5.

28. Answer the four questions presented in Section 7.10 to plan a spreadsheet that will list the name of each member of your class, his or her height in inches, and calculate the average height of your classmates. Produce a sketch of the spreadsheet on paper.

29. What steps are required to format a range of cells to display numbers to 1 decimal place?

30. a) What happens when you print a spreadsheet that is too large to fit on a single piece of paper?
    b) How can you print only selected cells in a spreadsheet?

31. Explain what must be done to print only the grades for Test 1 in the GRADES spreadsheet?

Exercises

1. The Ivy University Sports Car Club is testing different sports cars and storing the results in a spreadsheet.

   a) Create a new spreadsheet and enter the following data exactly as shown below. Save the spreadsheet naming it TRACK TEST.

Track Test (SS)

	A	B	C	D	E	F	G
1			Track Test				
2							
3	Car	Distance	Time				
4		(feet)	(seconds)				
5	Porsche	123.45	6.78				
6	Ferrari	145.67	7.77				
7	Lotus	123.66	5.99				
8	Aston-M.	148.99	7.89				
9	Corvette	156.34	6.68				
10	Jaguar	123.87	5.34				
11	Supra	136.98	7.11				
12							
13							
14							
15							
16							
17							

   b) In column D add the title Velocity and calculate the velocity for each trial by dividing the distance by the time. Make sure that any change made to a distance or time will automatically change the corresponding velocity.

   c) In cell D13 have the spreadsheet calculate the average velocity for the trials. Be sure to include a label for the average.

   d) Edit the formulas for velocity and average velocity to display their values to 2 decimal places. Save the modified spreadsheet on disk and print a copy.

2. The term spreadsheet was originated by accountants who spread out large sheets of paper containing financial figures. Computerized spreadsheets are useful in keeping track of personal finances as well.

   a) Create a spreadsheet that records your expenses for a week. Add any necessary rows for your expenses. Save the spreadsheet on disk naming it EXPENSES. It should be similar to:

Expenses (SS)

	A	B	C	D	E
1			Expenses		
2					
3	Expense	Week 1			
4					
5	Lunch	4.52			
6	Snacks	3.75			
7	Movies	8.35			
8	Clothes	12.35			
9	Supplies	9.75			
10					
11					
12					
13					

b) Add a row labeled TOTAL to the bottom of column B that calculates the total expenses for the week.

c) Format the row to display the totals to 2 decimal places.

d) Add columns C, D and E for your expenses in weeks 2, 3 and 4. Be sure to include proper titles and the total for each column.

e) Add a column F which displays the average cost per week of each item and then the total expenses for an average week.

f) Format column F to display the averages to 2 decimal places. Save the modified spreadsheet on disk and print a copy.

When complete your spreadsheet should be similar to:

Expenses (SS)

	A	B	C	D	E	F	G
1			Expenses				
2							
3	Expense	Week 1	Week 2	Week 3	Week 4	Average	
4							
5	Lunch	4.52	2.75	3.45	6.78	4.38	
6	Snacks	3.75	6.89	2.47	4.55	4.42	
7	Movies	8.35	0	7.55	3.45	4.84	
8	Clothes	12.35	9.99	78.65	0	25.25	
9	Supplies	9.75	0.56	2.34	2.13	3.70	
10							
11	TOTAL:	38.72	20.19	94.46	16.91	42.57	
12							
13							
14							
15							
16							
17							

3. Create a spreadsheet that displays a multiplication table. When a number is entered into cell C3 it is then shown multiplied by 1 through 12. Save the spreadsheet naming it MULTIPLY.

Your spreadsheet should be similar to the following. Make sure to format the columns so that they are properly justified:

Multiply (SS)

	A	B	C	D	E	F	G
1			Multiplication Table				
2							
3	Enter a number:		8				
4							
5	1	*	8	=	8		
6	2	*	8	=	16		
7	3	*	8	=	24		
8	4	*	8	=	32		
9	5	*	8	=	40		
10	6	*	8	=	48		
11	7	*	8	=	56		
12	8	*	8	=	64		
13	9	*	8	=	72		
14	10	*	8	=	80		
15	11	*	8	=	88		
16	12	*	8	=	96		
17							

4. Mr. Horatio von Money, Ivy University's major benefactor, keeps track of his stock portfolio in a spreadsheet named PORTFOLIO. Open this spreadsheet from your data disk. Note that the spreadsheet displays the price of each stock and the number of shares Mr. von Money owns.

    a) You are to assist Mr. von Money by adding a column to his spreadsheet that calculates the value of each stock he owns. The value is calculated by multiplying the price of the stock by the number of shares he owns.

    b) Format column D to display the value to 2 decimal places.

    c) Mr. von Money has decided that he will donate 25% of his portfolio to Ivy University. Total the value of all of his stocks and then display the amount of the donation. Be sure to label both figures.

    d) Format the spreadsheet to show the donation to 2 decimal places. Save the modified spreadsheet on disk and print a copy.

5. Varsity baseball coach Slugger Ryan needs a spreadsheet to store the statistics on each of his players. Below are listed the names, times at bat, and number of hits for the players:

Player	**At bats**	**Hits**
Attis	10	3
Baker	11	3
Connelly	9	5
Doucette	12	4
Enders	15	2
Fritz	10	6
Gold	14	4
Hernandez	12	6
Li	11	5

    a) Enter the above statistics into a new spreadsheet. Be sure to include proper titles. Save the spreadsheet naming it BASEBALL.

    b) Add a column to BASEBALL that calculates and displays each player's batting average to 3 decimal places. Batting averages are calculated by dividing the number of hits by the number of times at bat.

    c) Coach Ryan would like to know the overall team batting average. Use the average function to produce the calculation for him. Be sure to include formatting and a proper label. Save the modified spreadsheet on disk and print a copy.

6. Spreadsheets can be used to keep track of any type of numerical data. You are to produce a spreadsheet to help determine your caloric intake for a week.

    a) Create a spreadsheet which keeps a record of the calories you consume each day for a week. Your spreadsheet should be similar to the following. Save the spreadsheet naming it DIET.

Diet (SS)

	A	B	C	D	E	F	G
1				Calories			
2							
3	Meal	Mon	Tues	Wed	Thurs	Fri	
4							
5	Breakfast	560	640	680	780	890	
6	Lunch	789	450	450	1100	670	
7	Dinner	1250	1340	980	790	450	
8	Snacks	560	200	460	450	900	
9							
10							
11							
12							
13							
14							
15							
16							
17							

    b) Have the spreadsheet calculate the total number of calories consumed each day, the total for the week, and the average number of calories consumed per day. Be sure to include formatting and appropriate labels.

    c) It has been determined that aerobic exercise burns 360 calories per hour. Have the spreadsheet calculate the number of hours for a workout to burn off 50% of the total calories consumed for each day. Include an appropriate label. Save the modified spreadsheet on disk and print a copy.

7. Spreadsheets can be helpful in personal time management.

    a) Create a spreadsheet which stores the number of hours you spend each day of the week at each of the following activities:

        school classes
        athletics
        extra-curricular groups and clubs
        studying and doing homework
        eating
        sleeping
        watching television or listening to music
        talking on the phone
        doing chores at home
        working at a part-time job
        any other activities

    Save the spreadsheet on disk naming it ACTIVITY.

    b) For each activity have the spreadsheet calculate the total hours spent each week on the activity. Also calculate the average number of hours spent per day on each activity for the week.

c) Most people's schedules do not exactly account for all 24 hours in a day. Add a row which calculates and displays the amount of unaccounted time in your schedule for each day. Save the modified spreadsheet on disk and print a copy.

Chapter 8

Manipulating Data with the Spreadsheet

Edit - Fill Right ⌘R

Edit - Fill Down ⌘D

Options - Show Formulas

Edit - Absolute Cell Reference ⌘A

Select - Find Cell ⌘F

Select - Go To Cell ⌘G

Edit - Cut ⌘X

Chart - New Series Chart

Options - Freeze Titles Horizontal

Objectives

After completing this chapter you will be able to:

1. Plan a large spreadsheet including its layout.
2. Copy labels, values and formulas.
3. Search for a particular cell or label.
4. Use the Max and Min functions.
5. Use the If function to make decisions.
6. Insert and delete rows and columns.
7. Use a spreadsheet to answer "What if?" questions.
8. Create charts and graphs of spreadsheet data.

This chapter discusses how to plan a large spreadsheet and the techniques used to produce one on the computer. You will be taught how to format and manipulate data so that your spreadsheets are easy to read and use. Commands will be introduced which allow formulas to be copied from one set of cells to other cells. You will learn how to ask and answer "What if?" questions so that predictions can be made based upon the data stored in a spreadsheet. The chapter ends by demonstrating how to produce graphs and charts of the data stored in a spreadsheet. A special section on two advanced uses of the spreadsheet, lookup tables and loan amortization, is also included.

8.1 Planning a Large Spreadsheet

The spreadsheets produced in Chapter 7 required little planning because they were small and easy to understand. In this chapter planning will be more important as we develop large spreadsheets which can be continually modified and expanded.

As an example of the need for planning, we will produce a spreadsheet for Ivy University's accounting department to assist it in calculating its payroll. To do this we will follow the four steps for planning a spreadsheet presented in Chapter 7.

The first step in developing such a plan is to determine what new data the spreadsheet is to generate. This will be each employee's "gross pay" for the week. Gross pay is the pay earned before any deductions (such as taxes) are made.

The second step is to decide what data to include in the spreadsheet. This is:

1. Employee name
2. Payrate per hour
3. Hours worked per day for each of 5 days

The third step is to decide what calculations must be performed to produce the desired new data. Ivy's employees work by the hour for an hourly payrate which differs from employee to employee. Multiplying the total number of hours worked for the week by the payrate produces the gross pay.

The fourth step is to determine how the spreadsheet is to appear on the computer screen - its "layout." This is an important step. If we choose a proper layout the spreadsheet will not only be easy to use, but also easy to expand to perform additional tasks.

We begin planning the layout by determining what type of data is to be placed in each column. The placement of columns is important because we want related data grouped together in a form that is easy to read. Next we will decide how wide each column should be to display its longest entry. Because the 12 character default width may be either too small or too large, Works allows us to change column widths.

Before using the computer a sketch of the spreadsheet showing each column heading, the width of the column, and the type of data it will store should be drawn using paper and pencil. Here is a sketch of our plan for Ivy's payroll spreadsheet:

Name	Rate	Mon	Tue	Wed	Thu	Fri	Gross Pay
15 wide	9	7	7	7	7	7	12
(label)	(dollars)		(1 decimal place)				(dollars)

Note that each column width is shown along with the type of data it will store. Later we will add columns to the spreadsheet that contain other calculations.

8.2 Changing Column Widths

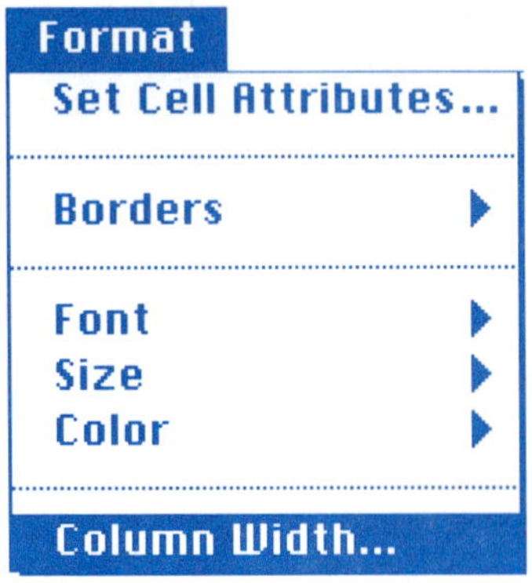

To change a spreadsheet layout the Format menu may be used. As we saw in Chapter 7 it allows single entries (one cell), rows, columns or blocks of cells to be formatted.

Often the default column width of 12 characters is insufficient to hold a column's data, requiring the width to be increased. This is done by selecting a cell in the desired column and then executing the Column Width command from the Format menu which displays the following dialog box:

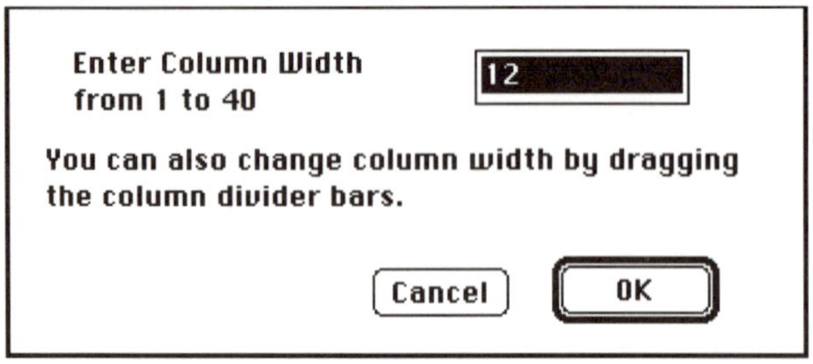

The Width dialog box is used to change the width of a column

Note the default width of 12 characters. This number can be changed to either increase or decrease a column's width from 1 to 40 characters. It is important to realize that the width of single cells cannot be changed, only whole columns.

The width of a column can also be changed by dragging its column divider bar. To do this the pointer is placed on the bar separating the column letters at the top of the screen and the mouse dragged to either increase or decrease the column width.

8.3 Formatting Cells For Dollar Amounts

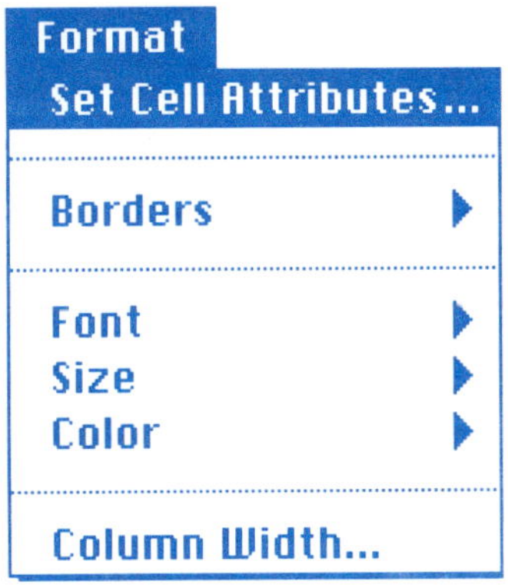

The Set Cell Attributes command from the Format menu allows cells to be formatted for dollar values by selecting Dollar. When this is done dollar signs are displayed in front of the values. An option is given by the Decimals box as to how many decimal places are to be displayed; usually the default value of 2 is accepted. To have commas displayed in the dollar amounts the Commas option must also be selected:

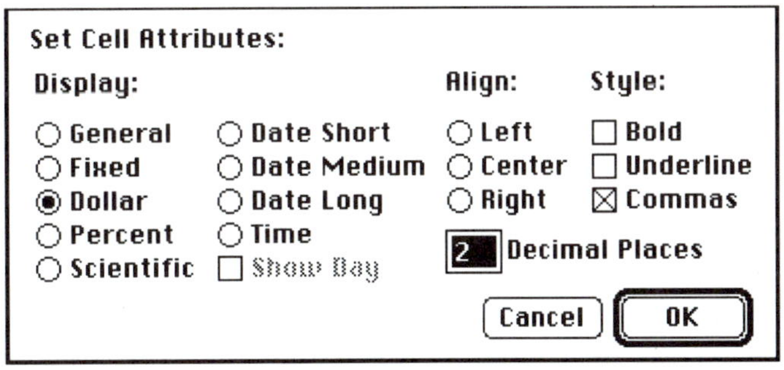

A cell with these attributes will displays dollar amounts with commas

It is important to realize that formatting options only affect the way that the data in a spreadsheet is displayed, and have no effect on the actual contents of the cells. For example, giving a Dollar format to a cell which stores the value 5 will display $5.00 in that cell. However, the contents of the cell can be seen to be only a 5 by checking the Entry bar. If the cell is not wide enough to store the value and its formatting, Works displays pound signs (**#####**) in the cell. The width of the column containing that cell should then be expanded to accomodate the value.

The following spreadsheet contains examples of each of the options discussed above as well as the Fixed format and Right-justification options discussed in Chapter 7:

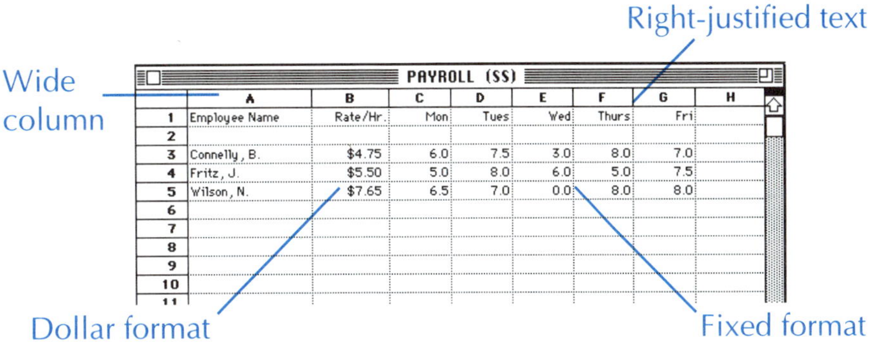

This spreadsheet shows several of the posible formatting options

Practice 1

In this Practice you will create a new spreadsheet named PAYROLL which stores the names, hourly wages and hours worked each day for three of Ivy University's employees. The spreadsheet will look like the one shown in Section 8.3 above.

1) START WORKS

2) CREATE A NEW SPREADSHEET

Select the Spreadsheet icon by double-clicking on it.

3) FORMAT COLUMN A TO 15 CHARACTERS WIDE AND COLUMN B TO 9 CHARACTERS WIDE

a. Select cell A1.
b. Select the Column Width command from the Format menu. The Width dialog box displays the default value of 12.
c. Type the new width, `15`, and click `OK`.
d. Select cell B1.
e. Repeat steps (b) and (c) to set column B's width to 9 characters.

4) FORMAT COLUMNS C THROUGH G TO 7 CHARACTERS WIDE BY DRAGGING

a. Place the pointer on the line separating the column letters C and D. A double arrow will appear.
b. Slowly drag the line to the left 5 spaces. The dotted line will flash as each space is passed. Column C is now 7 characters wide.
c. Repeat steps (a) and (b) to reduce the widths of columns D through G.

5) FORMAT CELLS B3 TO B5 TO DISPLAY DOLLAR AMOUNTS WITH 2 DECIMAL PLACES

a. Select cell B3.
b. Drag the mouse to cell B5. Cells B3, B4 and B5 are highlighted.
c. Select the Set Cell Attributes command from the Format menu.
d. Select Dollar and Commas and then click on `OK`. The default value of 2 Decimal places is left unchanged.

6) FORMAT BLOCK CONTAINING THE VALUES PORTION OF COLUMNS C THROUGH G TO DISPLAY 1 DECIMAL PLACE

a. Select cell C3.
b. Drag the mouse to cell G5. A block of cells is highlighted.
c. Select the Set Cell Attributes command from the Format menu.
d. Select Fixed and type a `1` for decimals and click on `OK`. All five daily hours columns are now formatted to display 1 decimal place.

7) RIGHT JUSTIFY THE COLUMN HEADINGS

The column headings in your spreadsheet should be right-justified to line up with the numbers in the columns.

a. Select cell B1.
b. Drag the mouse to cell G1. Cells B1 to G1 are highlighted.
c. Select the Set Cell Attributes command from the Format menu.
d. Select Right and click on `OK`. Cells B through G are now right-justified.

8) ENTER DATA

Enter all of the data shown in the spreadsheet in Section 8.3, including names and column headings.

9) SAVE PAYROLL ON DISK

When all of the data has been entered and formatted properly, press ⌘S. Type the file name `PAYROLL` and click on the `Save` button. The spreadsheet is now saved on disk.

8.4 Entering Formulas

We next calculate the Gross Pay column for PAYROLL. This calculation is performed by multiplying the payrate by the total number of hours worked for the week. To calculate B. Connelly's gross pay we will use the formula:

```
=B3 * Sum(C3:G3)
```

Remember, all formulas must begin with an equal sign (=).

Practice 2

In this Practice you will add a Gross Pay column to PAYROLL and calculate B. Connelly's gross pay for the week. Start Works and open the PAYROLL spreadsheet if you have not already done so.

1) ENTER THE GROSS PAY HEADING AND RIGHT JUSTIFY IT

a. Select cell H1 and enter the label: `Gross Pay`
b. With cell H1 still selected execute the Set Cell Attributes command from the Format menu and select Right. Click on `OK`.

2) FORMAT CELLS H3, H4 AND H5 TO DISPLAY DOLLARS

a. Select cell H3.
b. Drag the mouse to cell H5.
c. Select the Set Cell Attributes command from the Format menu and select Dollar and Commas. Click on `OK`.

3) ENTER GROSS PAY FORMULA IN CELL H3

a. Select cell H3.
b. Type: `=B3 *`
c. Select the Paste Function command from the Edit menu.
d. Select Sum() from the menu and click on `OK`.
e. Select cell C3 and drag the mouse the cell G3. Click on the Check box to enter the formula =B3 * Sum(C3:G3). The gross pay is calculated and displayed in cell C3.

4) SAVE PAYROLL ON DISK

Press ⌘S to save the latest version of PAYROLL on disk.

<u>Check</u> - Your spreadsheet should be similar to the one shown on the next page:

PAYROLL (SS)

	B	C	D	E	F	G	H	I
1	Rate/Hr.	Mon	Tues	Wed	Thurs	Fri	Gross Pay	
2								
3	$4.75	6.0	7.5	3.0	8.0	7.0	$149.63	
4	$5.50	5.0	8.0	6.0	5.0	7.5		
5	$7.65	6.5	7.0	0.0	8.0	8.0		
6								
7								
8								
9								
10								
11								

8.5 The Fill Right and Fill Down Commands

Draw On	⌘J
Move...	
Insert	⌘I
Paste Function...	
Absolute Cell Ref	⌘A
Fill Right	⌘R
Fill Down	⌘D
Open Cell Note...	

Often the same label, value or formula will be stored in a number of different cells. We can of course type it over and over again, but Works makes such copying easy with the Fill Right and Fill Down commands from the Edit menu. To copy the contents of a single cell the cell is selected and the mouse dragged to select the cells into which copies are to be made. If the cells are in a row the Fill Right command is issued, if in a column the Fill Down command issued.

The Fill Right and Fill Down commands are useful in placing a line of dashes across or down a spreadsheet to separate rows or columns. For example, to place dashes across a spreadsheet dashes are typed in the left-most cell in the row, the cells in the row selected by dragging, and the Fill Right command executed. The Command key shortcut for Fill Right is ⌘R and for Fill Down is ⌘D.

Practice 3

In this Practice you will place a line of dashes across row 2 of the PAYROLL spreadsheet using the Fill Right command. Start Works and open the PAYROLL spreadsheet if you have not already done so.

1) ENTER DASHES INTO CELL A2

a. Select cell A2.
b. Type 15 dashes (-) and click on the Check box.

2) USE FILL RIGHT TO COPY THE DASHES

a. With cell A2 still selected drag the mouse to cell H2.
b. Select the Fill Right command from the Edit menu. A row of dashes is copied between cells A2 and H2.

3) SAVE PAYROLL ON DISK

Press ⌘S to save this latest version of PAYROLL on disk.

Check - The spreadsheet should contain a line of dashes in row 2:

	A	B	C	D	E	F	G	H
1	Employee Name	Rate/Hr.	Mon	Tues	Wed	Thurs	Fri	Gross
2	---------------	----------	----------	----------	----------	----------	----------	----------
3	Connelly, B.	$4.75	6.0	7.5	3.0	8.0	7.0	$149
4	Fritz, J.	$5.50	5.0	8.0	6.0	5.0	7.5	
5	Wilson, N.	$7.65	6.5	7.0	0.0	8.0	8.0	
6								

8.6 Copying and Displaying Formulas

Another useful application of the Fill Down and Fill Right commands is in copying formulas. In our PAYROLL spreadsheet the formula to calculate B. Connelly's gross pay, `=B3 * Sum(C3:G3)`, is stored in cell H3. To calculate J. Fritz's and N. Wilson's gross pay the formula will have to be entered into rows 4 and 5 with the cell names adjusted for the new row numbers. For example, because J. Fritz's data is stored in row 4, the gross pay formula must be changed to refer to the values stored in row 4 instead of row 3: `=B4 * Sum(C4:G4)`

Works includes a most useful way of copying a formula with the computer automatically changing the cell references to apply to the new row or column. This is called "relative" copying. To produce relative copies in a column of cells the formula is entered into a cell and the cells into which relative copies are to be made selected by dragging. When the Fill Down command is executed, formulas are copied into the cells with their cell references automatically changed to reflect their location in the spreadsheet. The Fill Right command can be used to make relative copies in a row.

If we copy the formula that calculates B. Connelly's wage

```
=B3 * Sum(C3:G3)
```

from cell H3 into cells H4 and H5, the copied formula in H4 will automatically be changed to

```
=B4 * Sum(C4:G4)
```

and in H5 to:

```
=B5 * Sum(C5:G5)
```

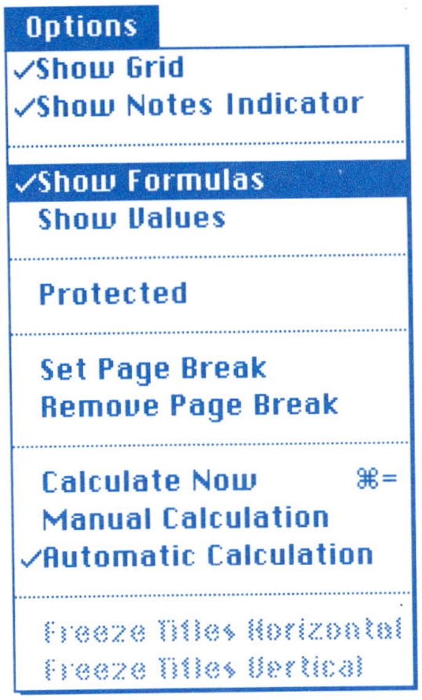

Although this technique of copying formulas is useful for making copies into only two cells, think how much time it would save if the spreadsheet contained a large number of employees. Another important advantage of this approach is that it avoids the possible errors that could be made if you were to type each formula separately, changing the cell names yourself each time.

When a spreadsheet becomes large it is helpful to view the many formulas it may contain at their cell locations. This can be accomplished by executing the Show Formulas command from the Options menu. When this is done Works displays the formula stored in each cell, rather than its value. To return to the regular screen the Show Values command is selected. If the Print command is executed when the Show Formulas command is executed the formulas contained in a spreadsheet will be printed.

8.7 Copying and Absolute References

In some situations we will want to copy formulas in which certain cell references do not change. For example, if we wanted to give all employees the same raise and wanted to enter the raise into cell A10 the formula in cell H3 would become:

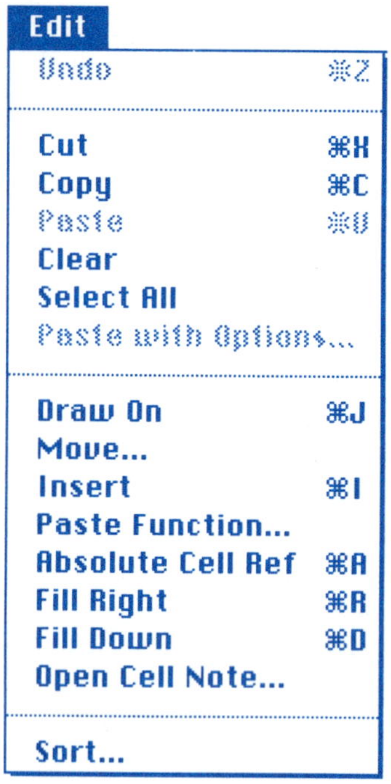


```
=B3 * Sum(C3:G3) + A10
```

If we make relative copies of this formula into cells H4 and H5, A10 would automatically become A11 and A12. To avoid this problem Works allows cell references to be kept constant by executing the Absolute Cell Ref command from the Edit menu. First, the cell to be copied is selected and its formula displayed on the Entry bar. Next the pointer is positioned immediately to the right of the cell reference which is to be kept constant and the Absolute Cell Ref command executed, ⌘A. Dollar signs will appear in front of both the column letter and row number (`$A$10`) and the new formula would be:

```
=B3 * Sum(C3:G3) + $A$10
```

When relative copies are now made, the cell reference A10 will not change. For example, if this formula were copied into row 4, it would become:

```
=B4 * Sum(C4:G4) + $A$10
```

When entering absolute references, it is not necessary to use the Absolute Cell Ref command. If you know that the cell reference is absolute, the dollar signs ($) may be entered by typing them on the keyboard when first creating the formula.

Practice 4

In this Practice you will store relative copies of the gross pay formula in cell H3 in cells H4 and H5. Start Works and open PAYROLL if you have not done so already.

1) COPY THE FORMULAS USING FILL DOWN

a. Select cell H3.
b. Drag the mouse to cell H5, highlighting cells H3, H4 and H5.
c. Select the Fill Down command from the Edit menu. Relative copies of the formula in cell H3 are now stored in cells H4 and H5 with their cell references changed. The gross pay is calculated for the other two employees.

2) VIEW THE FORMULAS ON SCREEN

Select the Show Formulas command from the Options menu. The formulas stored in each cell are now displayed. If the width of a cell is insufficient to display a formula the formula will appear truncated. The width of the column containing the cell can then be increased to display the complete formula.

3) RETURN TO THE REGULAR DISPLAY

Select the Show Values command from the Options menu. The formulas are replaced on screen by the values they calculate.

<u>Check</u> - The gross pay for J. Fritz and N. Wilson is shown in cells H4 and H5:

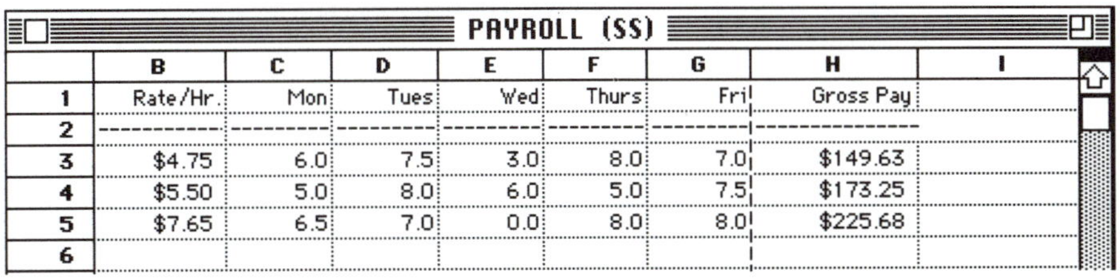

PAYROLL (SS)

	B	C	D	E	F	G	H	I
1	Rate/Hr.	Mon	Tues	Wed	Thurs	Fri	Gross Pay	
2	----------	---------	---------	---------	---------	---------	--------------	
3	$4.75	6.0	7.5	3.0	8.0	7.0	$149.63	
4	$5.50	5.0	8.0	6.0	5.0	7.5	$173.25	
5	$7.65	6.5	7.0	0.0	8.0	8.0	$225.68	
6								

4) **SAVE AND CLOSE PAYROLL**

a. Press ⌘S to save the modified spreadsheet on disk.
b. Press ⌘W to close PAYROLL.

8.8 The Find Cell and Go To Cell Commands

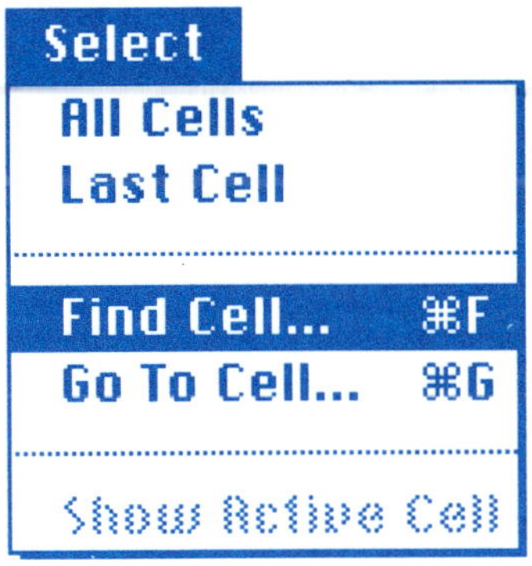

When working with a large spreadsheet it is sometimes cumbersome to locate the cell or cells that contain a particular value or label. To assist in such a search, Works contains the Find Cell command in the Select menu, ⌘F. When executed, the Find Cell command displays a dialog box which asks for the value or label to be searched for:

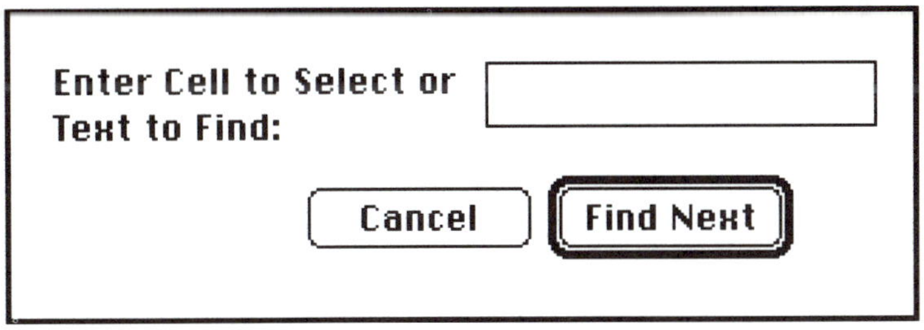

The Find Cell dialog box

When the search is executed the cell cursor jumps to the first occurrence of the label or value found after the currently selected cell. Works searches the cells across the spreadsheet by rows. Therefore, if the whole spreadsheet is to be searched for the first occurrence, cell A1 must be selected before the search is initiated. Executing the Find Cell command again finds the next occurrence of the same text, and so on until all occurrences have been found. A subsequent search would then produce the dialog box:

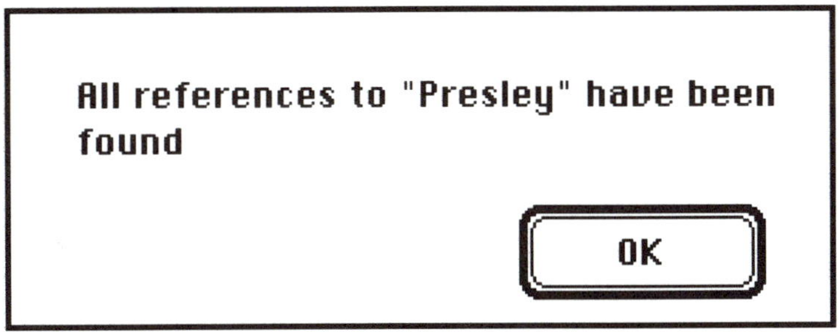

When all references have been found Works displays this box

If the label or value cannot be found anywhere in the spreadsheet Works displays the message:

If the search text is not found, Works displays this box

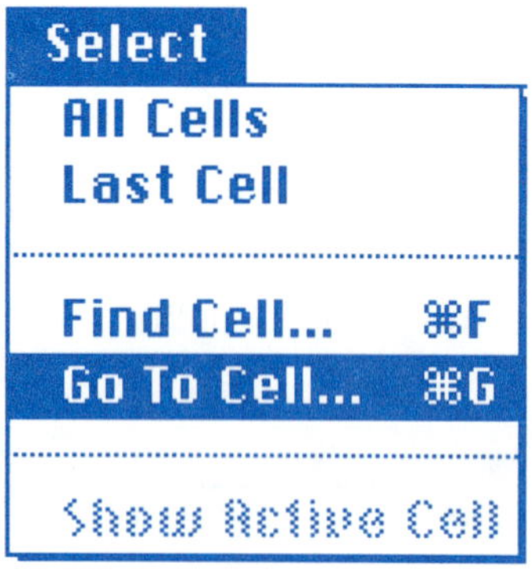

Searches are not case sensitive, which means that it does not matter if letters are typed in upper or lower case. Also, the search will stop if Works finds the text in any part of a value or label. That is, specifying a search text of "P" will find both "Presley" and "Roper".

To move the screen window so that a particular cell is displayed the Go To Cell command from the Select menu is used, ⌘G. When Go To Cell is executed the following dialog box is displayed:

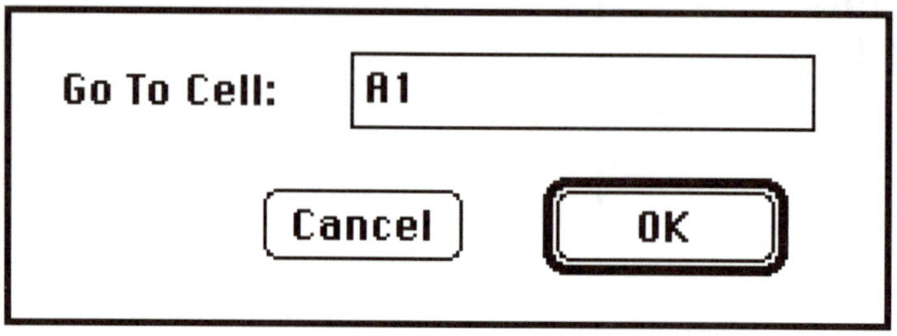

Entering a cell name in the Go To dialog box displays that cell

When a cell reference is entered the window moves only if the cell is not currently displayed otherwise nothing happens.

Practice 5

In this Practice you will search a large spreadsheet using the Go To Cell and Find Cell commands. A spreadsheet which calculates the payroll for 25 Ivy University employees will be used to demonstrate these commands.

1) OPEN THE IVY PAYROLL SPREADSHEET

From the Open File dialog box, select the spreadsheet named IVY PAYROLL from your data disk.

2) GO TO CELL H16

a. Select the Go To Cell command from the Select menu. A dialog box is displayed.

b. Type `H16` and click on `OK`. The screen window moves to include cell H16.

3) GO TO CELL A1

a. Press ⌘G to execute the Go To Cell command.
b. Type `A1` replacing the old value and click on `OK`. Cell A1 is displayed at the top of the window.

4) FIND THE TEXT "PRESLEY"

a. Select cell A1 to guarantee that the whole spreadsheet will be searched.
b. Select the Find Cell command from the Select menu. A dialog box is displayed.
c. Type `Presley` and click on the Find Next button. Cell A6 which contains the name Presley, B is selected.

5) FIND ALL OCCURRENCES OF THE LETTER P

a. Select cell A1.
b. Press ⌘F to execute the Find Cell command.
c. Type a `P` replacing the old value and click on the `Find Next` button. The cell containing the label "Gross Pay" which is the first cell after cell A1 to contain a P is selected.
d. Press ⌘F to execute the Find Cell command click on the Find Next button. The cell containing the label "Presley, B.", which is the next cell to contain a P is selected.
e. Repeat step (d). The search for P is repeated and the cell cursor moves to the label "Roper, M.", which is the next cell to contain a P. Note that it does not matter that the P is embedded in Roper or that it is in lower case.
f. Repeat step (d) until the message All references to "P" have been found is displayed. Click on `OK` to remove the message.
g. Select the Find Cell command from the Select menu.
h. Type `XYZ` and click on the `Find Next` button. Because that text does not appear in the spreadsheet the message "XYZ" not found is displayed. Click on `OK` to remove the message.

8.9 The Max and Min Functions

Works includes two functions which determine either the maximum or minimum value stored in a range of cells. These functions are useful to the Ivy University accounting department in determining the highest and lowest salaries earned by its employees. The Max function takes the form:

`=MAX(`<range of cells>`)`

For example,

`=MAX(C3:C10)`

displays the maximum value stored in the range of cells C3 to C10. The Min function takes the form:

`=Min(`<range of cells>`)`

For example,

`=Min(C3:F3)`

displays the minimum value stored in the range of cells C3 to F3.

8.10 Expanding a Spreadsheet

Data can be added to the right side of a spreadsheet by simply making entries into unused columns, but this should be done with care. If data is added without thought to the overall plan, the spreadsheet will quickly become a jumble of unrelated data.

To make the IVY PAYROLL spreadsheet more useful to the Ivy University accounting department we will modify it to calculate and deduct taxes and social security from each employee's gross pay. The taxes deducted will be 15% and the social security 6.5% of the gross pay. To display this data on the spreadsheet we add three columns titled Taxes, Soc. Sec., and Net Pay. Net pay is the actual pay an employee receives after deductions have been made, and is calculated by subtracting the taxes and social security from gross pay.

Practice 6

In this Practice you will add columns to IVY PAYROLL which calculate taxes, social security and net pay for each of the 25 Ivy University employees. The maximum and minimum net pay is also displayed. Start Works and open the IVY PAYROLL spreadsheet if you have not already done so.

1) ADD HEADINGS TO COLUMNS I, J AND K

a. Select cell I1 and enter the label: `Taxes`
b. Select cell J1 and enter the label: `Soc. Sec.`
c. Select cell K1 and enter the label: `Net Pay`

2) RIGHT-JUSTIFY THE HEADINGS

a. Select cell I1.
b. Drag the mouse to cell K1.
c. Execute the Set Cell Attributes command from the Format menu and select Right. Click on OK.

3) COPY THE LINE OF DASHES

a. Select cell H2.
b. Drag the mouse to cell K2.
c. Press ⌘R to execute the Fill Right command. The line of dashes now extends to column K.

4) FORMAT COLUMNS TO DISPLAY DOLLAR VALUES

a. Select cell I3.
b. Drag the mouse to cell K30. A highlighted block now runs from cell I3 to cell K30.
c. Select the Set Cell Attributes command from the Format menu.
d. Select Dollar and Commas and click on OK. Now all cells from I3 to K30 are formatted for dollar amounts of 2 decimal places.

5) ENTER FORMULAS FOR TAXES COLUMN

a. Select cell I3.

b. Enter the formula

`=H3 * .15`

to calculate the taxes by taking 15% of the gross pay.

6) ENTER FORMULAS FOR SOCIAL SECURITY COLUMN

a. Select cell J3.
b. Enter the formula

`=H3 * .065`

to calculate the social security by taking 6.5% of the gross pay.

7) ENTER FORMULAS TO CALCULATE NET PAY

a. Select cell K3.
b. Enter the formula

`=H3 - I3 - J3`

to calculate the net pay by taking the gross pay minus the taxes and social security deductions.

8) COPY RELATIVE FORMULAS INTO COLUMNS I, J AND K

a. Select cell I3.
b. Drag the mouse to cell K27. A block of all the cells that will have relative formulas copied into them is highlighted.
c. Press ⌘D to execute the Fill Down command. Note that the relative formulas are copied for all three columns.

9) DETERMINE MAXIMUM AND MINIMUM NET PAY

a. Select cell J29.
b. Enter the label: `Min pay =`
c. Select cell K29.
d. Enter the function:

`=Min(K3:K27)`

Note that a value of $58.88 is displayed.
e. Select cell J30.
f. Enter the label: `Max pay =`
g. Select cell K30.
h. Enter the function:

`=MAX(K3:K27)`

The value $273.38 is displayed.

10) SAVE IVY PAYROLL ON DISK

Press ⌘S to save the modified IVY PAYROLL on disk.

<u>Check</u> - The last 2 rows of IVY PAYROLL should contain the values:

Total =	$4,941.01		Min pay =	$58.88
			Max pay =	$273.38

8.11 Using the If Function

It is sometimes desirable to have simple decisions made based upon the data stored in a spreadsheet. In Works such a decision is made using the If function. The decision is based on a comparison entered into the function. If the comparison is true one value is placed in the cell; if not, a second value is used. The If function has the form:

```
=If(<comparison>, <true value>, <false value>)
```

For example,

```
=If(C5 < E7, 10, 20)
```

stores a value of 10 in the current cell if the value in cell C5 is less than the value in cell E7, and a 20 if it is not.

The comparison part of the If function can contain one of the following comparisons:

=	equals
<	less than
>	greater than
<=	less than or equal to
>=	greater than or equal to
<>	not equal to

The following are examples of valid Ifs:

```
=If(N1 <= 25, 50, 100)
=If(B2 < K25, 0, B2*0.15)
=If(C10 > Min(C3:C8), C12, C14)
=If(D22 <> F25, 0, Sum(E1:E10))
```

The If function can be used by Ivy University's accounting department to calculate two tax brackets rather than one in the IVY PAYROLL spreadsheet. For example, if an employee's gross pay exceeds $250, 25% should be deducted for taxes. If the gross pay is less than or equal to $250, 15% should be deducted. To recalculate all of the salaries by hand for the two tax brackets would be quite a job. Happily this can easily be done using the If function. Another advantage of our computerized spreadsheet is that when the taxes are recalculated the net pay will also be recalculated automatically.

To calculate B. Connelly's taxes to take into account the two tax brackets we will replace the formula in cell I3 with:

```
=If(H3 > 250, H3 * .25, H3 * .15)
```

This formula states that if the gross pay stored in cell H3 is greater than 250, multiply it by .25 to determine the 25% tax. If the value stored in H3 is less than or equal to 250 multiply it by .15.

Practice 7

In this Practice you will change the formulas in column I to allow for two brackets in calculating each employee's taxes. Start Works and open IVY PAYROLL if you have not already done so.

1) ENTER THE NEW TAX FORMULA

a. Select cell I3.
b. Enter the formula:

```
=If(H3 > 250, H3 * .25, H3 * .15)
```

2) COPY THE NEW FORMULA TO CELLS I4 THROUGH I27

a. Make sure cell I3 is still selected and then drag the mouse to cell I27.
b. Select the Fill Down command from the Edit menu.
c. Press ⌘S to save the modified file on disk.

Now all employees earning more than $250 a week are taxed at the rate of 25% while all others are taxed at the 15% rate.

Check - The last 2 rows of IVY PAYROLL should contain the values shown below. The Max pay value changes from $273.38 because J. Sowers is now taxed at the higher rate (25%):

Total =	$4,941.01		Min pay =	$58.88
			Max pay =	$238.55

8.12 Inserting and Deleting Columns and Rows

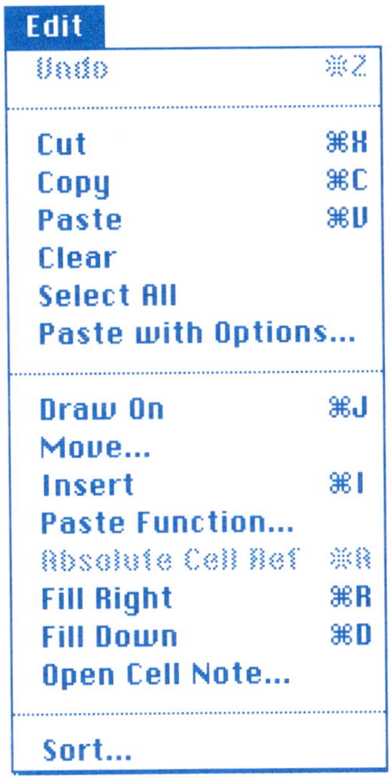

It is possible to insert or delete whole rows or columns in a spreadsheet. This is especially helpful to Ivy University when a new employee has been hired and a row must be inserted or an old employee leaves and a row must be deleted. It is also useful when columns must be inserted between existing columns. For example, a new column to deduct pension plan contributions can be inserted between the Soc. Sec. and Net Pay columns in IVY PAYROLL.

Inserting a new row is accomplished by moving the pointer to the row number below where the row is to be inserted, clicking to select the row, and then executing the Insert command from the Edit menu (⌘I). The selected row and all rows below it will move down to make room for the new row. To insert a new column the pointer is moved to the column letter where the column is to be inserted, clicking to select the column, and then executing the Insert command. The selected column and all columns to the right move to the right to make room for the new column. Newly inserted rows and columns are empty and contain no data or formulas. However, new rows retain the formatting of the row they were inserted above, and new columns the formatting of the column they were inserted before.

To delete a row the row is selected and the Cut command from the Edit menu executed (⌘X). All rows below the deleted row move up to fill the row. A column is similarly deleted by selecting the column and executing the Cut command. The columns to the right of the deleted column then move to the left to fill the space. Once a row or column has been deleted it cannot be recovered, so use caution when deleting. (The Undo command from the Edit menu, ⌘Z, will restore a deleted row or column as long as no other operation has been performed after the deletion.)

When a column or row is inserted or deleted Works automatically changes the range of any formulas that are involved. For example, if row 3 is deleted the formula =SUM(C1:C10) changes to =SUM(C1:C9). If a row is inserted between rows 1 and 10, the formula would become =SUM(C1:C11).

Practice 8

In this Practice rows will be deleted and inserted into the IVY PAYROLL spreadsheet. Employee H. Crane, who says she has found a much better job, will be deleted and a new employee, A. Nitrate, who cleans chemistry labs added. Start Works and open IVY PAYROLL if you have not already done so.

1) DELETE ROW FOR EMPLOYEE CRANE, H.

a. Select the row containing H. Crane's data by clicking on its row number, row 21.
b. Select the Cut command from the Edit menu. The row is deleted and all rows below moved up to fill the space.

2) INSERT ROW AND DATA FOR NEW EMPLOYEE

a. Select row 17 by clicking on its row number.
b. Select the Insert command from the Edit menu. A new row is inserted at row 17 and the rows below moved down to make room.
c. Enter the following data in the inserted row:

```
Nitrate, A.   5.5   6.5   7   8   2   1.5
```

3) TRANSFER FORMULAS TO THE NEW ROW

Note that the formulas needed to calculate A. Nitrate's salary and deductions do not appear in the newly inserted row. The new row will require the copying of the four formulas into columns H through K. We can copy all of the formulas at one time by selecting the formulas in row 16 and copying them into 17.

a. Select cell H16.
b. Drag the mouse to cell K17 extending the highlight.
c. Press ⌘D to execute the Fill Down command. The new formulas are copied into A. Nitrate's row and the values calculated.

4) SAVE IVY PAYROLL ON DISK

Press ⌘S to save the modified version of IVY PAYROLL on disk.

Check - A. Nitrate's salary and deductions should be shown in row 17:

Gross Pay	Taxes	Soc. Sec.	Net Pay
$137.50	$20.63	$8.94	$107.94

8.13 Asking "What If?"

One of the most powerful features of a spreadsheet is its ability to answer "What if?" questions. By making changes in a spreadsheet it is possible to perform calculations that make predictions based on the changes. Because spreadsheets perform such calculations rapidly, a number of different situations can be tested. This technique is widely used by businesses to predict their finances under a wide range of possible situations and is often called "forecasting." For example, if an automobile manufacturer uses a spreadsheet to determine the cost of producing cars, it could predict the cost under various price changes: What if the price of steel were to increase by 15%? What if the cost of labor were to increase by 6%? What if taxes were halved? The effects of such changes can be quickly calculated by entering the new information in the appropriate cell or cells. All formulas would then be automatically recalculated. It is in using a spreadsheet to produce such predictions that its calculation power is truly utilized.

Ivy University's employees have not had a pay raise in five years and have decided to strike if their demand for wage increases are not met. Because the budget at Ivy is already very tight, this threat has the administration concerned about how much the raises will cost. Using the IVY PAYROLL payroll spreadsheet the accounting department will do wage projections. The employees want an increase of 15% of their gross pay. Ivy plans to offer a 5% increase, but may have to compromise at 10% or may even be forced to accept the full 15%. To see how much each of these percentages will cost, three new columns are added to the spreadsheet which calculate the new gross pay for each of the raises and the total payroll for all employees.

Practice 9

In this Practice you will answer the "What If?" question described in the previous Section by adding 3 columns to the IVY PAYROLL spreadsheet which calculate raises of 5%, 10% and 15%. Start Works and open IVY PAYROLL if you have not already done so.

1) FORMAT THE NEW COLUMNS

a. Right justify cells L1, M1 and N1 using the Set Cell Attributes command from the Format menu.
b. Select cell K2 and extend the underline of dashes to include the 3 new columns using the Fill Right command, ⌘R.
c. Format the block of cells from cell L3 to N30 to display dollar amounts with commas and 2 decimal places.

2) CALCULATE 5% RAISES

a. Enter the heading `5% Raise` into cell L1.
b. Enter the formula

```
=H3 * 1.05
```

into cell L3. This formula calculates a new gross pay which is 5% higher than the original.
c. Make relative copies of the formula in cell L3 into cells L4 through L27 using Fill Down, ⌘D.

3) CALCULATE 10% AND 15% RAISES

a. Enter the heading `10% Raise` into cell M1.
b. Repeat parts (b) and (c) of step 2 for column M using the formula `=H3 * 1.10` to properly calculate a 10% raise.
c. Enter the heading `15% Raise` into cell N1.
d. Repeat parts (b) and (c) of step 2 for column N using the formula `=H3 * 1.15` to properly calculate a 15% raise.

4) SUM THE NEW GROSS PAYS

a. Using the Delete key erase the labels in cells J29 and J30 and then erase the formulas in cells K29 and K30.
b. Enter the label `Pay Raise =` into cell K29.
c. Enter the formula

   `=SUM(L3:L27)`

   into cell L29.
d. Make relative copies of the formula in cell L29 into cells M29 and N29 using the Fill Right command.

5) CALCULATE THE INCREASED COST OF RAISES

a. Enter the label `Raise Cost =` into cell K30.
b. Enter the formula

   `=L29 - $H$29`

   into cell L30. Note that we want copies of this formula to subtract the value stored in H29. This requires the dollar signs in the cell name.
c. Make relative copies of the formula in cell L30 into cells M30 and N30 using the Fill Right command.

Check - The last two rows of the new columns should be:

Pay Raise =	$5,118.70	$5,362.45	$5,606.20
Raise Cost =	$243.75	$487.50	$731.24

6) SAVE THE MODIFIED SPREADSHEET ON DISK

a. Press ⌘S to save the modified IVY PAYROLL spreadsheet on disk.
b. Close IVY PAYROLL by pressing ⌘W.

8.14 Charts and Graphs

Numeric data can be difficult to interpret when it is presented in rows and columns in a spreadsheet. For this reason data is often better displayed in the form of a chart or graph. Studies have shown that people remember more about information that is presented graphically. Also, charts show the relationships between the different pieces of data better than columns of figures. Works can produce two types of charts, Pie charts and Series charts, that display the data stored in a spreadsheet.

Pie Chart: Pie charts are used to show the relation between the fractional parts that make up a whole amount:

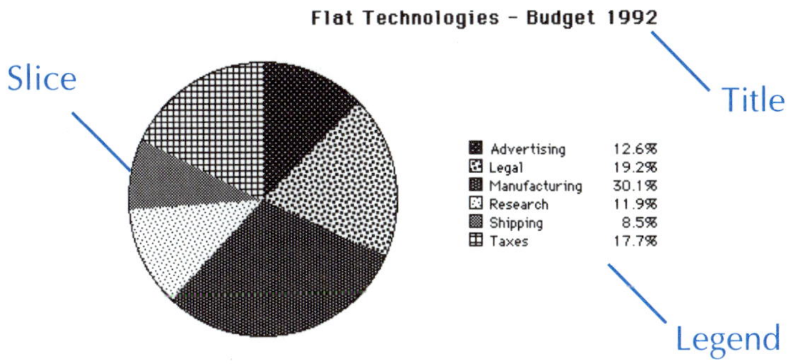

Each "slice" in the pie represents one fractional part of the whole, the size of the slice varying with the percentage of the total. Pie charts graph data from a spreadsheet column.

Series Charts

There are four types of series charts: bar charts, stack charts, line charts and combination charts. Series charts are used to show relationships between numbers and graph data from spreadsheet rows.

Bar Chart: One of the most common charts is the bar chart in which each piece of data is represented by a bar:

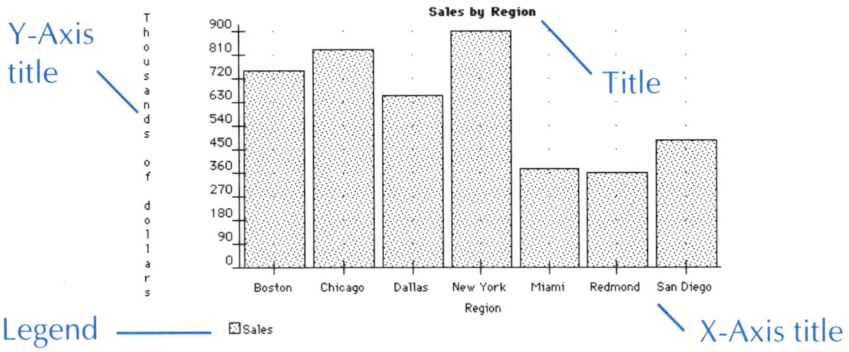

Longer (taller) bars are used to represent larger numbers. Bar charts are useful when comparing the differences between many values and may include titles as shown above.

Stack Chart: Stack charts are a variation of bar charts which illustrate component parts of a total as they change.

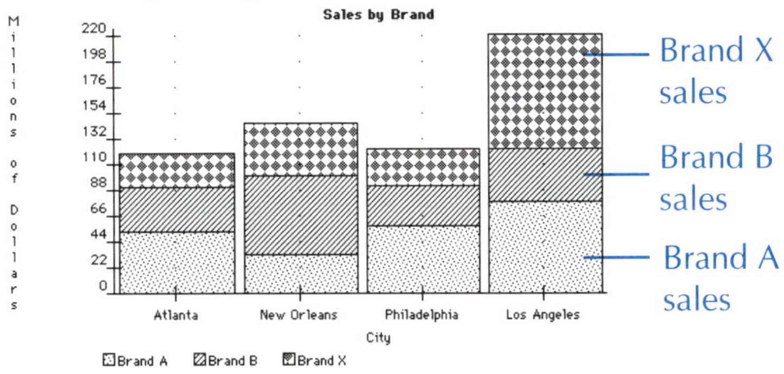

Line Chart:

Line charts, or "graphs", are normally used to show changes in a value over time. For example, this chart shows a city's average temperature for each month over the period of a year:

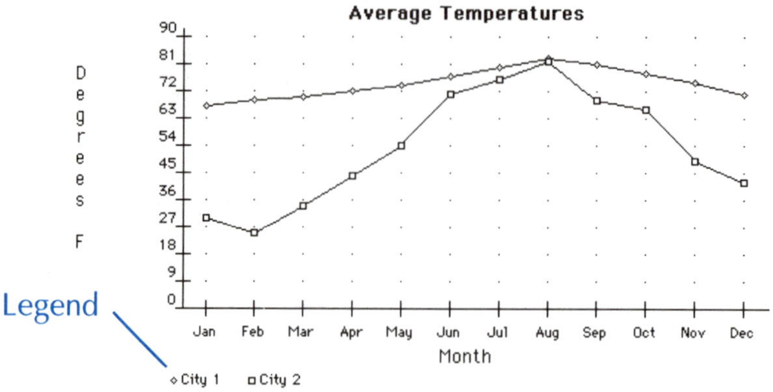

Combination Chart:

Combination charts combine a bar chart with a line chart allowing you to display one set of numbers with bars and another set of numbers with a line on the same chart. Combination charts are used to compare related data.

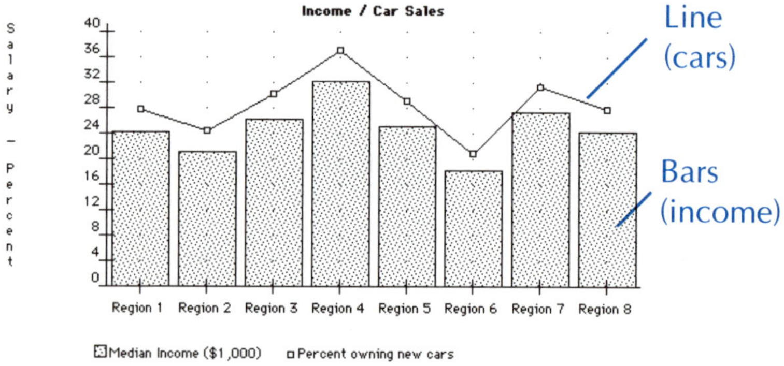

Just as with spreadsheets, a chart should be carefully planned. You must first decide what information the chart is to contain, and in what order. Next, consider what type of chart to use. Finally, thought should be given to the titles that make the chart easier to read and understand.

8.15 Creating Pie Charts

Works can create a number of different charts of the data stored in a spreadsheet. Once created, a chart is automatically linked to the spreadsheet from which its data is taken, so that if a number is changed in the spreadsheet, the chart also changes. After the chart has been created, titles may be added, and the chart printed. Works names the first chart created the first eight characters of the spreadsheet name followed by Chart 1, the second chart the spreadsheet name followed by Chart 2 and so on up to the maximum of 8 charts per spreadsheet. For example, if the spreadsheet is named IVY ENROLLMENT the first chart created for it will be named IVY ENRO Chart 1.

Pie charts are created by selecting the New Pie Chart command from the Charts menu. When New Pie Chart is selected the following dialog box is displayed:

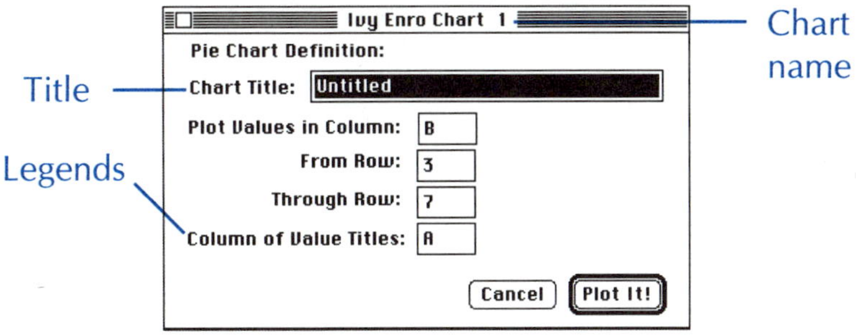

The Pie Chart dialog box

The defaults shown above may be changed by typing over them or simply deleted if they are not needed. The letter of the column which contains the values to be charted is entered into the Plot Values in Column: box. Row numbers are entered for the first and last row to be included from the column in the From Row: and Through Row boxes. The column letter for the column which contains the titles for the portions of the pie is entered into the Column of Value Titles box. The chart title is typed on the keyboard. When all the information has been entered the Plot It! button is clicked. Note that Pie charts are created from data contained in columns. This is different from Series charts which will be created from data contained in rows. To print a chart the Print Window command is selected from the File menu.

Practice 10

In this Practice you will create a pie chart using the data stored in the IVY ENROLLMENT spreadsheet on your data disk. Start Works if you have not already done so. IVY ENROLLMENT contains data on the Freshman course enrollment for Ivy University over a period of years. The pie chart will display the percentage enrollments for each department for the year 1991. Make sure that a printer is connected to your computer and ready to print.

1) OPEN THE IVY ENROLLMENT SPREADSHEET

2) PRODUCE A NEW PIE CHART

a. Select the New Pie Chart command from the Chart menu.
b. Type “Department Enrollments 1991” in the Chart Title: box.
c. Move the pointer to the Plot Values in Column: box and double-click. Type E which removes the default value of B.
d. Move past the From Row: box since we want the default value of 3.
e. Move the cursor to the Through Row: box and double-click then enter 10.
f. Since the department names are stored in row A we will not change the default value A in the Column of Value Titles: box.
g. Click on `Plot It!` and the pie chart is displayed on the screen.

3) PRINT THE CHART

With the chart still displayed, select the Print Window command from the File menu to print the pie chart on paper.

4) CHANGE A VALUE IN THE SPREADSHEET

a. Select IVY ENROLLMENT from the Window menu to return to the spreadsheet.
b. Select cell E4 and enter `975`.
c. From the Window menu select IVY ENRO Chart 1. Note how the percentages of the pie have changed to reflect the new biology value.

5) RETURN TO THE SPREADSHEET AND SAVE IT

a. Select IVY ENROLLMENT from the Window menu.
b. Press ⌘S to save the modified spreadsheet with chart on disk.

8.16 Creating Series Charts

A Series Chart is created by selecting the New Series Chart command from the Chart menu which produces the dialog box:

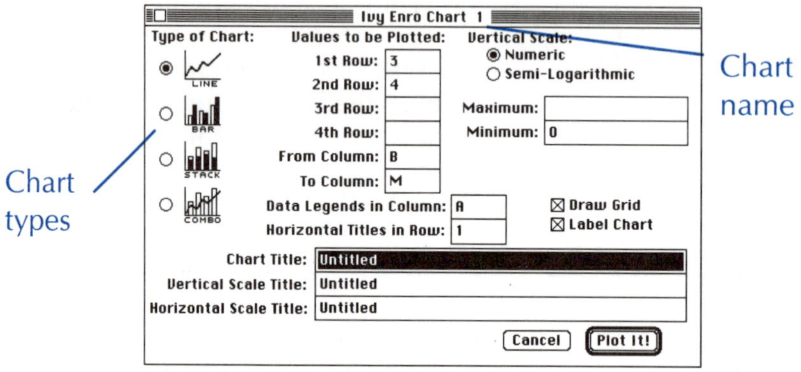

The Series chart dialog box

From this box the type of chart (line, bar, stack or combo) is selected. The row number of the row of data to be plotted is entered into the 1st Row box. Up to three additional rows or series may be plotted by entering row numbers into the appropriate boxes. The number of rows selected will determine how many separate lines or bars will be graphed on a single chart. The column letters for the first column and last columns to be charted are entered into the From Column: and To Column: boxes. Note that unlike Pie charts, Series charts display data from rows rather than columns.

Practice 11

In this Practice you will create a bar chart, stack chart, line chart and combination chart. Start Works and open IVY ENROLLMENT if you have not already done so. Make sure that a printer is connected to your computer and that it is ready to print.

1) CREATE A BAR CHART OF THE COMPUTER DEPARTMENT'S ENROLLMENT AND PRINT IT

a. Select the New Series Chart command from the Chart menu.
b. Click on BAR to select a Bar chart.
c. Move the pointer to the 1st Row: box and double-click. Enter a 5 to select the row containing the computer department's enrollments. The default value is replaced.

d. Move the pointer to the 2nd Row: box and double-click. Press the Delete key to remove the default value of 4.
e. Move the pointer to the To Column: box and double-click. Replace the default value with E. Since all other boxes contain proper values we do not have to change them.
f. Double-click on the Chart Title: box and type the title "Computer Department Enrollments".
g. Double-click on the Vertical Scale Title: box and type "Number of Students".
h. Double-click on the Horizontal Scale Title: box and type "Years".
i. Click on the `Plot It!` button. The bar chart is displayed.
j. Select the Print Window command from the File menu. The bar chart is printed on paper.
k. Return to the spreadsheet by clicking on the Close box at the upper left corner of the screen. Your chart should be similar to:

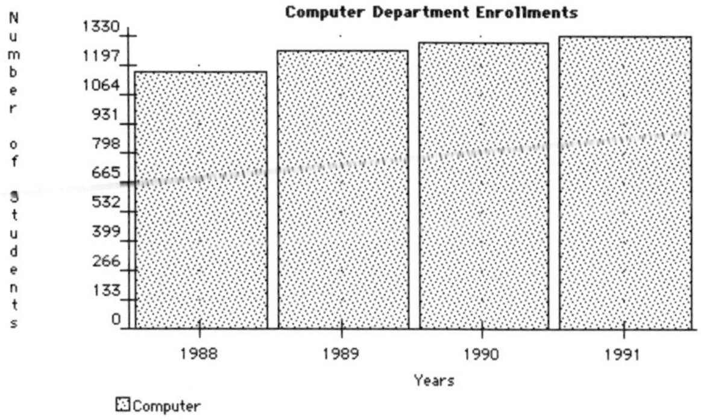

2) CREATE A STACK CHART OF THE BIOLOGY AND PHYSICS DEPARTMENT'S ENROLLMENT AND PRINT IT

a. Select the New Series Chart command from the Chart menu.
b. Select STACK.
c. Enter a 4 into the 1st Row box.
d. Enter a 10 into the 2nd Row box.
e. Enter E into the To Column: box.
f. Title the chart "Physics and Biology Enrollments".
g. Title the vertical scale "Number of students".
h. Title the horizontal scale "Years".
i Click on `Plot It!`. The stack chart is displayed. Note that the physics enrollment is shown stacked on top of the biology enrollment.
j. Select the Print Window command from the File menu. A copy of the chart is printed on paper.
k. Click on the Close box to return to the spreadsheet.

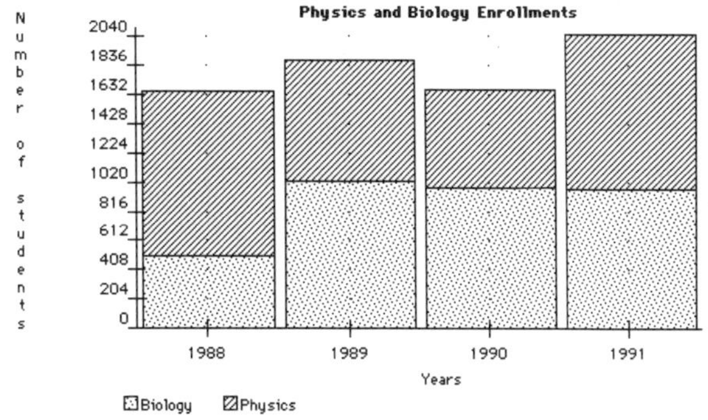

3) CREATE A LINE CHART OF FOUR DEPARTMENT ENROLLMENTS

a. Select the New Series Chart from the Chart menu. We do not have to change the type of chart since LINE is the default setting.
b. Enter the row numbers 5 and 6 into the 3rd and 4th row boxes.
c. Enter E into the To Column: box.
d. Enter appropriate titles for the chart and the two scales.
e. Click on `Plot It!`. Four lines are plotted, one for each of the four selected departments.
f. Select the Print Window command from the File menu.
g. Click on the Close box to return to the spreadsheet.

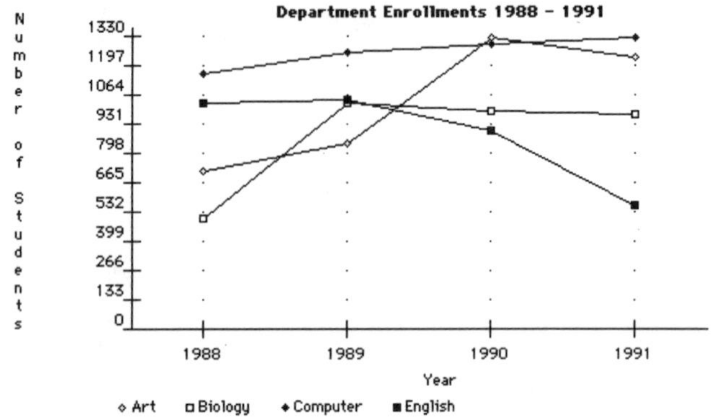

4) CREATE A COMBINATION CHART OF THE MUSIC AND LANGUAGE DEPARTMENTS' ENROLLMENTS

a. Select the New Series Chart command from the Chart menu.
b. Select COMBO.
c. Enter 7 for 1st Row (Language department) and 9 for 2nd Row (Music department).
d. Enter E in the To Column: box.
e. Enter appropriate titles.
f. Click on the `Plot It!` button. The combination chart is displayed with the language enrollment charted by bars and the music enrollment by a line.
g. Select the Print Window command from the File menu to print the chart.
h. Click on the Close box to return to the spreadsheet.
i. Press ⌘S to save Ivy Enrollment with its charts on disk.

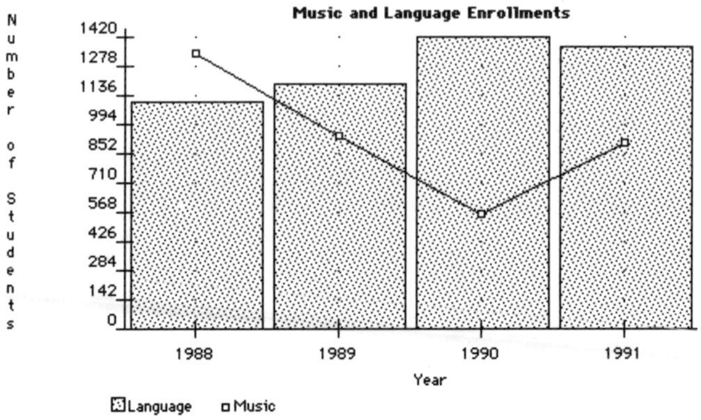

8.17 Loading and Erasing Previously Created Charts

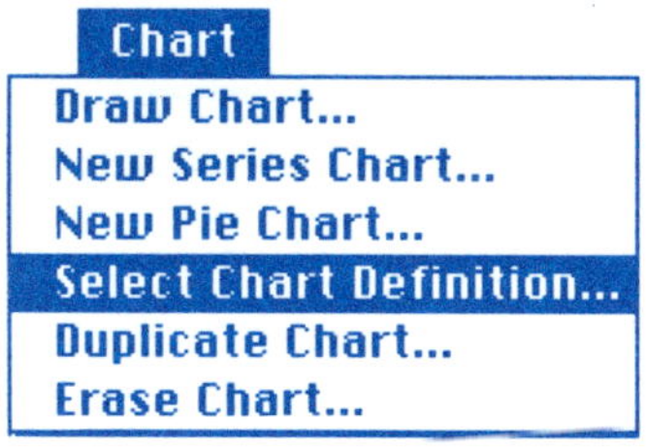

When a spreadsheet is saved the charts created for it are saved with it. To display a previously created chart its spreadsheet must be opened and then the chart using the Select Chart Definition command from the Chart menu:

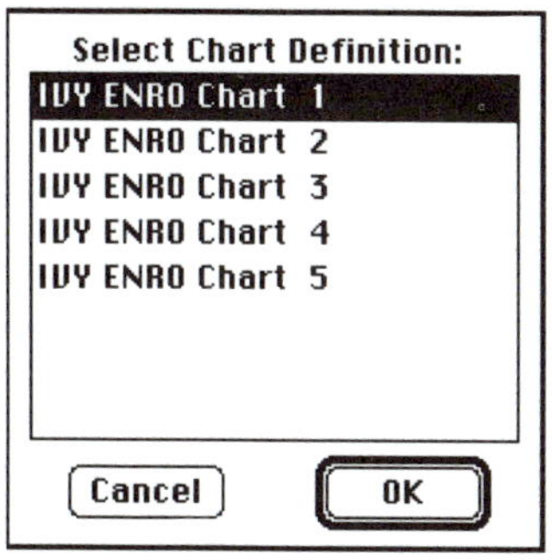

This box allows a previously created chart definition to be modified

Selecting a chart name from the dialog box will display its definition. Clicking on `Plot It!` will then display the chart.

Only 8 charts may be saved with a spreadsheet at a time. To erase a chart the Erase Chart from the Chart menu is selected:

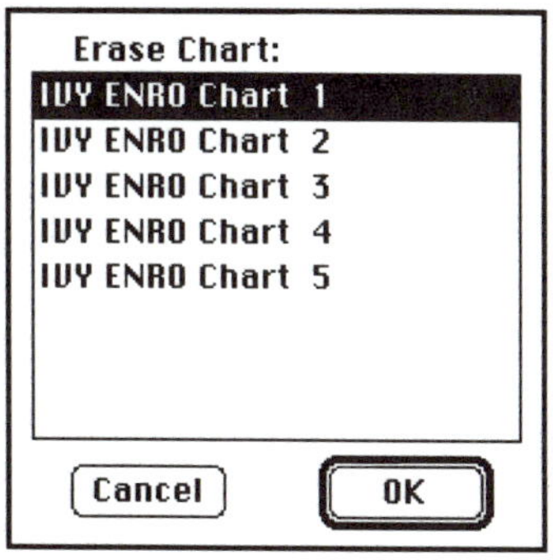

Chart definitions may be erased from this box

Selecting a chart name from the dialog box will erase the chart.

8.18 Displaying a Chart and Spreadsheet Together

Sometimes it is desirable to display a chart and its associated spreadsheet at the same time. To do this the adjust box at the lower right hand corner of the chart is dragged to reduce the size of the chart. As the chart becomes smaller the spreadsheet appears:

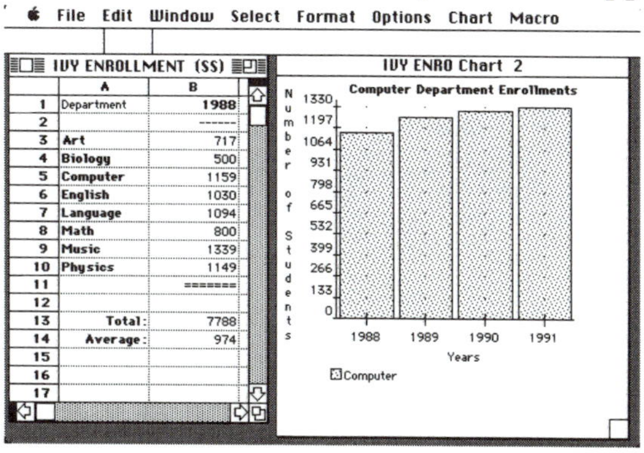

Charts and spreadsheets may be viewed on screen together in windows

It is important to note that if the chart is not returned to full size before it is saved, it will be displayed reduced the next time it is accessed. Also, a Print Window command issued at this time will print only the chart or the spreadsheet, not both even though both are currently visible on the screen.

Practice 12

In this Practice you will display a previously created chart along with its spreadsheet and then erase the chart. Open IVY ENROLLMENT if it is not already.

1) VIEW CHART 3

a. Select the Select Chart Definition: command from the Chart menu.
b. Select IVY ENRO Chart 3 and click on `OK`. The chart's definition dialog box is displayed.
c. Click on `Plot It!` to display the chart.

2) DISPLAY BOTH THE CHART AND SPREADSHEET

a. Drag the adjust box at the lower right hand corner of the chart until column D of the spreadsheet can be seen.
b. Unless you return the chart to full size, it will appear reduced in size the next time it is selected. Click on the Expand box to return the chart to full size.
c. Click on the Close box to close the chart and return to the spreadsheet.

3) ERASE CHART 5

a. Select the Erase Chart command from the Chart menu.
b. Select IVY ENRO Chart 5 from the dialog box and click on `OK`. Chart 5 is now erased.

4) SAVE IVY ENROLLMENT AND QUIT WORKS

a. Press ⌘S to save the spreadsheet on disk. The next time IVY ENROLLMENT is opened Chart 5 will not be available.
b. Press ⌘Q to quit Works.

Advanced Spreadsheet Techniques

In the earlier part of this chapter we presented the most commonly used spreadsheet functions. As you have become aware if you have scrolled through the list of available Works functions, there are many other functions available to you. In this section we present additional functions which may be used to produce advanced spreadsheets.

8.19 The Choose and Vlookup Functions

The If function allows a formula to be created which displays one value if a comparison is true, and another value if the comparison is false. The example given in Section 8.11 uses If to calculate tax withholdings using two different rates based on gross pay: 25% for those employees earning over $250 and 15% for all others. Suppose, however, that there were 10 or 15 different tax rates. The If required to calculate the tax would be extremely large and complex, and might exceed the maximum display length for formulas, 200 characters. To solve problem such as this, Works includes two functions which can be used to select one value from a list of many: `Choose` and `Vlookup`.

Choose: The Choose function has the form

=Choose(<position>, <value$_1$>, <value$_2$>, ... <value$_N$>)

where <position> is an expression that evaluates between 1 and *N*. Choose displays the value in the list which corresponds to <position>. If <position> is 1, Choose displays <value$_1$>, if it is 2 then <value$_2$> is displayed, and so on. For example, given the formula

```
=Choose(A1, 10, 15, 20, 25)
```

Works displays 10 if the value stored in cell A1 is 1, 15 if the value stored in A1 is 2, 20 if the value is 3, and 25 if it is 4. If <position> is negative or greater than *N* (the number of possible <values>) `*Error*` is displayed, meaning that a corresponding value is not available. Note that the integer portion of <position> is rounded to determine which <value> to display. If A1 stores 2.6, 20 is displayed because the 2.6 is rounded to 3. Choose could be used to calculate multiple tax rates by assigning each employee a numeric code between 1 and *N* which signifies which tax rate to use.

Vlookup: Vlookup is similar to Choose except that the <values> to be displayed are stored in cells in the spreadsheet, not listed in the function itself. This has two advantages; first, because they are in cells, the values may be calculated instead of being constants. Second, the values may be printed with the spreadsheet showing the table used. Vlookup has the form:

=Vlookup(<position value>, <range>, <columns>)

where <position value> is a numeric expression and <range> is the cell range where the values to be displayed are stored. When evaluated, Works finds the largest number in <range> which is less than or equal to <position value>, and then displays the value which is stored in the cell <columns> adjacent to the right of that cell (usually 2). This is similar to the manual operation of looking up a value in a two column table: the first column is searched for the desired data, then the value read from the adjacent column. As an example, assume the following spreadsheet fragment:

```
                 B          C
1                1          10
2 . . .          2          15
3                3          20
4                4          25
5                5          30
```

Given the function

```
=Vlookup(A1, $B$1:$C$5, 2)
```

if cell A1 stores the value 1, then 10 is displayed. This is because cell B1 stores the largest value which is less than or equal to 1 so Vlookup displays the value stored in the cell that is 1 column adjacent to B1, the 10 in cell C1. If A1 stores 3.5, this function would display 20, because cell B3 stores the largest value in <range> which is less than or equal to 3.5. (If A1 stored the value 0, `*Error*` would be displayed.)

Note that the values in <range> must be in ascending order for Vlookup to work correctly. If the <position value> is less than the first value stored in <range> an `*Error*` is displayed. For this reason it is important to make the first value in <range> less than any value that will be looked up. If <position value> is larger than the last value in <range>, the last value in the lookup table is displayed. For example, if A1 stores 100, the function above would display 30. Vlookup differs from Choose in that the <position value> may be negative or zero as long as it is greater than or equal to one of the values stored in <range>.

Note the use of dollar signs in the range. These are used to guarantee that the cell references in range will not change if Fill Down or Fill Right are used to copy the Vlookup function to other cells.

Assume that a payroll spreadsheet is to calculate withholding using the 7 tax rates shown below:

Gross Pay	**Tax Rate**
under $150	0%
$150-$199	8%
$200-$249	10%
$250-$299	12%
$300-$349	17%
$350-$599	28%
$600-up	33%

If gross pay were calculated in cell H1, the function

```
=H1 * Vlookup(H1, Y1:Z7, 2)
```

would properly calculate withholding if the tax lookup table was stored in the spreadsheet as:

	Y	Z
1	0	0
2	150	0.08
3	200	0.10
4	250	0.12
5	300	0.17
6	350	0.28
7	600	0.33

8.20 Splitting Windows and Freezing Titles

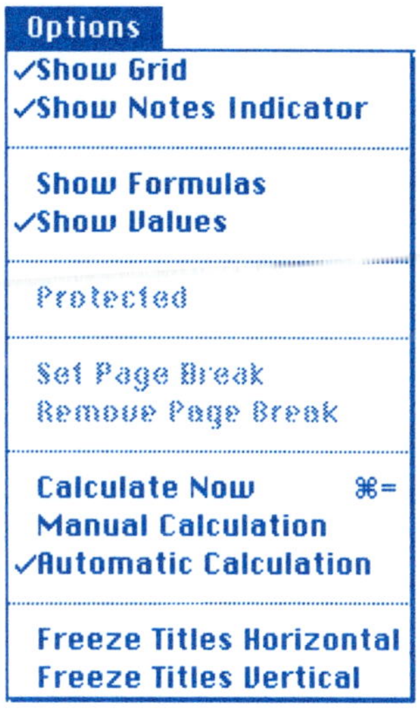

A problem encountered when working with large spreadsheets is that as you scroll across or down the spreadsheet the titles in row 1 or the labels in column A scroll off the screen making it difficult to determine what columns or rows displayed cells are in. Works solves this problem by allowing you to split the spreadsheet screen into a number of different windows, and then "freeze" the columns in the left window and rows in the top window so they may not be scrolled.

To freeze the top row of a spreadsheet point to the split bar located at the upper right hand corner of the screen:

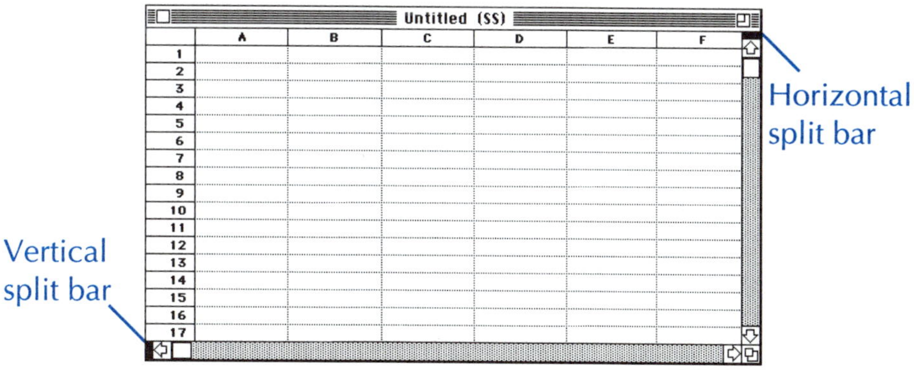

The split bars are located at the ends of the scroll bars

The pointer becomes a two-way arrow which can be dragged below row 2. The spreadsheet screen is now divided into two windows. Both windows may be scrolled separately, or left alone. Executing the Freeze Titles Vertical command from the Options menu eliminates any scrolling in the upper window. Rows 1 and 2 will now remain on screen.

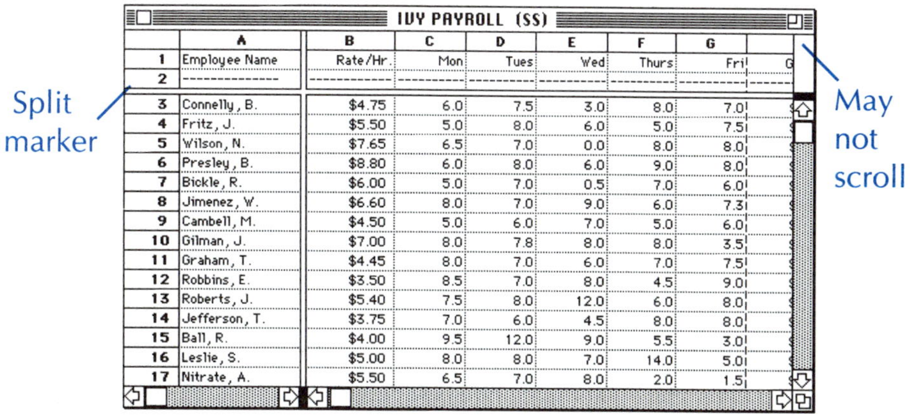

This spreadsheet has been split both horizontally and vertically

Similarly, to freeze the columns point to the split bar at the lower left of the screen and drag it to the right of the column to be frozen. Once split, executing the Freeze Titles Horizontal command from the Options menu will now freeze the columns in the leftmost window. To "unfreeze" the rows or columns select the Freeze Titles commands again and return the split bar to its original position at the edge of the screen.

Practice 13

In this Practice you will modify the IVY PAYROLL spreadsheet to include a retirement deduction which allows employees to contribute different percentages of their salaries. This will be done using the Choose function. An advantage to employees of contributing to the retirement plan is that they do not have to pay taxes on the contribution. The spreadsheet will also be modified to allow for seven tax rates using the Vlookup function. Freeze Titles will be used to keep Employee Names on the screen. Start Works and open IVY PAYROLL.

1) OPEN THE IVY PAYROLL SPREADSHEET

From the Open File dialog box, select the IVY PAYROLL spreadsheet from your data disk.

2) FREEZE EMPLOYEE NAMES

a. Drag the split bar at the left-bottom edge of the screen to the right edge of column A.
b. Select the Freeze Titles Horizontal command from the Options menu. The employee names will now remain on the screen when the spreadsheet is scrolled to the right.

3) INSERT COLUMNS TO CALCULATE RETIREMENT

a. Insert two new columns at columns I and J.
b. Title column I `Retire Code` and column J `Retirement`.
c. Extend the dashes in row 2 to cells I2 and J2 using Fill Right.

4) ENTER THE RETIREMENT CODES

There are five retirement codes (1 through 5) which determine the percentage of gross pay that will be deducted for each employee.

a. Format cells I3 to I27 for General display to eliminate the dollar signs.
b. Enter the following numbers in the cells indicated:

Cell	Code	Cell	Code	Cell	Code
I3	1	I12	4	I20	2
I4	3	I13	2	I21	3
I5	2	I14	1	I22	1
I6	4	I15	3	I23	4
I7	2	I16	2	I24	3
I8	2	I17	1	I25	2
I9	5	I18	5	I26	2
I10	3	I19	2	I27	5
I11	3				

5) ENTER THE CHOOSE FUNCTION TO CALCULATE RETIREMENTS

Each of the codes above correspond to the following percentages which will be used to calculate the retirement deduction:

Code	Percentage
1	0%
2	2%
3	5%
4	8%
5	10%

a. Enter the following function in cell J3:

```
=Choose(I3, 0, .02*H3, .05*H3, .08*H3, .1*H3)
```

b. Use the Fill Down command from the Edit menu to produce appropriate functions for the rest of column J.

6) CALCULATE TAXES USING THE VLOOKUP FUNCTION

The following tax rates will be used in calculating taxes:

Salary	Tax Rate
under $150	0%
$150-$199	8%
$200-$249	10%
$250-$299	12%
$300-$349	17%
$350-$599	28%
$600-up	33%

a. The tax table will be stored in cells R2 through S8. Enter the label `Tax Table` in cell R1 and right justify it.
b. Enter the following values into the indicated cells to create the tax table:

Cell	Salary	Cell	Tax Rate
R2	0	S2	0
R3	150	S3	0.08
R4	200	S4	0.1
R5	250	S5	0.12
R6	300	S6	0.17
R7	350	S7	0.28
R8	600	S8	0.33

c. Enter the formula

```
=Vlookup(H3-J3, $R$2:$S$8, 2) * (H3-J3)
```

into cell K3. Note that taxes are based on the gross pay minus the deduction for retirement. Dollar signs ($) are needed to keep the cell references for the lookup table from changing when Fill Down is used.

c. Use Fill Down to complete the calculations in column K.

7) RECALCULATE NET PAY AND SAVE THE SPREADSHEET

a. Enter the formula:

```
=H3 - J3 - K3 - L3
```

into cell M3.

b. Use Fill Down to recalculate the cells in column M. The new net pay is displayed.

c. Press ⌘S to save the modified file on disk.

8.21 Amortization Tables

One of the most useful applications of a spreadsheet is to produce an amortization table which displays how much interest and principal is paid on each payment of an installment loan. Principal paid is the amount of a loan that has been paid back. For example, the payment made each month on a 30 year loan of $150,000. borrowed at an interest rate of 10% is $1,316.36. On the first payment made $1,250.00 goes to paying the interest on the loan and $66.36 goes to reducing principal (i.e. the amount owed). On the 50th payment $1,223.88 goes to paying interest and $92.48 to reducing principal.

The `Pmt` function is used to calculate the periodic payments for an installment loan when given the interest rate, number of payments to be made, and the amount of the loan. It takes the form:

```
=Pmt(<rate>, <payments>, <pv>, <fv>, <type>)
```

where

rate: the interest rate per period

payments: the number of payments to be made

pv: the amount of the loan (its present value)

fv: future value is optional; we will not make use of it by setting it to 0.

type: another optional value, usually set to 0.

As an example, if you borrow $150,000 to purchase a home at an interest rate of 10% for 30 years the function will be:

```
=Pmt(10% / 12, 360, 150000, 0, 0)
```

Note the percent sign (%) which is needed to convert the 10 to 10%, the yearly interest rate. This is divided by 12 to calculate the monthly rate. The number of payments is 360, 30 years * 12 months. When calculated Pmt returns a value of -1316.36, the negative sign indicating that payment is to be made rather than received.

Practice 14

In this Practice you will complete an amortization table in a spreadsheet named LOAN which displays the interest and principal paid on the payments made on a loan. Start Works if you have not already done so.

1) OPEN THE LOAN SPREADSHEET

From the Open File dialog box, select the LOAN spreadsheet from your data disk.

2) ENTER THE LOAN'S INFORMATION

a. Enter the principal, `150000` in cell B3.
b. Enter the yearly interest rate, `10%` in cell B4.
c. Enter the number of payments, `360` (30 years × 12 monthly payments) in cell B5.

3) CALCULATE THE MONTHLY PAYMENT

Enter the formula

```
=Pmt(B4 / 12, B5, B3, 0, 0) * -1
```

into cell B7. The division by 12 is needed to convert the yearly interest rate in cell B4 to a monthly value. Multiplying by negative 1 makes the payment a positive number. The payment should be $1,316.36.

4) ENTER THE FIRST PAYMENT DATA

a. Enter the number `1` in cell A10.
b. Enter `=B3` in cell B10.
c. In cell C10, enter `=B10 * ($B$4 / 12)` to calculate one month's interest on the loan. Absolute cell referencing (the $B$4) is used because the interest rate will be the same for each payments. The value $1,250.00 should be displayed.
d. To calculate the amount of the payment which is applied to the principal, enter the formula `=$B$7 - C10` in cell D10 ($66.36).
e. To calculate the new principal, enter the formula `=B10 - D10` in cell E10 ($149,933.64).

5) ENTER FORMULAS FOR THE SECOND PAYMENT

a. Enter the formula `=A10 + 1` in cell A11.
b. To display the new principal, enter `=E10` in cell B11.
c. Use Fill Down (⌘`D`) to copy the formulas in cell C10 through E10 into cells C11 through E11. This completes the data for the second payment and the new principal should be $149,866.73 displayed in cell E11.

6) COMPLETE THE TABLE USING FILL DOWN

Use Fill Down to copy cells A11 through E11 into rows 12 through 369. Because of the large number of cells and formulas involved, it will take a moment for the computer to recalculate the spreadsheet.

7) SAVE THE TABLE ON DISK

Press ⌘`S` to save the modified LOAN spreadsheet on disk.

<u>Check</u> - Your spreadsheet should be similar to that shown below. This spreadsheet is now a "template" which may be used to calculate the payments on any 30 year loan. Experiment by changing the principal and interest rate values in cells B3 and B4 to see the effects on the monthly payment and the total amount of interest paid.

LOAN (SS)

	A	B	C	D	E
348	339	$26,360.33	$219.67	$1,096.69	$25,263.64
349	340	$25,263.64	$210.53	$1,105.83	$24,157.81
350	341	$24,157.81	$201.32	$1,115.04	$23,042.77
351	342	$23,042.77	$192.02	$1,124.33	$21,918.44
352	343	$21,918.44	$182.65	$1,133.70	$20,784.73
353	344	$20,784.73	$173.21	$1,143.15	$19,641.58
354	345	$19,641.58	$163.68	$1,152.68	$18,488.91
355	346	$18,488.91	$154.07	$1,162.28	$17,326.62
356	347	$17,326.62	$144.39	$1,171.97	$16,154.65
357	348	$16,154.65	$134.62	$1,181.74	$14,972.92
358	349	$14,972.92	$124.77	$1,191.58	$13,781.33
359	350	$13,781.33	$114.84	$1,201.51	$12,579.82
360	351	$12,579.82	$104.83	$1,211.53	$11,368.30
361	352	$11,368.30	$94.74	$1,221.62	$10,146.67
362	353	$10,146.67	$84.56	$1,231.80	$8,914.87
363	354	$8,914.87	$74.29	$1,242.07	$7,672.81
364	355	$7,672.81	$63.94	$1,252.42	$6,420.39
365	356	$6,420.39	$53.50	$1,262.85	$5,157.53
366	357	$5,157.53	$42.98	$1,273.38	$3,884.16
367	358	$3,884.16	$32.37	$1,283.99	$2,600.17
368	359	$2,600.17	$21.67	$1,294.69	$1,305.48
369	360	$1,305.48	$10.88	$1,305.48	$0.00
370			============	============	
371		Total Interest =	$323,888.65	$150,000.00	
372					
373		Total paid =	$473,888.65		

8.22 Where can you go from here?

The last two chapters introduced you to the concepts of a spreadsheet: how one is designed, created on the computer and used to produce calculations. There are other Works spreadsheet options we have not discussed which you may want to learn about. Reading the spreadsheet sections in the Works manual supplied by Microsoft is a good place to start.

Spreadsheets may be used to store laboratory data to produce scientific and statistical calculations as well as financial calculations. There are larger and more powerful spreadsheet programs available with names such as Lotus 123, Excel and Wingz which include many advanced calculating features. Although more complicated to use, these spreadsheet programs are similar to the Works program and would look familiar to you in many ways. Having learned the Works spreadsheet, you will be able to easily learn and use other spreadsheet software.

There is little doubt that spreadsheets will be employed in almost every type of endeavor that makes use of numbers. The introduction you have had should be helpful when you encounter these other applications, either in school or on the job.

Chapter Summary

Large spreadsheets require careful planning so that they are easy to use and may be modified and expanded. Consideration must be given to the placement of columns so that related data is located in adjacent columns. The width of a column may be changed either by dragging its column divider bar or by executing the Column Width command from the Format menu. Cells may be formatted to display dollar amounts by executing the Set Cell Attributes command from the Format menu.

Often the same label, value or formula must be stored in a number of cells. The Fill Down (⌘D) and Fill Right (⌘R) commands on the Edit menu can be used to copy what is stored in a cell into another cell or across a row or down a column of cells. One of their most useful applications is in copying formulas. When this is done Works automatically changes the cell names in the copies to reflect the new rows or columns they are in. This is called "relative" copying. To keep a cell reference constant when copied, the Absolute Cell Ref command from the Edit menu (⌘A) is used which places dollar signs in front of the column letter and row number ($B$25).

The Go To command from the Select menu (⌘G) can be used to move the cursor to a particular cell by giving its cell name. Searches for a label or value can be performed using the Find Cell command from the Select menu (⌘F).

The Max and Min functions display the maximum or minimum value stored in a range of cells. Decisions can be performed based on data in a spreadsheet using the If function. If a comparison is true the first value in the function is displayed in the current cell, if false the second value is shown.

New columns or rows can be inserted into a spreadsheet by executing the Insert command from the Edit menu (⌘I). Old columns or rows can be deleted by using the Cut command from the Edit menu (⌘X).

A spreadsheet can be used to answer "What If?" questions. By changing the data in a spreadsheet it is possible to produce calculations that make predictions based on the changes.

Works can use the data stored in a spreadsheet to produce bar, line, stack, pie or combination charts. Generally, a bar chart is used to compare different items, a line chart to track values over time, a stack chart to illustrate component parts of a total as they change, and a pie chart to show the relationship between different parts of a whole quantity. Combination charts combine a bar chart with a line chart. Up to 8 different charts can be created and stored with each spreadsheet.

The `Choose` and `Vlookup` functions can be used to select a value from a list of many. Choose includes the values as part of the function, Vlookup uses a lookup table stored in another part of the spreadsheet. The `Pmt` function calculates the period payment on an installment loan when given the interest rate, principal and number of payments.

Vocabulary

Absolute reference - keeping a cell reference constant when copied into cells by placing dollar signs in front of its column letter and row number ($B$25). This is done by executing the Absolute cell Ref command from the Edit menu: (⌘A).
Amortization table - displays the interest and principal paid on each payment of a loan.
Chart - graphical representation of numeric data.

Find Cell - moves the cursor to the next cell containing text specified in the Find Cell command from the Select menu: (⌘F).
Format - the way that data is displayed such as cell width. Formatting options include Dollar, Date, Align and Style, and are selected from the Set Cell Attributes command of the Format menu.
Go To Cell - moves the screen window to display a particular cell specified in the Go To Cell command from the Select menu: (⌘G).
Layout - the design of a spreadsheet including the placement of data in its rows and columns, column widths and the use of formatting options.
Pointing - moving the cell cursor to specify cell names in formulas.
Relative copy - copying formulas in a spreadsheet so that the cell names reflect the new rows and columns they are in. The Fill Right (⌘R) and Fill Down (⌘D) commands from the Edit menu are used to make relative copies.
What If? question - performing calculations to make predictions based upon the data stored in a spreadsheet.

Reviews

Sections 8.1-8.3

1. What factors should be considered when planning the layout of a spreadsheet?

2. Sketch a layout for a spreadsheet that will contain the inventory for an automobile dealership. The spreadsheet should include the names of the different automobile models, the number of each model in stock, and the price of each model. Show the width of each column and tell whether it stores a value or a label.

3. a) Explain two methods that may be used to increase the width of a column.
b) What will be displayed if a cell is not wide enough to display the value it stores?

Section 8.4-8.7

4. How may a column be formatted to display dollar values to 2 decimal places with commas.

5. What is meant by the term "relative" copying? Give an example.

6. What steps must be taken to copy the formula

```
=Average(C6:C20)
```

stored in cell C22, into the range of cells D22 to G22 so that the formula correctly calculates the average for each column?

7. a) When copying formulas how is it possible to keep one cell reference constant while allowing others to change?
b) Give two examples of when you would need to do this.

8. a) How can Works be instructed to display the formulas stored in the cells of a spreadsheet rather than the values they calculate?

b) What happens if the Print command is executed when the formulas are displayed?

9. What is the fastest way to move from cell A1 to cell Z14?

10. a) What steps must be taken to find each cell in a spreadsheet that contains the name "Harry?"
b) What is displayed if a search is performed for a label that does not appear in a spreadsheet?

11. Which of the following labels would be found in a repeated search for the characters PO?

```
hippo
Hoppy
opposite
Oprah
Porter
pox
```

Sections 8.8-8.10

12. Why is it not a good practice to keep adding columns to a spreadsheet without careful planning?

13. a) Write a formula that calculates the maximum value stored in the range of cells D5 to Y5.
b) Write a formula that calculates the minimum value stored in the range of cells C2 to C20.

14. What will be displayed by the following formulas if cell D5 stores a value of 30 and E7 a value of -12?

a) `=If(D5 <= E7, 10, 20)`
b) `=If(E7 * D5 < -5, E7, D5)`
c) `=If(D5 - 42 = E7, D5 * 2, E7 * 3)`

15. Write formulas that perform each of the following:

a) Store 50 in the current cell if the value stored in D20 equals the value in C90, or 25 if they are not equal.
b) Store the value contained in B50 in the current cell if the sum of the range of cells C30 to C430 exceeds 1000, otherwise store a 0.
c) Store the value of X20 * 10 in the current cell if X20 is less than 30; otherwise store just X20's value.

Sections 8.11-8.12

16. What steps must be taken to delete the Net Pay column from the IVY PAYROLL spreadsheet?

17. What steps must be taken to insert a column titled `Sat` into IVY PAYROLL that follows the column titled Fri?

18. a) The formula `=SUM(C3:C22)` is used to sum the values in cells C3 to C22. If a row is inserted directly above row 20, what must be done to include the new cell in the sum?
b) If a row is inserted directly above row 23, what must be done to include the new cell in the sum?

19. a) Explain what is meant by a "What if?" question.
    b) How can a spreadsheet be used to answer "What if?" questions?

20. Make a list of 5 "What if?" questions that could be answered using the IVY PAYROLL spreadsheet.

Sections 8.13-8.17

21. What type of chart: a bar chart, line chart, stack chart or pie chart would probably best be suited to displaying each of the following sets of data?

    a) a student's GPA over four years at college
    b) the percentages spent on different parts of Ivy University's budget
    c) the number of faculty members in each department at Ivy
    d) the number of books sold each day for a month at the college bookstore

22. a) How many charts can be created and stored with a single spreadsheet?
    b) What happens to charts stored with a spreadsheet if the data in the spreadsheet is changed?

23. Explain the steps required to create a bar chart from the IVY PAYROLL spreadsheet which displays the first four employee's net pay.

24. Describe a combination chart that could be produced from the data in the IVY PAYROLL spreadsheet.

25. Explain how a chart and its associated spreadsheet can be displayed together.

Section 8.18 - 8.19

26. Write a Choose function which displays 100 if cell B20 contains a value of 1, 500 if a 2, 900 if a 3 and 1200 if a 4.

27. The Lawrenceville Widget Company uses the following discount rates when large numbers of widgets are ordered:

Number of Widgets	**Discount %**
100 - 499	10%
500 - 999	30%
1000 - 1999	50%
2000 or over	70%

Write a Vlookup function that can be used to display the proper discount percent if cell C12 stores the number of widgets. In a diagram show the contents of the lookup table.

Exercises

1. The Ivy University Alumni Association has decided to use a spreadsheet to determine how much it must charge each member attending its annual Homecoming Dinner Dance so that it will not lose money. Below are listed the costs of each item based upon 50 members attending:

Expenses	50 members
Band	$1,500.00
Decorations	$185.00
Print tickets	$73.15
Electricity	$50.00
Advertising	$182.00
Clean up	$78.00
Appetizers	$56.00
Entrees	$111.00
Dessert	$34.50
Beverages	$150.00

a) Create a new spreadsheet named DANCE similar to the one above which calculates the cost per ticket when 50 members attend. All of the costs are summed and the total divided by the number of members to produce the cost per member. Save the spreadsheet on disk when complete.

b) In columns C, D and E calculate the cost per ticket when 100, 150 or 200 members attend. Consider the following when adding these columns:

(1) The expenses for Band through Clean up remain the same no matter how many members attend. Be careful to set up these values in the new columns so that if the value in column B is changed it will also change in the other columns. For example, if the Band cost is changed to $785.50 in column B, it should also appear as $785.50 in the three new columns.

(2) The values for Appetizers through Beverages change depending on how many members attend. Therefore, the cost for Dessert for 50 members must be multiplied by 2 to calculate the cost for 100 members, by 3 to calculate the cost for 150 members, and so on. The values for Appetizers, Entrees and Beverages are calculated similarly.

Your spreadsheet should be similar to the following:

DANCE (SS)

	A	B	C	D	E
1	Expenses	50 members	100 members	150 members	200 members
2					
3	Band	$1,500.00	$1,500.00	$1,500.00	$1,500.00
4	Decorations	$185.00	$185.00	$185.00	$185.00
5	Print tickets	$73.15	$73.15	$73.15	$73.15
6	Electricity	$50.00	$50.00	$50.00	$50.00
7	Advertising	$182.00	$182.00	$182.00	$182.00
8	Clean up	$78.00	$78.00	$78.00	$78.00
9	Appetizers	$56.00	$112.00	$168.00	$224.00
10	Entrees	$111.00	$222.00	$333.00	$444.00
11	Dessert	$34.50	$69.00	$103.50	$138.00
12	Beverages	$150.00	$300.00	$450.00	$600.00
13					
14	Cost/Member =	$48.39	$27.71	$20.82	$17.37
15					

c) Produce the following charts using the data in DANCE:

(1) a pie chart which displays the percent amounts of each cost when 50 members attend. Title the chart Dance Expenses.

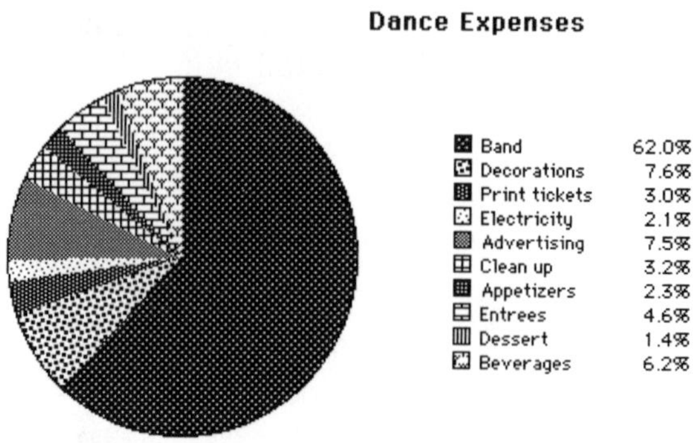

(2) produce charts similar to that created in (1) for 100, 150 and 200 members attending. Title and label the charts appropriately.

(3) a bar chart which displays the cost per member when 50, 100, 150 and 200 members attend. Title the chart as shown.

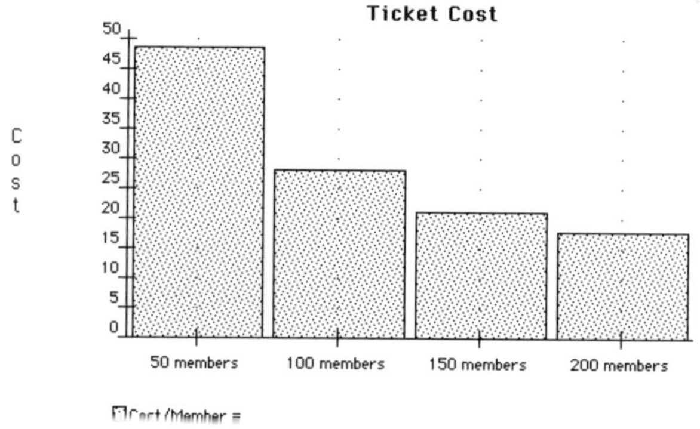

d) Perform the following What if? questions using your spreadsheet, save the modified file on disk and then print a copy:

(1) The Ivy alumni are unhappy about most of the plans. They hate the band, the Poison Ivy's. Many of the younger alumni want the Dreadful Greats instead, but they will cost $3,500. Calculate the cost per member with the new band.

(2) Many alumni want better desserts. Calculate the costs with Desserts doubled.

(3) A group of alumni do not want to hold the dance in Ivy Hall which the University will let them use if they pay for electricity and clean up. These members want to hold the dinner dance at the Newton Hilton which will cost $7,000. Add a row to your spreadsheet to include the new hotel cost and delete the rows for Electricity and Clean up because these costs are included in the Hilton's fee.

2. On your data disk is a spreadsheet named STOCK2 which stores the names, purchase price and number of shares for stocks owned by Grace van Ivy, a relative of Ivy University's founder. You are to assist her by producing the following calculations in the spreadsheet. Columns D through G should be set to 15 characters wide and formatted to display dollar values.

   a) Add the title `Original Value` to column D and calculate the original value of each stock. The original value is calculated by multiplying the shares bought by the purchase price.

   b) At the bottom of column D calculate the total paid for all of the stock.

   c) Ms. van Ivy wants to know how much money she has made or lost on each stock. Below is listed the current price per share for each stock:

Alex Car Wash	$23.12
American Exp.	$120.45
Freitas Fries	$30.12
Giorgio Pizza	$89.78
International	$45.23
Ivy Newspapers	$14.00
Jane's Cakes	$56.89
Johnson Co.	$45.32
Lucky Stores	$20.67
Mad Music Co.	$67.39
Mercedes Birdfood	$79.50
Micheal's Auto	$45.35
Photo Magic	$1.20
Ronald Indust.	$10.45
Sam's Pancakes	$67.00
Taco Willies	$15.89
Tasco Foods	$90.00
Zanadu Clothes	$123.45

   Add the title `Current Price` to column E and display the current price per share. Save the modified spreadsheet on disk.

   d) Add the title Current Value to column F and calculate the current value of each stock. Current value is found by multiplying the number of shares by the current price. Sum column F to find the current total value of the stocks.

   e) Ms. van Ivy wants to know what stocks have gained in value and which ones have lost in value. Add a column G titled `Gain or Loss` and calculate the gain or loss of each stock by subtracting the original value from the current value. Note that Works displays negative dollar amounts by enclosing them in parentheses.

f) Ms. van Ivy has decided that it would be best to sell the poorest performing stocks. She wants to know which stocks have lost more than 30% of their original value. Add a column H named Status which uses If functions to display 0's for stocks that should be sold or 1's for stocks that should be retained. Be careful in creating the If functions.

g) Produce a pie chart titled Percentage Value to show Ms. Ivy how her first 10 (Alex Car Wash to Mad Music) stocks are performing. Use the values stored in the Current Value column. The chart should look similar to the following:

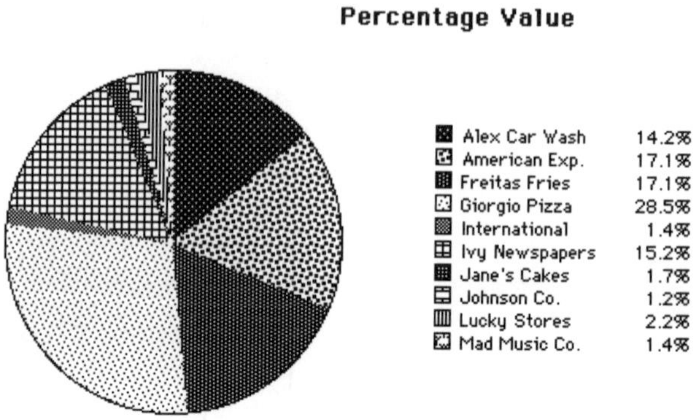

h) When she sells stock Ms. Ivy pays a commission to her stock broker based on the following scale:

Number of Shares	Commission %
0 — 29	5%
30 — 69	4%
70 — 99	2%
100 — 149	1%
150 and over	0.5%

The commission is calculated by multiplying the current value of the stock by the commission percent. Add a column I titled Commissions which calculates the sales commission on each of Ms. Ivy's stocks. Make use of the Vlookup function to produce the column.

i) Save the modified spreadsheet on disk and print a copy.

3. Fantasy Wheels Used Cars wants to use a spreadsheet to keep track of its inventory. The spreadsheet should record the year and model of each car for sale, and the price Fantasy paid for it. Fantasy will use the spreadsheet to determine how much to charge for each car (the selling price). Here is a partial list of Fantasy's inventory. Be imaginative and add three cars of your own to the list:

1972 Corvette price paid: $8,500	1978 Rolls Royce price paid: $34,460
1984 Ferarri price paid: $22,340	1967 Mustang price paid: $11,230

1985 Porsche
price paid: $31,000

1955 Studebaker
price paid: $950

1957 Bel Aire
price paid: $1,250

1975 Aston-Martin
price paid: $56,700

1978 Triumph
price paid: $4,560

1958 Thunderbird
price paid: $14,000

1958 Cadillac
price paid: $8,895

1948 Bentley
price paid: $49,500

1988 Jaguar
price paid: $24,650

1968 GTO
price paid: $12,000

1985 DeLorean
price paid: $28,999

1978 Bricklin
price paid: $36,200

a) Carefully design your spreadsheet using paper and pencil. Take into consideration all of the ways the spreadsheet might be used. In your plan make separate columns for each of three possible selling prices: 10% markup over price paid, 20% markup and 35% markup.

b) Using the design from part (a) create a new spreadsheet named CARS and enter the above data. Use proper formatting and labels. Display the following on your spreadsheet:

(1) total of prices paid for inventory
(2) average price paid per car
(3) total of the selling prices for each of the three markups
(4) profit for each car when it sells at the 20% markup price.
(5) total profit if all of the cars were to sell at the 20% markup price.

c) The 1972 Corvette has been sold. Delete its row from the spreadsheet. Be sure to modify any formulas that might need to be changed.

d) Fantasy has acquired two new cars. Add the following data to the spreadsheet, being sure to modify any formulas that might need to be changed:

1987 Honda
price paid: $6,500

1986 Jeep
price paid: $5,350

e) Fantasy is having a sale on all cars built before 1970. Create a properly formatted column titled Sale which displays a 7.5% markup on the price paid if the car is on sale, and 0 if it is not.

f) Create a properly formatted column titled Sale Profit which displays the profit that Fantasy would earn if all of the pre-1970 cars sold at the 7.5% markup price described in part (e). Total this column.

g) Save the spreadsheet on your data disk naming it CARS and print a copy.

h) Produce a bar chart which displays the price for the 35% mark up of the four most expensive cars. Your chart should be similar to the following:

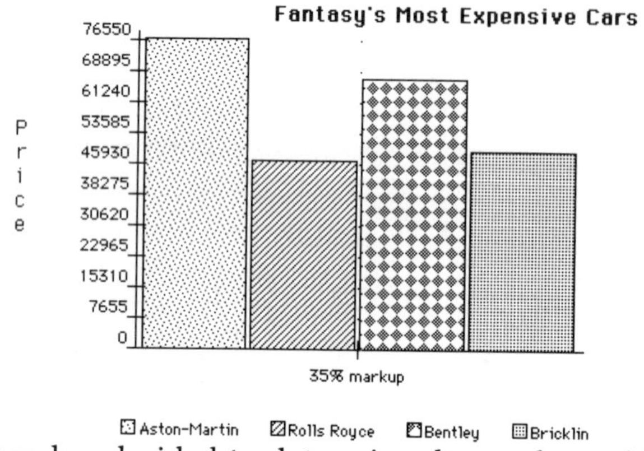

i) Fantasy has decided to determine the markup of its cars based on each car's condition. A rating system will be used of from 1 to 5. The rating for each car is shown below:

Type	**Cars**
1	Studebaker, Thunderbird, DeLorean, Bricklin
2	Mustang, Jaguar, Honda, Jeep
3	Ferarri, Acton-Martin, Triumph, GTO
4	Bel Aire, Rolls Royce, Cadillac
5	Porsche, Bentley

Insert a new column titled Rating which displays each car's rating.

The percent (%) mark up for each rating is listed below:

Rating	% markup
1	10%
2	20%
3	35%
4	50%
5	75%

Insert a new column titled Rating Markup which displays the price of each car after its markup. Use the Choose function to produce this column.

j) Save the modified CARS spreadsheet on disk and print a copy.

4. Your friend, Mike Entrepreneurial, is opening a lawn mowing service and wants you to set up a spreadsheet named LAWNS for his business.

   a) Using paper and pencil, design the spreadsheet so that Mike can enter his customers' names, and the lengths and widths of their lawns in feet. Have the computer display lawn area and the price of cutting the lawn. Mike charges $0.002 per square foot. Be careful to properly format each column and to use meaningful labels.

   b) Using the design from part (a), create the spreadsheet on the computer. Include data for a minimum of 15 customers. Display the total income Mike receives from mowing all his customer's lawns and the average income per lawn.

   c) Mike would like to increase his profit. He wants to ask "What if?" questions about raising his prices. Modify the spreadsheet so that he need only change one entry to raise his price per square foot. Determine what happens to his total income when he doubles and triples his prices.

   d) Mike's customers who have large lawns are complaining bitterly about his prices. In response to the complaints he has decided that all customers with lawns of less than 20,000 square feet will pay $0.003 per square foot and those with larger lawns will pay $0.002 per square foot. Use If functions to calculate the price each customer will pay.

   e) To help Mike better visualize which customers contribute most to his business produce a pie chart titled Income similar to the one below:

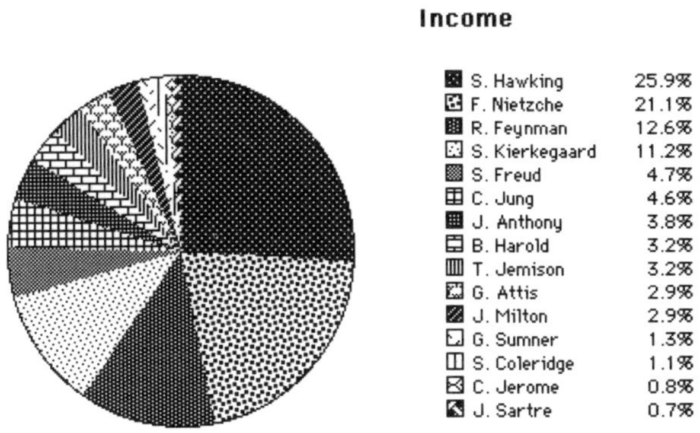

   f) Mike must pay taxes on the price he charges so he wants the following tax table built into the LAWN spreadsheet:

Price in Dollars	Tax %
0 — 14	0
15 — 39	5
40 — 59	7
60 — 99	12
100 — 199	15
200 and above	30

Add a column titled Taxes which displays the taxes Mike must pay for each of his customers. Use a lookup table to produce the calculations.

g) Create a bar chart titled Best Customers which displays the price and taxes for each of Mike's four best customers. Your chart should be similar to the following:

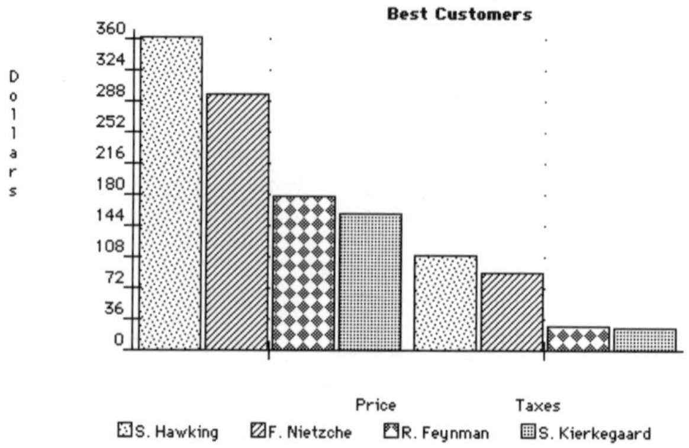

h) Save the spreadsheet on disk using the name LAWNS and print a copy.

5. You have been given an assignment to record the average yearly temperature for your city over a 50 year period. You can find this information in an almanac or at the town library or use the example data given below:

Year	Temp	Year	Temp	Year	Temp
1939	64	1956	49	1973	69
1940	73	1957	54	1974	74
1941	62	1958	65	1975	80
1942	51	1959	53	1976	76
1943	66	1960	55	1977	68
1944	55	1961	63	1978	59
1945	67	1962	75	1979	58
1946	78	1963	67	1980	67
1947	76	1964	76	1981	72
1948	65	1965	58	1982	65
1949	64	1966	69	1983	64
1950	53	1967	70	1984	58
1951	54	1968	65	1985	67
1952	65	1969	56	1986	68
1953	74	1970	57	1987	74
1954	73	1971	72	1988	73
1955	65	1972	70	1989	71

a) Create a spreadsheet named TEMPERATURE which shows the year and average temperature for the last 50 years. Place the Years in row 1 and Temperatures in row 2 so that the data in the spreadsheet runs horizontal rather than vertical. Use proper formatting and labels. To save typing include a formula to calculate and display the year.

Add formulas which calculate each of the following. Use proper formatting and labels:

c) The average temperature over the past 50 years.

d) The average of the first 25 years only.

e) The average of the last 25 years.

f) The minimum and maximum temperatures for the first 25 years.

g) The minimum and maximum temperatures for the last 25 years.

h) Save TEMPERATURE on disk and print a copy.

6. The following figures represent the data for the last 10 years for Flat Technologies, a one-product manufacturer:

Year	Expenses	Units Sold	Price/Unit
Year 1	$50,000.00	6,000	$14.50
Year 2	$60,000.00	7,500	$15.50
Year 3	$65,000.00	8,000	$16.00
Year 4	$75,000.00	10,000	$17.00
Year 5	$77,500.00	15,000	$17.75
Year 6	$70,000.00	14,000	$19.00
Year 7	$65,000.00	11,500	$19.00
Year 8	$63,500.00	10,250	$18.50
Year 9	$60,000.00	10,750	$18.25
Year 10	$62,500.00	11,000	$18.50

a) Create a new spreadsheet named FLAT and enter the above data into it. Be sure to use proper formatting.

b) Add a column titled **Profit** which calculates the profit (income minus expenses) for each year.

c) Add rows to the bottom of the spreadsheet which calculate the average of the yearly expenses, unit sales, price and profit columns. Be sure to include proper labels for these figures.

d) Produce a pie chart titled **Sales Pie** which shows the percentage of units sold each year for years 1 to 10.

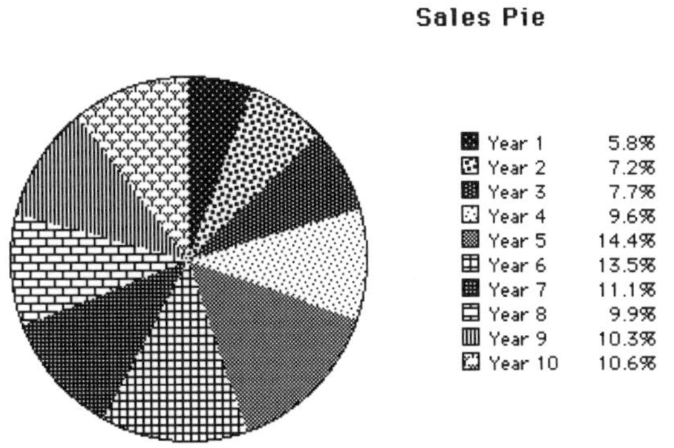

e) Flat's production department has estimated that expenses will rise by 5% each year for the next five years. Insert rows which calculate the expense costs for the next 5 years. Be sure to include this new data in the averages at the bottom of the spreadsheet.

f) Flat's marketing department has estimated that the unit sales will increase by 3.5% each year for the next five years. Extend the unit sales column to include these figures.

g) The marketing department has also determined that the product sells the most when it is priced at $17.45. Make this the selling price for years 11 through 15.

h) Add rows which calculate the average, minimum and maximum profit for years 11 through 15 only. Include proper labels for these rows. Print a copy of the modified spreadsheet.

i) The state in which Flat Technologies is located has a corporate tax based on the following rates:

Profit	Tax Rate
0 — 19,999	2%
20,000 — 39,999	4%
40,000 — 59,999	5%
60,000 — 99,999	6%
100,000 and above	8%

Add a column F to the spreadsheet titled State Tax which displays the taxes Flat has paid for each of its 15 years. Use a Vlookup table to calculate the tax.

j) Save the FLAT spreadsheet on disk when complete and print a copy.

7. You have been asked to get price quotes from several printers to have a small newsletter printed for your club:

Printer A: $.25 per copy up to 1000 copies
$.23 per copy for every copy over 1000

Printer B: $.27 per copy for up to 900 copies
$.15 per copy for every copy over 900

Printer C: $.28 per copy for up to 500 copies
$.20 per copy for every copy over 500

a) Create a new spreadsheet named PRINTER which shows the cost for printing 500, 1000 and 1500 copies of the newsletter for each of the three printers. Use an If to calculate the prices.

b) Add a row to the bottom of the spreadsheet which shows the minimum cost for printing each of the three numbers of copies.

c) The club president would also like quotes for 750 and 1250 copies. Add two columns to the spreadsheet which calculate and display the costs for these numbers of copies. Calculate which printer is cheapest for each of the five numbers of copies. Save the spreadsheet when completed and print a copy.

d) Produce a bar chart that displays the cost that each printer charges for the different number of copies:

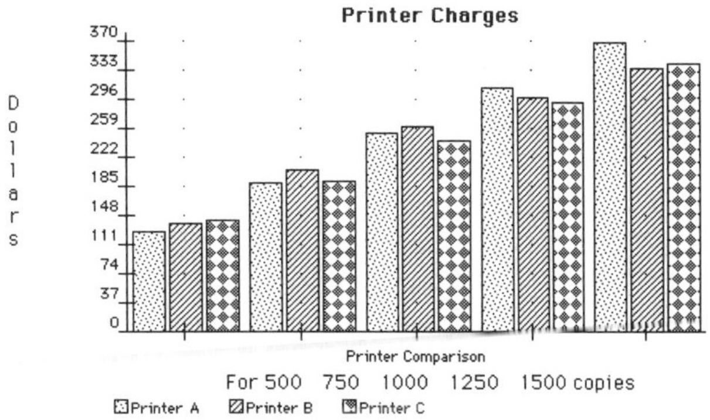

e) Printer C has heard about the other printer's prices and has decided to change his quote to the following:

$.27 per copy for up to 500 copies
$.21 per copy for every copy over 500

Change the formulas for Printer C to reflect this new price. Save the modified spreadsheet on disk and print a copy.

Chapter 9

Integrating the Word Processor, Data Base and Spreadsheet

Window

Edit - Open ⌘O

File - Close All

Edit - Prepare to Merge ⌘M

Edit - Show Field Data

File - Print Merge

Objectives

After completing this chapter you will be able to:

1. Open multiple files and switch between them.
2. Transfer text between word processor files.
3. Transfer data between data base files.
4. Transfer data between spreadsheet files.
5. Integrate spreadsheet data with a word processed document.
6. Use the word processor to create a mail-merge document for use with the data base.
7. Share data between the data base and spreadsheet.

Works is an "integrated" software package. That is, it is possible to use the three applications areas, word processing, data base and spreadsheet, by running only one program. There are two important reasons for using an integrated package. The first is that, because the applications are integrated, it is possible to share data between them. The second is that it is easy to learn and use such a package because it has similar commands in each of the applications areas. For example, pressing ⌘ S always saves the current file whether you are using the word processor, data base or spreadsheet. This chapter will discuss the different ways of sharing data between the applications areas and assumes that you have completed the previous chapters.

9.1 Using Multiple Windows

The operations in Works mimic the work done in an actual office: for example, a file is retrieved from storage and must be opened before it may be used. It is unlikely in a real office that only one file would be worked on at a time. For this reason Works allows up to 14 files to be open at any one time. This can include any mix of word processor, data base and spreadsheet files, but is limited by the size of the files and the amount of memory your computer has available.

When opening files, Works displays a list of the different files available on your data disk. It is possible to open a single file by highlighting its name in the list and double-clicking, which places a copy of the file on disk in the computer's memory. It is then possible to use the Open command (⌘O) again to open a second file. Up to 14 files can be opened simultaneously in this manner. Each file is placed in its own "window". The term window refers to the memory storing a particular file, as well as the boxed area on the screen displaying the file. Works displays the names of open files in the Window menu:

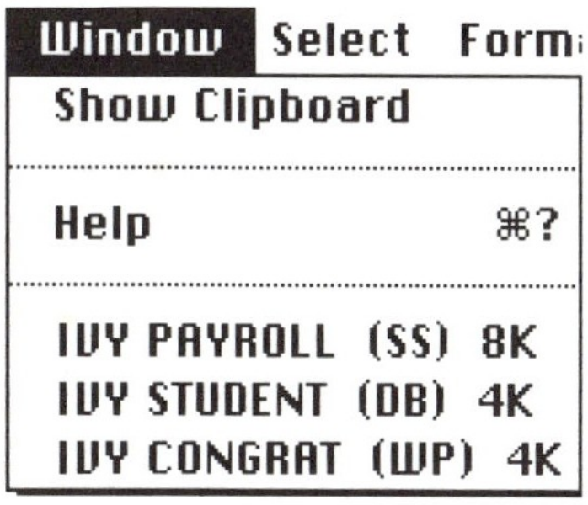

The Window Menu lists all open files, their types and sizes

Selecting a file name from this menu switches to that file in the corresponding window. When a file is selected, Works automatically switches to the proper application and displays that file. The two letters in parentheses after the file's name indicate the application: (WP) for Word Processor, (DB) for Data Base and (SS) for Spreadsheet. The number indicates the size of the file in kilobytes or "K" as described in Chapter 1.

There are many different reasons for switching between files. For example, you may be writing a letter in the word processor and wish to refer to some figures stored in a spreadsheet. With both files open in windows, you could call up the Window menu, switch to the spreadsheet file, view the figures and then switch back to the word processed letter. Other reasons include integrating the data between applications which will be described below.

Works maintains the current status of each open file, including any changes made, in that file's window. This includes the position of the cursor and any options set, so that it is possible to work with one file, switch to another, and return to the first file, picking up exactly where you left off. An option set in one window has no effect on any other. For example, it is possible to have a database displayed in List view in one window, and another displayed in Form view in a different window.

A file in a window does not have to be saved until you have finished working with it. However, it is a good idea to save modified files from time to time as a precaution. Pressing ⌘S saves only the file in the window currently displayed on the screen, so it is a good practice to save a modified file before switching to another.

Practice 1

The Practices in this Chapter deal with problems that require several open files at one time. We will start by opening several Ivy University files in different windows and switching between them.

1) BOOT THE MACINTOSH SYSTEM AND START WORKS

2) OPEN THREE FILES

a. Click once on the Word Processor icon and locate the IVY CONGRAT file in the files list. Double-click on the file name to open it. The IVY CONGRAT word processing file is placed in the first window and displayed on the Word Processor screen.
b. Press ⌘O to display the Open dialog box a second time.
c. Click once on the Data Base icon and select IVY STUDENT from the files list. The IVY STUDENT data base is placed in a new window and displayed on the Data Base screen. IVY CONGRAT is still open in a window, only not displayed.
d. Press ⌘O to display the Open dialog box a third time.
e. Click once on the Spreadsheet icon and select IVY PAYROLL from the files list. The IVY PAYROLL spreadsheet is placed in a new window and displayed on the Spreadsheet screen.
f. Use the mouse to select cell A5.

3) SWITCH TO THE IVY STUDENT DATA BASE

a. Use the mouse to display the Window menu. Note the three open files listed in the menu.

b. From the Window menu select IVY STUDENT. The application switches to data base and displays the IVY STUDENT file.

4) SWITCH TO THE IVY CONGRAT DOCUMENT

a. Display the Window menu.

b. Select IVY CONGRAT. The application switches to word processor and displays the IVY CONGRAT file.

5) SWITCH BACK TO IVY PAYROLL

Select IVY PAYROLL from the Window menu. The application switches back to the spreadsheet. Note that the cell cursor is still on cell A5, where it was placed in step 2 above.

Check - The IVY PAYROLL spreadsheet file should be displayed:

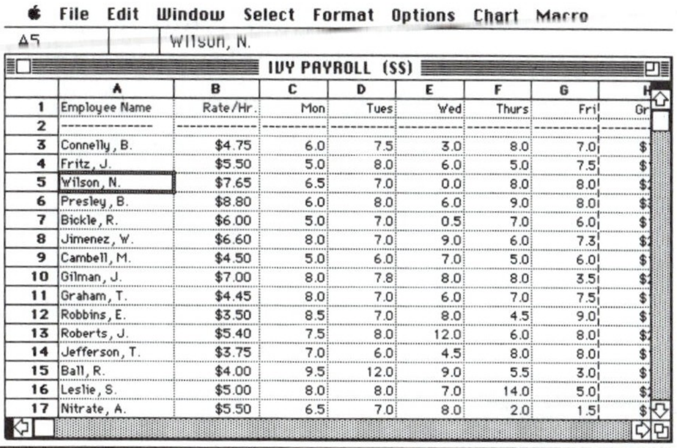

	A	B	C	D	E	F	G	H
1	Employee Name	Rate/Hr.	Mon	Tues	Wed	Thurs	Fri	Gr
2	-------------	----------	----------	----------	----------	----------	----------	------
3	Connelly, B.	$4.75	6.0	7.5	3.0	8.0	7.0	$
4	Fritz, J.	$5.50	5.0	8.0	6.0	5.0	7.5	$
5	Wilson, N.	$7.65	6.5	7.0	0.0	8.0	8.0	$
6	Presley, B.	$8.80	6.0	8.0	6.0	9.0	8.0	$
7	Bickle, R.	$6.00	5.0	7.0	0.5	7.0	6.0	$
8	Jimenez, W.	$6.60	8.0	7.0	9.0	6.0	7.3	$
9	Cambell, M.	$4.50	5.0	6.0	7.0	5.0	6.0	$
10	Gilman, J.	$7.00	8.0	7.8	8.0	8.0	3.5	$
11	Graham, T.	$4.45	8.0	7.0	6.0	7.0	7.5	$
12	Robbins, E.	$3.50	8.5	7.0	8.0	4.5	9.0	$
13	Roberts, J.	$5.40	7.5	8.0	12.0	6.0	8.0	$
14	Jefferson, T.	$3.75	7.0	6.0	4.5	8.0	8.0	$
15	Ball, R.	$4.00	9.5	12.0	9.0	5.5	3.0	$
16	Leslie, S.	$5.00	8.0	8.0	7.0	14.0	5.0	$
17	Nitrate, A.	$5.50	6.5	7.0	8.0	2.0	1.5	$

9.2 Removing Files from Memory

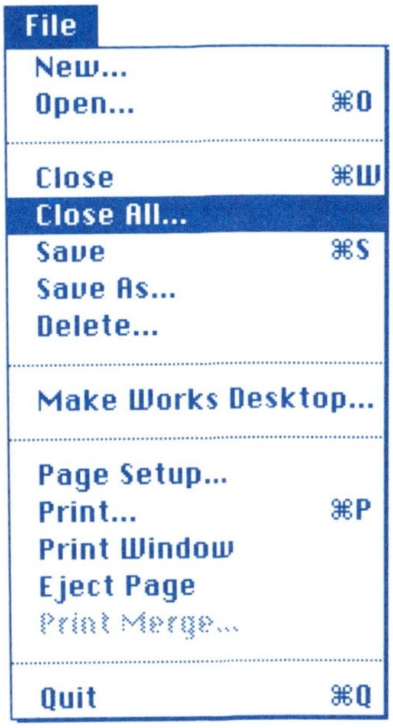

When work on an open file is complete, it should be closed (⌘W) to free memory for other files. Works performs certain operations faster when more memory is available. Also, should some accident occur that clears the computer's memory, limiting the number of open files to only those necessary means that less data from modified files would be lost. When a file is closed it is removed from its window, and Works automatically switches to the next open window.

If changes have been made to a file, it should be saved on disk before it is closed. If you attempt to close a file which has been modified before saving it, or to exit Works, you are warned that changes will be lost unless the file is saved.

It is possible to close all open files at one time using the Close All command from the File menu. To protect against accidental closures, Works displays a dialog box:

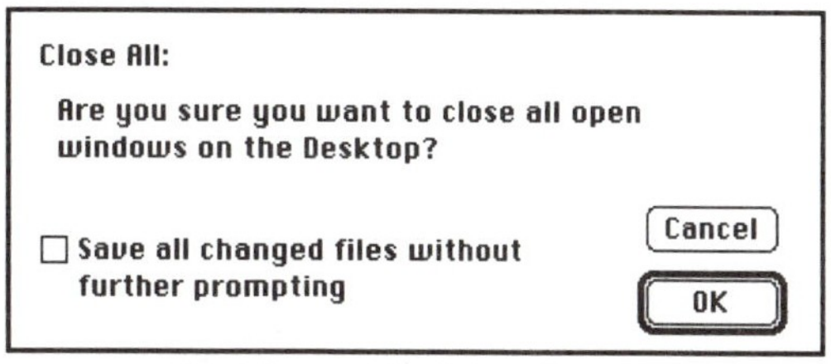

The Close All dialog box

Clicking on `OK` removes all files from the computer's memory. However, before attempting to close a modified file, Works will display a warning. If several files were modified and not saved, Works will display a warning for each file.

9.3 Displaying Multiple Windows

When several files are open, it is possible to display all of their windows simultaneously. While this is not necessary, it is sometimes helpful to see the contents of more than one file on the screen at a time.

To display more than one file, the size of the displayed window can be reduced using the adjust box in the lower right-hand corner:

Dragging the Adjust box makes windows smaller or larger

Dragging this box towards the upper left makes the window smaller. The modified window can then be moved to a new location on the screen by clicking on the file name at the top of the window and dragging. If needed, the expand box in the upper right corner of the window can be clicked to restore the file to full-screen size.

In the Practices that follow, it is your choice as to whether to display more than one window on the screen at the same time or not. Unless you are specifically directed, you may perform the Practice in the manner which is most convenient for you.

9.4 Using Windows to Integrate Word Processed Documents

As you saw in Practice 1, Works can open several files at one time and switch easily between them. It is possible to transfer data between different open files and applications areas using the Copy and Paste commands in a special way.

You have previously used the Copy command in the different applications areas, but only to copy data within the same file. To copy data between different open files, four steps are required:

1. The data to be copied is highlighted by dragging the mouse.
2. The Copy command is executed (⌘C).
3. The file to receive the copied data is displayed using the Window menu.
4. The cursor is placed at the position to copy the data and Paste executed (⌘V).

We will begin by copying data from one word processor document to another. This is a powerful tool, allowing blocks of text to be entered into the computer once, and then shared among different documents.

It is best that both the file providing the text to be copied, and the file receiving the text be open. Copying the text simply transfers a copy of the highlighted block to the receiving document; the original file remains unchanged. Because the file receiving the block is modified, it should be saved before it is closed or Works exited.

Practice 2

In this Practice you will copy a paragraph from one word processed document into another. The three files IVY CONGRAT, IVY STUDENT and IVY PAYROLL should still be open from the last Practice. We will first close IVY PAYROLL and IVY STUDENT, then copy a paragraph from the IVY HANDBOOK document into the IVY CONGRAT letter.

1) REMOVE THE UNNEEDED FILES FROM MEMORY

a. Press ⌘W to close the currently displayed file, IVY PAYROLL. That window is closed and the previous window displayed.
b. Select IVY STUDENT from the Window menu. Press ⌘W to close this file. The window is closed and the last window, containing IVY CONGRAT, displayed.

2) OPEN THE IVY HANDBOOK FILE

The IVY HANDBOOK file contains a passage from the Ivy University student handbook which we want to copy.

a. Press ⌘O to display the Open File dialog box.
b. Click once on the Word Processor icon and select IVY HANDBOOK from the files list. IVY HANDBOOK is opened and placed in a new window, on top of the first window. Two word processor files are now open in memory.

3) HIGHLIGHT THE TEXT TO BE COPIED

a. If not already, place the cursor at the beginning of the first paragraph, which begins "One of the most. . .".
b. Drag the pointer to the end of the paragraph, highlighting the entire paragraph.

4) COPY THE PARAGRAPH INTO THE IVY CONGRAT LETTER

a. Press ⌘C to execute the Copy command. The highlighted text is copied in the computer's memory.
b. Switch to IVY CONGRAT in the first window by selecting it from the Window menu.
c. Move the pointer to the position where the text should be inserted, the blank line after the sentence which reads "To quote the student handbook:". Click the mouse once to insert the cursor.
d. Press ⌘V to execute the Paste command. The highlighted paragraph from IVY CONGRAT is copied from the file and placed at the current cursor position.
e. Press ⌘S to save the modified congratulations letter on disk.

5) ADJUST THE WINDOWS TO DISPLAY BOTH FILES

a. Place the pointer on the adjust box at the bottom right-hand corner of the window.
b. Drag the box to the left, about halfway across the screen. The IVY HANDBOOK window is revealed below.

Check - The paragraph should be inserted in the congratulations letter. Both files should be visible in different windows:

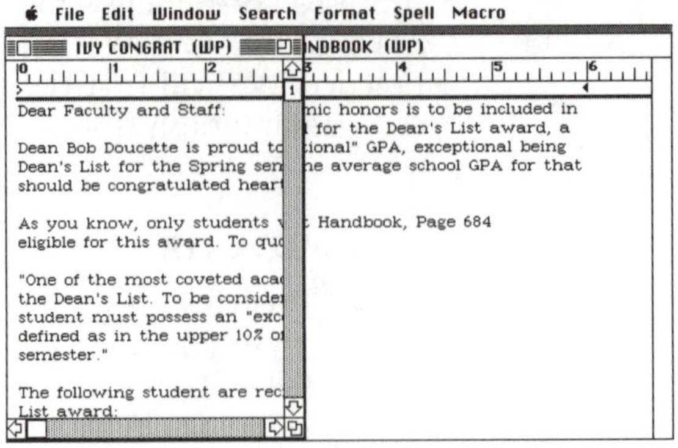

9.5 Sharing Data between Two Spreadsheets

It is possible to share data between two spreadsheets by opening both files and copying the data between them using Copy and Paste. Just as when copying within a single spreadsheet, cells copied from one spreadsheet to another retain their formulas and formatting.

To transfer data between two open spreadsheets, the following steps are taken:

1. The spreadsheet cells to be copied are highlighted using the mouse.
2. The Copy command is executed, ⌘C.
3. The Window menu is used to display the second spreadsheet.
4. The cursor is positioned where the copy is to be placed and the Paste command executed (⌘V) to copy the cells.

You must make room for the new data if you wish to insert the copied cells between already existing cells. For example, to copy a row from one spreadsheet into the center of another you must first insert a blank row in the receiving spreadsheet. Works displays a warning and the Paste command overwrites existing data if this is not done.

Practice 3

In this Practice you will copy a group of cells from one spreadsheet to another, adding the data for a group of new employees to the IVY PAYROLL spreadsheet. Start Works if you have not already done so.

1) PREPARE THE WINDOWS

a. Close any open files using ⌘W.
b. Press ⌘O and open the IVY NEW EMP spreadsheet. Note that there are seven new employees.
c. Press ⌘O again and open the IVY PAYROLL spreadsheet in a new window.

2) INSERT SEVEN EMPTY ROWS IN THE RECEIVING SPREADSHEET

a. Click on cell A19.
b. Press ⌘I 7 times to insert seven empty rows.

3) HIGHLIGHT THE CELLS TO BE COPIED

a. Use the Window menu to switch to IVY NEW EMP.
b. Make sure that the cell cursor is on cell A1. Drag the pointer to the end of the spreadsheet to select all of the cells through column I containing data for the seven employees.

4) COPY THE DATA INTO THE PAYROLL SPREADSHEET

a. Press ⌘C to execute the Copy command.
b. Switch to IVY PAYROLL using the Window menu.
c. Select the cell where the new cells are to be inserted, the blank rows starting at cell A19.
d. Press ⌘V to Paste the data. The highlighted cells from IVY NEW EMP are copied from that file and placed at the current position. The formulas are recalculated to reflect the new data.
e. Use Fill Down (⌘D) to copy the formulas in cells J18 through P18 to the new employees in rows 19 through 25.
f. Press ⌘S to save the modified spreadsheet on disk.

Check - The new employees inserted into the spreadsheet automatically change the totals displayed at the bottom of the spreadsheet:

IVY PAYROLL (SS)

	K	L	M	N	O	P
22	$14.86	$13.42	$157.48	$216.72	$227.04	$237.36
23	$15.12	$12.29	$161.60	$198.45	$207.90	$217.35
24	$0.00	$7.82	$102.81	$126.26	$132.28	$138.29
25	$101.67	$24.08	$237.34	$389.03	$407.55	$426.08
26	$15.05	$12.48	$160.63	$201.60	$211.20	$220.80
27	$16.00	$13.26	$170.71	$214.25	$224.46	$234.66
28	$0.00	$9.62	$130.98	$155.40	$162.80	$170.20
29	$0.00	$4.88	$70.13	$78.75	$82.50	$86.25
30	$23.00	$16.25	$190.75	$262.50	$275.00	$287.50
31	$0.00	$8.97	$122.09	$144.85	$151.75	$158.64
32	$51.69	$20.17	$232.19	$325.76	$341.27	$356.79
33	$58.02	$22.64	$260.63	$365.66	$383.08	$400.49
34	$15.55	$14.04	$164.81	$226.80	$237.60	$248.40
35						
36			Pay Raise =	$6,594.32	$6,908.34	$7,222.35
37			Raise Cost =	$314.02	$628.03	$942.05
38						

9.6 Sharing Data between two Data Bases

It is possible to transfer data between two data bases by using the Copy command. After opening both files, the desired records from the first file are highlighted, and then copied into the receiving file. If the first data base is displayed in Form view, only the displayed record may be copied. If the file is displayed in List view, a highlighted block of records and fields may be copied. Because of this, records are best copied when both files are displayed in List view.

The process of sharing records between data bases is made slightly more complex when the files contain different fields. When this occurs, the entries from the first field in the original file are copied to the first selected field in the second file, and so on, regardless of the field names. Therefore, care must be taken when transferring records from one data base to another to ensure that the entries are placed in the proper fields. Like the spreadsheet, if the copied records are to be inserted into the middle of a data base, empty records must first be created, otherwise existing records will be overwritten with the copied data.

Another problem occurs when the data being Pasted has more fields than the receiving data base. When this is attempted, any fields beyond the length of the receiving data base are truncated and not pasted. For example, attempting to paste a record with 5 fields into a data base which has only 4 fields causes the fifth field to be not copied.

Practice 4

In this Practice you will transfer records between two data base files. Start Works if you have not already done so.

1) PREPARE THE WINDOWS

a. Close any open files using ⌘W.
b. Open the IVY STUDENT data base. If the file is displayed in Form view, switch to List view using ⌘L.
c. Press ⌘O and open the IVY NEW STU data base in a second window. If the file is displayed in Form view, switch to List view using ⌘L.

2) HIGHLIGHT THE RECORDS TO BE COPIED

Select the first field in the first record. Drag the mouse to the end of the data base to select all fields in all of the records.

3) COPY THE HIGHLIGHTED RECORDS TO IVY STUDENT

a. Press ⌘C to execute the Copy command.
b. Switch to IVY STUDENT using the Window menu.
c. Scroll to the end of the file where the records are to be inserted. Click on the First Name field in the empty record at the bottom of the data base.
d. Press ⌘V to paste the records. The highlighted records from IVY NEW STU are copied from that file and placed at the current position.
c. Press ⌘S to save the modified data base on disk.

<u>Check</u> - The new records are pasted at the bottom of the data base:

First Name	Last Name	Address	City	State	Zip	
Kim	Kokonen	#5 Palm Tree Apts.	Stans Valley	VE	99999	Septe
Gina	Goida	221 Runaway Bay	Buffalo	TN	64830	Feb
Iggy	Pop	13 Big Time Circle	West Lafeet	AK	94857	Nov
Gill	Bates	123 Lotus Lane	Redmond	WA	02134	
Francis	Ford	9 Calculus Street	Calabash	MI	08753	
Sam	Adams	121 Carey Quadrangle	Leaftown	PA	19717	N
Robbie	Radar	1389 Kings Hiway	Haddonfield	PR	00123	Feb
Dan	Theman	945 Action Avenue	Baskerville	RI	04858	Oc
John	Zvetan	Hardenberg Hall	Stanford	CA	97654	
Bill	Russell	17 Slopes Street	Boyton	CO	34567	
Steve	Rohrman	212 Phillips Ave.	Magnolia	NJ	28131	Oc
John	Camper	12 Swan's Cove	Winter Park	UT	57735	Nove
Jane	Doe	35 Russel Street	Bumblebee	NM	34234	Fe
Jon	Heacock	63 Copper Place	Roxbury	KY	77538	N
Mary Ann	Nash	Runaway Road	Frost Proof	OR	78543	
Linda	Stratford	1 Winding Way	Capt. Cook	HI	56889	
Paul	Walpole	987 Forrest Court	St. Stephen	ID	56778	

9.7 Merging Spreadsheets with the Word Processor

One of the options when copying spreadsheet data is to paste the data into a word processed document. Businesses must often send memos and letters which contain the figures from a spreadsheet. The ability to place a spreadsheet within a word processed document is one of the most powerful features of an integrated package like Works.

Usually the files produced by a separate (non-integrated) spreadsheet are not compatible with a separate word processor, requiring the figures to be typed by hand. This is a time consuming and error prone process.

The steps required to place an open spreadsheet within an open word processor document are:

1. The desired spreadsheet cells are highlighted using the mouse.
2. The Copy command is executed, ⌘ C.
3. The Window menu is used to display the word processor document.
4. The cursor is positioned and Paste (⌘ V) used to copy the cells.

Cells copied into a document are automatically separated by tabs, forming a table like the ones created in Chapter 3. Works creates tab stops for the table which match the position and alignment of the original cells in the spreadsheet. You may wish to change the tab stops or other formatting options to better fit your document.

Practice 5

In this Practice part of a spreadsheet will be copied into a word processor document. Start Works if you have not already done so.

1) PREPARE THE WINDOWS

a. Close any open files using ⌘ W.
b. Press ⌘ O and open the IVY CONGRAT word processor file.
c. Press ⌘ O and open the GRADES spreadsheet in a new window. GRADES was created in the Practices of Chapter 7.

2) HIGHLIGHT THE CELLS TO BE COPIED

Make sure the cursor is in cell A1. Drag the pointer to cell D11 to select the cells in columns A to D of the spreadsheet.

3) COPY THE CELLS TO THE DOCUMENT

a. Press ⌘ C to execute the Copy command.
b. Switch to IVY CONGRAT using the Window menu.
c. Move the cursor to the blank line after the paragraph which begins "Dr. Sulfuric's Chemistry class. . .".
d. Press ⌘ V to execute Paste. The highlighted cells from GRADES are pasted at the current cursor position. Note how tabs are used to separate the different columns.
e. Press ⌘ S to save the modified letter on disk.
f. Print a copy of the letter using ⌘ P.

<u>Check</u> - The spreadsheet showing Dr. Sulfuric's grades should be inserted into the letter:

Dr. Sulfuric's Chemistry class once again led the school in highest percentage of Dean's List students. Here is a selection from her grade book showing the extraordinary performance of her students:

Name	Test 1 9/10/90	Test 2 10/20/90
J. Smith	50	83
W. Freitas	86	89
M. Porter	78	100
B. Presley	45	78
H. Crane	66	76
M. Lee	85	74

9.8 Merging Data Bases with the Word Processor

Data from a data base may also be copied into a word processor document. This is done when a word processed report must contain information from a data base. The ability to copy records from a data base to a document is another important feature of Works.

The steps required to place data from an open data base within an open word processor document are:

1. The desired data base information is highlighted using the mouse.
2. The Copy command is executed, ⌘C.
3. The Window menu is used to display the word processor document.
4. The cursor is positioned and the Paste command (⌘V) used to paste the data into the document.

List view is useful when copying records because it allows more than one record to be highlighted. Also, only the highlighted fields are copied, so the entire record does not have to be selected and queries can be used to limit the number of records copied. To make it easy to identify the copied records, Works automatically includes the field names along with the data. These may be deleted from the document if not needed. Fields copied into a document are automatically separated by tabs, with Works creating tab stops which match the position and alignment of the fields in the data base. You may change the stops to better fit the document.

Practice 6

In this Practice selected fields from a data base will be copied into a word processor document. A query will be used to limit the number of records copied. Start Works if you have not already done so.

1) PREPARE THE WINDOWS

a. Close the GRADES spreadsheet by switching to its window and then using ⌘W.

b. Press ⌘O and open the IVY STUDENT data base in a new window. If it is not already, press ⌘L to display the data base in List view.

2) APPLY A QUERY TO THE DATA BASE

a. Execute the Record Selection command from the Organize menu to create a new query. If they exist, delete any previous rules using the `Delete Rule` button.
b. Select GPA from the fields list.
c. Select "is greater than" from the comparison list.
d. Type `3.5` on the Comparison Information line.
e. Click on Select to apply the query. Note that only those student records with a GPA greater than 3.5 are displayed.

3) HIGHLIGHT THE DATA TO BE COPIED

a. Click on the first name field in the first record.
b. Drag the mouse down the First Name and Last Name fields, highlighting only those fields in each record.

4) COPY THE HIGHLIGHTED DATA IN TO THE DOCUMENT

a. Press ⌘`C` to execute the Copy command.
b. Switch to IVY CONGRAT using the Window menu.
c. Move the cursor to the blank line after the paragraph which begins "The following students. . .".
d. Press ⌘`V` to Paste the information. Only the highlighted fields from IVY STUDENT are copied from that file and placed at the current cursor position. Note the field names and how tabs are used to separate the data.
e. Press ⌘`S` to save the modified letter on disk.
f. Print the letter using ⌘ `P`.
g. Close the files selecting the Close All command from the File menu. Click on `OK` to close all files.
h. Click on `No` to ignore the changes caused by applying the query to IVY STUDENT.

Check - The first and last names of all students in IVY STUDENT with a GPA greater than 3.5 should be inserted into the letter. You may wish to change the position of the tab stops to better fit the document.

9.9 Mail Merge and Form Letters

One of the most useful applications provided by an integrated package is the ability to use "mail merge" to create personalized form letters. You have undoubtedly received such letters that begin "The next winner of 10 Million dollars could be" followed by your name. This is an example of a mail merged form letter.

Mail merge takes advantage of the computer's ability to integrate the information stored in a data base with a word processed letter and print the result. To create such a letter, open the data base which contains the personalized data which is to appear in the letter: name, address, etc. The letter is then typed into the word processor, indicating where the data from the data base fields is to be printed. When completed, the computer prints one copy of the letter for each record in the data base, inserting data from each record into the letter.

To mail merge a letter, the following steps are required:

1. The desired data base file is opened.
2. The letter is typed in the word processor, marking where you wish the data from the different fields to be printed.
3. The Print Merge command is executed from the File menu.

When the Print Merge command is executed, Works generates and prints a personalized copy of the letter for each record in the data base. If there are 50 records in the data base, 50 personalized letters will be printed. Works merges data only from visible records, making it possible to use queries to limit the number of letters printed. For example, Ivy University could print mail merge letters for only those students with an honors GPA by applying the appropriate query before executing Print Merge.

The position of the merged data in the letter is specified by inserting the name of a field into the document using the Prepare To Merge command from the Edit menu (⌘M). Works then displays a list of the open data base files. For example:

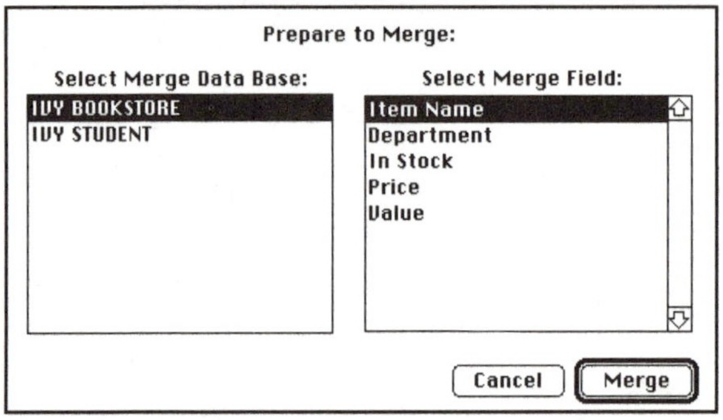

The Prepare to Merge dialog box lists open data base files and their fields

When you select the desired data base file, a listing of the Fields in that data base is displayed from which you may select:

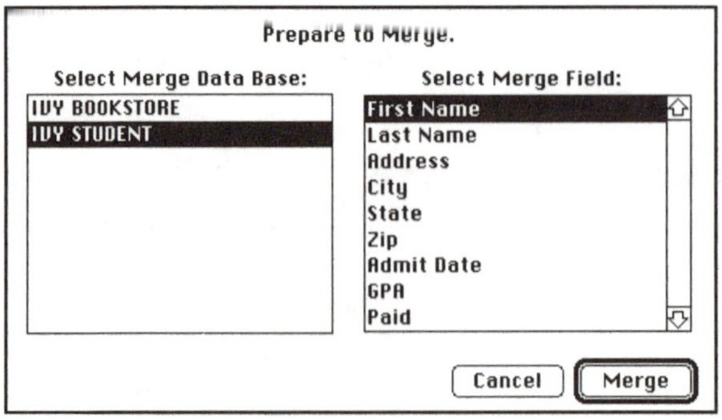

Selecting a data base file lists the field names in that file

When Merge is clicked, Works inserts a marker into the text showing both the name of the data base file and the selected field. For example, selecting First Name from the IVY STUDENT file as shown in the above dialog box would place the marker

IVY STUDENT:First Name

A mail merge marker lists both the data base and field name

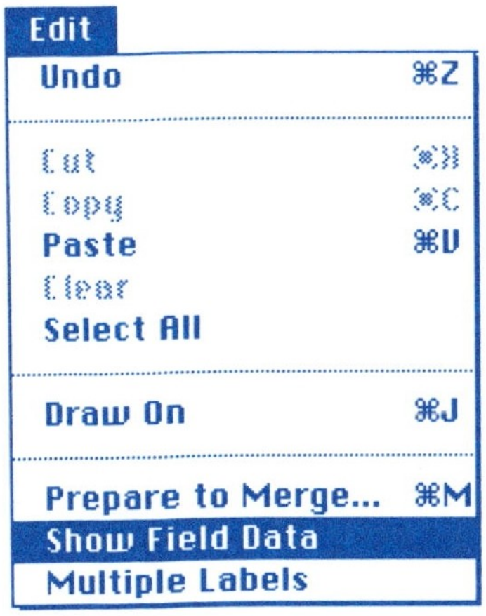

in the document at the current cursor position. These markers can be positioned throughout the document until all the required fields have been specified. Markers may be moved, copied, formatted and deleted like ordinary text. When the letter is printed you have the option of printing a plain or merged copy. Printing a plain document (⌘P) shows the markers, allowing you to review the placement of the fields. A merged document using the Print Merge command prints the actual information from the data base in place of the markers.

To see what a merged document will look like, it is possible to execute the Show Field Data command from the Edit menu. When this is done, the markers are replaced on screen by the data from the first record in the data base. This is a useful option for checking the formatting of a merged document. The markers may again be displayed by executing the Show Field Names command from the Edit menu.

Practice 7

In this Practice you will modify and print a mail merged letter. Although this letter contains data from only two fields, it is possible to create a mail merged document which contains data from any field in an open data base. Start Works if you have not already done so.

1) PREPARE THE WINDOWS

a. Close any open files using ⌘W.
b. Press ⌘O and open the IVY STUDENT data base.
c. Press ⌘O and open the IVY TUITION word processed letter in a second window.

2) INSERT THE FIRST MERGE FIELD INTO THE LETTER

a. Place the cursor after "Dear" and type a space.
b. Select Prepare to Merge from the Edit menu to display the dialog box. Because it is the only open data base, a list of the fields in IVY STUDENT is shown in the Select Merge Field list. Note that First Name is already selected.
c. Click on the `Merge` button to accept First Name. A marker is inserted into the letter.
d. Press the Space bar to insert a space after the First Name marker.

3) INSERT THE NEXT MERGE FIELD INTO THE LETTER

a. Press ⌘M to display the Prepare To Merge dialog box.
b. Click on Last Name in the Select Merge Field list.
c. Click on `Merge` to select Last Name. A second marker is inserted into the letter.
d. Type a colon (`:`).

Check - The First Name and Last Name markers should be inserted into the letter so that the line appears on the screen as:

Dear [IVY STUDENT:First Name] [IVY STUDENT:Last Name]:

4) VIEW AN EXAMPLE MERGED DOCUMENT

a. Select the Show Field Data command from the Edit menu. The markers are replaced on screen by the data from the first record in IVY STUDENT:

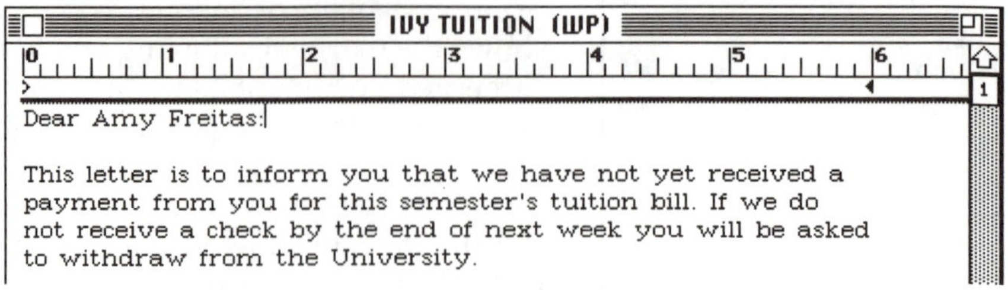

b. Select the Show Field Names command from the Edit menu. The markers are again displayed.

5) PRINT PLAIN AND MERGED COPIES OF THE TUITION LETTER

a. Press ⌘S to save the modified letter on disk.
b. Press ⌘P and click on OK to print a plain (non mail-merged) copy of the letter. Note the position of the field markers in the text. Only one copy of the letter is printed and the word processor screen is again displayed.
c. Execute the Print Merge command from the File menu. Click on OK. A personalized copy of the letter will be printed for each record in the data base. After three or four letters have printed press ⌘. (period) to terminate the printing. Note how the markers have been replaced by the different names from the data base in the printed copies.

9.10 Expanding Mail Merge

In Practice 7 you created and printed a simple mail merge document. While this document contained the data from only two fields, it is important to realize that any field from the open data base may be included in a mail merge. In addition, it is possible to re-use fields. For example, the recipient's first name could appear in the mail merged letter twice: once in the address and once in the greeting. Also, data from fields may be printed inside other text. That is, a field marker may be placed inside a sentence, and Works will adjust any text following the marker to make room for the merged data.

Another mail-merge technique involves using queries to limit the number of mail merged documents produced. It is not usually the case that a mail merge document will be printed for every record in a database. Normally a query will be first used to limit the number of records displayed. When the Print Merge command is then executed, documents are produced for only those selected records which meet the query's criteria.

Practice 8

In this Practice you will modify and print a more complex mail merged letter. A query will be used to limit the number of letters printed. The IVY STUDENT data base and IVY TUITION letter should still be open from the last Practice.

1) PREPARE THE WINDOWS

a. Close IVY TUITION using ⌘W.
b. Press ⌘O and open the IVY GPA letter in a second window. Note that several field markers have already been inserted into this letter.

2) INSERT A FIELD INTO THE LETTER

a. If it is not already there, place the cursor on the blank line below the Last Name marker in the address.
b. Press ⌘M to display the Prepare To Merge dialog box. A list of the fields in IVY STUDENT is shown in the Fields option because IVY STUDENT is the only open database.
c. Highlight Address in the Merge Field list.
d. Click on Merge to select Address. A marker is inserted into the letter.

3) INSERT THE NEXT FIELDS INTO THE LETTER

a. Place the cursor on the blank line below the Address marker.
b. Press ⌘M to display the Prepare To Merge dialog box.
c. Double-click on City in the Merge Field list to insert a City marker.
d. Type a comma (,) followed by a space.
e. Press ⌘M to display the Prepare To Merge dialog box.
f. Double-click on State in the Merge Field list to insert a State marker.
g. Type a space.
h. Press ⌘M to display the Prepare To Merge dialog box.
i. Double-click on Zip in the Merge Field list to insert another marker.

Check - Markers should be inserted into the letter so that the heading appears on the screen as:

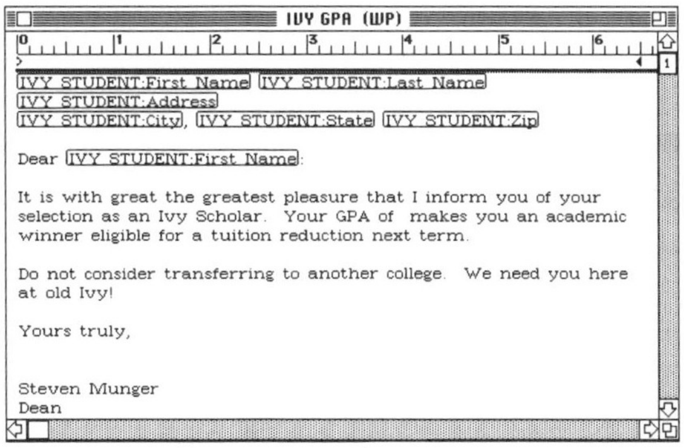

IVY STUDENT:First Name IVY STUDENT:Last Name
IVY STUDENT:Address
IVY STUDENT:City, IVY STUDENT:State IVY STUDENT:Zip

Dear IVY STUDENT:First Name:

It is with great the greatest pleasure that I inform you of your selection as an Ivy Scholar. Your GPA of makes you an academic winner eligible for a tuition reduction next term.

Do not consider transferring to another college. We need you here at old Ivy!

Yours truly,

Steven Munger
Dean

4) INSERT THE GPA INTO THE LETTER AND VIEW THE DATA

a. Move the cursor into the body of the letter, on the blank space after "Your GPA of. . .".
b. Press ⌘M to display the Prepare To Merge dialog box.
c. Double-click on GPA in the Merge Field list. A GPA marker is inserted into the text.
d. Execute Show Field Data from the Edit menu to see the contents the first record.
e. Execute Show Field Names to again display the markers.

5) APPLY THE QUERY "GPA is greater than 3.5" TO THE DATA BASE

a. Switch to the IVY STUDENT data base using the Window menu.
b. Execute Record Selection from the Organize menu to define a new query. Delete any old rules using the `Delete Rule` button.
c. Select GPA from the field list, and "is greater than" from the comparisons list.
d. Type `3.5` on the Comparison Information line.
e. Click on Select to apply the query. Note that only those student records with a GPA greater than 3.5 are displayed.

6) PRINT PLAIN AND MERGED COPIES OF THE TUITION LETTER

a. Display the IVY GPA letter using the Window menu.
b. Press ⌘`S` to save the modified file on disk.
c. Press ⌘`P` and click on `OK` to print a plain (non mail-merged) copy of the letter. Note the position and number of the field markers.
d. Execute the Print Merge command from the File menu and print one copy. A personalized copy of the letter is printed for only the records which meet the query's criteria (GPA is greater than 3.5).

Check - Your letters should be similar to:

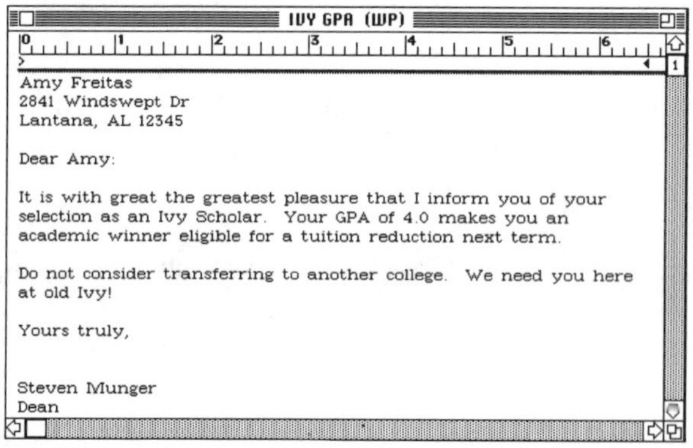

9.11 Integrating the Data Base and Spreadsheet

It is sometimes desirable to have the information stored in a data base available for use in a spreadsheet. This allows users to employ the power of the spreadsheet to ask "What If?" questions and perform calculations on numerical data base fields. For example, the Ivy University Bookstore data base could be transferred into a spreadsheet to determine the profit that would result from raising the cost of all items by 10 percent.

So far, we have used the Copy and Paste commands to transfer data into previously opened file. These can also be used to transfer data to a new file. When this is desired, the new file can be created using New from the File menu after the Copy command has been executed.

Creating a new spreadsheet from a data base file is a four step process:

1. The desired entries are highlighted in the data base using the mouse.
2. The Copy command is executed, ⌘C.
3. The New command from the File menu is used to create a new, empty spreadsheet.
4. Paste (⌘V) is used to copy the fields into empty cells.

When the records are copied the data from the first field is placed in the first column, the second field in the second column, and so on. The new spreadsheet can then be used in the same ways as any other spreadsheet, including performing calculations, formatting, etc. To copy more than one record, the data base must be displayed in List view. If the data base is displayed in Form view, only the visible record may be copied. When the records are copied, the formats of the entries in the data base are retained in the spreadsheet cells.

Practice 9

In this Practice you will create a new spreadsheet named BOOKS using the information from the IVY BOOKSTORE data base file. Start Works if you have not already done so.

1) PREPARE THE WINDOWS

a. Close any open files using ⌘W.
b. Open the IVY BOOKSTORE data base.
c. If the data base is displayed in Form view switch to List view using ⌘L.

2) HIGHLIGHT THE RECORDS TO BE COPIED

Select the first field of the first record. Drag the pointer to the end of the data base to select all of the records.

3) COPY THE HIGHLIGHTED RECORDS INTO THE NEW SPREADSHEET

a. Press ⌘C to execute the Copy command.
b. Select New from the File menu to display the New dialog box.
c. Double-click on the Spreadsheet icon. A new, empty spreadsheet is shown on the screen.
d. Select cell A1. Press ⌘V to paste the data into the spreadsheet. The highlighted records from IVY BOOKSTORE are copied from that file and placed at the current position, each field in a separate column.
e. Press ⌘S to display the Save dialog box.
f. Type `BOOKS` and press Return to save the new spreadsheet on disk.

Check - Data from the Ivy Bookstore data base has been copied into a spreadsheet. Formatting commands could now be used to change the layout of the spreadsheet and formulas added to perform calculations:

BOOKS (SS)

	A	B	C	D	E	F
1	**Item Name**	**Department**	**In Stock**	**Price**	**Value**	
2	Avocado Dip	Food	105	$0.99	$103.95	
3	Ball point pen	Pens/Pencils	150	$0.89	$133.50	
4	Chips	Food	77	$0.65	$50.05	
5	Class Ring	Clothing	50	$212.50	$10,625.00	
6	Dictionary	Books	22	$12.95	$284.90	
7	Doritos	Food	145	$2.49	$361.05	
8	Felt-tip pen	Pens/Pencils	76	$0.98	$74.48	
9	Logo T-Shirt	Clothing	250	$9.99	$2,497.50	
10	Pencil	Pens/Pencils	200	$0.15	$30.00	
11	Pepsi	Food	444	$0.65	$288.60	
12	School Jacket	Clothing	100	$34.95	$3,495.00	
13	School Tie	Clothing	15	$17.50	$262.50	
14	Theasaurus	Books	12	$15.00	$180.00	
15	Three-Hole Pape	Paper	200	$1.98	$396.00	
16	Three-Ring Bind	Supplies	122	$3.50	$427.00	
17						

Chapter Summary

This chapter presented the commands necessary to share data between the applications areas and different files produced by the same application. The ability to share data between applications is the primary reason for using an integrated package such as Works.

Works is capable of opening up to 14 different files, each in its own window. This can include any mixture of word processor, data base and spreadsheet files. It is possible to switch between any open file using the Window menu. Several windows may be displayed simultaneously by dragging them to adjust their sizes. When work has been completed on a file, it should be Saved ⌘S and then Closed ⌘W to make room for other files.

To transfer data between different files the files are opened in separate windows and the following steps executed:

1. The data to be copied is highlighted by dragging the mouse.
2. The Copy command is executed from the Edit menu, ⌘C.
3. Using the Window menu the file to receive the copied data is displayed.
4. The cursor is placed at the position to copy the data and the Paste command executed from the Edit menu, ⌘V.

The chapter explained how data may be transferred between:

2 word processor documents (section 9.4)
2 spreadsheets (section 9.5)
2 data bases (section 9.6)
a spreadsheet and word processor document (section 9.7)
a data base and word processor document (section 9.8)
mail merging a data base and word processor document (sections 9.9 and 9.10)
a data base and spreadsheet (section 9.11)

One of the most powerful abilities of an integrated package is the ability to produce mail merge documents. In mail merge, a document is created in the word processor with markers showing where data should be inserted. When the document is printed, the markers are automatically replaced with information from a data base, creating a different copy of the document for each record. In this way, the computer can produce personalized form letters. Queries can be used to limit the number of records displayed, which has a corresponding effect on the number of mail merged documents printed.

Vocabulary

Integrated - A software package that contains different applications. Because Works is integrated, data may be shared between its three applications areas.

Mail merge - Using the contents of a data base file and a word processor document to have the computer produce personalized form letters.

Window - Location in the computer's memory used to store an open file. Works may have up to 14 files open at one time.

Window menu - Listing of the files currently open which allows switching between files.

Reviews

Sections 9.1-9.6

1. a) What is meant by an integrated software package?
   b) What are two advantages of using such a package?

2. What is the purpose of having more than one file open at any one time?

3. a) What is a "window"?
   b) What is the maximum number of windows Works allows to be open at one time?
   c) What steps are required to switch from one window to another?
   d) How may the contents of 3 different windows be displayed simultaneously?

4. Give 3 examples of when you might want to switch between windows. Explain what files would be stored in the different windows.

5. a) Why should files be closed after you are through working with them?
   b) What steps are required to close 3 currently open files?

6. The file NEW PRESIDENT contains a paragraph which describes the inauguration of Ivy University's new president. Explain the steps required to copy this paragraph into a file named ALUMNI which contains a letter to be sent to all Ivy alumni.

7. a) What steps are required to copy two columns from a spreadsheet named OWED and insert them between two existing columns in a spreadsheet named ASSETS?
   b) Must the formulas in ASSETS be changed to include the new columns?

8. Fantasy cars has just bought out Luxury Autos and wants to merge into a single file the data bases which contain both dealerships inventories. Explain the steps required to do this.

9. What problems can occur when transferring records between two data bases?

Sections 9.7-9.11

10. Give 3 examples when you might want to merge part of a spreadsheet with a word processor document.

11. List the steps required to copy the name and GPA of each student from California or Idaho from the IVY STUDENT data base into a word processor document named WESTERN.

12. What does "mail merge" mean?

13. a) Explain the steps required to mail merge the names and addresses of customers from Fantasy Cars customer data base into a letter to be sent each customer.
    b) What additional steps would be required to send the letters to only customers living in Boca Raton, Florida?

14. Give 3 examples where you might want to copy information from a data base into a spreadsheet. For each example explain what the spreadsheet would be used for.

Exercises

1. Ivy University must raise next semester's tuition in order to cover its increasing labor costs.

   a) Create and save a letter named INCREASE using the Word Processor which notifies students of the upcoming tuition increase. INCREASE should be similar to:

   ```
   Dear Student:

   We are sorry to inform you that due to
   rising labor costs we are forced to raise
   your tuition by $1,000 dollars.  This
   increase is effective next semester.

   Sincerely,

   The Administration
   ```

   The administration has decided that students might take the news of a tuition increase better if it came in a personalized letter.

   b) Using the IVY STUDENT data base, modify the INCREASE letter to mail merge the students' first name in place of the word "Student." Save the modified version on disk.

   c) Print mail merged letters for the first three students in the data base. Use ⌘. (period) to cancel the printing.

   d) In order to keep its better students from transferring to less expensive schools, the Ivy administration has decided that the tuition increase should be on a sliding scale based on the student's GPA. Each student's tuition will increase by $500. An additional $100 will be charged for each tenth of a GPA point below 4.0, for example:

GPA	INCREASE
4.0	$500.00
3.9	$600.00
3.8	$700.00
...	
0.1	$4,400.00
0.0	$4,500.00

   Modify the IVY STUDENT data base to contain a calculated field named `Increase` which displays the amount of the tuition increase. Format the new field to display dollar values.

   e) Modify the INCREASE letter to merge the actual tuition increase in place of the "$1,000."

f) Save the modified versions of INCREASE and IVY STUDENT on disk. Using the new INCREASE, print mail merged letters for the first three students. Use ⌘ . (period) to cancel the printing.

2. The Fantasy Wheels pre-owned car company would like to transfer their inventory data base FANTASY into a spreadsheet so that they can perform "What if?" questions with the data. This data base was created in Chapter 5 exercise 3.

   a) Create a new spreadsheet named WHAT IF which lists the year, model, amount paid and asking price for each car from the data in FANTASY. Format the spreadsheet, adding titles and labels.

   b) Add two columns to the spreadsheet. The first calculates a new asking price which is a 10% increase of the current asking price. The second displays the additional profit gained by selling the cars at these new prices.

   c) Acting as Fantasy's sales manager, use the word processor to write a letter named NEW PRICE to the owner of Fantasy Wheels describing your plan to raise prices.

   d) Place a copy of the WHAT IF spreadsheet into the NEW PRICE letter. Print a copy of NEW PRICE and save the file on disk.

3. When using a computerized data base to store inventory figures, the numbers stored in the file can be incorrect when items have been added or removed from inventory without notifying the computer operator to update the data base. To keep the figures up to date, a worker must periodically count the actual number of items on hand for each product and report this number to the operator who updates the data base.

   a) Using the PRODUCT data base created in Chapter 5 exercise 5 create a mail merged form that could be used by the worker to record the actual amount on hand for each item. An example form is shown below:

Plasma-Tech Industries

Manual Inventory Update Form

Product ID: A1000
Product Name: Widgets
Presumed amount on hand: 920

Actual amount on hand: ____________

Save the form under the name UPDATE and print mail merged copies for the first three items.

b) Using the PRODUCT data base, prepare a mail merged document named REORDER listing the product ID, name and amount on hand for only those items with less than 100 units on hand. The document should inform the purchasing manager that these items must be reordered.

4. In Chapter 7 exercise 4 an alumnus used a spreadsheet named PORTFOLIO to calculate a donation to Ivy University. Apply appropriate formatting to the columns and then copy the spreadsheet into a word processed letter informing the I.U. Board of Trustees of the donation. Save and print the letter.

5. Use the IVY STUDENT data base to display the students who have not yet paid their tuition bills. Create a mail merge letter warning them to pay the bill or face expulsion from the university. Print a copy of the letter for each student. Use ⌘. (period) to interrupt the printing if you wish.

6. Your friend Jill is searching for a new car and has written to you for information.

   a) Using the CAR PRICE data base display all cars with air conditioning which cost less than $9,000. Copy those records into a new spreadsheet named JILL CARS. Include proper labels and formatting in the spreadsheet. Have JILL CARS calculate the minimum, average and maximum costs for these cars.

   b) Create a letter informing Jill of her choices. Include the JILL CARS spreadsheet in the letter. Save the letter naming it TO JILL and print a copy.

7. You have been asked to gather some statistics about car prices for your economics class.

   a) Create a new spreadsheet named PRICES which contains all of the data about new car prices from the CAR PRICE data base. Use proper labels and formatting.

   b) Modify the PRICES spreadsheet to calculate each of the following:

      average base price of a new car
      average price for a new car with air
      average price for a new car stereo
      average price for a new car with sunroof
      maximum base price of a new car
      minimum price of a new car with air conditioning

   c) Using the word processor, create and print a report detailing your findings for the class. Include the actual calculated figures from PRICES in the report.

8. Use the word processor to create the following file named MEMO:

```
Memo to: Steve Munger, Asst. Headmaster
From: Bob Doucette, Dean

Steve:

The following students have received Dean's
List status:


Please update their records.  Thank you.
```

Copy the table of Dean's List students from the IVY CONGRAT letter created in Practice 6 into this memo. Save and print a copy of MEMO.

9. You have moved. Using the ADDRESS data base created in Chapter 5 exercise 1, prepare and print a personalized mail merged letter to each of your friends which gives your new address. Use ⌘. (period) to interrupt the printing if you wish. An example letter is shown below:

```
Amy Eppelman
343 Nenue Street
Honolulu, HI 08033

Dear Amy:


This is just a short note to let you know
my new address:

     1389 Southwest Drive
     Atlantic, FL 76800

Of course, we'll still get together on your
birthday, 7/5/65, or I'll call you at (767)
145-5937.

See you soon,

A. Friend
```

10. In Practice 8 you created a spreadsheet named BOOKS by transferring records from the Ivy Bookstore data base file. Open BOOKS and make the following changes to it:

    a) Insert rows at the top of the spreadsheet and add proper column titles.

    b) Increase the Item Name column width to display complete item names.

    c) Format all prices to display dollar values with 2 decimal places.

d) Calculate and display the average price of all items available. Use proper formatting and include a label for this value.

e) Format the Department column, making it right justified and change its width.

f) In column E create a formula which displays the value of the items in stock for each item (price per item times the number of items in stock).

g) At the bottom of column E calculate and display the total value of all items available.

h) Format column E to display dollar values, and include a proper title and label for the total.

i) Save the modified spreadsheet on disk and print a copy.

Chapter 10

Using the Drawing Tools

Edit - Draw On ⌘J

Edit - Draw Off ⌘J

Format - Bring to Front ⌘F

Format - Send to Back ⌘B

Objectives

After completing this chapter you will be able to:

1. Switch to the Draw layer using the Draw On command.
2. Describe and use each of the drawing tools to produce drawings.
3. Create a word processed document containing drawings.
4. Merge a spreadsheet graph with a document.

The Macintosh was the first personal computer designed to display an accurate representation of printed text on the screen. Because of this, it was easy for the computer to use the same techniques needed to produce characters to display drawings. Macintosh Works includes an option which allows you to create and print drawings. We will introduce each of the drawing tools and tdemonstrate their uses.

10.1 The Draw Layer

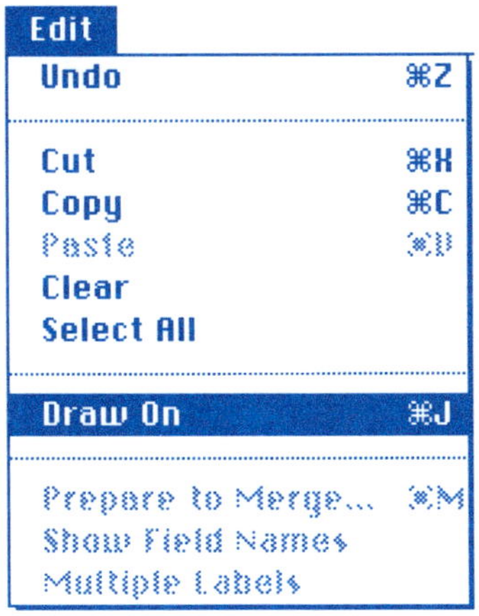

Drawings produced in Works are considered to be placed on a different "layer". It is helpful to think of this layer as a transparent sheet or "overlay" which may be placed over text. To access the draw layer, the Draw On command is executed from the Edit menu, ⌘ J. When executed, the drawing Tools menu is displayed:

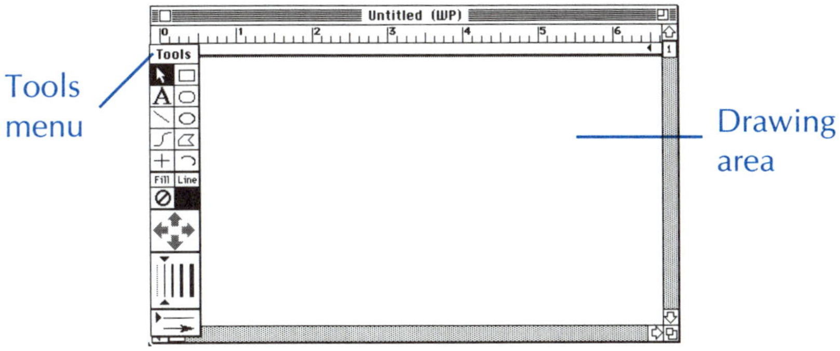

The Tools menu is displayued on the Draw layer

Each "tool" in this menu is used to produce a different type of drawing or effect, and is selected by clicking the mouse pointer on the appropriate shape. Below we describe how to use each of the tools.

10.2 The Box Tool

The Box tool is used to draw rectangular boxes. This is done by selecting the box from the Tool menu and indicating the upper-left and lower-right corner of the box. When the mouse is then placed over the Draw layer, it changes to a cross-hair shape:

The Cross-hair pointer indicates that a graphic is being drawn

Clicking the mouse creates the upper-left corner of the box. As the pointer is dragged, Works displays lines showing where the box will be drawn:

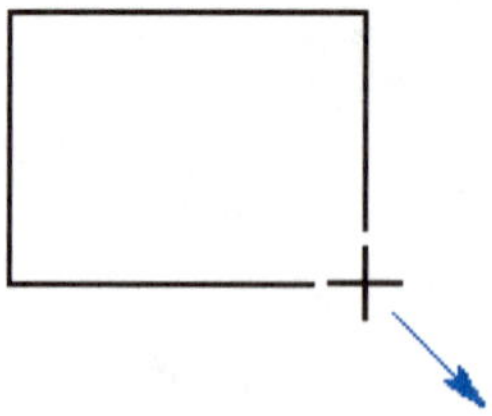

Dragging the cross-hair pointer creates the box

When the pointer is in the correct location, releasing the button draws the box on the Draw layer.

Therefore, drawing a box is a three step process:

1. The Box tool is selected from the Tool menu.
2. The cross hair pointer is placed at the position of the upper-left corner of the box.
3. The pointer is dragged to the lower-right corner of the box. When the mouse button is released, the box is placed on the Draw layer.

Practice 1

In this Practice you will create a new word processor document and draw a box on the Draw layer.

1) START WORKS AND CREATE A NEW WORD PROCESSOR DOCUMENT

a. Boot the Macintosh system and click on the Microsoft Works icon to start Works.
b. Double-click on the Word Processor icon to create a new document.

2) SWITCH TO THE DRAW LAYER

Select the Draw On command from the Edit menu. Works switches to the Draw Layer and displays the drawing Tools menu.

3) SELECT THE BOX TOOL FROM THE TOOLS MENU

a. Click once on the Box tool in the Tools menu.
b. Move the pointer on to the Draw layer. The pointer changes to cross-hairs.

4) DRAW THE BOX

a. Press and hold down the mouse button.
b. Drag the mouse down and to the right. Note how lines are shown, indicating where the box will be drawn.
c. Release the button. Works places the box on the Draw layer. Note that the pointer is returned to the default arrow shape.

Check - Your box should be similar to:

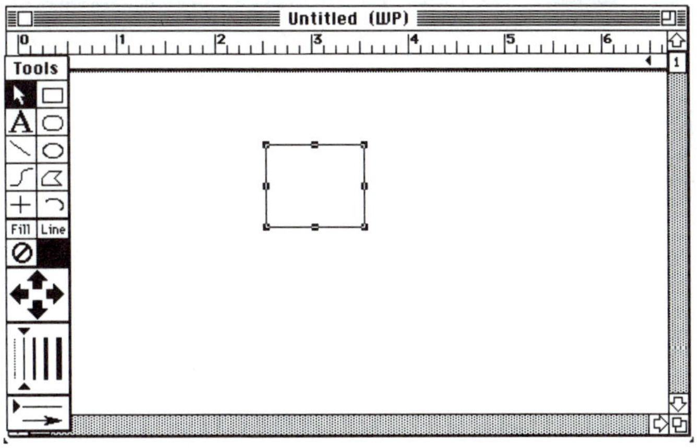

10.3 Using Handles

The black boxes displayed with a drawing are called "handles" and are used to adjust a previously drawn item:

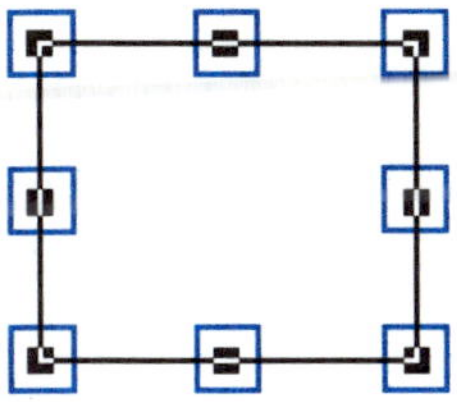

Each of the handles may be used to stretch the graphics in a different direction

When handles are shown, a drawing is said to be selected. Using the arrow pointer, is possible to reshape a selected drawing by dragging one of the handles. For example our box could be made longer by dragging the handle on the left side:

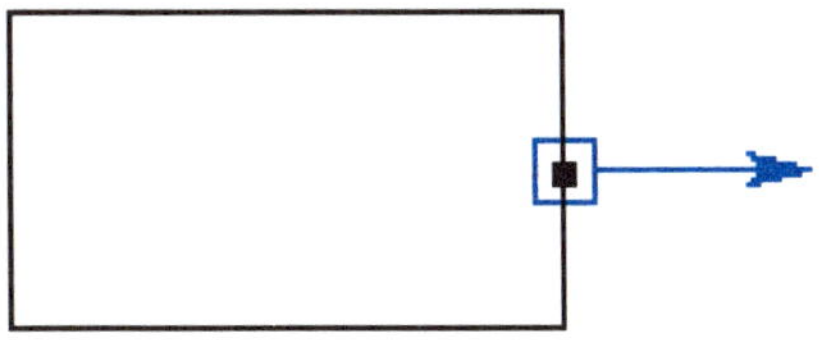

Dragging the handle to the right stretches the drawing

This is called "stretching". Dragging other handles can make the box taller, shorter or more narrow.

10.4 "Perfect" Shapes using Shift

The box created in the last Practice was more of a rectangle than a square. Unless you are an experienced artist, it would be difficult to create a perfect square using the Box tool alone. For this reason, Works allows "perfect" shapes (such as a square) to be drawn by holding down the Shift key while dragging the mouse. When this is done, Works automatically adjusts the sides of the box being drawn to be a square. When using this technique it is important to release the mouse button before the Shift key to insure that the box drawn will be a square.

Practice 2

In this Practice you will create a new box which is a perfect square, and modify the box drawn in the last Practice. The box drawn in the last Practice should still be selected.

1) DRAW A SQUARE

a. Click on the Box tool in the Tools menu. The original box is no longer selected and the handles are removed.
b. Move the pointer to a blank area on the Draw layer.
c. Press and hold down the Shift key.
d. With the Shift key held down, drag the mouse down and to the right. Note how the lines shown are a perfect square. Move the mouse up and down and from side to side. Because the Shift key is depressed, the box is always a square.
e. Release the mouse button first and then let up the Shift key. Works places the square on the Draw layer and changes the pointer back to an arrow. Note the handles on the newly drawn square.

Check - Your screen should be similar to:

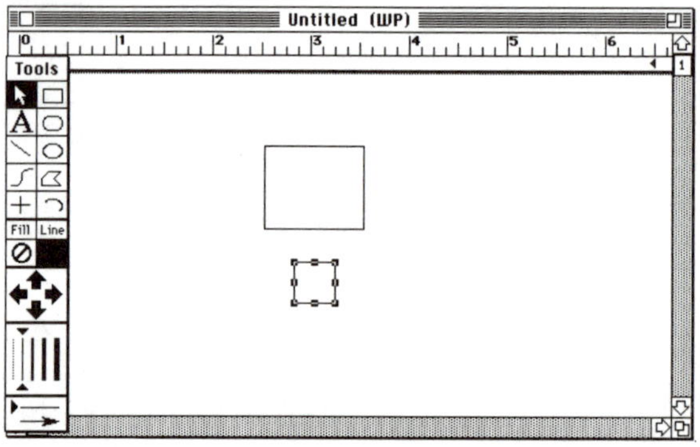

2) SELECT THE ORIGINAL BOX

Place the pointer on one of the lines which make up the original box and click. The box is selected and the handles are again shown. Note that the square drawn in step 1 above is no longer selected.

3) STRETCH THE BOX

a. Place the pointer on the handle in the lower-right corner.
b. Drag the mouse down and to the left. The box becomes taller and thinner.
c. Release the mouse. The new box is shown on the screen.

Check - Your screen should be similar to:

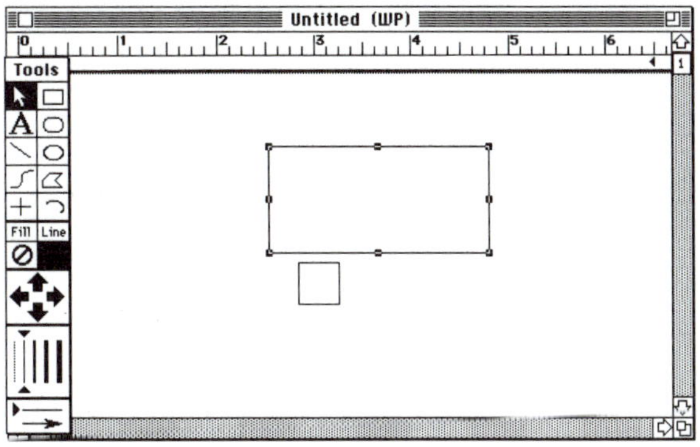

4) SAVE THE FILE ON DISK

a. Press ⌘S to display the Save dialog box.
b. Type the file name `GRAPHICS` and click on `Save`. The file with Draw layer is saved on disk.

10.5 The Rounded Box Tool

The Rounded Box tool draws rectangular boxes with round corners. Similar to the Box tool, the mouse is placed at the position of the upper-left corner of the box and then dragged. When the button is released the box is placed on the Draw layer. Pressing the Shift key while dragging creates a square with rounded corners.

10.6 Using Cut, Paste and Undo

A selected object may be removed from the Draw layer using the Cut command from the Edit menu, ⌘X. Once cut, the object remains in the computer's memory and may be Pasted (⌘V) back into the file if so desired.

Works can reverse the effect of the last drawing operation using the Undo command from the Edit menu, ⌘Z. Undo-ing a cut places the deleted object back on the Draw layer. Undo-ing a stretch returns the object to its original size.

Practice 3

In this Practice you will create a new rounded corner box and remove the original rectangle drawn in the first Practice. Start Works, open the GRAPHICS file and switch to the Draw layer using ⌘J if you have not already done so.

1) DRAW A ROUNDED CORNER BOX

a. Select the Rounded Corner Box tool from the Tools menu.
b. Move the pointer on to the Draw layer.
c. Drag the mouse down and to the right and release the button. A box with rounded corners is displayed.

2) DELETE THE ORIGINAL BOX

a. Click on the original rectangular box, selecting it.
b. Select the Cut command from the Edit menu. The rectangular box is removed from the screen.

3) PASTE THE DELETED BOX BACK INTO THE FILE

Select the Paste command from the Edit menu. The deleted box is returned to the screen.

4) UNDO THE PASTE COMMAND

Select the Undo command from the Edit menu. The effects of the last command, the Paste, are undone and the box is again removed from the screen.

5) SAVE THE MODIFIED FILE ON DISK

Press ⌘ S to save the modified GRAPHICS file, without the original box, on disk

<u>Check</u> - Your screen should be similar to:

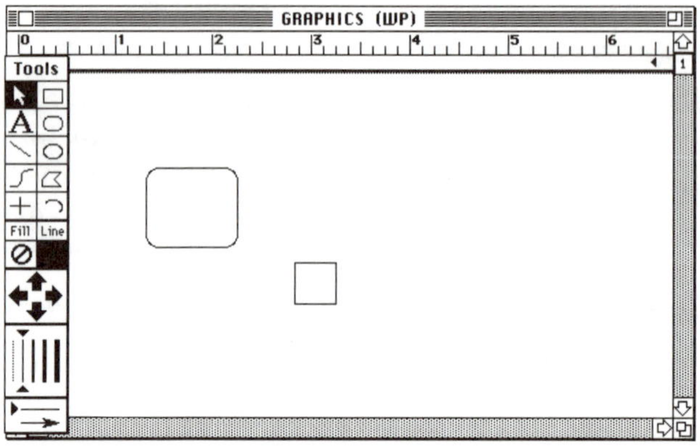

10.7 The Oval Tool

Circles and ovals are created using the Oval tool. Holding down the Shift key while drawing an oval creates a perfect circle.

The process for creating an oval is slightly different than that for drawing a box:

1. The Oval tool is selected from the Tool menu.
2. The cross hair pointer is dragged, creating the oval. When the mouse button is released, the circle is placed on the Draw layer.

10.8 Moving Objects and Changing Line Widths

Because they have no corners, it is sometimes difficult to judge the starting position when drawing ovals. For this reason, Works allows a graphic object to be moved to a new location on the Draw layer by dragging. To do this, select the object to be moved by clicking on it. Place the pointer on any part of the selected object <u>except</u> a handle and drag. When the button is released, the object is left in its new position.

The drawings you have created so far have used the same line width. Works has five different widths which may be selected from the Tools menu:

The line width tool is used to change the thickness of the line

The dashed line furthest to the left means no line width - an invisible line. This will be of use in later drawings. Line widths may be selected at two different times; either before the object is drawn, or after. If selected before, that width becomes the default and all future objects will be drawn using it until changed. The line width of a previously created object may be changed by selecting that object and clicking on the desired width.

Practice 4

In this Practice you will create a circle using the Oval tool and change its line width. The rounded box drawn in the previous Practice will be moved. Start Works, open the GRAPHICS file and switch to the Draw layer using ⌘ J if you have not already done so.

1) DRAW A CIRCLE

a. Select the Oval tool from the Tools menu.
b. Move the pointer on to the Draw layer.
c. Hold down the Shift key and drag the mouse down and to the right to create a circle. The default line width is used.

2) CHANGE THE LINE WIDTH OF THE CIRCLE

a. The circle should still be selected from the last step. Click on the widest line width in the Tools menu. The circle is shown in that width.
b. Click on the dashed line width. The circle disappears because it is drawn using invisible lines, but the handles still remain.
c. Click on the fourth line width, the second thickest. The circle reappears using that line width.

3) SELECT THE ROUNDED BOX AND MOVE IT

a. Click on the rounded box, selecting it. The handles are shown around it.
b. Place the pointer on a line in the box, being careful to avoid the handles.
c. Drag the box next to the circle and release the button. The rounded box is moved to that location.
d. Press ⌘ S to save the modified GRAPHICS file on disk.

Check - Your screen should be similar to:

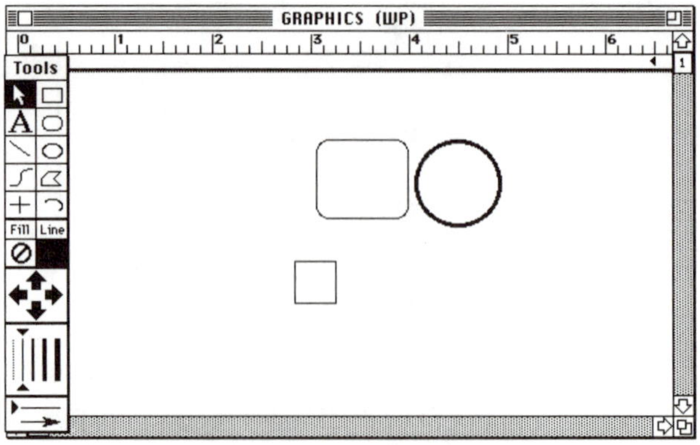

10.9 The Line and Arrow Tools

The Line tool is used to add straight lines to the Draw layer. Lines are created by clicking the pointer at the starting point of the line, and then dragging to the end point. When the mouse is released, the line is drawn. Holding down the Shift key when drawing forces the line to be vertical, horizontal or diagonal.

A special option when drawing lines is to create arrows using the Arrow tool:

The Arrow tool places an arrowhead at the end of the line

When selected, the Arrow tool adds an arrowhead to the end point of the line. The Arrow tool may be selected either before the line is drawn, or after. If selected before, all future lines will be drawn with an arrowhead until changed. Arrowheads may be removed from a previously created line by selecting the line and clicking on the Plain line tool.

Practice 5

In this Practice you will create two straight lines using the Line tool and change one of them into an arrow. Start Works, open the GRAPHICS file and switch to the Draw layer using ⌘ J if you have not already done so.

1) DRAW A LINE

a. Click on the Line tool in the Tools menu.
b. Move the pointer on to the Draw layer.
c. Drag the mouse down and to the right to create a diagonal line. The default line width is used.

2) DRAW A HORIZONTAL LINE

a. Select the Line tool from the Tools menu.
b. Hold down the Shift key and drag the mouse down and to the right to create a horizontal line. Note how the line does not follow the pointer, but remains horizontal because the Shift key is pressed.

3) CREATE AN ARROW

a. The horizontal line should still be selected from the last step. Click on the arrow tool. An arrowhead is shown at the end point of the line.
b. Click on the Plain tool. The arrowhead is removed.
c. Press ⌘Z to execute the Undo command. The effects of the Plain command are undone, and the arrowhead is displayed.
d. Press ⌘S to save the modified GRAPHICS file on disk.

Check - Your screen should be similar to:

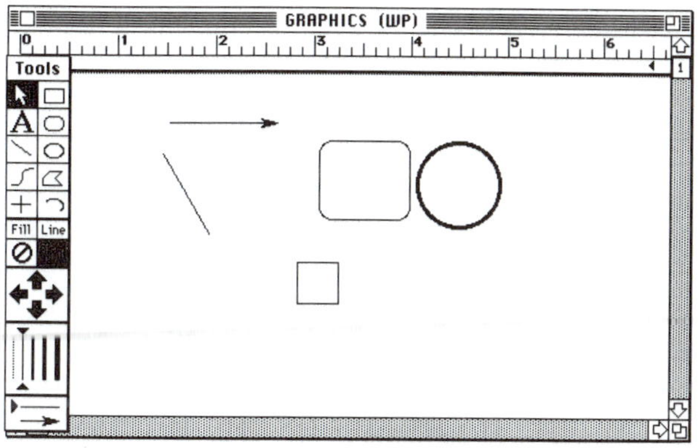

10.10 The Freehand and Perfect Line Tools

Works provides two other line drawing tools. The Perfect Line tool draws only vertical or horizontal lines. This is the same as using the Line tool with the Shift key as described in the previous section. The Freehand tool allows any type of line to be drawn: curved, straight, crooked, etc. Freehand lines are different because they have many handles, allowing them to be reshaped in a variety of ways. Lines produced with the Line and Perfect Line tools only have two handles, one at each end point.

Practice 6

In this Practice you will create two new lines, one using the Perfect Line tool and another using the Freehand tool. The Freehand line will be adjusted using some of the handles. Start Works, open the GRAPHICS file and switch to the Draw layer using ⌘J if you have not already done so.

1) DRAW A VERTICAL LINE

a. Select the Perfect Line tool from the Tools menu.
b. Move the pointer on to the Draw layer.
c. Drag the mouse down to create a vertical line.
d. With the mouse button still held down, move the mouse in a slow circle around the starting point of the line. Note how this tool will only allow vertical, horizontal or diagonal lines to be drawn.
e. Bring the mouse below the starting point to create a vertical line and release the mouse.

2) DRAW A FREEHAND LINE

a. Click on the Freehand tool in the Tools menu.
b. Move the cursor on to the Draw layer.
c. Drag the cursor in an "S" shape and release the mouse. The Freehand line is shown with many handles.

3) MODIFY THE FREEHAND LINE

a. The Freehand line should still be selected from the last step. Place the pointer on a handle near the middle of the "S" and drag it to the left. The segment of line between two handles is stretched. This process could be repeated for any of the handles on the Freehand line.
b. Press ⌘S to save the modified file on disk.

Check - Your screen should be similar to:

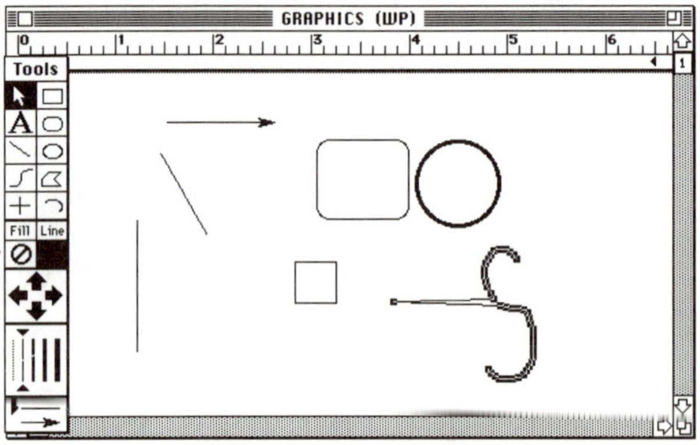

10.11 The Polygon Tool

Works has a special tool for creating "polygons." A polygon is simply a figure created by joining the starting points of several lines with the ending points of others. While this could be accomplished using the Line tool, the Polygon tool makes it easy by automatically making the end point of the current line the starting point of the next. To create a polygon, the pointer is moved to create one side of the object. Clicking the mouse then draws a line for that side, and starts a new line from the end point of the previous one, creating a corner.

Polygons may be either "open" or "closed". In a closed polygon, the end point of the last side is connected to the starting point of the first line. A rectangle is an example of a closed polygon which has four sides. In an open polygon, the sides are not connected:

Closed *Open*

To create an open polygon, double-click on the final end point. To create a closed polygon, click on the starting point of the first side.

The process for creating a polygon is slightly different than that for the other tools:

1. Select the Polygon tool from the Tool menu.
2. Click the cross hair pointer at the starting position for the first side of the polygon.
3. For each side in the polygon, move the pointer to the next corner and click.
4. To create a closed polygon, click on the starting point. For an open polygon, double-click on the last end point.

10.12 Selecting Multiple Objects

It is possible to select more that one object at a time by holding down the Shift key when selecting. This allows multiple objects to be Cut or moved at the same time. When several objects are selected, it is possible to "de-select" one by holding down the Shift key and clicking on it.

Practice 7

In this Practice you will create a closed and an open polygon. Some of the previously created objects will first be removed to make room. Start Works, open the GRAPHICS file and switch to the Draw layer using ⌘ J if you have not already done so.

1) REMOVE SOME OF THE OBJECTS

a. Click on the diagonal line, selecting it.
b. Hold down the Shift key and click on the Freehand "S" line. Both the diagonal and Freehand lines are now selected.
c. Hold down the Shift key and click on the arrow, then on the vertical line. Four lines are now selected.
d. De-select the arrow by holding down the shift key and clicking on it. Only three objects are now selected.
e. Execute the Cut command by pressing ⌘ X. All of the select objects are removed as a group.

2) DRAW A CLOSED TRIANGULAR POLYGON

a. Select the Polygon tool from the Tools menu.
b. Move the pointer on to the Draw layer.
c. Click the mouse to begin the polygon.
d. Move (not drag) the mouse down and click. The first side is drawn.
e. Move the mouse to the right and click, drawing the second side.

f. Place the pointer on the starting point of the first side and click. Works joins the end point of the third side with the starting point of the first side to create a closed triangular polygon.

3) DRAW AN OPEN "U-SHAPED" POLYGON

a. Select the Polygon tool from the Tools menu.
b. Move the pointer on to the Draw layer.
c. Click the mouse to begin the polygon.
d. Move the mouse down and click. The first side is drawn.
e. Move the mouse to the right and click, drawing the second side.
f. Move the mouse up and double-click, drawing the third side. The double-click indicates that this is an open polygon.

Check - Your screen should be similar to:

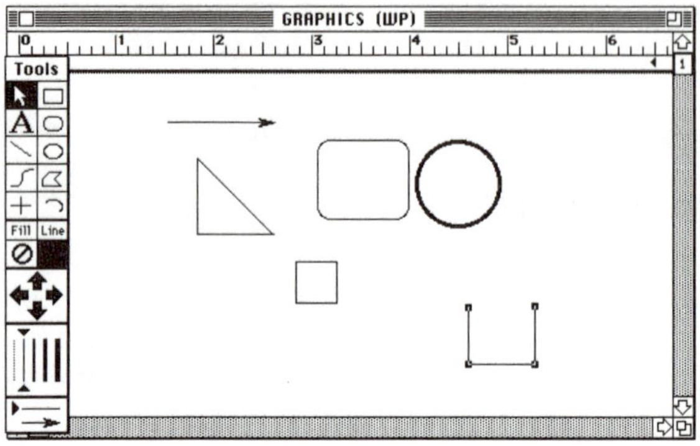

4) MODIFY THE OPEN POLYGON

a. The open polygon should still be selected from the last step. Place the pointer on the lower-right handle and drag it to the right. The second and third sides are stretched.
b. Press ⌘ S to save the modified file on disk.

Check Your screen should be similar to:

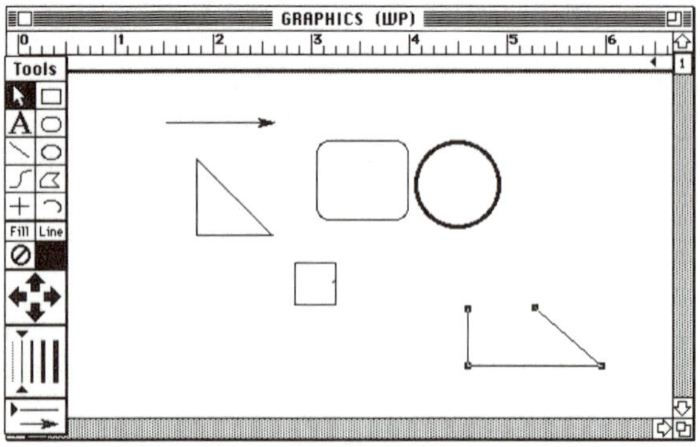

10.13 The Arc Tool

Works can draw arcs using the Arc tool. An arc is a segment of a circle. The Arc tool always creates 90 degree arcs, or one quarter of a circle. Larger arcs may be created by dragging one of the handles on a previously drawn arc.

Practice 8

In this Practice you will create and modify an arc. Start Works, open the GRAPHICS file and switch to the Draw layer using ⌘ J if you have not already done so.

1) DRAW AN ARC

a. Select the Arc tool from the Tools menu.
b. Move the pointer on to the Draw layer.
c. Drag the mouse up and to the right drawing a 90 degree arc.
d. Release the mouse. Note the handles at both ends of the arc.

2) STRETCH THE ARC

a. The arc should still be selected from the last step. Place the pointer on the upper handle.
b. Drag the handle to the right, stretching the arc to a half circle (180 degree arc).
c. Press ⌘ S to save the modified GRAPHICS file on disk.

Check - Your screen should be similar to:

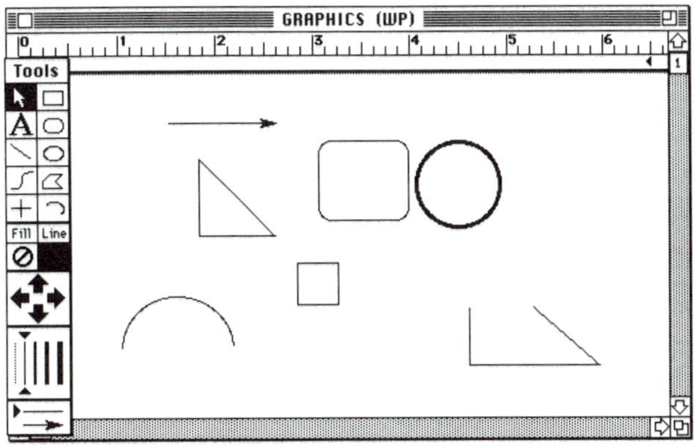

10.14 Line and Fill Patterns

In addition to widths, lines may also have patterns. That is, instead of drawing in solid black Works allows a line to be drawn in one of a number of patterns selected from the Line Pattern menu:

The Line Pattern menu has many different choices for lines

Patterns may be selected before beginning to draw, or may be applied to a selected object, and work best with thicker line widths. The current pattern is displayed on the Tools menu under the word "Line."

Closed objects such as a box or closed polygon may be filled with a pattern. The default pattern is none, meaning that closed objects are hollow. A solid object may be created by selecting a fill pattern from the Fill Pattern menu:

The Fill Pattern menu

The default is no fill, as indicated by the ⊘ symbol on the Tools menu. As with line patterns, fill patterns may be selected before beginning to draw, or applied to a selected object. The current fill pattern is displayed on the Tools menu under the word "Fill."

Practice 9

In this Practice you will modify several objects by applying line and fill patterns. Start Works, open the GRAPHICS file and switch to the Draw layer using ⌘ J if you have not already done so.

1) CHANGE THE LINE PATTERN OF THE CIRCLE

a. Select the circle by clicking the pointer on it.
b. Using the mouse, select a new pattern from the Line Pattern menu. The circle changes on screen to display the new pattern.
c. Select several different patterns from the Line Pattern menu and observe the changes to the circle. Select solid black as the last pattern.

2) CHANGE THE FILL PATTERN OF THE POLYGON

a. Select the triangular polygon by clicking the pointer on it.
b. Using the mouse, select a new pattern from the Fill Pattern menu. The triangle changes on screen to display the new pattern.
c. Select several patterns from the Fill Pattern menu and observe the changes to the triangle. Select no fill, ⊘, as the last pattern.
d. Press ⌘ S to save the modified GRAPHICS file on disk.

10.15 Clear and the Clipboard

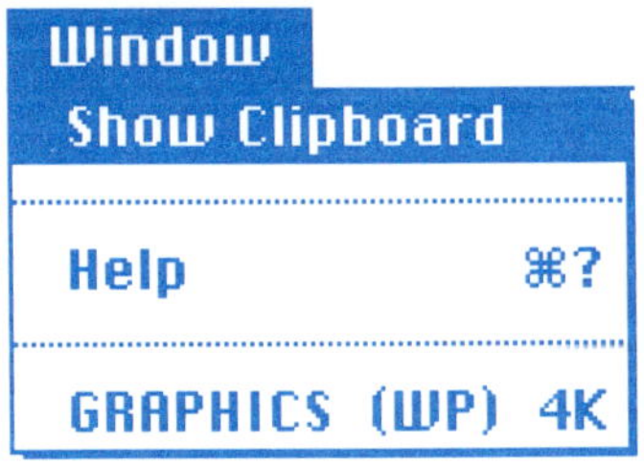

After an object has been Cut (⌘X), it is possible to Paste (⌘V) it back into the document. Cut objects are stored in a special place in the computer's memory called the "Clipboard." It is possible to view the contents of the Clipboard by selecting Show Clipboard from the Window menu. Show Clipboard displays a small window on the screen which contains the contents of the Clipboard, if any:

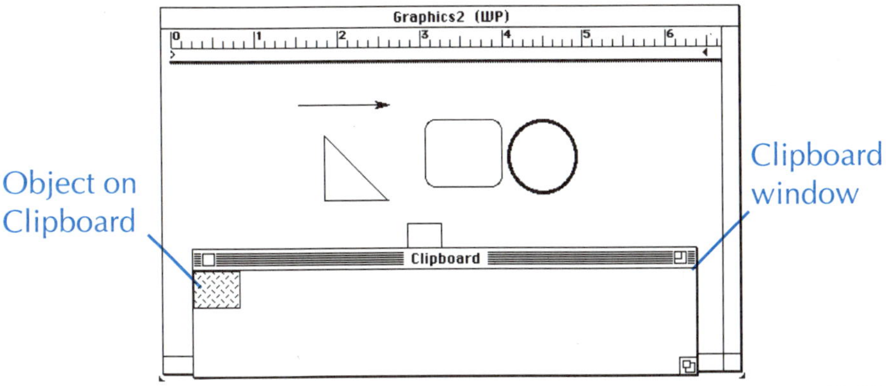

Selecting Show Clipboard displays the Clipboard window

No changes may be made to the contents of the Clipboard. The Clipboard may store only one object at a time - the next Cut or Copy command will replace the current contents. The Clipboard window may be removed by clicking its Close box or selecting Hide Window from the Window menu. Both the Clipboard and the document may be displayed at the same time by adjusting the size of their windows.

It is sometimes be necessary to remove an object from the Draw layer without disturbing the contents of the Clipboard. To accomplish this, Works includes the Clear command on the Edit menu. Clear deletes a selected object, but does not place it on the Clipboard.

10.16 Bring to Front, Send to Back

As you have seen, it is possible to move objects on the Draw layer by dragging them. It is possible to place an object over top of another. If the top object is filled, the bottom object is then no longer visible. It is possible to think of these objects as being "stacked" on top of each other. Works can change the order in which stacked objects are displayed using the Bring to Front and Send to Back commands from the Format menu. Bring to Front (⌘F) moves a selected object to the top of the stack, while Send to Back (⌘B) moves it to the bottom.

Practice 10

In this Practice you will display the Clipboard and use the Bring to Front and Send to Back commands. Start Works, open GRAPHICS and switch to the Draw layer if you have not already done so.

1) DISPLAY THE CLIPBOARD

a. Select the Show Clipboard command from the Window menu. The Clipboard window is displayed on the screen.

b. Using the adjust box at the lower right-hand corner, shrink the Clipboard window to about half its current size.

c. Place the pointer in the word "Clipboard" at the top of the window and drag the Clipboard to the right side of the screen.
d. Click the pointer on the Draw layer. The Clipboard window is placed behind the document window.
e. Using the adjust box, decrease the size of the document window so that the Clipboard and the document are visible on screen at the same time.

2) CUT AN OBJECT FROM THE DOCUMENT

a. Click on the rounded corner box, selecting it.
b. Execute the Cut command by pressing ⌘ X. The box is removed from the document and placed on the Clipboard.

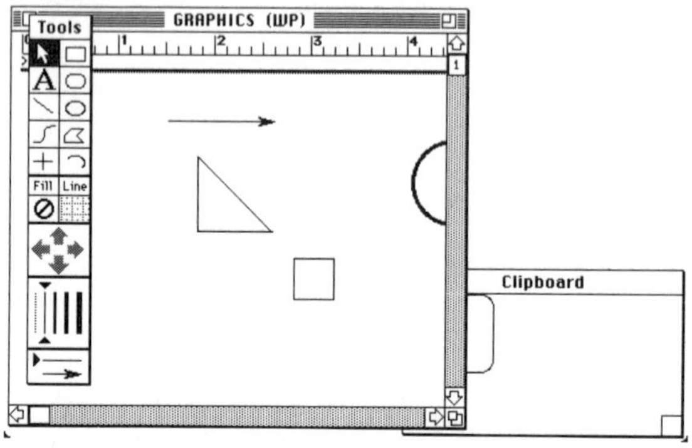

3) CLEAR AN OBJECT FROM THE DOCUMENT

a. Click on the arc, selecting it.
b. Execute the Clear command from the Edit menu. The arc is removed from the document but the contents of the Clipboard are unchanged.

4) REMOVE THE CLIPBOARD

a. Select the Hide Clipboard command from the Window menu to remove the Clipboard window from the screen. Even though the Clipboard is not displayed, it contents remain unchanged.
b. Using the adjust box, increase the size of the document window so that fills the entire screen.

5) PASTE AN OBJECT ON TOP OF ANOTHER

a. Click on the circle, selecting it.
b. Select a pattern from the Fill Pattern menu, making a solid circle.
c. Execute the Paste command by pressing ⌘ V. The rounded corner box is copied from the Clipboard and Pasted into the document over top of the circle.

6) REVERSE THE ORDER OF THE STACKED OBJECTS

a. The rounded corner box should still be selected from the previous step. Execute the Send to Back command by pressing ⌘ B. The rounded corner box is placed behind the circle. Part of the box is no longer displayed because it behind the filled circle.
b. Press ⌘ S to save the modified file on disk.
c. Press ⌘ W to close the GRAPHICS file.

10.17 Inserting a Chart in a Document

Works' ability to create charts from the data stored in a spreadsheet was described at the end of Chapter 8. Once a chart has been created, Works can insert it into a word processor document, so that when the document is printed, the chart will be included. This feature is especially important to businesses and other organizations which produce reports that include charts.

To insert a chart into a document, the following steps are required:

1. The document is word processed, leaving room where you wish the chart to be printed.
2. The spreadsheet which contains the desired chart is opened.
3. The chart is displayed and copied to the Clipboard.
4. The word processed document is displayed and the chart Pasted into the document on the Draw layer.

When the Print command is executed, Works prints a copy of the chart inside the document.

The size and position of the chart in the document may be modified using the drawing tools. For this reason, when a chart is pasted into a document, Works automatically switches to the Draw layer and displays the Tools menu.

Practice 11

In this Practice you will insert a chart into a word processor document and print it. Start Works if you have not already done so.

1) OPEN THE DOCUMENT AND SPREADSHEET

a. Close any open files using ⌘ W.
b. Open the IVY REPORT word processor document in the first window. Space in the file has been left for the chart.
c. Press ⌘ O and open the IVY ENROLLMENT spreadsheet in a second window.

2) COPY THE CHART ONTO THE CLIPBOARD

a. With IVY ENROLLMENT still displayed, execute the Draw Chart command from the Charts menu.
b. Double-click on IVY ENRO Chart 2 to display that chart.
c. Press ⌘ C to copy the displayed chart to the Clipboard.

3) PASTE THE CHART INTO THE REPORT

a. Select IVY REPORT (WP) from the Window menu to return to the document.
b. Press ⌘ V to paste the chart on the Clipboard into the document. The chart is placed on the Draw layer and the drawing Tools menu displayed.
c. Using the pointer, drag the chart so that it is in the blank space in the center of the document.
d. If the chart is too big, drag one of the corner handles to make it fit in the space provided.

4) PRINT THE REPORT WITH THE CHART

a. Press ⌘ S to save the modified document on disk.
b. Press ⌘ P and click on OK to print the document. Because charts are complex, printing a document which contains a chart can take considerable time.
c. Press ⌘ Q to quit Works.

Check - The printed document contains a copy of the chart as shown on the screen:

Chapter Summary

This chapter explained the Macintosh Works drawing tools and how they may be employed to create a professional-looking document. The Draw On command from the Edit menu (⌘ J) is executed to access the Draw layer which displays the Tools menu. Each tool produces a different type of drawing.

The Box tool draws rectangular boxes while the Rounded Box tool draws rectangular boxes with rounded corners. Circles and ovals are created using the Oval tool and the Line tool produces straight lines. The Arrow tool adds an arrow head to the end point of a line. To adjust a drawing the black boxes shown around a graphic, called handles, are used. Perfect shapes are drawn by holding down the Shift key while dragging.

The Perfect line tool draws only vertical or horizontal lines. Any type of line: curved, straight, crooked, etc. can be drawn using the Freehand Tool. Polygons are created using the Polygon tool while the Arc tool creates 90 degree arcs.

Lines may be drawn in a number of patterns selected from the Line Pattern menu and closed objects may be filled with a pattern by selecting from the Fill Pattern menu. Objects may be stacked on top of each other and then the order of stacking changed using the Bring to Front (⌘F) or Send to Back (⌘ B) commands from the Format menu.

An object may be removed from the Draw layer by using the Cut command (⌘ X). Once cut, the object can be Pasted (⌘V) back into that file, or another file. Cut objects are stored in an area of computer's memory called the Clipboard. The contents of the Clipboard may be displayed by selecting the Show Clipboard command from the Window menu. A chart can be inserted into a word processor document by copying it to the Clipboard and then pasting it on the Draw layer. The effect of the last drawing operation can be reversed using the Undo command (⌘ Z).

Vocabulary

Arc - a segment of a circle.
Clipboard - a place in the computer's memory where cut objects are stored.
Draw layer - area in the computer's memory where drawings are made; accessed by executing the Draw On command.
Freehand drawing - any type of line which can be drawn; can be curved, straight, crooked, etc.
Handle - black box used to adjust a previously drawn item.
Perfect shape - an exact shape drawn by Works (such as a square, circle or straight line).
Polygon - a multi-sided figure which can be open or closed.
Stretching - reshaping a selected drawing by dragging one of its handles.
Tool - used by Works to produce a type of drawing.

Chapter 11

Telecommunications and the Future of Computing: Social and Ethical Implications

Communications - Dial ⌘D

Communications - Settings ⌘S

Communications - Hang Up ⌘=

Objectives

After completing this chapter you will be able to:

1. Define telecommunications and describe its uses.
2. Describe artificial intelligence and its use in expert systems and natural language processing.
3. Understand how robots may be used to automate tasks.
4. Describe different careers in computing and their educational requirements.
5. Understand the ethical responsibilities of computer use and programming.
6. Describe several objectives for the future of computing.

In this concluding chapter we discuss the future of computing, including the effects on computers of various technological developments, the career possibilities created by computers, and the social and ethical consequences of living in a computerized society. After having studied the previous chapters you should have a good understanding of how useful and powerful a computer is. In the first chapter of this text we stated that computers, unlike people, could not actually think but could store huge amounts of data and process it at very high speeds. This chapter describes how these capabilities will be exploited in the future to perform an ever increasing and varied number of tasks.

11.1 Telecommunications

One of the most important advances made in computing has been in the field of "telecommunications". By telecommunications we mean the sending of computer data over telephone lines. To do this an additional piece of hardware called a "modem" is required to translate the binary data of the computer into waves which can then be transmitted over phone lines. To receive data a modem must also have the capability of translating the waves back into binary form. This process involves what is called signal modulation and demodulation, hence the name modem. In addition to the modem, special telecommunications software is required so that the computer can transmit and receive data.

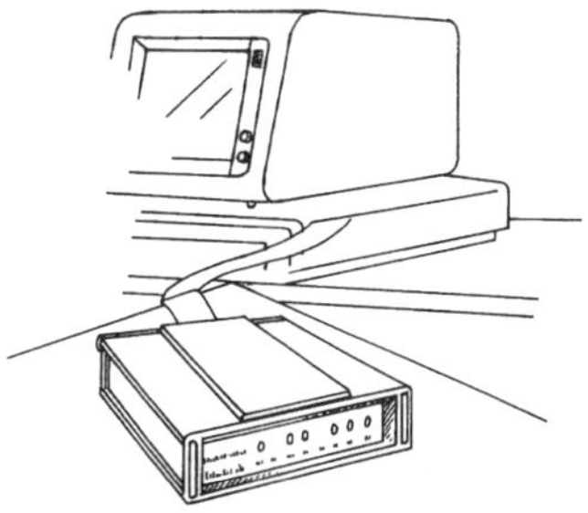

Some modems are "external" - outside of the computer

With a modem a microcomputer is capable of transmitting and receiving data between any two locations connected by phone lines. The rate at which each character of data is sent is measured in "baud", one baud representing the transmission of one character per second. Currently the most common rates are 300, 1200 and 2400 baud which means 300, 1200 and 2400 characters per second. However, newer modems are being created which are capable of communicating at 9600 baud and higher.

Any type of data that a computer is capable of storing can be sent and received by modem. Using a modem it is possible to access and search very large data bases which might store financial data, news reports, travel information or a company's sales data. If you go to a travel agent to book a flight, the agent will most likely use a computer to check the availability of flights and then make your reservation. The agent's computer is connected by modem to a large computer that contains a data base of flight information. This data base is similar to the ones you created using Works, only much larger.

Because of telecommunications it is now possible for many people to work at home rather than in an office. News reporters and writers often write their stories at home on a word processor and then transmit their word processing files to a central office many miles away. Financial consultants, accountants and travel agents are sometimes able to work at home accessing needed data bases using a computer and modem.

In many states it is possible to do your banking by computer, paying bills and making deposits from your home. Companies are also establishing computer services that allow you to shop at home, make your own travel reservations, even play a game of chess with someone in another state or country all by using a computer and modem. As you can see it is becoming increasingly apparent that the impact of telecommunications on our society will be significant.

11.2 Electronic Bulletin Boards and E-Mail

One of the most popular forms of telecommunication is the "electronic bulletin board" or "BBS." People who subscribe to a bulletin board service can call another computer and transmit messages to it which are then stored. When other subscribers of the service call the bulletin board it allows them to list all of the messages that have been "posted". Many companies and other organizations maintain bulletin boards to keep their employees aware of important events. For example, the Ivy University Alumni Association could have an electronic bulletin board which lists the month's events including athletic events and alumni reunions. All an Ivy alumnus need do to get a list of all of the events is call up the bulletin board using a modem and computer. Some BBS are run by individual users and are normally free. Others called "information services" are controlled by large companies and offer a variety of different services such as shopping or international weather forecasts for a fee.

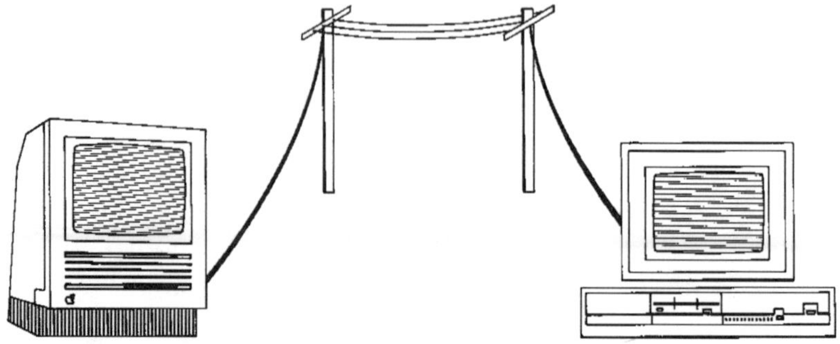

Bulletin boards and E-mail allow computers to communicate over phone lines

Electronic mail or "E-Mail" is similar to an electronic bulletin board, but is used instead to send and receive messages meant for one person or a small group. The person sending the message contacts the electronic mail service using a computer and modem, and then types in the name of the recipient and the message. When the recipient calls the electronic mail service he or she receives the message. The advantage of this system is primarily speed. Often letters sent through the mail take days to receive, even when sent across a town, while electronic mail can be received instantly. Another advantage of this service is that recipients can receive messages when they want them rather than when they are sent. This is especially useful when messages are sent around the world. A message sent from New York at 9:00 A.M. will be immediately received and stored by a computer in Tokyo at 1:00 A.M. Tokyo time, but the person in Tokyo need not call the electronic mail service until a more convenient time. Most larger information services offer E-Mail.

To keep electronic mail private a password system is employed. When first calling to receive messages, a person is asked to enter a secret password which must then be verified by the computer before the messages are transmitted.

It is possible to create a copy of a message left on a BBS or E-Mail system on your computer. This is called "downloading" and involves having the system's computer send a copy of the message file to your computer, where it is stored on disk. Similarly, the process of sending files to a BBS or E-Mail system is called "uploading".

Electronic mail is especially popular in universities where students and faculty can easily send messages to each other. If a University instructor wants to change her homework assignment she can send the new assignment to each member of her class using the university's E-mail system. She can also find out if the messages have been received (downloaded) because the system keeps a record of when each member of her class has checked for messages. It would be possible for a student to complete the assignment using a word processor and send the answers as another message (upload).

A growing number of universities now require all of their students to purchase microcomputers and modems. Among many other advantages, it has allowed everyone on their campuses to make use of electronic mail services.

11.3 Telecommunicating with Works

The fourth application area in Works is Communications. If your computer is equipped with a modem this application allows you to contact electronic bulletin boards and information services to send and receive data.

Telecommunicating can be complex, involving many different options such as baud rates and data sizes. In order for telecommunications to take place, both computers must use the same options. New subscribers to an information service normally receive a large packet describing the options which must be used to access that particular service. Fortunately, Works allows the options for each service to be saved in a different communications file, meaning that once saved, the user does not have to be concerned about setting the proper options again.

Double-clicking on Communications from the Open File dialog box displays the Communications screen:

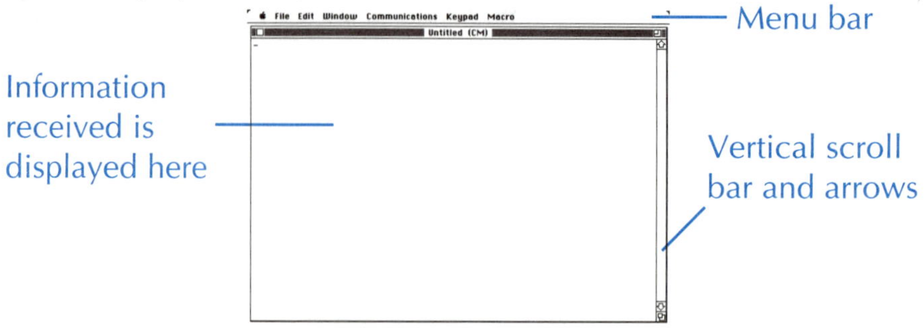

The Communications Screen

For two computers to communicate, they both must use the same options. The four most important of these are:

Baud Rate: The speed at which each computer will send and receive data. 300, 1200 and 2400 are common values, but newer modems are capable of transmitting data at 9600 baud or above.

Data size: The number of bits (binary digits) that make up one piece of data. This can be 7 or 8.

Stop bits: The number of bits, 1 or 2, sent to indicate the end of a piece of data.

Parity: How the receiving computer will determine if an error occurred in the transmission of data. Parity choices are named None, Odd and Even.

These four items are so important that bulletin boards (BBS) and information services are often classified by the settings that they expect. For example, a BBS may list itself as "1200, 8, None, 1" meaning that its computer communicates using 1200 baud, 8 data bits, None parity and 1 stop bit. Works controls the values of these options using the Settings command from the Communications menu:

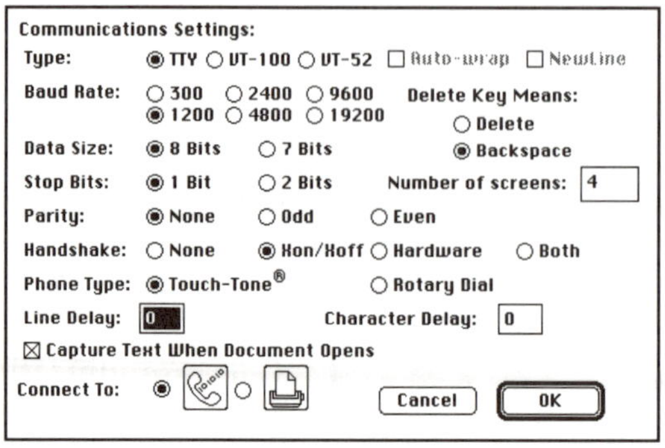

The Settings box controls the communications options

When a new communications file is created, this box is shown first.

Once the Settings options have been set, all that is needed is to tell Works what phone number to dial using the Dial command from the Communications menu, ⌘ D:

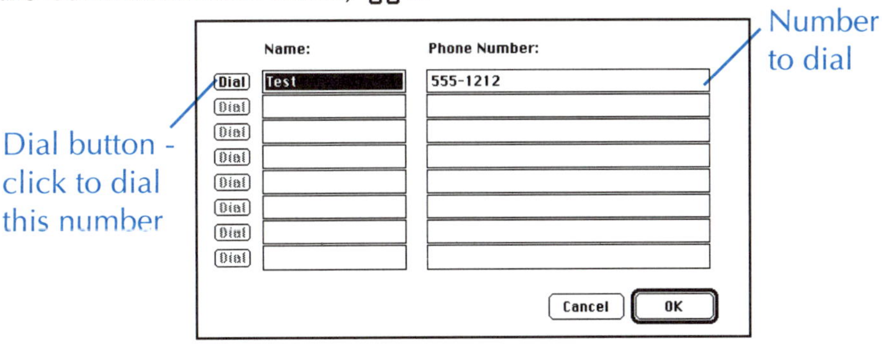

The Dial box lists up to 8 numbers which may be dialed using the current Communications options set from the Settings box

The Dial command's dialog box is used to tell Works what number to dial, including the area code if needed. Each number may also be give a name for identification purposes. Works allows dialing to be either Rotary (for older, pulse-dial phones) or Touch Tone as selected from the Settings box.

Once the proper options for Baud, Phone number, etc. have been set, a communications file can be created using ⌘ S which saves your choices on disk. Opening a previously saved communications file recalls the options you have set. In this way, Works simplifies the process of setting communications options by allowing you to create a different communications file for each service you contact.

After the options have been set and saved, Works can be told to contact the information service by clicking of the Dial button next the desired number in the Dial dialog box. Once done, Works dials the phone number and attempts to contact the other computer:

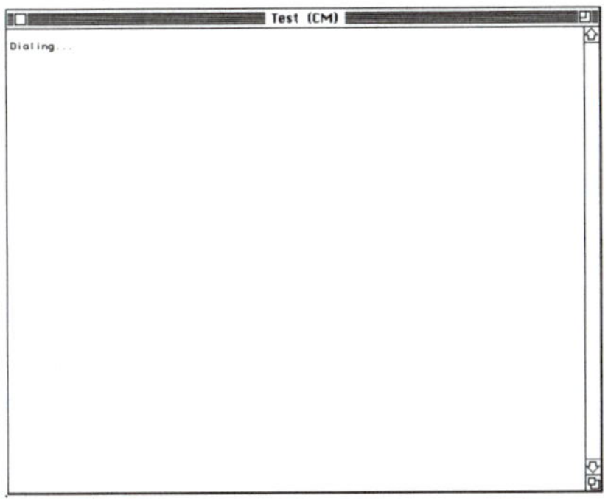

Works keeps you informed of the status of the communications session

If a connection is made, Works displays "Connect". The other computer then takes control of your computer, and anything that you type is sent to it. For this reason, the remote computer is often called the "host". Executing the Hang Up command from the Communications menu, ⌘ = (equals), terminates communications with the host and hangs up the phone.

Practice 1 - Connecting to a BBS

In this Practice you will set options to access a BBS, and create a communications file for that BBS's options. If you do not have a modem attached to your computer you will not be able to perform this Practice.

Make sure that your modem is connected to a phone line and is turned on. As examples for this exercise we will use the options "1200, 8, None, 1" and the local telephone number 555-1212. You may be able to get information about a local BBS from your computer dealer or a computer users group.

1) **BOOT THE MACINTOSH SYSTEM AND START WORKS**

2) **OPEN A NEW COMMUNICATIONS FILE**

   Double-click on the Communications icon to create a new Communications file. The Communications screen with the Settings dialog box is displayed.

3) **SET THE COMMUNICATIONS OPTIONS**

   a. Note that the default options for Baud Rate (1200), Data Size (8), Stop Bits (1) and Parity (None) are the ones we want. If you are using a pulse-dial phone, select Rotary for the Phone Type.
   b. Click on the Capture Text When Doucment Opens option to remove it.
   c. Click on `OK` to apply the options.

4) **ENTER THE PHONE NUMBER AND DIALING OPTIONS**

   a. Select the Dial command from the Communications menu to display the Dial dialog box.
   b. Type the name of the communication service in the Name option, `Test`.
   c. Press Tab and type the number in the Phone Number option, `555-1212`. (You may wish to enter an actual BBS phone number here.)
   d. Click on `OK` to set the phone number.

5) **SAVE THE OPTIONS IN A FILE NAMED BBS TEST**

   a. Press ⌘`S` to display the Save dialog box.
   b. Type the file name `BBS TEST` and click on `SAVE`. Works saves the phone number and communications options in a file named BBS TEST.

6) **INITIATE COMMUNICATIONS**

   a. Display the Dial dialog box by typing ⌘`D`. Works displays the phone number on the screen
   b. Click on the `Dial` button next to Test's phone information. Works removes the dialog box and displays "Dialing..." on the screen. Depending on the type of modem you have, you may be able to hear the phone being dialed.

c. When the host computer answers the phone and establishes communications with your modem, Works displays "Connect...". Press the Return key.

Note: If the host is already connected to another computer, or if your communications options are not set correctly Works displays "No Carrier". If this occurs, check your communications settings and tell Works to dial again using ⌘ D.

Check - When communications have been established, the host computer transmits a welcome message. Messages differ from service to service, but most ask for your name or account number:

```
WELCOME TO ELECTRONIC INFORMATION SERVICES

There are 17 new messages

Enter your First name: _
```

Because you are connected, anything typed on your keyboard will be sent to the host computer. You could now enter your name and receive information by following the instructions that the host sends to your machine.

7) **TERMINATE COMMUNICATIONS**

Execute the Hang Up command by pressing ⌘= (equals). Works displays the message "Hanging Up...".

11.4 The Future of Computing

In Chapter One we traced the history of computing and discovered that, as technology improved, computers increased in speed, stored more data, decreased in size and most importantly became less expensive. This trend will, in all probability, continue. As it does, one of the advances will be the continued development of small microprocessors which will be found in an ever increasing number of appliances and devices. Microprocessors can already be found in telephone answering machines, cameras, television sets, refrigerators, washing machines and automobiles.

One example of the use of a microprocessor is in the anti-lock braking system (ABS) found on many cars. A computer connected to sensors on a car's wheels detects when, as the brakes are applied, the car begins to skid. The computer then takes over control of the brakes, pumping them rapidly to keep the wheels from locking. This process avoids the skidding which often results when brakes are applied on wet roads. Other microprocessors are being developed which increase the efficiency of an automobile engine or control how safety devices will perform in case of an accident.

Microprocessors are also found in auto-focusing cameras which both focus themselves and set the proper exposure. To focus the camera a high frequency sound is sent from the camera to the subject. The sound then bounces off of the subject and back to a receiver on the camera. A microprocessor measures the time for the sound to return and then calculates the distance, setting the focus accordingly. To set the proper exposure the camera uses a photocell to measure the intensity of light and then, using a microprocessor, calculates the correct exposure.

One of the most promising areas of microprocessor development is in the diagnostic systems of complex electronic devices. Many devices such as computers and photocopiers have become so complicated that it is difficult to determine what is wrong when they malfunction. Therefore microprocessors have been developed which pinpoint what component is not working properly and then alerts the user. These types of systems will soon be commonly found on automobiles, aircraft or any device which contains a large number of complicated parts. Undoubtedly many new applications for microprocessors will be found in the future in areas which we can only begin to imagine.

Besides the development of better microprocessors, software will also improve. Most software developers are attempting to make their software increasingly "user friendly", which means easier to use. In learning the three applications areas you were required to familiarize yourself with a number of commands. By making the commands have similar effects in each of the applications areas, the program was made easier to learn. This process will continue to become less complicated as better software is written. Later in this chapter we discuss attempts to produce computers that allow the user to use voice rather than typed commands.

11.5 Artificial Intelligence

Although computers cannot think, one of the major areas of research continues to be the development of software programs that are capable of making increasingly complex decisions. The concept of using computers to make decisions which would normally be made by human beings is called "artificial intelligence". Herbert Schorr, a computer scientist at IBM, has declared that the development of artificial intelligence is the "second wave" of the information revolution. The first wave was the development of automated data processing which you studied when producing data bases and spreadsheets. According to Schorr "the second wave will automate decision making".

In a recent newspaper article the Internal Revenue Service (I.R.S.) defined artificial intelligence as "the science of making machines do things that would require intelligence if done by man". As an example, there are currently computers which can play chess so well that they can beat all but the best players. Universities actually challenge each other's computers to play chess to determine which has the best chess playing program. Are these computers really intelligent? Most computer scientists would say no. They are simply programmed to make a series of decisions in response to the moves made by their opponents. It is merely their speed and ability to access huge amounts of stored data which make them appear to be intelligent.

Some specialized computers are capable of playing master level chess

In 1950 the brilliant English mathematician Alan Turing wrote a paper entitled "Computing Machinery and Intelligence" in which he raised the question "Can machines think?". To answer the question he invented the "Imitation Game." Briefly summarized, the game involves placing a person and a computer in separate rooms and an interrogator in a third room. Communicating by typed questions and answers, the interrogator questions the human and computer to determine which is the computer. If the interrogator cannot tell the difference between the responses then, according to Turing, the machine has human thought capabilities. Since not even psychologists can agree on a definition of intelligence, this is probably as good a test as any. Currently, no computer or software package has been shown to be capable of passing Turing's test.

11.6 Expert Systems

One of the most promising areas of research into artificial intelligence is the development of what is called "expert systems." An expert system is programmed to produce the same solution a human expert would if asked to solve the same problem. The concept was first employed in research done in the 1960's at Stanford University by Professor Edward Feigenbaum and Doctor Edward Shortliffe. They developed a computer program named "Mycin", named for a group of antibiotics, which was designed to perform medical diagnosis of infectious diseases and suggest possible treatments. The program worked by asking questions about a patient's symptoms. A diagnosis was then given based upon the answers. Was this program actually thinking? Again, we answer no. The program was making its decisions based upon over 500 rules given it by human experts. For example, such a rule might specify that if a patient had a low-level infection and was allergic to penicillin, then the antibiotic Erythromycin should be prescribed.

Mycin, which took more than 20 man-years to develop, turned out to be more accurate than the human experts against whom it was tested. In one test Mycin prescribed the correct treatment 65% of the time, in contrast to the experts who were right in 42% to 62% of the cases. One of the problems with Mycin was that it did not know whether it was diagnosing a human being or not. In fact, it was capable of prescribing penicillin to fix a broken window. However, programs such as Mycin are useful when used to aid a human doctor in diagnosing a patient.

Since the Mycin experiment at Stanford, many expert systems have been developed in fields as diverse as accounting, biology, law and automobile repair. Although expert systems can be helpful in reducing the time it takes a professional to analyze and solve a problem, it has so far been apparent that a computer is sometimes a poor substitute for a human expert. This is because human experts may use "intuition" to solve a problem. In making a diagnosis a doctor uses intuition when making a decision which is not based on systematic logic. By looking at a patient and discussing his or her feelings and moods, a doctor is often able to ascertain important information which could not be used by a computer. We consider these to be "human" or "psychological" factors which, while very important, can not be programmed into a computer.

An example of an expert system that works quite well is one installed by the credit card division of American Express. In the past when a store called to get approval for a large charge, a trained credit expert would have to decide if approval should be given. By asking a series of questions about the amount being charged, the type of item being purchased, and so on, the expert would then make a decision. Now if an American Express card holder wants to make a large purchase, for example a $10,000 oriental rug, in many cases the computer will decide whether or not to approve the purchase.

Another useful expert system involves the repair of automobiles. In the past when Ford automobile dealers were confronted by a hard-to-diagnose engine problem they called expert Gordy Kujawski. Now they simply run an expert system program developed to duplicate the reasoning Kujawski uses to solve a problem. Creating this expert system involved describing Kujawski's thought processes in terms of rules, like the Mycin program. Programmers watched Kujawski at work and asked "Why did you test the battery?" and "How did you know to look at the carburetor?" and programmed the computer to respond as he did.

One of the more secretive uses of expert systems is that used by U.S. intelligence agents to avert terrorist acts. Programmed with the knowledge of a handful of terrorism agents, the system has proven surprisingly accurate in its ability to predict when and where terrorist activities will occur. Another similar system is used by the F.B.I. to predict the activities of criminals. Both systems have been programmed with rules that experts have developed based on many years of experience.

We earlier referred to the I.R.S. definition of artificial intelligence. They have developed an expert system which analyzes tax returns to determine if a person is correctly reporting income or making improper deductions. Programmed to look for suspicious patterns, the I.R.S. computer decides when a human agent should consider initiating a tax audit.

Currently there are about 3,000 expert systems in use with the number increasing at the rate of 50% per year. To date the expert systems that work the best are those for which a series of rules can be used to make a decision. When specific rules do not apply, as when intuition must be used, expert systems are usually not successful.

11.7 Natural Language Processing

Designing a computer system that can recognize human speech has long been a goal of computer scientists. After almost three decades of slow progress, machines are now being developed that can recognize spoken words and then translate them into digital form. This is called "speech recognition" and involves "natural language processing", a field of artificial intelligence which attempts to translate a sentence into its separate parts and understand its meaning.

The difficulties in producing natural language processing systems are many. First, many words have different meanings based upon the context in which they are used. The word "change", for example, could mean money as in "Here's your change" or a different order as in "Change my order to a hot dog". Second, there are almost an unlimited number of ways of giving the same instructions. And finally, a speech recognizing computer needs to be able to understand many different voice patterns and accents.

Solving these problems highlights the difference between human and machine "intelligence." A person would have little problem overcoming the difficulties mentioned above, but to a machine, which is programmed to follow instructions in a logical sequence, the difficulties are considerable.

A recent advance in natural language processing has been the development of the Sphinx software package by Carnegie-Mellon graduate student Kai-Fu Lee. Sphinx is an experimental system capable of recognizing continuous speech based on a vocabulary of almost 1,000 words. Most previous systems have been limited to individual words or words separated by pauses. One of the major advances made by Sphinx is its ability to recognize speech from many different speakers.

The potential applications for natural language processing systems are numerous. One such development will allow users of car telephones to dial their phones by speaking the numbers. Other potential uses include allowing people to dictate letters to their word processors or ordering airline tickets over a telephone connected to a computer. Voice messages might also be sent in digital form to computers as electronic mail.

One very useful application of natural language processing would be in language translation. A person calling France could speak in English with the computer translating and speaking in French at the other end. Although systems have already been developed which allow the user to type in English and have the output printed in French, machines which can handle spoken language appear to be well off in the future.

Today there are hand-held computers capable of translating a limited vocabulary of English to French or Spanish as it is being spoken

A major problem faced by language translation programs is that most languages such as French, German, and especially Asian languages such as Japanese and Chinese are structured differently than English. Also, as you have learned if you have studied a foreign language, many words have a number of different meanings. For all of these reasons even the best translation programs are at present not very accurate, often producing humorous results. A computer asked to translate the biblical passage "the spirit is willing, but the flesh is weak" from English into Russian and then back into English produced the result "the wine is agreeable, but the meat is spoiled".

Many computer scientists believe that future advances in artificial intelligence will depend upon the development of radically new technologies. To be truly useful as artificial intelligence machines, computers will have to possess some form of "common sense". They will have to be able to distinguish, for example, between a person and a window, as Mycin cannot. Until this is accomplished we would be wise to give artificial intelligence systems only limited trust, being on guard against the errors in judgement they may make.

11.8 Robotics

Another application of artificial intelligence is in "robotics". To be defined as a robot a machine must be able to be programmed and also be able to move. Most robots, unlike an R2D2 or C3PO, are simply moveable arms that can be directed to perform a task by moving. Because they can be programmed, robots can make simple decisions and then act upon them.

Of the robots currently "employed", most are used in the automobile industry to spot weld and spray paint cars. As robots become capable of performing increasingly complicated tasks, they will undoubtedly be used in many more industries.

There are a number of advantages to using robots. One is their ability to perform tasks too dangerous for humans. Robots have been developed which can remove and defuse bombs, work in highly radioactive environments, or under conditions of extreme noise or temperatures. Their use in aiding handicapped people is also a very promising area. A major advantage of robots is that they can perform their tasks tirelessly, willing to work twenty-four hour days without rest or vacations.

To date robots have been used only to perform simple, repetitive tasks. They have often been both expensive and unreliable. A task as simple as picking up an egg has proven extremely difficult for them to perform. The eye-hand coordination which we take for granted requires an extremely complex set of actions which are difficult to duplicate mechanically. Even a task as simple as moving through a room without hitting objects is currently difficult for today's robots.

We have all seen science fiction movies where a robot becomes so human-like that it exhibits emotions and temperament, but so far no real robot has been developed which has any of these traits. In all probability such a robot is a very long way off, if indeed one can ever be invented.

When natural language processing and artificial intelligence programs are perfected, the use of robots will undoubtedly increase. The dream of having a machine you can order around like a personal servant may then become a reality.

The factory of the future will probably contain numerous robots performing a wide variety of tasks. As manufacturers produce an increasing number of highly complicated products, robots will be easier to train than human beings.

11.9 Careers in Computing

As computers become more powerful they will play an ever increasing role in the world in which we live. Consequently most people, no matter what field they are employed in, will encounter computers. It is estimated that by the end of the 1990's over 90% of all office personnel will have a computer terminal or PC at their desks.

Doctors, lawyers, accountants, business people, educators, farmers and almost any profession you can think of are currently using or will soon make use of computers. It is the purpose of this text to introduce you to the many varied tasks that a computer can perform to help and prepare you for almost any career you might consider.

If you have become especially interested in computers you might consider a career in computing. According to recent government projections the computer field will continue to hire people at an increasing rate. In this section we discuss some of the careers that you might consider and the education required to enter them.

Data Processing

The area of computing that employs the largest number of people is data processing. Data processing, as you have already learned, involves the electronic storage, manipulation and retrieval of data. Banks, businesses, educational institutions - almost any organization requires large amounts of data and therefore people capable of data processing. Data processing careers are usually divided into six categories:

1. System Analyst
2. System Developer - Programmer
3. System Manager
4. Computer Operator
5. Data-entry Operator
6. Computer Science and Research

We will consider each area separately, outlining the qualifications expected of a person entering the area.

Systems operators get hands-on experience with the computer hardware

System Analyst

Before a data processing system can be set up a system analyst must first analyze and design the system. The analyst must determine how an organization will use their computer system, what data they will store, how they will access it, and how they expect the system to grow in the future. The success or failure of the data processing system will be primarily determined by how well the analyst does his or her job. The data base chapters emphasized the importance of carefully planning how a data base is to be structured. This type of planning gave you an introduction to what a system analyst does.

System analysts should possess the following characteristics:

(1) A good knowledge of the organization installing the data processing system including its goals and objectives.

(2) A comprehensive knowledge of both data-processing methods and the current software and hardware available.

(3) A knowledge of programming languages and how they might be used to produce required software.

(4) The ability to work well with both technical and nontechnical personnel.

Most system analysts are college graduates who have majored in computer science or business administration or both. A good way to start preparing yourself to be a system analyst is to take the programming courses offered by your school in languages such as BASIC and Pascal and business courses such as management and accounting.

System Developer - Programmer

After the system analyst has determined what type of system should be installed, it is the job of the system developer to provide the necessary software. This is accomplished by writing three types of programs:

(1) system programs - are programs that operate the system's hardware. The disk operating system (DOS) booted on your microcomputer is an example of a system program.

(2) applications programs - are programs that solve specific problems. In a business these might be problems such as customer billing or inventory control. The word processing, data base and spreadsheet programs you have used are applications programs.

(3) program maintenance - many businesses need their programs expanded or changed to meet new demands or to correct errors. This is called program maintenance.

Programmers should possess the following characteristics:

(1) A detailed knowledge of the programming language being used.

(2) A detailed knowledge of the organization for which the program is being written.

(3) An ability to reason analytically and pay close attention to details.

(4) Creativity to develop problem-solving strategies.

(5) Considerable patience to work out the fine details of a program and to discover the "bugs" it may contain.

(6) Knowledge of how the programs and computer hardware will interact

The education required to be a programmer is usually determined by the needs of the employer. Many businesses employ programmers who have taken only technical school or junior college programming courses. Large or specialized companies, which need highly sophisticated programming, usually require college graduates. A good way to start in preparing for a career as a programmer is to take the programming and computer science courses as well as the mathematics courses offered by your school.

System Manager

Companies with large data processing requirements usually employ a manager who is responsible for running the Management Information Systems department (MIS). The MIS manager must organize the computer and human resources of the department in order to best achieve the organization's goals.

System managers should possess the following characteristics:

(1) A detailed understanding of the organization's goals.

(2) The ability to motivate and work closely with technical personnel.

(3) A detailed understanding of data-processing methods, hardware, and software.

A college degree in business administration with a concentration in information systems is desirable to be a system manager. Since a system manager is an administrator he or she will usually possess previous management experience.

Computer Operator

A computer operator is responsible for setting up equipment, mounting and removing tapes and disks, and monitoring the computer's operation. Often the computer operator must help the programmers and users of a computer when problems arise.

The following are characteristics a computer operator should possess:

(1) A good understanding of how the computer equipment operates.

(2) The ability to read and understand technical manuals.

(3) Be able to detect and correct operational errors.

(4) Good communication skills to explain to computer users problems they may encounter.

Most computer operators have technical school or junior college educations. Because of the many different types of computers, the majority of their training is usually received on the job. A good way to prepare for a career as a computer operator is to take computer courses in school and assist, if possible, in the operation and maintenance of the school's computers.

Data-Entry Operator

It is the job of a data-entry operator to type data into a computer. This is usually done at a computer terminal which is much like the computer you have been using. Data-entry operators may work for banks entering cancelled checks, department stores entering inventory figures, or educational institutions entering student records.

Often data is entered from various locations and then sent over phone lines to a central computer. Because of this it is sometimes possible for data-entry operators to work at home.

The following are characteristics a data-entry operator should possess:

(1) The ability to type fast and accurately.

(2) Attention to detail in order to pick up errors that may occur.

Usually a high school diploma is sufficient to gain a job as a data-entry operator. Often several weeks of on the job training will be offered by the employer. To begin to prepare for a position as a data-entry operator it is advisable to take courses in typing and word processing.

Computer Scientist

The study of computer science is a very broad field involving many disciplines including science, electronics and mathematics. A computer scientist often works in research at a university or computer manufacturer developing new computer applications software and hardware. It is computer scientists who first design robots, natural language processors, or any of the other many applications that we have mentioned.

The following are characteristics a computer scientist should possess:

(1) A sense of curiosity.

(2) An aptitude for science and mathematics.

(3) Patience to perform experiments that may take years.

A computer scientist usually has both undergraduate and graduate school degrees. To prepare to be a computer scientist it is advisable to take science courses, especially physics, mathematics courses including calculus, and programming and computer science courses.

11.10 The Social and Ethical Consequences of Computers

The society in which we live has been so profoundly affected by computers that historians refer to the present time as "the information age". This is due to the computer's ability to store and manipulate large amounts of information (data). Computers have become such a dominant force that if all of them were to disappear much of our society would be unable to function. Because of computers we are evolving out of an industrial into an information society much as over a hundred years ago we evolved from an agricultural into an industrial society. Such fundamental changes in society cause disruptions which must be planned for. For this reason it is crucial that we consider both the social and ethical consequences of our increasing dependence on computers.

We have already mentioned the impact of telecommunications. By allowing people to work anywhere that telephones or satellite communications are available, we are likely to become a more diversified society. Large cities with their centralized offices will no longer be as necessary. This diversification could reduce traffic congestion, air pollution and many of the other consequences of an urban society. Stock brokers or writers, for example, can now consider the benefits of working outside a city and yet still have all of the facilities they need readily available to them at home through a computer. Because of this, Alvin Toffler in his book "The Third Wave" called this the age of the "electronic cottage".

In our discussion of robots we mentioned their ability to work twenty-four hour days without vacations. While this is obviously a major benefit to an employer, it could have a negative impact on employees. Manufacturers are increasingly able to replace factory workers with machines, thereby increasing efficiency and saving money. This trend, however, also leads to increased unemployment of those factory workers who lack technical skills.

The argument is often used that new technologies such as robotics create jobs for the people who design, build, install and service them. While this is true, these new jobs require well educated, highly trained people. For this reason it is important to think carefully about the educational requirements needed for employment. As we become an increasingly "high-tech" society, those properly prepared for technical jobs will be the most likely to find employment. In response to this problem many states have instituted programs to train laid-off factory workers so that they may enter technical fields.

One of the probable benefits of our information society will be a reduction in the work week. In the agricultural age people often worked 80 or more hours per week just to grow enough food to feed their families. During the early part of the industrial age most factory workers worked 60 hours per week. Presently most people work 40 hours or less per week, and with increased technology the work week will likely continue to decrease.

11.11 The Right to Privacy

With computers impacting on our lives in an ever increasing number of ways, serious ethical questions arise. By ethical questions we mean asking what are the right and wrong ways to use computers. As human beings we want to insure that our rights as individuals are not encroached upon by the misuse of these machines.

Probably the most serious problem created by computers is in invading our right to privacy. Because computers can store vast amounts of data we must decide what information is proper to store, what is improper, and who should have access to the information. Every time you use a credit card, make a phone call, withdraw money from the bank, reserve a flight on an airplane, or register to take a course at school a computer records the transaction. Using these records it would be possible to learn a great deal about you - where you have been, when you were there, and what you have done.

Computers are also used to store information dealing with your credit rating, which determines your ability to borrow money. If you want to buy a car and finance it at the bank, the bank first checks your credit records on a computer to determine if you have a good credit rating. If you are able to purchase the car and then apply for automobile insurance, another computer will check to determine if you have traffic violations or have been involved in any activities which would make you a poor risk. How do you know if the information being used is accurate? To protect both your privacy and the accuracy of data stored about you, a number of laws have been passed.

The Fair Credit Reporting Act of 1970 deals with data collected for use by credit, insurance and employment agencies. The act gives individuals the right to see information maintained about them. If a person is denied credit they are allowed access to the files used to make the credit determination. If any of the information is incorrect, the person has the right to have it changed. The act also restricts who may access credit files to only those with a court order or the written permission of the individual whose credit is being checked.

The Privacy Act of 1974 restricts the way in which personal data can be used by federal agencies. Individuals must be permitted access to information stored about them and may correct any information that is incorrect. Agencies must insure both the security and confidentiality of any sensitive information. Although this law applies only to federal agencies, many states have adopted similar laws.

The Financial Privacy Act of 1978 requires that a government authority have a subpoena, summons, or search warrant to access an individual's financial records. When such records are released, the financial institution must notify the individual of who has had access to them.

Laws such as the three mentioned above help to insure that the right to privacy is not infringed by data stored in computer files. Although implementing privacy laws has proven expensive and difficult, most people would agree that they are needed.

11.12 Protecting Computer Software and Data

Because computer software can be copied electronically it is easy to duplicate. Such duplication is usually illegal because the company producing the software is not paid for the copy. This has become an increasingly serious problem as the number of illegal software copies distributed by computer "pirates" has grown. Developing, testing and marketing software is an expensive process. If the software developer is then denied rightful compensation, the future development of all software is jeopardized. Suppose for example that a programmer has written a piece of software which you like. If you illegally make copies and distribute them to your friends, that programmer loses income and may not be able to continue developing new software. Because most software is continually being updated and improved you could be denied these better versions.

Software companies are increasingly vigilant in detecting and prosecuting those who illegally copy their software. Therefore, when using software it is important to use only legally acquired copies, and to not make illegal copies for others.

Another problem that is growing as computer use increases is the willful interference with or destruction of computer data. Because computers can transfer and erase data at high speeds, it makes them especially vulnerable to acts of vandalism. Newspapers have carried numerous reports of home computer users gaining access to large computer data bases. Sometimes these "hackers" change or erase data stored in the system. These acts are usually illegal and can cause very serious and expensive damage.

One especially harmful act is the planting of a "virus" into computer software. A virus is a series of instructions buried into a program which cause the computer to destroy data when given a certain signal. For example, the instructions to destroy data might wait until a certain time or date is reached before being executed. Because the virus is duplicated each time the software is copied it spreads, hence the name virus. This practice is illegal and can result in considerable damage.

Most people are becoming aware that the willful destruction of computer data is no different than any other vandalization of property. Since the damage is done electronically the result is often not as obvious as destroying physical property, but the consequences are much the same. It is estimated that computer crimes may cost the nation as much as 30 billion dollars a year and be rising each year.

11.13 The Ethical Responsibilities of the Programmer

Increasingly computers are being used to make decisions in situations which can threaten human life. In one incident a patient being treated for cancer received five times the prescribed amount of radiation due to an error in the computer program operating the radiation machine. The consequences were a serious hazard to her life and health. As the use of computers to control medical equipment increases, this type of error may become more common.

It is extremely difficult, if not impossible, for a computer programmer to guarantee that a program will always operate properly. The programs used to control complicated devices contain millions of instructions and as the programs grow longer the likelihood of errors increases. What is a special cause for concern is the increased use of computers to control potentially dangerous devices such as aircraft, nuclear reactors, military weapons or sensitive medical equipment. This places a strong ethical burden on the programmer to insure, as best he or she can, the reliability of computer software.

The Defense Department is currently supporting research aimed at detecting and correcting program errors. Because it spends an estimated 18 billion dollars annually developing software, much of it for use in situations which can be life threatening, the department is especially interested in having reliable programs.

As capable as computers have proven to be, we must be cautious in allowing them to replace human beings in areas where judgement is crucial. Because we are intelligent, humans can often detect that something out of the ordinary has occurred and then take actions which have not been previously anticipated. Computers, on the other hand, will only do what they have been programmed to do, even if it is to perform a dangerous act.

We must also consider situations in which the computer can protect human life better than humans. For example, in the space program astronauts place their lives in the hands of computers which must continuously perform complicated calculations at very high speeds. No human being would be capable of doing the job as well as a computer. Computers are also routinely used to monitor seriously ill patients. Since computers are able to work 24-hours a day without becoming distracted or falling asleep, they probably perform such tasks better than most humans would.

11.14 Computers and Biological Systems

Computer scientists are now researching the possibility of developing computer circuits made from living proteins and enzymes. The chips created from these circuits are called "biochips". Signals would be sent through the biochips the same way as signals are sent through the human brain, but at speeds many thousands of times faster. The potential would then exist to create computers with reasoning power approaching that of the human mind.

Although the development of useful biochips is probably well in the future, it is both exciting and frightening to ponder their possibilities. It has been suggested that biochips could be implanted into the human brain. Thus, a person could become an instant expert in any field of interest. Obviously if such a possibility were to be realized, the social and ethical questions that would be raised would dwarf the problems we have considered.

Desktop Publishing, Presentations and Graphics

The popularity of computers has spawned a new generation of software applications geared to the presentation of information. This has made it possible for computers to be used to produce and manipulate art work, pictures and the layout of documents in much the same way as word processors manipulate text. These applications, for example, allow a small business, educational institution, or individual to produce professional looking documents without the use of artists, designers or typesetters. Below we discuss three of the most popular applications, and the technology that has made them available.

11.15 Laser Printers and Output Devices

Probably the most important advance which made these applications possible was the creation of a low-cost, dependable *laser printer*. The printer that you have most likely used is called an "impact" printer. Like a typewriter, impact printers require that an inked ribbon be pressed against paper to produce an image of the character. The most common impact printer is the "dot matrix" which prints characters as a series of small dots. Because the characters are made up of dots, dot matrix print can appear jagged, especially on curved letters:

`This is an example of dot matrix print.`

Examining the print closely shows how the dots are used to create a character:

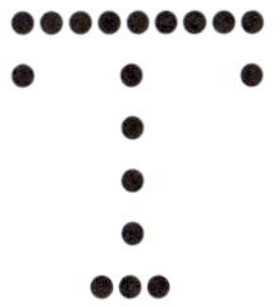

A character produced by a dot-matrix printer is composed of small dots

Because they are not very precise, dot matrix printers are not very good at printing graphics, and their output often appears sloppy or unfinished.

A laser printer, on the other hand, uses a beam of light to draw each character on the page, employing a process similar to a photocopier. This allows the characters to be fully formed, eliminating the use of dots. A close examination of a character produced by a laser printer illustrates this:

A character produced by a laser printer is smoother

Laser printers are also able to produce graphics such as pictures and diagrams with the same level of clarity.

11.16 Desktop Publishing

One of the most popular uses for laser printers is in the field of "desktop publishing", or DTP. In desktop publishing, special software is used to allow persons not trained in art or layout to create professional looking documents using a personal computer and a laser printer. It is the purpose of desktop publishing software to combine text (created in a word processor) with illustrations (created by a graphics program) to produce the final document. Before desktop publishing existed, creating a document such as an advertising brochure was a complicated procedure, often involving many people:

1. A writer to create the text of the brochure.
2. An artist to produce the illustrations.
3. A typesetter to print the text.
4. A layout person to combine the text and illustrations into the completed brochure using scissors and glue.

Now a single person can perform all of these tasks using a computer. A major advantage of using desktop publishing software is that changes can be made to a document in much the same way as changes are made to text using a word processor. Illustrations and text can be added or deleted, changed in size or the whole layout redone - all on a computer screen.

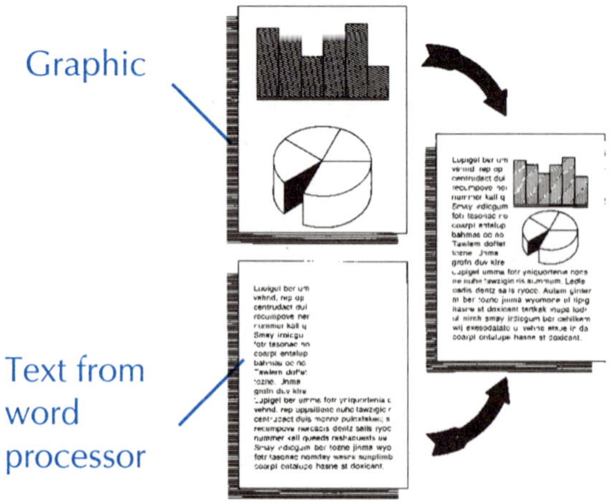

DTP software combines graphics and text into one file

By performing the layout of a document on the computer screen instead of on paper, changes may easily be made. Different layouts can be created and printed until the desired combination is found. Once completed, the final version can be printed and the document saved on disk so that it can be edited or reprinted at any later time.

Three of the most commonly used desktop publishing programs are *PageMaker*, *Ventura Publisher* and *Quark Express*. Less powerful and inexpensive programs such as Publish It!, First Publisher and PrintShop allow DTP documents to be created and printed on dot matrix printers. Often these packages contain collections of prepared illustrations called "clip art" which can be included in whatever document is produced, often eliminating the need for an artist.

11.17 Elements of Desktop Publishing

It must be remembered that the primary purpose for producing a desktop published document is to convey information to the readers of that document. For this reason, publishers must consider the appearance of the information and determine whether it is appropriate to the type of document being produced. The document could be a sales flyer, technical manual, or corporate report - it is unlikely that each would use the same format. One of the most powerful features of DTP is that it gives the user the opportunity to experiment with different formats until the one which best fits the information they are trying to communicate is produced.

Elements of format

There are several different elements which contribute to a document's format. In the word processing chapters of this text you learned about margins, indents, bold and italic text, and other formatting options. Documents produced using DTP software have these, and several other formatting options to consider.

Typeface: One of the first and most important decisions that must be made is to determine what *typeface* will be used in producing a document. The typeface is a description of how the text characters are formed. Laser printers have hundreds of typefaces which they can print while professional typesetting equipment has thousands. Some typefaces are better than others, however, when used for certain tasks. For example, a typeface which is good when used for a headline may not be as good when used in long paragraphs. Many laser printers and typesetting machines operate using a system called PostScript which is used to identify typefaces. Below we show examples of several PostScript typefaces along with descriptions of what each typeface is best used for.

Body text The following faces are well suited for use in the paragraphs which make up the body of a document.

Bookman: ABCDEF abcdef 123456789 *ABCD* **ABCD**

New Century Schoolbook: ABCD abcd 123456 *ABC* **ABC**

Times-Roman: ABCDEF abcdef 123456789 *ABCD* **ABCD**

Palatino: ABCDEF abcdef 123456789 *ABCD* **ABCD**

Headlines and headings

The following faces are well suited for headlines and captions, and other short pieces of text such as a menu or table.

Avant Garde: ABCDEF abcdef 123456789 *ABCD* **ABCD**

Helvetica: ABCDEF abcdef 123456789 *ABCD* **ABCD**

Optima: ABCDEF abcdef 123456789 *ABCD* **ABCD**

Special or decorative

There are several typefaces which are designed to be used in special applications such as displaying computer output, or to add decorative flair to a publication.

Zapf Chancery: ABCDEF abcdef 123456789 "?!&$(%#*

`Courier: ABCDEF abcdef 123456789` *ABCD* **ABCD**

`Symbols:` ABXΔEΦ αβχδεφ 123456789 !≅#∃%⊥&∗()−=

`Zapf Dingbats:` ✚✢✆★✱✳✈ ❖✎❍❑▼❚ ⚭✝✔✕✖✗✙✠✂

Usually a document will have several typefaces, one for the body, another for titles, etc. Again, the DTP software makes it easy to experiment, trying typefaces in different combinations until the most pleasing combination is found.

Graphics:

Another element to consider when creating a DTP document is the use of graphics, which often determine how a document will be perceived. Questions involving graphics include where to place them, how large they should be and whether to use photographs or drawings. The proper use of graphics can often make the difference between a professional looking document and one that looks amateurish.

One of the most popular uses for DTP is the creation of newsletters. In an Exercise of Chapter 3 you were asked to create a newsletter with two columns. Because the Works word processor can not do this automatically, it is a tedious task to produce the columns. Desktop publishing software can create multi-column pages automatically making column text easy to read. The software can also draw horizontal and vertical lines called "rules".

Besides the options described above, DTP programs can perform such additional tasks as printing text in color, drawing boxes around paragraphs, rotating type so that it appears on an angle, and controlling the space between lines, words and letters.

11.18 Graphics and Illustration Software

Using specialized software it is possible to create graphic images on the computer. By graphic images, we mean non-text items such as drawings, photographs, charts, logos, etc. The advantage of using a computer rather than drawing on paper is that the image can then be manipulated; changed in size, rotated, etc. When an artist wants to make a change to a picture drawn on paper, he or she must either use an eraser or start from scratch. Using graphics software, the artist could instead draw the picture on a computer screen. If changes were then desired, they could be made to the picture stored in the computer's memory. When the final version had been created, it could be printed in black and white using a laser printer, or in color using a special, color printer.

There are several powerful programs available for creating and editing graphics images. Several of these are *Adobe Illustrator*, *Aldus Freehand* and *Corel Draw*. Most require the use of a specialized input device to aid in the drawing. The most popular of these devices are the mouse and the drawing tablet. These devices are used to translate the movements of the artist's hand onto the computer screen.

In addition to allowing the easy modification of a graphic, illustration software often has a variety of advanced tools that would be difficult or time consuming to duplicate manually. For example, suppose a business hires an artist to design a logo. Using pen and paper, the artist would then sketch the logo and add any colors using paint. Suppose the artist choose green as the color for the logo and painted it on paper. If the company then wanted to see what the logo looked like in red, the artist would have to start from scratch, drawing the outline, and painting it red. If the logo was instead prepared using illustration software, the artist could move the cursor to the desired location on the screen, issue a command which said "Change this green area to red" and print the version. Other examples of editing options include changing line widths, erasing lines and objects in a diagram, and changing the size or position of objects. Once complete, the final graphic can be saved in a file on disk, similar to a data base or spreadsheet, that could be edited or reprinted at a later date.

Another advantage to using illustration software is that any graphics produced can easily be placed in a desktop-published document. Most DTP software packages can read the files produced by illustration software, and place a graphic directly into a DTP document. Some DTP packages can even perform basic editing on the image, allowing it to be scaled (made larger or smaller), rotated, or clipped (choosing to display only part of the graphic).

11.19 Desktop Presentations

Many business people are required to give presentations; new employees must be trained, financial information disseminated, advertising campaigns tested, etc. These presentations often require the use of visual aids such as slides and charts. One of the fastest growing areas for personal computer use is in the field of *desktop presentation* where the computer is used to create and display such visual aids.

Suppose that a business hires 10 new employees, all of whom must be trained to perform certain tasks. One of the most common ways to train employees is to give them a series of lectures explaining the tasks they will perform. Visual aids such as charts or slides will probably help the new employees to learn the information being presented. With desktop presentation software, a personal computer could be used to prepare and present the visual aids.

Most desktop presentation software has two parts, an editor where graphics are created and manipulated (similar to the illustration software described above), and a display controller where the created graphics may be displayed in sequence on the computer's screen. Many packages are also able to display graphics which were created using separate illustration software.

There are several ways to use presentation software. The first is for the creation of slides. Graphics are created and then output to a "film recorder" which produces a photographic slide capable of being projected. Because the film recorder hardware is expensive, smaller companies often send a diskette containing their graphic files to a "service bureau"; a company that owns a film recorder and makes slides for customers.

A second way to use presentation graphics is to store the graphics on a diskette, and then use a computer screen to display them to an audience. Often the computer will be connected to a large monitor or projection system. Two advantages of this method is that the computer can be used to easily change the order of a presentation and to produce animated sequences by changing the displayed images very quickly.

The third use is to print black and white copies of the graphics on a laser printer for use by the audience as handouts. This is often done in conjunction with one of the other two methods, giving the audience take-home notes which they may review after the lecture.

11.20 How do we face the future?

In this text we have presented the history of computing, showed you how to word process, use a database and a spreadsheet, and have considered the future of computing. Our hope is that you are excited by computers and realize the tremendous potential they have to serve us in a wide variety of ways. We also hope that you have been made aware of how computers might be misused. It is therefore the duty of each one of us, as responsible citizens, to insure that the awesome power given to us by computers be used only to benefit mankind.

Chapter Summary

This chapter began by discussing the future of computing. One of the most important advances in the field of computing has been in telecommunications, which means the sending of computer data over phone lines. Modems are used both to transmit and receive computer data. Because of telecommunications many people may be able to work at home.

A popular form of telecommunications is the electronic bulletin board which allows users to transmit and receive messages. A similar form of telecommunications is electronic mail (E-mail) where single users are able to receive messages meant only for them.

The continued development of microprocessors will effect many products including automobiles and home electronic devices. With their ability to make simple decisions, microprocessors can automate many of the functions performed by these devices.

Using computers to make decisions normally made by human beings is called artificial intelligence. Although computers cannot think, they can be programmed to make decisions which, for example, will allow them to play chess. Expert systems are a form of artificial intelligence where a computer is programmed with a set of rules that can solve a problem - producing the same solution a human expert would. Credit card companies, automobile manufacturers and hospitals are a few of the organizations currently using expert systems.

Recognizing spoken words and translating them into digital form is called speech recognition which involves natural language processing, a field of artificial intelligence that attempts to translate a sentence into its separate parts and understand its meaning. Numerous problems face the successful development of language processing systems.

A robot is a machine that can be programmed and also move. Robots are currently used to perform simple manufacturing tasks. When natural language processing and artificial intelligence programs are perfected, the use of robots will increase.

Careers in computing were discussed in this chapter and the educational requirements needed to pursue them. Careers which required only a high school education as well as those requiring a college education were presented.

Historians refer to the present time as the "information age" due to the computer's ability to store and manipulate large amounts of data. As the use of computers increases they will profoundly effect society including what jobs will be available and the length of the work week.

A problem created by computers is their potential for invading our right to privacy. Laws have been passed to protect us from the misuse of data stored in computers.

Because computer software is easy to copy, illegal copies are often made, denying software manufacturers of rightful compensation. Another problem has been the willful destruction of computer files by erasing data or planting a "virus" into programs that can spread when the programs are copied.

As computers are increasingly used to made decisions in situations which can threaten human life it becomes the responsibility of programmers to do there best to insure the reliability of the software they have developed. We must continue to be cautious not to replace human beings with computers in areas where judgement is crucial.

Vocabulary

Artificial intelligence - Using computers to make decisions which would normally be made by a human being.
Baud rate - Rate at which characters of data are transmitted. One baud represents the transmission of one character per second.
Biochips - Computer circuits made from proteins and enzymes.
Data size - The number of bits (binary digits) that make up one piece of data sent during telecommunications. (7 or 8.)
Download - To transfer a message or computer file from a bulletin board or E-Mail service computer to another computer.
Electronic bulletin board - (BBS) Telecommunications service which allows subscribers using a computer and modem to transmit messages that can be received by all the other subscribers.
Electronic mail - (E-Mail) Telecommunications service which allows a person using a computer and modem to send a message to another person's computer.
Expert system - System programmed to produce the same solution a human expert would if asked to solve the same problem.
Hacker - Person who uses a computer and modem to enter a computer system without authorization.
Information service - A company that provides different telecommunications services, usually for a fee.
Modem - Device which translates binary data into waves and waves back into binary data so that computer data can be sent over telephone lines.
Natural language processing - Using a computer to recognize spoken words and then translate them into digital form.
Parity - When telecommunicating, how the receiving computer determines if an error occurred in the transmission of data. Parity choices are None, Odd and Even.
Pirate - Person who illegally copies computer software.
Robot - Machine which can be programmed and is also capable of motion.
Stop bits - The number of bits, 1 or 2, sent to indicate the end of a piece of data.
Telecommunications - Sending of computer data over telephone lines.
Upload - To transfer a message or computer file from a computer to a bulletin board or E-Mail service computer.
Virus - Program which hides within another program for the purpose of destroying or altering data.

Reviews

Sections 11.1-11.3

1. Name four databases that you would like to be able to access using telecommunications. State why each of them would be useful to you.

2. Besides those listed in the text, list three occupations where people would be able to work at home rather than in an office using telecommunications.

3. What is the difference between an electronic bulletin board and electronic mail?

4. If all of the students in your school had computers and modems at home, in what ways could they be used by teachers and students?

Sections 11.4-11.5

5. What tasks do you think automobile microprocessors may perform in the future?

6. What is artificial intelligence?

7. a) What devices owned by your family contain microprocessors and what are they used for?
   b) What devices would you like to see include microprocessors? Why? What tasks would the microprocessors perform?

8. State three questions you would ask to determine which was the human and which the computer when playing Turing's Imitation Game. Asking "Are you the computer?" is not fair!

Sections 11.6-11.8

9. What did the computer program Mycin do?

10. List four jobs where you think expert systems could be used to help the people performing the jobs. Explain why the systems would be helpful.

11. List four jobs where expert systems could probably not be used, and explain why.

12. Would an expert system be helpful to you in selecting clothes to buy? Explain why or why not.

13. What are some of the difficulties being encountered in the development of natural language processing systems?

14. Why should we be careful in trusting expert systems? What do they lack that humans possess?

15. If you could have a robot built to your own specifications, what would you have it be capable of doing?

Section 11.9

The six computer careers mentioned in this chapter include:

(1) system analyst
(2) system developer - programmer
(3) system manager
(4) computer operator
(5) data-entry operator
(6) computer scientist

16. Which of the above careers require only a:

    a) high school diploma
    b) college diploma
    c) college and graduate school degrees

17. For each of the following students list the careers above that he or she should consider:

    a) a student who likes mathematics.
    b) a student who wants to be involved in the management of a business.
    c) a student who wants to work in the development of rocket guidance systems.
    d) a student who likes to think through problems in a methodical, logical way.

Sections 11.10-11.14

18. Alvin Toffler named his book "The Third Wave". What were the first two waves?

19. What is meant by the term "high-tech" society?

20. a) How do you believe society will benefit from the information age?
    b) What might be the negative aspects of the information age?

21. How can a computer be used to invade your privacy?

22. What can you do if you are turned down for credit at a bank and believe that the data used to deny credit is inaccurate?

23. What is necessary for a federal government authority to access an individual's financial records? What must the authority do after accessing the records?

24. What ethical responsibilities does a programmer have when writing a program that will be used to design a bridge? Can the programmer absolutely guarantee that the program will operate properly? Why?

25. Do you think the development of biochips will benefit mankind? Why?

Sections 11.15-11.19

26. What is the primary advantage of using a laser printer rather than a dot matrix printer?

27. What is desktop publishing?

28. List three advantages of using desktop publishing to produce a newsletter.

29. List three advantages of saving desktop published documents on disk.

30. The two primary elements which contribute to a document's format are typeface and graphics. Briefly explain what each is.

31. Why are different typefaces usually employed to produce a brochure?

32. Who do many artists produce graphic images on a computer rather than directly on paper?

33. What is desktop presentation? Give three examples where you might use it.

34. Explain three methods that can be used to display graphics produced by desktop presentation software. Which method would probably be the best to use if you expected to make changes to the presentation?

Appendix A - Works Command Summary

The following commands are grouped by application area. A list of functions which may be used in the spreadsheet and data base is given at the end of this list.

Word Processor

The File Menu

The File menu is used to create new files, open previously created files, save files, close files, print, and to quit Works.

New...	
Open...	Command-O
Close	Command-W
Close All...	
Save	Command-S
Save As...	
Delete...	
Make Works Desktop...	
Page Setup...	
Print...	Command-P
Print Window	
Eject Page	
Print Merge...	
Quit	Command-Q

The Edit Menu

Use the Edit menu to undo the previous action, cut, copy, paste or delete highlighted text, create drawings and graphics, include data base fields for mail merge and show their field names, and print labels.

Undo	Command-Z
Cut	Command-X
Copy	Command-C
Paste	Command-V
Clear	

Select All	
Draw On	Command-J
Prepare to Merge...	Command-M
Show Field Names	
Show Field Data	
Multiple Labels	

The Window Menu

Use the Window menu to show the Clipboard, access the Help system, and switch between open files by selecting the desired file's name from this menu.

Show Clipboard	
Help	Command-?

The Search Menu

Search contains the commands to search for and replace text and to go to a specific page.

Find...	Command-F
Replace...	Command-R
Go To Page #...	Command-G

The Format Menu

The Format menu is used to set character formats such as bold, italic and underline, to control paragraph justifications and spacing, and to insert and delete page breaks.

Hide Ruler	
Font	
Size	
Style	
Color	
Copy Format	Command-K
Paste Format	Command-Y
Justification	
Spacing	
Insert Page Break	
Remove Page Break	
Title Page	
Set Page #...	

The Spell Menu

Spell includes checking the spelling, setting spell options, and locating the spell dictionary file.

Correct Spelling...
Options...
Dictionary...

Word Processor Keyboard Commands

The following Command key shortcuts may be executed from the Word Processor screen.

Command-B	Make text bold
Command-C	Copy
Command-F	Find
Command-G	Go To Page #
Command-I	Make text italic
Command-J	Draw On / Draw Off
Command-K	Copy Format
Command-M	Prepare to Merge
Command-N	Normal (no emphasis) text
Command-O	Open file
Command-P	Print
Command-Q	Quit
Command-R	Replace
Command-S	Save
Command-U	Underline
Command-V	Paste
Command-W	Close
Command-X	Cut
Command-Y	Paste Format
Command-Z	Undo
Command-?	Help

Data Base

The File Menu

The File menu is used to create new files, open previously created files, save files, close files, print, and to quit Works.

New...	
Open...	Command-O
Close	Command-W
Close All...	
Save	Command-S

Save As...	
Delete...	
Make Works Desktop...	
Page Setup...	
Print...	Command-P
Print Window	
Eject Page	
Quit	Command-Q

The Edit Menu

Use the Edit menu to move, copy or erase highlighted data, and insert and delete records and fields.

Undo	Command-Z
Cut	Command-X
Copy	Command-C
Paste	Command-V
Clear	
Select All	
Paste Function...	
Insert Record	Command-I
Change Field Name...	
Add New Field...	
Delete Field	

The Window Menu

Use the Window menu to show the Clipboard, access the Help system, and switch between open files by selecting the desired file's name from this menu.

Show Clipboard	
Help	Command-?

The Organize Menu

Organize contains the commands to search for data, apply and remove queries, and sort the records.

Find Field	Command-F
Match Records...	Command-M
Record Selection...	
Show All Records	
Sort...	Command-A

The Format Menu

The Format menu is used to switch between list and form views, set display formats for the field names and the data stored in a field.

Show List	`Command-L`
Show Form	`Command-L`
Show Grid	
Bold Field Name	
Bold Field Data	
Border Field Name	
Border Field Data	
Font	
Size	
Color	
Set Field Attributes...	

The Report Menu

The Report menu allows report formats to be created, modified, copied and renamed, and allows formats to be viewed on the screen.

Select Report...
New Report...
Duplicate Report...
Erase Report...

Data Base Keyboard Commands

The following Command key shortcuts may be executed from the Data Base screen.

`Command-A`	Sort
`Command-C`	Copy
`Command-D`	Enter Current Date
`Command-F`	Find Field
`Command-I`	Insert Record
`Command-L`	Show List / Show Form
`Command-M`	Match Records
`Command-O`	Open file
`Command-P`	Print
`Command-Q`	Quit
`Command-S`	Save
`Command-T`	Enter Current Time
`Command-V`	Paste
`Command-W`	Close
`Command-X`	Cut

Command-Z	Undo
Command-"	Copy field from last record
Command-?	Help

Spreadsheet

The File Menu

The File menu is used to create new files, open previously created files, save files, close files, print, and to quit Works.

New...	
Open...	Command-O
Close	Command-W
Close All...	
Save	Command-S
Save As...	
Delete...	
Make Works Desktop...	
Page Setup...	
Print...	Command-P
Print Window	
Eject Page	
Quit	Command-Q

The Edit Menu

Use the Edit menu to move, copy, fill or delete highlighted data, paste functions, insert rows and columns, and sort rows.

Undo	Command-Z
Cut	Command-X
Copy	Command-C
Paste	Command-V
Clear	
Select All	
Paste with Options...	
Draw On	Command-J
Move...	
Insert	Command-I
Paste Function...	
Absolute Cell Ref	Command-A
Fill Right	Command-R
Fill Down	Command-D

Open Cell Note...	
Sort...	
Change Chart Name...	(from Chart Screen)

The Window Menu

Use the Window menu to show the Clipboard, access the Help system, and switch between open files by selecting the desired file's name from this menu.

Show Clipboard	
Help	`Command-?`

The Select Menu

Select contains the commands to highlight cells, find data, go to a specific cell, and to return to the currently selected cell.

All Cells	
Last Cells	
Find Cell...	`Command-F`
Go To Cell...	`Command-G`
Show Active Cell	

The Format Menu

The Format menu is used to set display formats for the data stored in a cell or highlighted group of cells. A format set in a cell affects only the way the data is displayed, not what is actually stored in that cell. Columns widths may also be changed from this menu.

Set Cell Attributes...
Borders
Font
Size
Color
Column Width...

The Options Menu

Options includes governs the display of grids, notes, formulas or values, protects cells so their contents may not be changed, inserts and removes page breaks, controls when Works performs calculations, and the freezing and removing of titles.

Show Grid
Show Notes Indicator
Show Formulas
Show Values

Protected	
Set Page Break	
Remove Page Break	
Calculate Now	Command-=
Manual Calculation	
Automatic Calculation	
Freeze Titles Horizontal	
Freeze Titles Vertical	

The Chart Menu

The Chart menu allows charts to be created, modified, copied, and erased, and allows charts to be viewed on the screen.

Draw Chart...
New Series Chart...
New Pie Chart...
Select Chart Definition...
Duplicate Chart...
Erase Chart...

Spreadsheet Keyboard Commands

The following Command key shortcuts may be executed from the Spreadsheet screen.

Command-A	Absolute / Relative Cell Reference
Command-B	Bold
Command-C	Copy
Command-D	Fill Down
Command-F	Find Cell
Command-G	Go To Cell
Command-I	Insert
Command-J	Draw On / Draw Off
Command-N	Normal (no emphasis) text
Command-O	Open file
Command-P	Print
Command-Q	Quit
Command-R	Fill Right
Command-S	Save
Command-V	Paste
Command-W	Close
Command-X	Cut
Command-Z	Undo
Command-=	Calculate Now
Command-?	Help

Functions

The following is a partial list of functions that may be placed in a spreadsheet cell, or in the formula for a computed field in a data base. A complete list is given in the Works manual supplied by Microsoft.

In the discussion that follows, <value> may be replaced by:

- a single value (such as `10`)
- a cell reference (such as `C5`)
- an expression that evaluates to a single value (such as `C5*2`)
- a field reference (such as `GPA`)

<range> may be replaced by:

- a list of cells separated by commas (such as `A1, B12, D5`)
- a continuous range (`A1:A10`)
- a mixture of both (`A1, B1:B5, C3`)
- a field reference (such as `GPA`)

`Abs(`<value>`)` Returns the absolute value of <value>: ABS(10) returns 10, ABS(-10) returns 10.

`ACos(`<value>`)` Returns the arccosine of <value> in radians. The <value> must be between -1 and +1.

`ASin(`<value>`)` Returns the arcsine of <value> in radians. The <value> must be between -1 and +1.

`ATan(`<value>`)` Returns the arctangent of <value> in radians.

`Average(`<range>`)` Returns the average of the values in <range>. Cells which contain text or are blank are ignored.

`Cos(`<value>`)` Returns the cosine of <value> where <value> is measured in radians.

`Count(`<range>`)` Returns the number of non-blank cells in <range>.

`Degrees(`<value>`)` Returns the degrees measurement of a <value> radians angle.

`Exp(`<value>`)` Returns *e* raised to the <value> power.

`If(`<condition>`,`<true value>`,`<false value>`)` Returns the <true value> if the <condition> is true, and the <false value> if the <condition> is false.

`Int(`<value>`)` Returns the integer value of <value>: ABS(1.9) returns 1.

`Ln(`<value>`)` Returns the natural logarithm (base *e*) of <value>. <value> must be positive.

`Log10(`<value>`)` Returns the base 10 logarithm of <value>. <value> must be positive.

`Max(`<range>`)` Returns the largest value in <range>.

Min(<range>)	Returns the smallest value in <range>.
Mod(<value1>,<value2>)	Returns the remainder of <value1> ÷ <value2>. <value2> may not be 0.
Pi()	Returns the constant 3.1415..., π (pi). No argument is used.
Rand()	Returns a random number between 0.0 and 0.9999999. No argument is used.
Round(<value>,<decimals>)	Returns <value> rounded to <decimals> decimal places. When <decimals> is 0, <value> is rounded to the nearest integer.
Sin(<value>)	Returns the sine of <value> where <value> is measured in radians.
Sqrt(<value>)	Returns the square root of <value>. <value> must be positive.
Sum(<range>)	Returns the total of the values in <range>. Cells which contain text or are blank are ignored.
Tan(<value>)	Returns the tangent of <value> where <value> is measured in radians.
Var(<value1>,<value2>,...)	Returns the sample variance of the <values>. Cells which contain text or are blank are ignored.

Making Backup Copies of Your Data

The Importance of Backups

Files you saved have been stored on disks, or on a network's hard disk. These files have taken time and effort to create. Businesses and institutions that use computers have even more time invested in the data stored on their disks, and often that data is invaluable because it cannot be replaced. Chapter 2 lists several sources of potential disk damage. The most common threat is the invisible magnetic radiation which surrounds us: computer monitors, electric motors, even the small magnet found in many paper clip holders. All generate sufficient magnetic radiation to destroy the files stored on a disk. Because computer disks are susceptible to different types of damage it is important to keep copies of them called *backups*, which are used should the original files become damaged.

Creating Backups of Important Data

Although it is easy to create backups of a file or disk many people do not take the time to do so. There are businesses that have lost thousands of dollars when their only copy of an important file such as a client list data base or accounts receivable spreadsheet has been lost or damaged.

Copying an Entire Disk

The simplest way to create a backup of your Works files is to make a copy of your data disk. This can be accomplished using the following procedure:

1. Boot a Macintosh System disk. Do not run Works but leave the System screen visible.
2. Insert your data disk into the drive.
3. From the System screen's File menu, select the Eject command (`Command-E`). The data disk's icon will remain on screen but be dimmed.

An Ejected disk's icon is shown dimmed on the System screen

4. Place a blank disk in the drive.
5. If the disk has not been formatted, follow the commands given in the resulting dialog boxes to initialize it.

Inserting a blank disk displays this dialog box

Give the disk a meaningful name such as "Backup Data".

Before it may be initialized, Works requires a name for the disk

6. Drag the dimmed data disk icon over top of the new disk. Works will respond with a message:

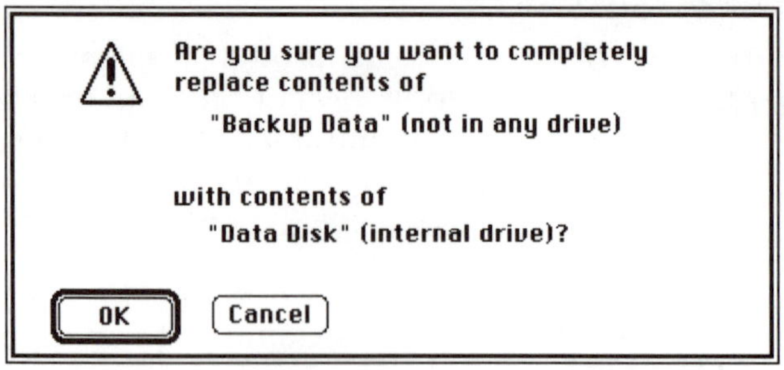

To prevent accidental erasure, Works allows the copy to be canceled

7. Swap the disks as requested by Works. When the copy is complete, remove the backup and store it in a safe place.

When the process is finished, a complete copy of the data stored on the original disk is made on the backup disk. The entire routine takes only a few minutes. At the end of the process, the disk left in the drive is a backup copy and should be stored in a safe place, away from the original disk.

Copying a Single File

A backup copy of a single file can be made dragging that file's icon onto another disk. For example, suppose you want to make a copy of a Works database file named CLIENTS:

1. Place the data disk containing CLIENTS in the drive.
2. Double click on the data disk icon to display its contents.
3. Select the Eject command from the System screen's File menu, (`Command-E`). The data disk is ejected.
4. Place an initialized disk in the drive for use as a backup.

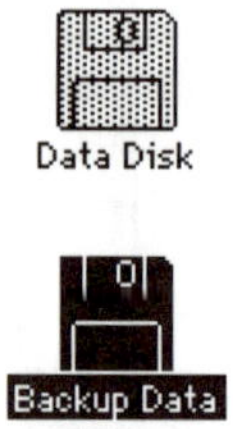

Both disk icons shown on the System Screen - Data Disk has been Ejected

5. Drag the Clients icon on to the backup disk's icon. Swap disks as directed.

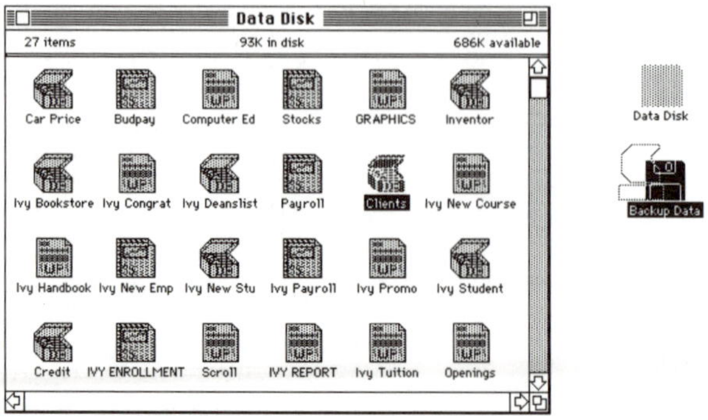

Drag the Clients icon on to the Backup Disk icon to make the copy

When the process is complete, a copy of the Clients data base has been made on the backup disk.

Saving a Backup Copy from Works

It is also possible to create backup copies of Works data files from within Works by using the `Save As` command to save the file on an initialized backup disk. To do this:

1. Open the desired file and select the `Save As` command from the File menu.
2. Click on the Eject button to eject the current Data Disk.

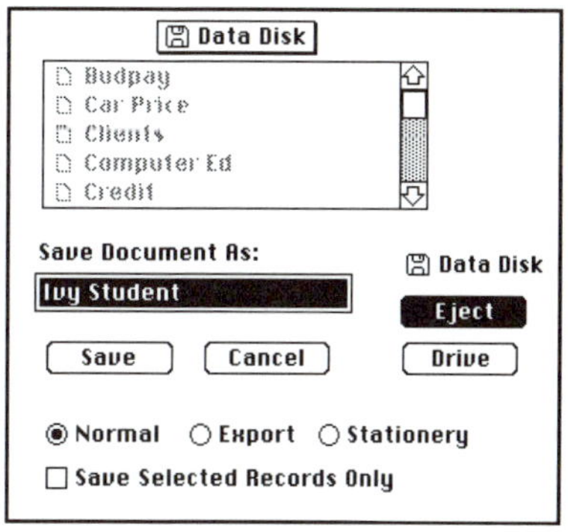

Clicking the Eject button ejects the current data disk

3. Insert the backup disk and click on the Save button:

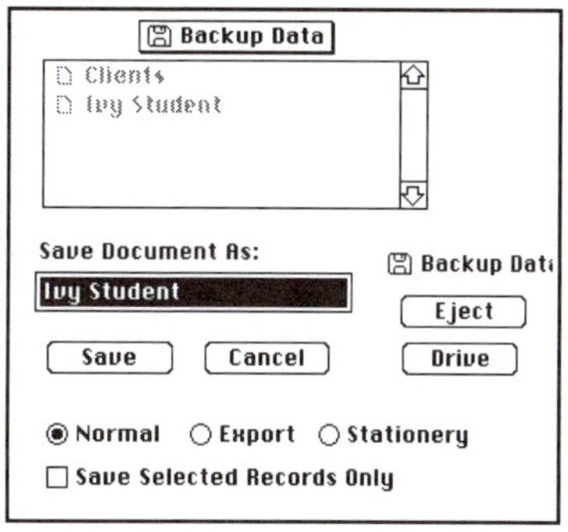

Clicking Save will save the open file on the new disk

This creates a copy of the open file on the backup disk.

For extra security, you can also save a file under another name on the same disk. For example, use Save As to create a copy CLIENTS using the file name CLIENTS BACKUP. This will protect you should something happen to the original CLIENTS file, but not if the data disk itself is damaged.

It is important to keep backup disks in a different location than the original copies. That way, the chances of both copies being destroyed are low. For example, if you keep your Works data diskette at school, keep your backup copy at home. Businesses often store their backup copies in special fire-proof safes, or in safe-deposit boxes at a bank. Several companies have been created just to provide safe "off-site storage" for computer data.

Remember, the data stored on a diskette is not permanent, and may easily be erased or damaged. Following the diskette handling rules given in Chapter 2 and keeping backup copies of important files in a safe place are the best insurance against data loss.

Appendix B - Developing Keyboarding Skills

Learning to Touch Type

The ability to "touch type" is especially helpful in using a computer. When touch typing you place your hands on the keyboard in a position which allows you to strike any of the keys without looking at your fingers. The advantage of learning how to do this is that while typing you can keep your eyes on the copy you are typing from. You will also be able to type with greater accuracy and speed then you could using the "hunt and peck" method where you must search for each key before striking it.

Before you begin to type it is important to have your hands and body in their proper positions. Your hands should be placed lightly on the keyboard with the slightly curved fingers of the left hand on the keys **ASDF** and the right hand on the **JKL;** keys. The right thumb will be placed on the space bar. This is called the "home row" or "home position."

Place the chair you are sitting in so that your arms reach out leaving the elbows loosely at your side. Sit in a relaxed but erect position with both feet flat on the floor. Maintaining proper posture will help to keep your body from tensing. Try not to slouch or bend over the keyboard. The proper posture is shown in the diagram:

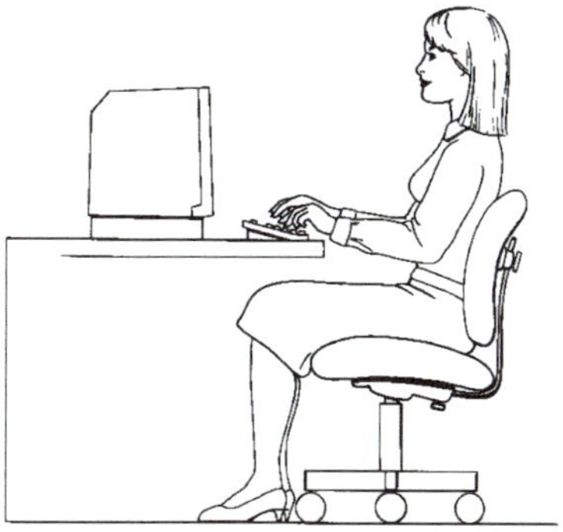

Always maintain proper posture when touch typing

To touch type it is necessary to memorize the location of each of the keys on the keyboard. This is best accomplished by learning just a few keys at a time which you will do when performing the following Lessons. Developing an even, smooth rhythm as you type is important. You want to strike each of the keys with the same pressure using a steady pace. To help you develop speed and accuracy the later Lessons ask you to keep track of how fast you are typing and the number of mistakes being made.

Before beginning the following lessons read pages 2-1 to 2-19 in *Chapter 2 - Introducing the Word Processor* and perform Practices 1 through 4 in that chapter to learn how to use the Works word processor. Next the lessons in this Appendix should be performed and then Chapter 2 completed.

Lesson 1

Start Works and create a new word processor file following the instructions given in Chapter 2.

Place your hands on the keyboard in the "home" position described above: the left hand on the keys **ASDF** and right hand on the keys **JKL;**. The right thumb is placed on the space bar. Type the following letters and press the Return key at the end of each row using your right pinky . Do not look at your hands while you type, look only at the picture of the keyboard below.

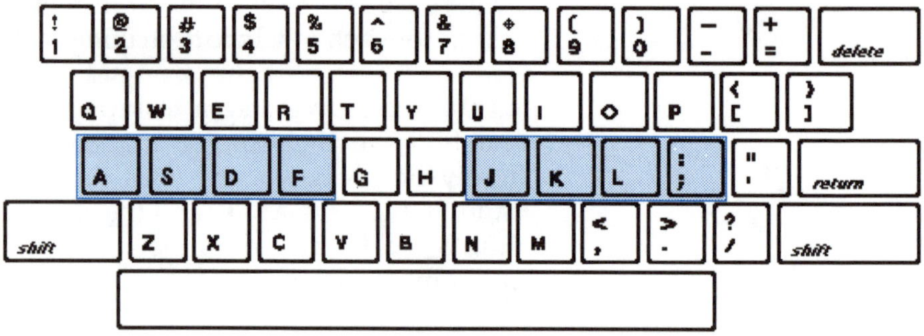

Always place your fingers on the home row *when beginning to touch type*

`aaa sss ddd fff jjj kk` <Press Return>

```
k lll ;;; asd asd dasf
sad sadf saj daf djkfl
dkd fjf sls a;f dad as
ask sad lad fad jak ka
sls fl; dja ksl fasjdl
add lass fall sad ads;
all fad salad falls ak
lad ask a;d aldf kjsdl
adds dklj ajds fasd fk
ld skja sdklja alskjd;
dksjl jak falls salads
```

Repeat the lesson above until you can type the keys without referring to the keyboard diagram. When you are finished, save the file following the instructions on page 2-12, naming it Lesson 1.

Lesson 2

In this Lesson the keys **RTYU** are added. Open a new word processor file and enter the following text pressing Return at the end of each line.

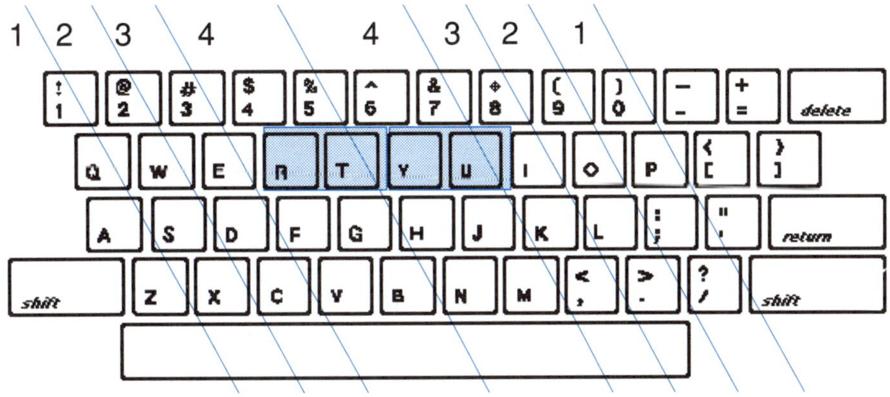

Press the R *and* T *keys with the left hand, and the* Y *and* U *keys with the right*

The letters RT are typed using the right finger of your left hand and the letters YU by the left finger of your right hand. Note the finger lines in the diagram which show which finger is used to type which keys: "1" for the pinky, "2" for the ring finger, "3" for the index and "4" for the pointer.

```
rrr ttt yyy uuu rtjufj

frt yuj sat fat jakfsd

dar yard jury duty fas

just dark dust data kl

jars rut say lass tar;

hat sat rat yur yards;
```

Repeat the Lesson until you can type the keys without referring to the diagram. When you are finished save the file naming it Lesson 2.

Lesson 3

Create a new word processor file. In this Lesson the keys **EGHI** are added. Note the finger lines which show which finger is used to type each of the keys.

Press the E *and* G *keys with the left hand, and the* H *and* I *keys with the right*

```
eee ggg hhh iii eighty

did lug tug hit sight

age hair red right lit

rake dirt sake height

fight saddle kettle us

huddle gerry jail sale

tuggle dirt yet little

rut side ask rail kiss

jilt hale said elk gas

right juggle her; rid

ted that fight federal

fester justify sight fist
```

When you are finished save the file naming it Lesson 3.

Lesson 4

Create a new word processor file. In this Lesson the letters **CVB MNO** are added as well as capital letters. Note the finger lines to determine which finger is used to type the new letters. To type capital letters use either your left or right pinky to hold down one of the Shift keys and type the letter.

Press the C, V and B keys with the left hand, and the M, N and O keys with the right. Use the pinky to hold down the Shift key.

```
ccc vvv bbb nnn mmm oo

money Tony convert Ned

Bill bend odd nod vex

boy Bob night vent Sam

avoid mad bite buried;

Lara Nina monkey said

Gray is a pretty color

Has Harry come home

Janet will not be at

school today

It is too late to

make up for yesterday
```

When you are finished save the file naming it Lesson 4.

Lesson 5

Create a new word processor file. In this Lesson the letters **QZXP** are added along with the period (.), comma (,), and question mark (?). Note the finger lines in determining which finger to use for each key.

Press the Q, Z *and* X *keys with the left hand, and the* P, comma, period, *and* question mark *with the right*

```
qqq zzz xxx ppp ... ,,
??? Ziggy quiet zinc
people zero exit quiz?
Zeke quay Walt Zoie,?
mix maximum next quash
oxen zest zing jinx .?
Jake quit his job.
What do you want?
Exit from the west.
Zinc is not pretty.
Would you be quiet?
I do not like quizzes.
```

When you are finished save the file naming it Lesson 5.

Lesson 6

Create a new word processor file. In this lesson the colon (:) and quote marks (") are added, each pressed with the right pinky. Allow Works to determine the end of each line:

```
":, ,:" :", "What is that?"
"This is a quote from Shakespeare."
Janet is a good student; John is
only fair. The "team" is:
Zeke, Jake, and Quent.
The following states are in the
west: Washington, Oregon,
California, and Nevada.
```

When you are finished save the file naming it Lesson 6.

Lesson 7

Create a new word processor file. Allow Works to determine the end of each line. Press Return at the end of each line. There are 100 "words" in this Lesson (when measuring typing speed, a "word" is considered to be 5 keystrokes) so dividing 100 by the number of minutes you take to type the words will give your speed in words per minute. Count the number of mistakes you make and divide by the time. Record both your speed in words per minute and the number of errors per minute. Repeat the Lesson a few times recording the results of each attempt. Your speed and accuracy should improve each time. Try for a minimum of at least 10 words per minute and only 1 error per minute.

```
dale rail flight word, solve draft general

writers rough writing correct difficulty

instead rise part important work order

going head; taken advantages club send

gift week disaster create advantage been

skills oral remember success gaining:

sharpen your insure smile do desire

achieve smile coal miner to done type

Zack exit press suspend flower beginning

stroke reunite, having determined;

carriage blooms crowd work quite document

fashion computer: gallery library

having options print transfer undo Marcia
```

When you are finished save the file naming it Lesson 7.

Lesson 8

Create a new word processor file. In this Lesson allow Works to determine the location of the end of lines. Time yourself and count the number of errors made to determine your speed in words per minute and accuracy in mistakes per minute. There are 244 words in the three paragraphs below. If you wish to check your speed and accuracy with just one of the paragraphs there are 75 words in the first paragraph, 84 words in the second and 85 words in the third.

```
     Many of the advances made by science and
technology are dependent upon the ability to
perform complex mathematical calculations and to
process large amounts of data. It is therefore
not surprising that for thousands of years
mathematicians, scientists and business people
have searched for "computing" machines that
could perform calculations and analyze data
quickly and accurately.

     As civilizations began to develop, they
created both written languages and number
systems. These number systems were not
originally meant to be used in mathematical
calculations, but rather were designed to record
measurements. Roman numerals are a good example
of this. Few of us would want to carry out even
the simplest arithmetic operations using Roman
numerals. How then were calculations performed
thousands of years ago?

     Calculations were carried out with a device
known as an abacus which was used in ancient
Babylon, China and throughout Europe until the
late middle-ages. Many parts of the world,
especially in the Orient, still make use of the
abacus. The abacus works by sliding beads back
and forth on a frame with the beads on the top
of the frame representing fives and on the
bottom ones. After a calculation is made the
result is written down.
```

When you are finished save the file naming it Lesson 8.

Lesson 9

Create a new word processor file. In this Lesson you will make use of the top row of keys which contain both numbers and symbols. Note which finger is to used to press each key. The Shift key is used to type symbols.

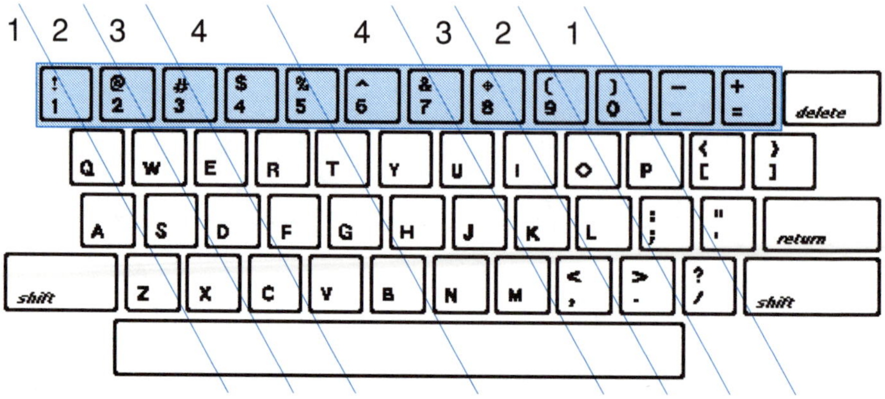

The Shift key must be held down when typing symbols

Type the following pressing Return at the end of each line:

```
123 456 789 101 256 23.890 1534.235 1,200,000.00

$42.89  #345  68.25%  45^12  26@ 34*29 = 986

23 & 79 are odd numbers!

(34 + 78) / (245 *12.8) = 0.0357
```

Type the following paragraph allowing Works to determine the end of each line:

```
     Hortense Bargain has decided to reduce the
price of stock items #3485 (paint), #7431 (elec-
tric plugs) and #2945 (lawn furniture) by 45%.
The new prices will be $38.50@, $72.95@ and
$14.98@.
```

When you are finished save the file naming it Lesson 9.

Glossary

A

Absolute reference - keeping a cell reference constant when copied into cells by placing dollar signs in front of its column letter and row number (`$B$25`). This is done by executing the Absolute Cell Ref command from the Edit menu: **`Command A`**.
ALU - Arithmetic Logic Unit, the part of the CPU that handles math operations.
Amortization table - displays the interest and principal paid on each payment of a loan.
Arc - a segment of a circle.
Arrow keys - Four keys that move the cursor up, down, right and left on the screen without changing any text.
Artificial intelligence - Using computers to make decisions which would normally be made by a human being.
ASCII - American Standard Code for Information Interchange, the code used for representing characters in the computer.

B

Baud rate - Rate at which characters of data are transmitted. One baud represents the transmission of one character per second.
Biochips - Computer circuits made from proteins and enzymes.
Bit - Binary Digit, a single 0 or 1 in a binary number.
Block - A highlighted section of text, created by dragging the mouse, which may contain anything from a single character to an entire document. Once highlighted, operations such as Copy and Move may be performed on the block or text formats such as bold applied.
Bold text - Darker letters, used for emphasis.
Boot - To turn on the computer and load the operating system (the Macintosh System).
Button - Similar to a switch which initiates an action within a dialog box. Buttons are selected by clicking the mouse on them.
Byte - A group of 8 bits.

C

Cell - Where a row and column intersect. A cell is identified by its column letter and row number, for example G8.
Cell indicator - Shows the current location of the cell cursor at the top of the screen.
Centered text - Text positioned evenly between the left and right margins.
Character - Any letter, number or symbol which can be displayed on the computer screen.
Character field - A field which stores only characters such as a name or address.
Chart - graphical representation of numeric data.
Check box - Indicator on Entry Bar clicked when data entered is correct. Also called "accept" box.
Clicking - Selecting an object that has been pointed to by pressing the button on the mouse.
Clipboard - a place in the computer's memory where cut objects are stored.
Close - To remove a file from the work area when it is no longer needed: **`Command W`**.
Column - Vertical line of data identified by a letter.
Command key - Key used to execute menu commands without using the mouse.
Computed field - Numeric field which is calculated based on the value(s) stored in other fields using a formula.
Conjunctions - Operators such as "and" and "or" used to join criteria in a selection rule.
Copy text - Creates an exact copy of a highlighted block in a new location: **`Command C`**.
CPU - Central Processing Unit, the device which electronically controls the functions of the computer.
Criteria - Description of the data that records must meet to be displayed. Refers to the contents of specific fields. Also called a "selection rule."
Criteria - Rule a field must satisfy in order to have the record displayed which contains the field. For example, "GPA is less than 2.0".
Cursor - A blinking line on the screen which indicates where characters entered from the keyboard are placed.

Cursor control keys - Keys used to move the cursor without having any effect on the text. See also Arrow keys.
Cut command - Removes the current record from the data base: **`Command X`**.

D

Data - Information either entered into or produced by the computer.
Data base - A collection of related information.
Data base file - A file on disk which is created by the data base application and which stores a computerized data base.
Data size - The number of bits (binary digits) that make up one piece of data sent during telecommunications. (7 or 8.)
Date field - A field which stores a date.
Default - A command or option that is selected automatically if no other command or option is chosen.
Delete key - A key that erases the character directly to the left of the cursor.
Delete text - Removes a highlighted block from a document using the Clear command from the Edit menu.
Delete text - The removal of a character or group of characters from a document.
Dialog box - Screen used to enter information and select options required by a command.
Document - Any material that can be typed in the word processor, such as a letter, research paper or story.
Double space - Leaving a blank line between each line of text when a document is printed.
Double-Clicking - Selecting an object that has been pointed to by pressing the mouse button twice in rapid succession.
Download - To transfer a message or computer file from a bulletin board or E-Mail service computer to another computer.
Dragging - Placing the pointer on an object, then depressing the mouse button while moving the object to a new location.
Draw layer - area in the computer's memory where drawings are made; accessed by executing the Draw On command.

E

Electronic bulletin board - (BBS) Telecommunications service which allows subscribers using a computer and modem to transmit messages that can be received by all the other subscribers.
Electronic mail - (E-Mail) Telecommunications service which allows a person using a computer and modem to send a message to another person's computer.
Entry - The information stored in one field in one record.
Entry Bar - Line at the top of the screen where data entered from the keyboard is displayed before it is entered into a cell.
Expert system - System programmed to produce the same solution a human expert would if asked to solve the same problem.

F

Field - A specific piece of information stored in each record, such as Last Name.
Field attribute - Determines how the data in a field will be displayed.
Field name - Name by which the computer identifies the different pieces of information in a record.
File - Information created by Works which is stored on a disk. A word processor file stores a document.
File name - A name for a file stored on disk, up to 32 characters in length. Colons (:) may not be used in file names.
Find - The computer searches a document for specified text: **`Command F`**.
Find Cell - moves the cursor to the next cell containing text specified in the Find Cell command from the Select menu: **`Command F`**.
Find Field command - Performs a general search which displays the next record containing a specified search for text in any field: **`Command F`**.
Font - Description of the shape of a set of characters such as Boston or Helvetica.
Footer - Line which is printed at the bottom of each page.
Form - The arrangement and number of fields in a record.
Form - The arrangement, length and order of the fields in a data base record.

Form view - All of the fields for a single record displayed on the screen at one time. Useful when updating a record or adding new records.
Form View - The fields for a single record displayed on the screen. Useful when updating a record.
Format - How the records in a data base are displayed, Form view (one at a time) or List view (up to 21 at a time).
Format - The arrangement of text on a page.
Format - the way that data is displayed such as cell width. Formatting options include Dollar, Date, Align and Style, and are selected from the Set Cell Attributes command of the Format menu.
Format - The way that text appears on a page, including options such as font, indents, emphasized text and headers and footers.
Format menu - Menu from which formatting options such as font, style, size and justification are set.
Formatting - Determines how the data stored in a cell will be displayed.
Formulas - Mathematical statements used to calculate values which are stored in cells. The statement **=C5+D7+E8** is a formula.
Freehand drawing - any type of line which can be drawn; can be curved, straight, crooked, etc.
Functions - Used in formulas to perform common calculations. **=SUM(B5:B10)** is a function.

G

Go To Cell - moves the screen window to display a particular cell specified in the Go To Cell command from the Select menu: **Command G**.
Go To Page # command - Used to move the cursor directly to the top of a specified page: **Command G**.

H

Hacker - Person who uses a computer and modem to enter a computer system without authorization.
Handle - black box used to adjust a previously drawn item.
Hardware - Physical devices which make up the computer and its peripherals.
Header - Line which is printed at the top of each page.
Hidden records - Records which do not meet the currently applied selection rule's criteria, and are not displayed but remain in the file.
Highlighted text - Text that has been selected as a block by dragging the mouse.
I-beam pointer - Shape the mouse pointer becomes when moved into the text of a document. Clicking the mouse places the cursor at the current location of the I-beam pointer.

I

Icons - Small pictures contained in a dialog box which have effects similar to buttons.
Indent - Paragraph formatting option which increases the left or right margin.
Information service - A company that provides different telecommunications services, usually for a fee.
Input - Data used by the computer.
Insert command - Adds a new, empty record to the data base before the current record: **Command I**.
Insert text - Adding words or characters to a document.
Integrated - A software package that contains different applications. Because Works is integrated, data may be shared between its three applications areas.

J

Justification - See Paragraph alignment.
Justified - Paragraph format in which each line of text is made to extend from the left margin to the right by adding extra space between words.

K

K, kilobyte - Measurement of computer memory capacity, 2^{10} or 1024 bytes.
Key Field - Field which stores the data used when determining the order during a sort.
Key field - Field which stores the data used when determining the order during a sort.
Keyboard - Device resembling a typewriter used for inputting data into a computer.

L

Label - Words or characters stored in a cell that cannot be used in calculations.
Layout - the design of a spreadsheet including the placement of data in its rows and columns, column widths and the use of formatting options.
Left alignment - Default paragraph format where text is even with the left hand margin, while the right side is ragged.
List - Group of items from which you may choose.
List view - Displays the first few fields for a number of records. Useful when comparing records to one another or determining the results of a query.
List View - Up to 21 records displayed on the screen at one time.

M

Macintosh System - Operating System programs that the computer needs to run.
Mail merge - Using the contents of a data base file and a word processor document to have the computer produce personalized form letters.
Margin - Blank spaces on a printed page which surround text.
Memory - Electronic storage used by the computer.
Menu - A list of commands that are available at a particular point in a program.
Menu bar - Line at the very top of the screen showing names of available menus.
Microprocessor - CPU on a single chip.
Modem - Device which translates binary data into waves and waves back into binary data so that computer data can be sent over telephone lines.
Modify - To change the contents of a record or entry.
Monitor - Television-like device used to display computer output.
Mouse - A device used to position the pointer on the screen.
Move text - Removes a highlighted block from its current position and places it in a new one: `Command X` and `Command V`.

N

Natural language processing - Using a computer to recognize spoken words and then translate them into digital form.
Numeric field - A field which contains only numbers.

O

Open File dialog box - Dialog box displayed by the Open command which contains options for creating new files or opening previously saved files.
Output - Data produced by a computer program.

P

Pagination - Works calculates and displays a dotted line showing where text will be broken into pages when printed.
Paragraph alignment - How text is printed in relation to the margins: left (default), right, centered or justified.
Paragraph format - Use of options affecting a paragraph including alignment, spacing, tabs and indents.
Parity - When telecommunicating, how the receiving computer determines if an error occurred in the transmission of data. Parity choices are None, Odd and Even.
PC - Personal Computer, a small computer employing a microprocessor.
Perfect shape - an exact shape drawn by Works (such as a square, circle or straight line).
Peripheral - Secondary hardware device connected to a computer such as a printer, monitor or disk drive.
Pirate - Person who illegally copies computer software.
Pointing - moving the cell cursor to specify cell names in formulas.
Pointing - Placing the mouse pointer on an object located on the screen.
Polygon - a multi-sided figure which can be open or closed.
Print command - Command on File menu which prints the currently displayed file: `Command P`.
Program - Series of instructions written in a special language directing the computer to perform certain tasks.

Q

Query - Limiting the number of records that are displayed using criteria that displayed records must meet. A query is based on criteria which refer to specific fields and contain comparisons such as 'is less than' or 'is not equal to'.
Quit - To leave the Works program and return to the Macintosh System.
Quit command - Command on File menu used to exit Works: **Command Q**.

R

RAM - Random Access Memory, memory which the computer can both read from and write to.
Range - Partial row or column of adjacent cells.
Record - A complete collection of data for one item.
Relative copy - copying formulas in a spreadsheet so that the cell names reflect the new rows and columns they are in. The Fill Right (**Command R**) and Fill Down (**Command D**) commands from the Edit menu are used to make relative copies.
Replace text - The computer replaces one specified piece of text with another: **Command R**.
Report - Information extracted from a data base, usually printed on paper.
Report - Printed description of the information stored in a data base.
Report definition - Description of the order and placement of fields in a report. May include titles and summaries.
Return key - Key used to indicate the end of an entry such as a dialog box option or response to a prompt. In word processing Return is pressed at the end of each paragraph. In general, pressing Return transfers the information typed into the computer's memory.
Right alignment - Paragraph format where text is set even with the right hand margin, while the left side is ragged.
Robot - Machine which can be programmed and is also capable of motion.
ROM - Read Only Memory, memory from which the computer can read only.
Row - Horizontal line of data identified by a number.
Ruler - Line at the top of the work area showing placement of tab stops, indents and margins.

S

Save - Transfer of data from the computer's memory to a file on disk.
Save command - Command on File menu used to save a file on disk: **Command S**.
Screen scroll - Moving through a document, the screen acts as a window showing only part of the document.
Scroll - Moving the screen "window" to view different parts of a spreadsheet.
Scroll bars - Used to move the screen window and are located below and on the right of the screen.
Search - Locate specific text in a document: **Command F**.
Search - Operation where the computer searches through the fields in a data base, displaying the first one to contain a specified text.
Search for text - Text entered by the user during a Find Field which records are compared to.
Search text - Text entered by the user to be found or replaced.
Selection Range - Selection rule criteria that includes an operator such as 'less than' or 'greater than'.
Selection rule - Limiting the number of records in a data base that are displayed by defining criteria that they must meet.
Single space - Leaving no space between each line of text when a document is printed.
Software - Computer programs.
Sort - Places data base records in order, based on the value stored in a specific (key) field: **Command A**.
Spelling checker - Words in a document not found in Works' dictionary file are displayed along with possible correct spellings.
Spreadsheet - Rows and columns of data on which calculations can be performed.
Stop bits - The number of bits, 1 or 2, sent to indicate the end of a piece of data.
Stretching - reshaping a selected drawing by dragging one of its handles.
Style - How text is displayed; for example, bold or italic.
Subscript - Text printed slightly below the normal line.
Superscript - Text printed slightly above the normal line.

T

Tab stop - Position(s), shown on the ruler, where the cursor jumps to when the Tab key is pressed. Used to create columns or indent text.
Telecommunications - Sending of computer data over telephone lines.
Terminal - Keyboard and monitor combination used to communicate with a mainframe or minicomputer.
Text - Any character or group of characters in a document.
Text format - How the letters making up the text are printed: bold, underlined, italic, superscript, subscript or plain.
Time field - A field which stores a time.
Tool - used by Works to produce a type of drawing.

U

Undo command - Reverses the effect of the last command issued: **Command Z**.
Unjustified - Left-aligned text, with the right side jagged.
Update - See Modify.
Update a record - Changing the contents of an entry or entries in a record.
Upload - To transfer a message or computer file from a computer to a bulletin board or E-Mail service computer.

V

Values - Numeric data that can be stored in cells and used in calculations.
Virus - Program which hides within another program for the purpose of destroying or altering data.

W

What If? question - performing calculations to make predictions based upon the data stored in a spreadsheet.
Window - Area of the screen where data is displayed.
Window - Location in the computer's memory used to store an open file. Works may have up to 14 files open at one time.
Window - Part of the computer's screen displaying a file that may be used by Works.
Window menu - Listing of the files currently open which allows switching between files.
Word processor - A computer application program that allows text to be manipulated, printed and stored.
Word wrap - When the computer decides whether to keep a word on the current line, or move it to the next based on the amount of space left on the line.
Work area - Center of the word processor screen, where text is typed and edited.

X

X box - Indicator on Entry Bar clicked when data entered is incorrect. Also called the "reject" or "cancel" box.

Index

D

E

F

W

Z